Slave Emancipation, Christian Communities, and Dissent in Post-Abolition Tanzania, 1878–1978

RELIGION IN TRANSFORMING AFRICA
ISSN 2398-8673

Series Editors
Barbara Bompani, Joseph Hellweg, Hassan Ndzovu and **Emma Wild-Wood**

Editorial Reading Panel
Robert Baum (Dartmouth College)
Dianna Bell (University of Cape Town)
Ezra Chitando (University of Zimbabwe)
Martha Frederiks (Utrecht University)
Paul Gifford (SOAS)
David M. Gordon (Bowdoin College)
Jörg Haustein (University of Cambridge)
Paul Lubeck (Johns Hopkins University-SAIS)
Philomena Mwaura (Kenyatta University, Nairobi)
Ebenezer Obadare (University of Kansas)
Abdulkader I. Tayob (University of Cape Town)
M. Sani Umar (Northwestern University)
Stephen Wooten (University of Oregon)

Series description
The series is open to submissions that examine local or regional realities on the complexities of religion and spirituality in Africa. Religion in Transforming Africa will showcase cutting-edge research into continent-wide issues on Christianity, Islam and other religions of Africa; Traditional beliefs and witchcraft; Religion, culture and society; History of religion, politics and power; Global networks and new missions; Religion in conflict and peace-building processes; Religion and development; Religious rituals and texts and their role in shaping religious ideologies and theologies. Innovative, and challenging current perspectives, the series provides an indispensable resource on this key area of African Studies for academics, students, international policy-makers and development practitioners.

Please contact the Series Editors with an outline or download the proposal form at www.jamescurrey.com:
Dr Barbara Bompani, Reader in Africa and International Development, University of Edinburgh: b.bompani@ed.ac.uk
Dr Joseph Hellweg, Associate Professor of Religion, Florida State University: jhellweg@fsu.edu
Professor Dr Hassan Ndzovu, Associate Professor of Religious Studies, Moi University: hassan.ndzovu@gmail.com
Professor Emma Wild-Wood, Professor of African Religions and World Christianity, University of Edinburgh: emma.wildwood@ed.ac.uk

Previously published titles in the series are listed at the back of this volume.

Slave Emancipation, Christian Communities, and Dissent in Post-Abolition Tanzania, 1878–1978

Salvatory S. Nyanto

© Salvatory S. Nyanto 2024

All Rights Reserved. Except as permitted under current legislation
no part of this work may be photocopied, stored in a retrieval system,
published, performed in public, adapted, broadcast, transmitted,
recorded or reproduced in any form or by any means, without the
prior permission of the copyright owner

The right of Salvatory S. Nyanto to be identified as the author of this work has been
asserted in accordance with sections 77 and 78 of the
Copyright, Designs and Patents Act 1988

First published 2024
James Currey

ISBN 978-1-84701-358-3

James Currey
is an imprint of
Boydell & Brewer Ltd
PO Box 9, Woodbridge
Suffolk IP12 3DF (GB)
www.jamescurrey.com
and of
Boydell & Brewer Inc.
668 Mt Hope Avenue
Rochester, NY 14620-2731 (US)
www.boydellandbrewer.com

A CIP record for this book is available from the British Library

The publisher has no responsibility for the continued existence or accuracy of URLs for
external or third-party internet websites referred to in this book, and does not guarantee
that any content on such websites is, or will remain, accurate or appropriate

In memory of Mwalimu Stephen Nyanto Rukurugu (*Kabhabhi*)

Contents

List of Illustrations	viii
Acknowledgements	x
List of Abbreviations	xiii
Glossary of Kinyamwezi and Kiswahili Words	xv
Prologue: Maria Leo Kalenga: Society, Gender, and Christianity in Post-Abolition Tanzania	xviii
Introduction: Slave Emancipation, Christian Communities, and Dissent in Post-Abolition Tanzania	1
1 Authority, Adaptation, and Dissent in Nineteenth-Century Unyamwezi, 1840–77	36
2 Slave Emancipation, the Beginnings of Mission Communities, and Everyday Life in Missions, 1878–1914	61
3 Translation as Dissent: Language, Society, and Christianity in Unyamwezi, 1906–20s	97
4 Catechists, Women, and Dissent in Villages beyond the Catholic Missions, 1930–50s	122
5 Teachers, Women, and Kinship Networks in Villages beyond the Moravian and Swedish Free Missions, 1930–50s	149
6 Christians, the Revival Movement, and Dissent in Moravian Missions and Villages, 1950–60	177
Conclusion	209
Appendix	217
Bibliography	219
Index	236

Illustrations

Maps

1	Location of Missions in Unyamwezi in the Nineteenth Century, 1878–98	28
2	Location of the LMS Mission and Milambo's Ikulu	30
3	Location of the White Fathers' Mission and Ntabo's Ikulu	32
4	Trade Routes from the Interior to the Coast, *c*.1890	44
5	The Spread of Catechists in Villages of the Ndala Catholic Mission, 1930–60s	131
6	The Spread of Christianity in Villages of Unyamwezi (Moravians)	173
7	The Spread of the Revival Movement and Dissent in Unyamwezi	183

Figures

1	Ancestral Veneration in Unyamwezi (Undated Image)	38
2	Mtemi Mpandashalo, Successor of Mirambo, *c*.1890	42
3	Mtemi Hwami of Msalala and His People, *c*.1880s	43
4	Sirboko's Slaves (Men and Women) Carrying Wood Fuel and Harvesting Rice in Unyamwezi, *c*.1860s	56
5	LMS Mission at Urambo Kilimani in 1883	65
6	The Orphanage Centre at Kipalapala Mission in 1889	89
7	The Mission Community near the White Sisters Convent in Ushirombo, *c*.1900	95
8	Ndala Catechists' School (*Misongeni*)	127
9	Undated Image of a Catechist Teaching Children in the Village Outstation	133
10	Incidence of Sleeping Sickness in Tabora District, *c*.1925–50	152
11	Movement of Produce by Rail in Tabora District in Tons, 1929–40	154

ILLUSTRATIONS ix

12	Baptized Christians in the Moravian Missions of Unyamwezi, 1931–50	174
13	African-ordained Pastors in the Moravian Missions of Unyamwezi, 1940s–50s	174

Tables

1	Slaves, Owners, and Their Witnesses, 1908–09	73
2	Certificates of Freedom (*Freibriefe*) Granted to Slaves Living at Tabora and Ushirombo, 1900–14	80
3	Certificates of Freedom (*Freibriefe*) Granted to Slaves Living at Ndala and Uyui, 1897–1914	82
4	Changing Concepts and Meanings of Words in the Kinyamwezi New Testament	107
5	Translation of Kinyamwezi Songs and the Lord's Prayer	118
6	Number of Catechists in Catholic Missions, 1928–46	136
7	Number of Baptized Christians in Catholic Missions, 1937–56	137
8	Movement of Produce by Rail in Tabora District in Tons, 1929–40	155
9	Names, Shame, and Slave Antecedents in Mission Registers, c.1937–44	158
10	Baptized Christians in the Moravian Missions of Unyamwezi, 1931–50	173
11	Names of Women, Girls, and Children at the White Sisters' Convent, 1909–10	217
12	Former Slaves in Christian Communities, Vicariate of Unyanyembe, 1907–10	218
13	Redeemed Slaves, Village Communities, and Christians in the Vicariate of Unyanyembe, 1906–07	218

Acknowledgements

This book would not have been completed without the moral and material support I received from various individuals and institutions. I am indebted to the European Research Council (ERC), grant number 818908 ASEA, for financing the research and writing of this book as part of my postdoctoral research on the aftermath of slavery in East Africa. Professor Felicitas M. Becker, principal investigator of the project on the aftermath of slavery in mainland East Africa, deserves my heartfelt gratitude for her generosity, inspiration, and immensurable scholarly support and advice on shaping the arguments presented in the book. Professor Becker maintained a guiding hand in the research and publication of this book. The African History Group at Ghent University provided me with a friendly working environment as a postdoctoral fellow. Professor Elisabeth McMahon of Tulane University and Professor Jörg Haustein of the University of Cambridge offered constructive and thought-provoking feedback on my earlier draft that shaped my thinking about the subject matter. The book would not have had its shape without their input. I thank Dr Faraja Kristomus Lugome, Ruthmarie Mitsch, and Dr Nicholas Di Liberto for rigorously editing the manuscript. They read it thoroughly with inquisitive minds and provided me with valuable comments on some parts of the manuscript.

At the University of Iowa, Professor James L. Giblin gave me unwavering moral and material support. His scholarship has inspired me, and his influence is evident in all chapters of this book. His limitless fortitude and advice motivated me to apply for the doctoral programme at Iowa when we met at his home in Dar es Salaam in 2012. He taught me to be focused and coherent and encouraged me to write 'an African-centred story' from primary sources. His insistence that I draw an African-centred story from the documents has shaped my approach to the primary sources that missionaries, colonial officials, and individual travellers produced about African history. My profound debt and admiration go to Mama Blandina Giblin, whose motherly care invariably made me feel at home in the most trying moments of the graduate programme at Iowa. Professors Jeffrey L. Cox, Richard B. Turner, Raymond Mentzer, and Evan M. Fales extended unfailing support and mentorship throughout the graduate programme. Regrettably, Professor Cox could not see the final publication of this book. I am equally grateful to the history department members at Iowa, especially Professors Elizabeth Heineman and Landon Storrs. Professors Colin Gordon and Jacki T. Rand shaped my ideas during the predissertation seminars. My colleagues in the graduate programme, Marlino E. Mubai, Aldrin T. Magaya, Andrew Steck, and Justin Kirkland, provided me with an intellectually engaging environment.

At the University of Dar es Salaam, Vice Chancellor Professor William A.L. Anangisye relieved me from my duties as Director of the Office of the Vice Chancellor to concentrate on the research and writing of this book. The Deputy Vice Chancellor-Academic, Professor Bonaventure S. Rutinwa; the Deputy Vice Chancellor (Planning, Finance and Administration), Professor Bernadeta Killian; and Deputy Vice Chancellor (Research), Professor Nelson Boniface, provided me with unreserved and timely support. My colleagues in the history department provided me with indescribable backing and a pleasant working environment. Professor Frederick J. Kaijage and the late Professor Kapepwa I. Tambila inspired me to join the department. Professor Kaijage's survey course 'Africa and World Religions' influenced me to think further about historical questions concerning religion. As my advisor, Professor Isaria N. Kimambo inspired me to dig deeper into the field between 2010 and 2012. I remain indebted to the advice and support of Professors Isaria N. Kimambo, Frederick J. Kaijage, and Yusufu Q. Lawi, and Drs Oswald Masebo, Maxmilian J. Chuhila, Hezron Kangalawe, and James Zotto. Dr Reginald Kirey, as a doctoral candidate at the University of Hamburg, helped me access the Kinyamwezi Bible and other books deposited in the Universitätsbibliothek Hamburg. Ms Olipa Simon Mwakimi of the University of Dar es Salaam Institute of Resource Assessment (IRA) prepared all the maps in this book.

I benefited at various stages of research and writing from the University of Iowa Graduate College Post-Comprehensive Research Award; T. Anne Clearly International Dissertation Research Fellowship; Gordon and Anne Prange Dissertation Fellowship; Marcus Bach Fellowship; Ballard Seashore Dissertation Fellowship; and the University of Dar es Salaam research grant. Among the archivists who assisted me at various stages of research were the staff of the Tanzania National Archives and the White Fathers Archives at Atiman House in Dar es Salaam. I thank the late Sr Frediana Kabafunzaki and Sr Perpetua Kyomugisha, who devoted their time to assisting me in locating potential documents from the archives of the Archdiocese of Tabora. At the University of Iowa, the interlibrary loan staff and Dr Edward Miner obtained various documents for me from other university libraries in the United States. Others who assisted me were staff of the UK National Archives at Kew; Joanne Ichimura of the School of Oriental and African Studies (SOAS) in London; Anne George, Mark Eccleston, and Vicky Clubb of the Cadbury Research Library Special Collections at the University of Birmingham; and

Fr Dominique Arnauld, MAfr, of the Archives Générales des Missionnaires d'Afrique in Rome (AGMAfr).

In addition to these archivists, I am grateful to Archbishop Paul R. Ruzoka of the Archdiocese of Tabora for his permission to read church records in the diocesan archives. At the same time, Rev. Elias Shija of the Free Pentecostal Church of Tanzania (FPCT) allowed me to pursue research into the Swedish Free Mission. Oscar E. Kisanji made his family collection available to me, and Fr William Crombie, MAfr, assisted me in translating into English some parts of the French diaries of the Ndala and Ushirombo missions. In Tanzania and Rome, Fr Dr Francis Nolan, MAfr, shared his knowledge of the White Fathers, the Church Missionary Society (CMS) and London Missionary Society (LMS) in Unyamwezi. At the same time, Bishop Dr Methodius Kilaini, auxiliary of Bukoba Catholic Diocese, supported and encouraged me in this endeavour. In the UK, Dr Maxmillian J. Chuhila accommodated me in Coventry and devoted his time to accompanying me to SOAS and the UK National Archives.

My profound gratitude goes to my research assistants, Mzee Theodori Kulinduka, Mzee Mikaeli Katabi, and Mzee Oscar E. Kisanji. Without their support, this project would not have been completed. I am beholden to Maria Leo Kalenga and Paulina Mwanamihayo of Ndala village, and Anastazia Maturino Mulindwa of Ushirombo. Maria and Paulina's memories of slavery in Unyamwezi increased my curiosity about the subject matter, and accordingly, I made frequent trips to the Ndala village to learn more from them. Unfortunately, Maria and Paulina joined their ancestors before they could see this book completed.

Indeed, writing this book has left me with profound gratitude and admiration for the assistance of these individuals and institutions. Nevertheless, they should not be held accountable for my statements and judgements in this book. The shortcomings of this work remain my responsibility, and I apologize in advance for possible misrepresentations of statements, conclusions, and arguments.

Ad majorem Dei gloriam!

Abbreviations

AAT	Archives of the Archdiocese of Tabora
AGM	Afr Archives Générales des Missionnaires d'Afrique
CMG	Companion of the Order of St Michael and St George
CMS	Church Missionary Society
CWM	Council for World Mission
DRC	Democratic Republic of Congo
EAF	East Africana
FPCT	The Free Pentecostal Church of Tanzania
Fr	Father (Priest)
IFRA	Institut Français de Recherche en Afrique
KFC	Kisanji Family Collection
LMS	London Missionary Society
MAfr	Missionaries of Africa
MC	Military Cross
MCWT	Moravian Church in Western Tanganyika
MdA	Les Missions d'Afrique des Pères blancs
Msgr	Monsignor
MUTU	Moravian Unyamwezi Teachers' Union
OBE	Officer of the Order of the British Empire
OMS	Overseas Missions Series
Rev.	Reverend
RSV	Revised Standard Version (Bible)
Rt Rev.	Right Reverend
SFM	Swedish Free Mission
SOAS	School of Oriental and African Studies
Sr	Religious Sister
TAC	Tanganyika African Church
TANU	Tanganyika African National Union
TMP	Tanganyika Mission Press
TNA	Tanzania National Archives

xiv ABBREVIATIONS

UDSM	University of Dar es Salaam
UKNA CO	United Kingdom National Archives (Colonial Office)
UMCC	Unyamwezi Moravian Church Council
URT	United Republic of Tanzania
WFA	White Fathers Archives

Glossary of Kinyamwezi and Kiswahili Words

Bafumbuzi/vafumbuzi: Wise men, from the Kiswahili -*wafumbuzi*

Bafumu/vafumu (sing. *mfumu*): Fortune tellers, some of whom used their power for malicious activities

Bahembeki/vahembeki (sing. *mhembeki*): Teachers or evangelists who worked in the village outstations

Bakombe/vakombe (pl. *mukombe*): Messengers

Balogi/valogi: People, usually witches, who use supernatural power for malicious ends

Balokole (sing. *mlokole*): The saved ones or born-again Christians

Balungwana/valungwana: Men with a reputation for being 'civilized' or 'free' in contrast to enslaved men

Bamalaika/vamalaika: Angels, from the Kiswahili -*malaika*. Etymology: Arabic -*malak*

Banangwa (sing. *mwanangwa*): Sons of chiefs who could succeed in chieftaincy or serve as subchiefs

Bandari: Harbour

Bandeba/vandeva (sing. *mundeba/mundeva*): An occupational group in Unyamwezi

Baraza: A practice of communal meetings. Etymology: Kiswahili -*baraza*

Basese (sing. *msese*): Slaves, both men and women

Basomi/vasomi: Literate people (Christians, especially those who could read and write)

Basugwa: Voluntary slaves who returned to their families; pawns

Batemi/vatemi (sing. *mtemi*): Nyamwezi chiefs with political and ritual authority

Buswezi: Nyamwezi secret society

Butemi/vutemi: Chiefdom

Changilo: *Boys' dormitory, or* boarding school. An extension of the culture of the Nyamwezi chiefs in accommodating young men at chiefly headquarters to train them to become soldiers

Data: Father/Parent

Data wiswe: Our Father (the Lord's Prayer)

Fibula ja Kinyamwezi: Kinyamwezi primer reader; handbook. Etymology: German *-fibel*

Fitabu: Book, from Kiswahili *-kitabu*. Etymology: Arabic *-kitāb*

Freibrief: *Certificate of* emancipation

Fundi: Artisan; construction technician; builder of houses

Guku: Grandfather

Ibuku: Book. Etymology: English *-book*

Ifungu: Tithe

Ikulu/kuikulu: The headquarters of Nyamwezi chiefs

Ilagano Ipya: New Testament. Etymology: Kiswahili *-agano jipya*

Injili: Gospel

Ivanza lya chalo (pl. *mavanza ga chalo*): Council of church elders

Ki-: Prefix used to denote a language, for example, Kinyamwezi, Kiswahili

Kitabu (pl. *vitabu*): Book. Etymology: Arabic *-kitāb*

Kulokoka: To be saved or to be born again

Kujitawala: self-governance

Kunakili: Copying; translation intending to avoid change of meaning

Luduko: Hardship and suffering; also, excommunication

Lusangi: Neighbourhood

Lwanga: Libation of sorghum flour mixed with water. Etymology: Kiswahili *-wanga*

Mama: Mother

Masala: The mind (Kinyamwezi); also, temptation

Masika: The rainy season

Mbuga: Low-lying grasslands dominated by thorny bush

Mchungaji: Pastor

Mfalme: King

Mhola ya Chelu: Good News (the Gospel)

Migabo/migawo: Nonancestral spirits of water bodies, groves, and forests

Migani ja vutemi vwa Mulungu (Kiny): Stories about God's kingdom

Milangale: Trumpet

Mimbo ga bupiji: Songs of praise (Nyamwezi)

Miombo: Light forest dominated by Brachystegia

Misheni: Mission station or parish. Etymology: English *-mission*

Mpina: Poor person; one who renounces worldly wealth

Mšyolo/kumšyolo: Curse; also, sin

Mudugu (pl. *vadugu*): Relative. Etymology: Kiswahili *-ndugu*

Mulungu: God. Etymology: Kiswahili *-Mungu*

Mupilofeti (pl. *vapilofeti*): Prophet

Muungu: God. Etymology: Kiswahili *-Mungu*

Mwalimu (pl. *Walimu*): Teacher. Etymology: Arabic *-mu'allim*

Mwinjilisti: Evangelist

Mwongofu (pl. *waongofu*): Born-again Christian

Mzee: Old person. Honorific for a man

Mzungu: White person from Europe

Nimbo: Hymns. Etymology: Kiswahili *-nyimbo*

Posho: Remuneration

Roho: Spirit (holy). Etymology: Arabic *-rūh*

Roho nsondo: Holy Spirit

Rugaruga (pl. *barugaruga*): Young, unmarried, professional soldier

Safari kuu: A grand march to the coast between Unyamwezi and the Indian Ocean coast

Shamba: Farm or plantation

Sinagogo: Village outstation

Tarumbeta: Trumpet

Tembe: A traditional mud-roofed house, quadrangular in shape

Udongo mgumu: Hard soil

Ugome: Opposition; the movement of opposition against revivalism

Ustaarabu: A reputation of being 'civilized' or 'free' in contrast to men in enslavement

Valola masonda (sing. *mlola nsonda*): Messengers

Vasenzi (sing. *msenzi*): Barbarians. Etymology: Kiswahili *-washenzi*

Vasomi (sing. *msomi*): Literate people. Etymology: Kiswahili *-wasomi*

Vayaga/Vamakoba: Nyamwezi professional elephant hunters

Waganga (sing. *mganga*): Diviners; healers

Wahenga (sing. *mhenga*): Ancestors

Wakristu (sing. *mkristu*): Christians

Wakristu wapya (sing. *mkristu mpya*): New Christians; born-again Christians

Waongofu (sing. *mwongofu*): Born-again Christians

Waungwana (sing. *Muungwana*): Men with a reputation for being 'civilized' or 'free' in contrast to men in enslavement

Wazee wa Kanisa (sing. *mzee wa kanisa*): Church elders

Welelo: Universe

Wokovu: Salvation

PROLOGUE

Maria Leo Kalenga: Society, Gender, and Christianity in Post-Abolition Tanzania

I first interviewed Maria Nyamizi Leo Kalenga on 7 January 2016. She spent hours telling me about her parents, Leo Kalenga and Marina Sitta, and other men and women who had joined the mission community of Ndala as formerly enslaved people. Her father, Mzee Leo Kalenga, fled to the Ndala mission as an enslaved person from Congo.[1] I arrived at Maria's house in Ndala village for the second interview on 5 September 2016, and this time I was still curious to learn more about her work at the State House between 1960 and 1985. Born in 1926, Maria Kalenga was the only surviving daughter of Leo Kalenga. Unfortunately, she did not live to see this final product, as she died in May 2017, at ninety-two.

Maria Kalenga cited the war of *mbulumbulu* as the cause of the enslavement of many Nyamwezi. But evidence shows that what she called *wambulumbulu* or *bulamatari* was the name the Nyamwezi used for the Belgian troops. As the First World War reached Unyamwezi, the Belgian troops destroyed houses, kidnapped women, and took men and the young as porters.[2] Perhaps the name of the war that enslaved many Nyamwezi escaped Maria's memory. Undoubtedly, wars between chiefdoms caused much of the instability in the region, with so many Nyamwezi taken as captives and prisoners of war. Like other runaway enslaved persons, Maria's father lived in the Ndala mission community. Maria's mother was also a formerly enslaved person who came from present-day Iramba in central Tanzania. Maria's recollection indicates that her mother was enslaved because her family could not withstand hunger and poverty. She was therefore offered as a slave in return for food. However, she ran away to the mission, escaping enslavement.[3] The two formerly enslaved people were married at Ndala mission church on 20 April

---

[1] Interview with Maria Leo Kalenga, Ndala, 7 January and 6 September 2016.

[2] Francis P. Nolan, 'Christianity in Unyamwezi, 1878–1928' (PhD thesis, University of Cambridge, 1977), 300.

[3] Maria's mother's escape from her master demonstrates the many strategies female slaves used to free themselves from enslavement. For details of women's

1913.[4] Maria Kalenga and her brothers and sisters were baptized at the Ndala Catholic mission, attended the Ndala mission school, and served in different capacities during the colonial and postcolonial periods. One of Maria's sisters, Anastazia Ndumbagwe Leo Kalenga, worked at the Muhimbili national hospital in the 1950s.

Maria recalled that she 'studied because of Father Simon Sequin' ('nilisoma sababu ya Padri Sequin'), acknowledging how the relationship her parents had established with the Ndala mission after their marriage allowed them to move from the mission community to build a house in the village. Father Sequin, Maria recalled, 'told my father to take his children to the mission school to learn to read, write, and arithmetic [sic]'.[5] Father Sequin helped Maria pursue her studies, becoming a new patron as he had done for many slave women at the Ndala mission and the village.[6] Maria passed her primary education examination at Ndala mission school and was subsequently enrolled at Tabora Girls' Secondary School under the sponsorship of Father Sequin. Maria returned to Ndala when she completed her secondary education and married in 1942. Unfortunately, her husband (Isakala) died seven years later in 1949.

After her husband died, Father Sequin took her to Nairobi for a six-month secretarial course in 1950. She recalled how she 'was efficient and typed letters so fast', which impressed her instructors.[7] After the course, Maria returned to Ndala and worked temporarily at the Ndala mission. The newly independent government announced a secretarial post at the State House in 1962. Father Sequin encouraged Maria to apply for the advertised position and helped her prepare the application letter, which he mailed to the State House in October 1962. Rashid Kawawa, the prime minister of Tanganyika, called Maria for an interview at the State House. When Maria arrived in Dar es Salaam, she sought accommodation at the sisters' convent at Msimbazi centre, and the next day she went for an interview. Maria recalled that President Julius Kambarage Nyerere, Prime Minister Kawawa, and the Minister of Education, Mr Saidi

---

strategies, see Marica Wright, *Strategies of Slaves and Women: Life-Stories from East/Central Africa* (London: James Currey, 1993).

[4] Ndala Diary, 20 April 1913, WFA 01.43.

[5] Interview with Maria Leo Kalenga, Ndala, 6 September 2016.

[6] Andreana C. Prichard, *Sisters in Spirit: Christianity, Affect, and Community Building in East Africa, 1860–1970* (East Lansing: Michigan State University, 2017), 59; James Giblin, *The Politics of Environmental Control in Northeastern Tanzania, 1840–1940* (Philadelphia: University of Pennsylvania Press, 1992), 60–69.

[7] In Kiswahili, 'niliweza kuchapa maandishi haraka'.

Mswaya, wanted her to work in their offices. Eventually, Maria said, 'Kura ikaangukia Ofisi ya Nyerere' (the vote was in favour of Nyerere's office).[8]

As a typist, Maria earned a monthly salary of between 150 and 200 shillings. Besides her monthly salary, Maria won a Volkswagen car in a 1963 lottery. Mwalimu Nyerere presented the car to Maria in front of the crowd at the national stadium, but unfortunately, Maria said, 'They have stolen my car's picture'.[9] The police kept the car because Maria could not drive. Mwalimu Nyerere suggested that the government buy the car. Maria accepted Mwalimu's suggestion and was paid 150,000 shillings, half of which she gave to her father in Ndala village. In addition to working as a secretary in Nyerere's office, Maria Kalenga remembers how she always carried Madaraka Nyerere, son of Mwalimu Nyerere, on her back every Saturday, and that 'Mwalimu and his wife Mama Maria loved her so much'.[10] Mwalimu Nyerere retired as president of the United Republic of Tanzania in 1985. Shortly after his retirement, he encouraged Maria to retire, saying, as Maria recalled, 'Ng'atuka wakupe hela zako' ('retire so they pay you money').[11] After her retirement, Maria returned to Ndala village and continued attending the Sunday services at Ndala mission. Her friendship with the family of Mwalimu Nyerere continued, and Mama Maria Nyerere said that Maria Kalenga 'invariably wrote me letters along with Christmas gift cards', confirming the ties of friendship that continued between the two families after Maria Kalenga left the State House in Dar es Salaam.[12]

The story of Maria Leo Kalenga is one of the many stories of formerly enslaved people and their descendants in western Tanzania that offer insight into our understanding of the afterlives of slavery in the late colonial and postcolonial periods. The experience of Maria Leo Kalenga demonstrates the continued ties between formerly enslaved people, their descendants, and the mission stations in western Tanzania. It also shows how the descendants of the marginalized shaped the course of nationalism and nation building. Maria's employment at the State House not only shows how descendants of formerly enslaved people in western Tanzania engaged in the nation-building project but also demonstrates how formerly enslaved people and their descendants transcended the social binaries and ideas of race and citizenship to create 'intimacies of national belonging' in postcolonial Tanganyika.[13] We learn

---

[8] In Kiswahili, 'wote walikuwa wananihitaji'.

[9] In Kaswahili, 'bahati mbaya wameiba picha ya gari yangu'.

[10] She said, 'Mwalimu alinipenda na Mama Maria alinipenda pia'.

[11] Interview with Maria Leo Kalenga, 6 September 2016.

[12] In Kaswahili, 'Mara nyingi Mama Maria Nyerere alikuwa ananitumia barua pamoja na kadi za Noeli'.

[13] Prichard, *Sisters in Spirit*, 211.

from the story of Maria that during the struggle for independence, the colonial government did not give Mwalimu Nyerere access to medical care; it was her sister Anastazia who 'took pills from Muhimbili to Nyerere's house at Majumba Sita (Magomeni)'.[14] That Mwalimu Nyerere named his daughter Anastazia in honour of Maria Kalenga's sister, Anastazia Ndumbagwe Leo Kalenga, suggests 'relationships of familiarity and/or commonality' between Maria and Nyerere's family that were akin to the intimacy between 'relative, kin, sibling, cousin [and] close friend'.[15] The story of Maria and her sister represents the many stories of formerly enslaved people and their descendants that have been muted in much of the existing scholarship and, of course, in the mainstream narratives of nationalism and nation building. They can only be recovered through conversation with the descendants of the enslaved in the villages.

[14] Interview with Maria Leo Kalenga, 6 September 2016.
[15] Prichard, *Sisters in Spirit*, 219.

INTRODUCTION

Slave Emancipation, Christian Communities, and Dissent in Post-Abolition Tanzania

Setting the Context: Missions as Melting Pots

On 20 April 1913, two runaway slaves, Leo Kalenga from Congo (in the present-day Democratic Republic of Congo, DRC) and Marina Sita from central Tanganyika, married at Ndala Catholic Mission. People living in the village and residents in the mission, mostly formerly enslaved people, attended mass in the Ndala mission church. Immediately after the ceremony, the people brought the bride and groom to their new home, with the women singing with loud ululations. There were many people, commented an unnamed diarist, 'more than had been invited', but 'all went well'.[1] After the marriage, Leo Kalenga left the mission community and built his house in the village while maintaining his relationship with the mission. He continued attending Sunday services and worked as a cook for the mission and later as a catechist, teaching the young and adults in preparation for baptism and confirmation. He had eight sons and daughters who were baptized at the mission and attended the Ndala mission school, and some of them worked as teachers and civil servants. Of his eight children, Maria Leo Kalenga continued living on her father's land until May 2018, when she breathed her last at ninety-two. She, too, maintained her ties with the mission, as she attended the Sunday services there and participated in other activities that demanded the presence of Christians in the mission.[2]

The marriage of Leo Kalenga to Marina Sita is an example of the daily life of many runaway slaves in western Tanzania who formed early Christian communities. Slaves saw missions as breathing spaces that removed them

---

[1] Ndala Diary, 20 April 1913, WFA 01.43 (White Fathers Archives).

[2] Interview with Maria Leo Kalenga, Ndala, 7 January 2016 and 6 September 2016. Maria Leo Kalenga's siblings included Donadi Tungu, Elizabeth Mweru, Anastazia Ndumbagwe, Margareta Mbiku, Daudi Kalenga, Zakaria, and Sesilia.

from the horrors of slavery, wars, and insecurity. As a result, mission stations attracted slaves from various parts of the East African interior. Slaves in Unyamwezi originated from parts of central and western Tanzania, Rwanda, Burundi, and eastern Congo – a region considered in the nineteenth century as 'arguably the richest in slaves'.[3] These slaves had lived in the region for quite some time before joining mission communities, and they had learned the Kinyamwezi language while living in the region as slaves.[4] Mission communities in western Tanzania varied in size, composition of inhabitants, degree of discipline, and the social context in which they came into being. Despite residents' diverse languages and cultures, mission communities were places where European culture, rather than the culture of African residents, controlled the day-to-day undertakings, including work patterns and attendance of religious services that became mandatory for all residents.[5] At the Ndala mission, Leo Kalenga and Marina Sita, along with other runaway slaves, lived in separate houses, Leo with the men in one and Marina in another house with women. Orphans – both boys and girls – lived together in the orphanage centre under the close supervision of missionaries. Both adults and children in the orphanage attended church services and performed various kinds of work in the mission, including farming and brickmaking.[6]

Notwithstanding the range of activities performed in the mission under a tight schedule, weekly dances on Saturdays not only created a 'cultural landscape' for residents from various parts of the East African interior but also strengthened networks of friendship between adult residents and unmarried young men and women, as well as between mission residents and villagers at Ndala.[7] Adults tried to socially integrate the orphans, children, and elderly who joined the communities by creating kinship relations that were not based on blood bonds but amounted to 'fictive' or 'networked' relationships based

---

[3] Karin Pallaver, 'Nyamwezi Participation in the Nineteenth-Century East African Long-Distance Trade: Some Evidence from Missionary Sources', *Africa*, Vol. 61, Nos 3/4 (2006), 516.

[4] See, for instance, Freibrief no. 102, 11 December 1903, AAT 526.503; Freibrief no. 275, 26 October 1909, AAT 526.503; and Freibrief no. 733, 7 May 1912, AAT 526.503.

[5] Adrian Hastings, *The Church in Africa, 1450–1950* (Oxford: Clarendon Press, 1996), 214.

[6] Interview with Maria Leo Kalenga, Ndala, 6 September 2016.

[7] In formulating an argument about the place of weekly dances in shaping the cultural landscape for the formerly enslaved in missions, I am indebted to Herman O. Kiriama, 'The Landscapes of Slavery in Kenya', *Journal of African Diaspora Archaeology and Heritage*, Vol. 7, No. 2 (2018), 192–206.

INTRODUCTION   3

on shared experiences of enslavement and mission life.[8] Unmarried young men could choose their spouses in the mission because they were not bound to pay bridewealth. Therefore, as Leo Kalenga matured, recalled Maria Kalenga, 'The priests told my father to find himself a wife from the women's house'. In addition to friendship and support in the mission villages, slaves like Leo Kalenga, who worked as teachers, catechists, or domestic servants, interacted with missionaries, forming relationships that would facilitate the translation of religious texts and songs into the Kinyamwezi language.[9] As centres of everyday life for the formerly enslaved people with diverse linguistic and cultural backgrounds, mission stations formed what Norman Etherington has described as 'melting-pot societies' for the growth and consolidation of Christianity, observing that 'without the presence of such individuals, missionaries might have failed to attract adherents altogether' in missions and village outstations.[10]

This book examines the intersection of post-slavery and Christian evangelism. It shows how formerly enslaved people came together to create new Christian communities in the missions of western Tanzania. It documents the cultural, intellectual, and linguistic creativity of African evangelists who created a Kinyamwezi-speaking Christian culture from inspiration offered by European missionaries on the one hand and African villagers on the other. In so doing, the book casts light on the fate of the hundreds of thousands of people who had laboured as slaves in the region, tracing the emergence of slave descendants into educated, professional roles. As mission residents, the formerly enslaved men and women became the first generation of Christians, some working as teachers, pastors, and catechists in missions and villages. This study shows that translating the New Testament, religious texts, and songs into the Kinyamwezi language and culture was reciprocal, with Africans and European missionaries teaching each other. Translation of religious texts produced first-generation African teachers and catechists, who laid the basis for the growth of African Christianity in villages.[11] In villages far from the mission centres, catechists and teachers helped adherents translate the Christian

---

[8] Elisabeth McMahon, *Slavery and Emancipation in Islamic East Africa: From Honor to Respectability* (Cambridge: Cambridge University Press, 2013), 196.

[9] Interview with Maria Leo Kalenga, Ndala, 6 September 2016.

[10] Norman Etherington, 'Mission Station Melting Pots as a Factor in the Rise of South African Black Nationalism', *International Journal of African Historical Studies*, Vol. 9, No. 4 (1976), 593.

[11] The concept of 'African Christianity' is shaped by Andrew Walls' understanding as 'Christian history in its own right, not an appendage of the missionary narrative.' See Wanjiru Gitau, 'The Life Work of Andrew Walls for African Theology: Re-centering Africa's Place in Christian History', November 2022,

Word into the Kinyamwezi and later the Kiswahili languages. In addition to translation, teachers and catechists administered churches in villages, taught catechism, and prepared the young and adults for baptism and confirmation. Other responsibilities included leading prayers on Sundays and at festivals, visiting families in villages at least once a week, offering instruction every evening, and teaching religious classes in nearby schools.[12]

In the earlier years of evangelization, slaves fled to the mission communities. Later, many slaves made public declarations and used certification of emancipation (*Freibriefe*) as ways to join the missions.[13] Public declarations developed in missions as a preliminary step towards the certification of emancipation to avoid tensions between slave owners and missionaries and between missionaries and officials of the German colonial state. The increasing numbers of fugitive slaves and those who desired to leave their masters prompted the German colonial state at Tabora military headquarters (*boma*) to mandate that individuals declare their desire to join mission communities before groups of witnesses as a legal prerequisite for certification of emancipation.[14] Both individual flights to the mission and certification of emancipation increased the number of slaves (adults and the young) in the Catholic missions in Unyamwezi. In 1906, about fifteen boys and ten girls lived in the orphanage at the Tabora mission, while fifty people lived in the mission village. At the Ushirombo mission, fifty-eight boys and sixty-five girls lived in the orphanage; forty older women lived in one house; and about 489 people lived in three surrounding mission villages. At the Ndala mission, there was one orphanage with twenty boys and nine families living in the mission village. And in 1909, there was one orphanage centre with twenty-eight boys at the Ngaya (Msalala) mission and about 178 people living in the village near the mission.[15] The increasing number of girls and boys living in the orphanages of Tabora, Kipalapala, Ushirombo, Ndala, and Ngaya resulted in the growth of mission villages. In 1905, at Ushirombo alone, the Christian village consisted of 192 homesteads, with twenty-two new families emanating from the two orphanages of the mission. At Tabora between 1909 and 1910, the number of girls and children in the orphanage centre at Tabora increased to forty-nine, while fifty-one adult women joined the mission community.[16]

Lausanne Movement, https://lausanne.org/global-analysis/the-lifework-of-andrew-walls-for-african-theology-2 (accessed 11 April 2024).

[12] See, for instance, 'School for Catechists', July 1962, AAT 325.299; 'The Pastoral Institute', 28 January 1964, AAT 325.299.

[13] For details about public declarations in Tabora, see Chapter 3.

[14] Rachats d'esclaves, 1908–1909, AAT 322.399.

[15] Annual Report, 1905–1906, 51–52, UDSM/History.

[16] Notre Dame de Tabora, 1 July 1909–1 July 1910, AAT 350.002; Aylward Shorter,

INTRODUCTION 5

In missions beyond centres of slavery, the residents, including porters, employees, and Nyamwezi students, extended networks of friendship to missionaries. These interactions in the missions created the basis for the reciprocal translation of religious texts and songs into the Kinyamwezi language, with Africans and missionaries teaching each other.[17] The involvement of the Nyamwezi in the translation process stimulated the independent reading of religious texts. It allowed the Nyamwezi people to incorporate Christianity into their everyday village life. The daily interaction between teachers, catechists, and European missionaries in mission stations inspired the adaptation of Christian culture. It led to the growth of African Christianity in villages where the influence of European missionaries was marginal. African teachers and catechists took the ethos of the mission stations and added their own cultural and intellectual creativity.[18] Nyamwezi women (often the wives of catechists and teachers) joined these intellectuals (*vasomi*) in shaping the growth of African Christianity, providing a model of Christian womanhood that attracted village women to Christianity. Nyamwezi women also found that 'home visits' and 'neighbourhood' (*lusangi*) gatherings offered greater opportunities for reaching more women and Christians in villages because they fostered the long-standing Nyamwezi practice of communal meals.[19]

The growth of Christianity in twentieth-century western Tanzania corresponded with tensions and divisions in the Catholic and Moravian churches. Catechists' demands for a salary, remunerations, and greater recognition within the church divided the clergy between European missionaries who supported their demands and African priests who objected to their claims.[20] For the Moravians, divergent interpretations of the teachings about salvation, sin, and public confession of sins split Christians in the established mission churches into born-again pastors and Christians who supported revivalism,

---

Cross and Flag: The 'White Fathers' during the Colonial Scramble (1892–1914) (Maryknoll, NY: Orbis Books), 74. See also Francis P. Nolan, 'Christianity in Unyamwezi, 1878–1928' (PhD thesis, University of Cambridge, 1977), 102.

[17] See, for instance, Teofilo H. Kisanji, *Historia Fupi ya Kanisa la Kimoravian Tanganyika Magharibi* (Kipalapala: TMP, 1980), 37–43.

[18] Ibid., 253–60; 'Catechist Benedicto Inega-Kitangiri Mission', 25 October 1956, AAT 325.297.

[19] Rev. Blackburn to Mr Lang, CMS Uyui, 24 June 1884, CMS/B/OMS/G3 A6/O/113; 'School for Catechists at Ndala', July 1962, AAT 325.299; interviews with Samweli Saimon Mhoja, Nhazengwa, 22 November 2016, and Jonas Kulwa Msubi, Nhazengwa, 23 November 2016.

[20] Fr J.B. Cuivrier to Fr Maguire, Ndala mission, 26 August 1970, AAT 325.298; letter to Archbishop Mihayo, Ndala, 20 October 1969, AAT 325.298; Fr Peter Dalali, Lukula Parish, 16 July 1962, AAT 325.298.

and Christians who opposed the revival movement. This book shows for the first time that lay Christians dissented against the revival movement, preventing born-again pastors and evangelists from holding church services. With growing tensions, some Christians seceded from the mainstream churches to form their own churches and installed pastors who worked independently of the Moravian church authority.[21] By the mid-1950s, religious dissent had become a significant force to be reckoned with, as the influence of revivalism in Tabora town grew. It attracted enough dissatisfied Christians from far and wide into the newly formed church to become a centre of religious dissent. Dissent against born-again pastors and Christians filtered into villages through a network of teachers, pastors, and Christians who had decamped from the Moravian mainstream churches.[22]

Dissent in missions and villages coincided with the Second World War that had a far-reaching impact on Tanganyika. The war's end ushered in a new era of intensive exploitation to revamp the dilapidated British economy, and, accordingly, the need for resources from Tanganyika intensified, as the empire was restructured through what has been called the 'second colonial occupation'.[23] By the mid-1950s, as the crisis reached the point of no return, decolonization in Tanganyika seemed inevitable to curb the dilemmas of increased colonial exploitation. Subsequently, ideas of independence spread in rural and urban Unyamwezi under party leaders of the Tanganyika African National Union (TANU) and dominated political and religious spheres such that formerly enslaved people, their descendants, and Christians in general 'began to talk about independence in churches' ('walianza kuzungumza kuhusu uhuru makanisani') and that idioms of 'self-governance from European missionaries' ('kujitawala kutoka kwa Wamisionari') dominated the everyday life of Christians in missions and villages.[24] Catechists and teachers demanded greater prominence and administration of churches in villages and mission stations amid the political and cultural shifts of the 1950s in

---

[21] Kisanji, *Historia Fupi*, 215.

[22] See, for instance, Moravian Mission Sikonge Diary, 28 October 1955, KFC; Moravian Mission Milumbani Diary, 19–20 May 1957, KFC.

[23] Donald A. Low and John Lonsdale, 'Introduction: Towards the New Order 1945–1963', in D.A. Low and Alison Smith (eds), *Oxford History of East Africa*, Vol. 3 (Oxford: Clarendon Press, 1976), 1–64. See also John Iliffe, *A Modern History of Tanganyika* (Cambridge: Cambridge University Press, 1979), 342; Salvatory S. Nyanto, 'Priests without Ordination: Catechists and their Wives in Villages beyond Missions, 1948–1978', *Catholic Historical Review*, Vol. 108, No. 3 (2022), 570.

[24] Interview with Oscar E. Kisanji, Tabora, 4 March 2020. See also Nyanto, 'Priests without Ordination', 571.

Tanganyika. For the Moravian teachers, the quest for Tanganyikan independence inspired them to push for the agenda of self-governance (*kujitawala*), complete authority (*mamlaka kamili*), and the creation of a synod (*sinodi*) and a provincial board (*halmashauri Kuu ya Jimbo*) within the Moravian Church of Western Tanganyika.[25]

In 1967, the Tanzania government launched the Arusha Declaration, which delineated the policies of 'Socialism and Self-Reliance' and 'Socialism and Rural Development' to promote people-centred development. The policies advocated egalitarianism, social and spatial equality, and communal life and production in settled *ujamaa* villages.[26] Catechists and their wives accommodated the principles of socialism in village outstations in small Christian communities ('*jumuiya ndogo ndogo*') because they regarded both *ujamaa* and *Gaudium et Spes* as integral to human dignity, development, and peace.[27] In the same vein, the Moravians responded to the call of the government and TANU party to 'build the new nation' ('kujenga taifa changa') and 'rid the country from the exploitation of the few' by insisting on the equality of people in villages as 'the central objective and effort of the church' ('lengo la juhudi za shughuli za kikanisa'), and by calling on teachers and evangelists in villages 'to cooperate with village government leaders' ('kushirikiana na viongozi wa serikali') on various campaigns and programmes in *ujamaa* villages.[28]

This book combines the narratives of religious experience from multiple Christian communities in Catholic and Moravian missions and village outstations. The experience in Unyamwezi in western Tanzania was somewhat different from other parts of East Africa, where Catholic and Protestant missionaries were invariably at loggerheads in the nineteenth and twentieth centuries. In Unyamwezi, the colonial authority policies of 'first come, first served' and a 'three-mile limit' helped thwart religious conflict between Catholic and Protestant missionaries. In places where missionaries of different faiths applied for land near one another, the colonial state authority would turn down the request in order to prevent tensions from arising between missionaries.[29]

---

[25] Oscar E. Kisanji, *Nimesema, Askofu Teofilo Hiyobo Kisanji: Baadhi ya Maandiko aliyoandika Hotuba alizotoa na Mahubiri aliyoyafanya kati ya mwaka 1955 na 1982* (Tabora: Frontex Associates, 2023), 25–27.

[26] Julius K. Nyerere, 'Socialism and Rural Development', in *Freedom and Socialism: A Selection from Writings and Speeches, 1965–1967* (1968; repr. Dar es Salaam: Oxford University Press, 1973), 7–9.

[27] Juvenalis B. Rwelamira, *Tanzanian Socialism, Ujamaa and Gaudium et Spes: Two Convergent Designs of Integral Human Development* (Rome: Academia Alfonsiana, 1988), 60; Nyanto, 'Priests without Ordination', 575.

[28] Kisanji, *Nimesema*, 128 and 198.

[29] Salvatory S. Nyanto, 'Empire, Religious Conflicts, and State Intervention in

SLAVE EMANCIPATION, CHRISTIAN COMMUNITIES, AND DISSENT IN TANZANIA

Consequently, the White Fathers established themselves in present-day northern Unyamwezi, placing missions along the central caravan route in Ushirombo, Tabora, Ndala, and Kipalapala between 1881 and 1902.[30] The Moravians, on the other hand, established themselves in southern Unyamwezi between 1898 and 1908. A German missionary, Rudolf Stern, adopted the Society's plan of establishing a mission presence with a chain of mission stations from Lake Victoria to the Nyasa Province. Later on, the Moravians established mission stations in southern Unyamwezi, particularly Kitunda, Kipembawe, Ipole and Sikonge. Ultimately, the southern part of Unyamwezi remained under Moravian influence. It was left unattended by other missionary societies, especially the White Fathers, until the beginning of the First World War in 1914.[31]

The Arguments: Gender, Adaptation, and Dissent in the Making of Christianity

The arguments of this book focus on how themes of gender, adaptation, and dissent came together in the making of Christian communities in post-abolition Tabora. I will particularly emphasize how the assimilation of Christianity reflected the concerns of former slaves who were seeking to escape marginalization under existing social hierarchies. By joining mission communities, former slaves not only adapted to the Christian culture but also dissented from authority, and some challenged religious authorities in the later decades of the twentieth century. Porters and the formerly enslaved living among the Nyamwezi were an essential part of the multilingual context of early Christians and played an important role in translating the Bible,

---

Buha and Unyamwezi, Colonial Tanganyika, 1920s–1960', *Tanzania Journal of Sociology*, Vol. 5 (June 2019), 79. For instance, in 1941, the White Fathers applied for a site at Kitangiri, about four miles from Nzega town, but the colonial state restricted the White Fathers from opening a new mission station because missionaries of the Swedish Free Mission had already set up their first mission station at Tazengwa, a few miles from Nzega town. For details, see Annual Report for Nzega Division, Kahama District, 1941, TNA 967.821.1.

[30] Nolan, 'Christianity in Unyamwezi', 157 and 196; Ushirombo Diary, 5 February 1891, WFA 01.43; Ndala Diary, 8–9 January 1896, WFA 01.43.

[31] Aylward E.M. Shorter, 'Ukimbu and the Kimbu Chiefdoms of Southern Unyamwezi: The History and Present Pattern of Kimbu Social Organisation and Movement', n.d., WFA 11-03; Kisanji, *Historia Fupi*, 37; J. Taylor Hamilton and Kenneth G. Hamilton, *History of the Moravian Church: The Renewed Unitas Fratrum, 1722–1957*, 2nd edn (Bethlehem, PA: Interprovincial Board of Christian Education, Moravian Church of America, 1983), 611; and Angetile Y. Musomba, *The Moravian Church in Tanzania Southern Province: A Short History* (Nairobi: IFRA, 2005), 85.

religious texts, and songs into Kinyamwezi, the language widely spoken in the region. In so doing, they departed from the ʿAjamī script of Kiswahili and influenced missionaries' inclination to Kinyamwezi as the language of translation and evangelization in missions and villages.[32] Indeed, this intellectual process embodied African adaptation and agency in shaping Christianity in nineteenth- and twentieth-century western Tanzania, in that Africans successfully integrated the Nyamwezi culture, social relations, and chiefly authority into the translated versions of the religious texts.[33]

Evidence from archives and documentary sources show that most runaway slaves were women (adults and children) who joined the missions of Tabora with hopes of finding alternative spaces free from the abuses of slavery.[34] The list of names of formerly enslaved women and orphan girls between four and forty years of age who sought refuge in the mission communities at Tabora, Ushirombo, and Ndala in the Vicariate Apostolic of Unyanyembe reveal the importance of gender in shaping the course of African Christianity and culture in nineteenth- and twentieth-century Tanzania. The experience of converts as 'part of the mission workforce' and 'workers in the mission' indicates how they negotiated their terms of freedom in the village communities of the missions.[35] After marriage, women maintained their ties to the missions as lay Christians, catechists, and the wives of catechists. As the wives of catechists, women proved to have a 'wholesome influence on their environment, especially on the women of the place where they [were] stationed'.[36] Village women learned from the wives of catechists the skills, including handicrafts and reading and writing, that the latter had acquired during their two-year stay at the Ndala mission, thereby contributing to the creation of a 'race of intellectual Christians' in villages.[37]

---

[32] See Chapter 3.

[33] Kisanji, *Historia Fupi*, 43.

[34] See, for instance, Notre Dame de Tabora, 1 July 1909–1 July, 1910, AAT 350.002.

[35] See, for instance, Noms des femmes, filles et enfants à Notre Dame, 1909–1910, 1 July 1910, AAT 350.002; Noms des autres réfugiées à Notre Dame, 1909–1910, AAT 350.002. See also Jean Claude Ceillier and François Richard, *Cardinal Charles Lavigerie and the Anti-Slavery Campaign* (Rome: Society of Missionaries of Africa, 2012), 156–60. In formulating an argument about women as 'workers of the mission', I am indebted to the work of Michelle Liebst, 'African Workers and the Universities' Mission to Central Africa in Zanzibar, 1864–1900', *Journal of Eastern African Studies*, Vol. 8, No. 3 (2014), 370 and 373.

[36] Archbishop, Marcus Mihayo, Tabora, to Rt Rev. Msgr H. Goertz, Gen. Sekr. Päpstliches Werk der Glaubensverbreitung, Hermannstrasze, 27 March 1967, AAT 325.299.

[37] School for Catechists, 11 July 1962, AAT Box 325.299; Andreana C. Prichard,

Women's agency in 'domesticating a religious import' and 'translating the message' created spaces for negotiating kinship ties and mutual relations with the wider communities in missions and villages through weekly dances and annual festivals.[38] In the Moravian and Swedish Free missions, women's prominence proved a more formidable force in shaping Christianity in villages beyond the missions. In addition to itinerant visits to village outstations, women in the Moravian and Swedish Free missions launched home-visit campaigns that were essential for the creation of 'affective spiritual communities', 'spiritual bonds and connections', and for forging 'kinships and friendships' with women based on their shared experiences.[39] Women capitalized on 'home visits' and 'neighbourhood' (*lusangi*) gatherings to reach out to more women and Christians in villages and to reinforce the long-standing Nyamwezi culture of the neighbourhood and communal meals. The involvement of women in the *lusangi* festivals and home visits as scripture readers, teachers, and translators of Christian texts offered them, missionaries, and African teachers the means to reinforce friendships and network–kin relations within and beyond mission communities.[40]

Formerly enslaved people also adapted themselves to the culture of mission communities and Nyamwezi society in nineteenth- and twentieth-century Tabora. Indeed, weekly dances and *lusangi* festivals bound formerly enslaved people to Christian and Nyamwezi culture because they offered them avenues for integration into mission communities and villages.[41] While some slaves adapted to the new culture by retaining their names with slave antecedents, others did not accept this practice and instead adopted Christian names to obscure their former identity.[42] The concealment of slave status through name changes increased from the second decade of the twentieth century and reflected a generational shift as formerly enslaved people and their descendants

---

Sisters in Spirit: Christianity, Affect, and Community Building in East Africa, 1860–1970 (East Lansing: Michigan State University Press, 2017), 8.

[38] Nicholas M. Creary, *Domesticating a Religious Import: The Jesuits and the Inculturation of the Catholic Church in Zimbabwe, 1879–1980* (New York: Fordham University Press, 2011), 619; and Lamin Sanneh, *Translating the Message: The Missionary Impact on Culture* (Maryknoll, NY: Orbis Books, 2009), 51.

[39] Prichard, *Sisters in Spirit*, 7–8.

[40] 'School for Catechists at Ndala', July 1962, AAT 325.299; interviews with Samweli Saimon Mhoja, Nhazengwa, 22 November 2016, and Jonas Kulwa Msubi, Nhazengwa, 23 November 2016.

[41] Ibid.

[42] Listi ya Vakristo Vahanya, Kanisa ya Ulilwansimba, Sikonge, Listi No. 2, entry 1944, KFC; Listi ya Vakristo Vahanya, Kanisa ya Vutyatya-Sikonge, Listi No 3, entry 527, 1944, KFC; and Listi ya Vakristo Vahanya, Kanisa ya Vutyatya-Sikonge, entry 711, 1944, KFC.

joined missions as adults and the development of binary distinctions in post-abolition Unyamwezi society between 'indigenous' (*wazawa*) and 'foreigners' (*wakuja*) and between 'Nyamwezi Christians' and 'former slaves' and their descendants who were marked as 'simply slaves' (*watumwa tu*).[43] Name changes to hide one's slave past suggest that shame (*aibu*) became a shorthand for the gamut of emotions associated with the trauma of enslavement. It is also suggestive of the hardships endured by the descendants of enslaved people who had to face persistent social tensions and new distinctions between slave and free, between those deemed 'civilized' Christians and unconverted slaves, and between *bona fide* residents and foreigners that shaped the discourses of slavery in twentieth-century Tanganyika.[44]

Dissent characterized the social history of slavery and the creation of mission communities in nineteenth- and twentieth-century Unyamwezi. Dissent began in nineteenth-century Unyamwezi with marronage – runaway slaves who defied the chiefly authority that hinged on the assumption that 'all people belonged to the chief'.[45] By joining mission communities, runaway slaves defied the authority of chiefs in Unyamwezi. They became a source of contention between chiefs and missions on the one hand and between chiefs, catechists, and teachers on the other.[46] Because most missionaries were relatively unversed in the Kinyamwezi language and culture, catechists and teachers served as translators because they knew the indigenous languages and culture. Their mastery of the Kinyamwezi languages allowed African catechists to revise accepted dogma in the work of translation. They interpreted scripture in their own way, appropriated Christianity, and were seen as 'masters of new ways' in the villages because they could read and write and were deeply immersed in their own culture.[47]

The East African revival (*ulokole*) which began in the 1930s on the evangelical wing of the CMS mission at Gahini in northern Rwanda had a far-reaching impact in East Africa in general and Tanganyika in particular. By the 1940s, its influence culminated in dissent, and in class and family divisions. Derek Peterson's authoritative work on the East African revival approaches revivalists as theological, social, and political innovators who challenged a

---

[43] Interviews with Eli William Makenge, Tabora, 4 October 2021, and Issa Ndima Kipakila, Kipalapala village, 11 March 2020.

[44] See for instance Paul V. Kollman, *The Evangelization of Slaves and Catholic Origins in East Africa* (Maryknoll, NY: Orbis Books, 2005), 265.

[45] For details see Rev. Blackburn to Mr Lang, CMS Uyui, 3 December 1883, CMS/B/OMS/G3 A6/O/8.

[46] Nolan, 'Christianity in Unyamwezi', 317.

[47] J.D.Y. Peel, *Religious Encounter and the Making of the Yoruba* (Bloomington: Indiana University Press, 2000), 156–61.

growing Christian establishment that had been slow to respond to dramatic social change.[48] For Peterson, opposing ideas between revivalists and patriotic critics stirred disagreements in their societies because each had its own version of community building.[49] Catherine Robins also shows the conflict between the revival brethren (*Balokole* or 'Saved Ones') and church leaders and the laity whom revivalists referred to as 'unsaved' Christians.[50]

By contrast, this book shows that dissenters in western Tanzania broke away from the established mission churches and village outstations. Divergent interpretation of sin, conversion and salvation aroused tensions between born-again pastors who supported revivalism and Christians who opposed the movement. In Unyamwezi, as revivalism took hold in villages, some women 'threw away their decoration beads as a sign of being born-again'.[51] Groups of saved women and men visited the homes of Moravian women in villages and missions to convince kin to join the revival movement. Nevertheless, their efforts encountered a formidable challenge from kin members who wanted to maintain the Moravian liturgy and doctrine traditions.[52] Revivalism also had a bearing on divisions in the Moravian church between born-again pastors in western Tanzania who worked from within the established church and Christians who were critical of them. Persistent inequality between the rich and the poor in Unyamwezi society accentuated doctrinal controversies over salvation, sin, and tithes (*zaka*), and increased dissent against revivalism, as dissenters questioned the role of wealth in salvation.[53] Growing tensions led some Christians to form their own churches and recognize their own pastors, drawing other dissatisfied Christians into their new churches. In some parts of East Africa, revivalists appealed to Christians' lives and became agents of social, political, and moral reform. Nevertheless, evidence from western Tanzania shows that the Moravian believers strongly opposed the movement and seceded to form an independent church with its own leadership and liturgy.[54]

---

[48] Derek R. Peterson, *Ethnic Patriotism and East African Revival: A History of Dissent, c. 1935–1972* (Cambridge: Cambridge University Press, 2012).

[49] Peterson, *Ethnic Patriotism*, 128, 150–51.

[50] Catherine E. Robins, 'Tukutendereza: A Study of Social Change and Sectarian Withdrawal in the Balokole Revival of Uganda' (PhD thesis, Columbia University, 1975), 27.

[51] Interview with Rev. Paulo Isai Misigalo, Tabora, 27 June 2017. Misigalo, in Kiswahili: 'wanawake walitupa shanga zao kama ishara ya kuokoka'.

[52] Interview with Sesilia Nikodemo Msogoti, Isevya-Tabora, 12 June 2018.

[53] See for instance 'Barazani kuna Baba zako Wengi', 1938, KFC.

[54] Sikonge Diary, 13–14 October 1942, KFC.

The administration of village outstations and the ingenuity in translating the message inspired teachers to join the nationwide nationalist movement calling for self-governance (*kujitawala*) and the Africanization of churches. By the 1950s, complaints that Africans were 'denied complete authority' (hawakupewa madaraka kamili) had become increasingly common in churches, education, and healthcare institutions because European missionaries 'accomplished tasks which Africans could easily do'. The formation of the Unyamwezi Moravian Council (UMCC) under the auspices of African pastors signalled the need for the Africanization of the church in the region because pastors and Christians used it as an effective forum to challenge the inequalities and bigotry between Africans and missionaries in mission churches, schools, and healthcare institutions. Within the UMCC, Africans exercised their intellectual creativity in challenging the hierarchies imposed by the European authorities in missions and village outstations. They used it to 'assume the authority of managing their affairs to become self-reliant'.[55]

Nevertheless, the quest for Africanization and self-governance was difficult, as it divided congregants and teachers within churches into missions and villages. While most pastors pushed for complete authority, others remained silent as Africans assumed the positions held by European missionaries.[56] The latter 'helped the colonial authority to prevent Africanization' and, therefore, slowed down the 'devolution of power' in churches and governments at provincial, district, and local levels.[57]

In 1967, following the Arusha Declaration and the implementation of *ujamaa* policies, dissent manifested in divisions between church authorities and the clergy and catechists in the villages. Unfair treatment coupled with economic hardships in the villages encouraged catechists to rebel against the church authority by demanding a salary and remuneration (*posho*) to ameliorate their untenable situation. Nevertheless, the decision to subsidize catechists aroused controversy between the White Fathers and the Nyamwezi clergy. The White Fathers argued that catechists should be paid a salary and other remuneration through donations from Europe because their busy schedule in villages – spending much of their time going to churches, waiting for catechumens, teaching, and visiting Christians – prevented them from cultivating crops like other villagers.[58] Although the Nyamwezi priests acknowledged the struggles endured by catechists in fulfilling their work in the villages, they opposed the idea of remuneration. Instead, they strongly believed that catechists should be taught to become self-reliant by cultivating the land allocated to them. The

---

[55] 'Minuti zya mkutano', October 1958, 4, KFC.

[56] Kisanji, *Nimesema*, 4–5.

[57] Ibid., 6–7.

[58] Letter to Archbishop Mihayo, Ndala, 20 October 1969, AAT 325.298.

Religious Experience and Missionary Sources in East African Historiography

Nyamwezi insistence on the need for the church authority to make catechists learn to become self-reliant largely stemmed from the ideals of socialism and self-sufficiency that had filtered down into rural areas during the first decade of Tanzania's independence.[59]

Religious Experience and Missionary Sources in East African Historiography

The abundant literature on Christianity has played a significant role in East African historiography. Scholars rely on missionary sources in multiple languages from the many archives to tell the stories of missionaries and evangelization in nineteenth- and twentieth-century East Africa. Despite the many erudite studies based on missionary sources, the religious experience of formerly enslaved people and the place of adaptation, gender, and dissent in the making of Christianity remain largely unexplored in the existing literature on East African Christianity. Thomas Spear and Isaria Kimambo published a collection of essays about East African expressions of Christianity in which the contributors draw examples from the myriad of missionary sources to show how Africans interpreted Christianity for themselves and appropriated it within the context of their own experiences.[60] While some of the volume's contributors document individual aspects of social change that are 'often considered part of Christianization', the book's overall analysis makes little effort to probe into the entanglements resulting from multiple interpretations, divisions, and class conflict within and beyond churches.[61]

In their studies of runaway slaves in Eastern and Central Africa, Fred Morton and Marcia Wright show various strategies and struggles for freedom. Fred Morton's study draws examples from the written records of missionaries, British officials, and formerly enslaved Christians in late nineteenth- and early twentieth-century Kenya to show that although slaves on the Kenyan coast who were pejoratively marked as 'children of Ham' found it easier to escape and organized self-governing runaway slave communities, colonial conquest in the late nineteenth century 'increased violence against and exploitation of freed and fugitive slaves', and the 'abolition of slavery seldom improved their

---

[59] Fr Peter Dalali, Lukula Parish, 16 July 1962, AAT 325.298.

[60] Tomas Spear, 'Introduction: Toward the History of African Christianity', in Thomas Spear and Isaria N. Kimambo (eds), *East African Expressions of Christianity* (Oxford: James Currey, 1999), 1.

[61] The exception in this volume is James L. Giblin, 'Family Life, Indigenous Culture and Christianity in Colonial Njombe', in Spear and Kimambo (eds), *East African Expressions of Christianity*, 309–22.

social and economic prospects'.[62] In her study of various strategies of slave emancipation, Marcia Wright explores how the life-histories of slaves (one man and five women) shed light on the experience of the transition from slavery to 'some sort of freedom'; these changes were not formal acts of emancipation because formerly enslaved people belonged to or were sheltered by a Christian community.[63] Her argument builds on the work of Edward Alpers about the story of Swema in nineteenth-century East Africa. Although Swema remained tied to the mission, Alpers suggests that her story embodied 'female vulnerability', 'struggles to embrace Christianity', and 'an opportunity to publicize the work of the mission'.[64] While acknowledging the contribution of these works to shedding light on the limited freedom experienced by formerly enslaved people in mission communities, they overlook how formerly enslaved people not only adapted to the mission experience and integrated their culture but also dissented from mission and colonial authorities and played a crucial role in inducing other slaves to join mission communities.

Missionaries in Eastern Africa relied on slaves as the basis for evangelization, and slaves who joined missions formed the first generation of Christians. Adrian Hastings argues that the White Fathers in Ushirombo, western Tanzania, 'made annual shopping expeditions to the slave market of Ujiji' and bought children to emancipate who were then to be Christianized as part of the socializing process in mission villages.[65] We also learn from Paul Kollman's work that the Spiritan missionaries (Holy Ghost) concentrated on evangelizing freed slaves along the Tanzanian coast. He argues that the missionary influence over formerly enslaved people depended on the 'control of space and time' but also emphasizes that African responses to the formative process in missions 'did not always fulfill the missionaries' hopes'.[66] Though these works provide glimpses into the challenges encountered in evangelizing the freed slaves, they position slave emancipation as a triumph of missionary enterprise. Little attention is devoted to individual experiences, such as the flight to the mission and public declarations of slaves' intent to become free, and slaves' agency in shaping early mission communities and integrating their own culture and experiences of slavery into Christianity.

---

[62] Fred Morton, *Children of Ham: Freed Slaves and Fugitive Slaves on the Kenya Coast, 1873–1907* (Boulder, CO: Westview Press, 1990), 1–2.

[63] Marcia Wright, *Strategies of Slaves and Women: Life Stories from East/Central Africa* (London: James Currey, 1993), 1.

[64] Edward A. Alpers, 'The Story of Swema: Female Vulnerability in Nineteenth-Century East Africa', in Clarie C. Robertson and Martin Klein (eds), *Women and Slavery in Africa* (Madison: University of Wisconsin Press, 1983), 185–86.

[65] Hastings, *The Church in Africa*, 213.

[66] Kollman, *Evangelization of Slaves*, 6.

Both enslaved and free women were central to the growth and spread of Christian culture in East Africa. Dorothy Hodson, Cynthia Hoeler-Fatton, and Heike Behrend have examined the place of gender in the development of African Christianity.[67] In extending the discussion on gender, Andreana Prichard's work draws examples from missionary sources and personal stories of female evangelists to show that African Christian women exploited the culture of Christianity in missions and networks of 'affective spirituality' that spread throughout Zanzibar and the adjacent mainland to create 'cultural nationalisms'.[68] Nevertheless, as Michelle Liebst argues, the work focuses on how missions, rather than the individuals within them, forged communities in nineteenth- and twentieth-century Zanzibar and Tanganyika.[69] While Prichard's book contributes to our understanding of how slaves became mothers and shaped networks of affective spirituality, discussion of how formerly enslaved people created effective communities and dissented from mission authority would have aided our knowledge of their experience in post-abolition Zanzibar and Tanganyika.

More recently, Liebst's work has extended the discussion on the labour history of Christian missions to show how missions acted as 'places of work' for skilled and unskilled African workers, enabling formerly enslaved people 'to establish an ideal setting for their core aims: the conversion of souls and the eventual establishment of an African ministry'.[70] She argues that many formerly enslaved African workers earned their living within the mission and drew upon and *adapted* knowledge and networks from the mission to make a living elsewhere. That African workers adapted to networks from the mission suggests that they were active participants in the transformation of Christianity and that 'with the pursuit of status and that of wages at odds, conversion and the adoption of a mission-centred career was a high-risk life strategy'.[71]

Meanwhile, studies about missionary translation have established the link between translation and idioms of knowledge and power, exhibiting how missionaries and colonial authorities drew parallels between conquest,

---

[67] Cynthis Hoehler-Fatton, *Women of Fire and Spirit: History, Faith and Gender in Roho Religion in Western Kenya* (Oxford: Oxford University Press, 1996); Dorothy L. Hodgson, *The Church of Women: Gendered Encounters between Maasai and Missionaries* (Bloomington: Indiana University Press, 2005); and Heike Behrend, *Alice Lakwena and the Holy Spirits: War in Northern Uganda, 1986–1997* (Oxford: James Currey, 1999).

[68] Prichard, *Sisters in Spirit*, 14 and 22.

[69] Michelle Liebst, *Labour and Christianity in the Mission: African Workers in Tanganyika and Zanzibar, 1864–1926* (Woodbridge: James Currey, 2021), 6.

[70] Liebst, *Labour and Christianity*, 1.

[71] Ibid.

conversion, and translation.[72] The works of Derek Peterson and John Peel show the intellectual responses of the Yoruba of Nigeria and the Gikuyu of Kenya to the evangelization efforts of missionaries. Although the two ethnic groups regarded 'European knowledge as powerful', their agency in the translation of religious texts was instrumental in shaping the course of Christianity because they incorporated Christian knowledge into their own culture and beliefs, employing these works of translation to show the connection between Christianity and vernacular languages, as well as between Christianity and indigenous religious concepts, and the difficulties of finding adequate synonyms for words associated with religion and authority.[73] Yet, as pointed out by Liebst, in both Yoruba and Gikuyu, the thrust of missionary education was closely linked with 'elitism and the beginnings of an African middle class'.[74]

As for revivalism and dissent in East Africa, scholarship has concentrated on conflicts between revivalists and church authorities, portraying revivalists as social, political, and moral agents of reform. In her work about revivalism and dissent, Catherine Robins shows that the conflict between revivalists (*balokole*) and church leaders intensified in twentieth-century Uganda because revivalists criticized the clergy and refused to 'compromise their sectarian principles'.[75] Revivalists' criticism of and refusal to compromise with the principles in established churches and the endurance of the revivalist movement have encouraged Kevin Ward, Emma Wild-Wood, Jason Bruner, and Daewon Moon to undertake further studies of the history, legacy, and politics

---

[72] Saurabh Dube, *After Conversion: Cultural Histories of Modern India* (New Delhi: Yoda Press, 2010), 40; Saurabh Dube, 'Conversion to Translation: Colonial Registers of a Vernacular Christianity', *South Atlantic Quarterly*, Vol. 101, No. 4 (2000), 815–16; Naoki Sakai, *Translations and Subjectivity: On Japan and Cultural Nationalism* (Minneapolis: University of Minnesota Press, 2008); Vicente Rafael, *Contracting Colonialism: Translation and Christian Conversion in Tagalog Society under Early Spanish Rule* (Ithaca, NY: Cornell University Press, 1988), 21; Johannes Fabian, *Language and Colonial Power: The Appropriation of Swahili in the Former Belgian Congo 1880–1938* (Cambridge: Cambridge University Press, 1986).

[73] Peel, *Religious Encounter*, 156–61; Derek R. Peterson, 'Translating the Word: Dialogism and Debate in Two Gikuyu Dictionaries', *Journal of Religious History*, Vol. 23, No. 1 (1999), 31; and Derek R. Peterson, *Creative Writing: Translation, Bookkeeping, and the Work of Imagination in Colonial Kenya* (Portsmouth, NH: Heinemann, 2004), 118.

[74] Liebst, *Labour and Christianity*, 5.

[75] Catherine E. Robins, 'Tukutendereza: A Study of Social Change and Sectarian Withdrawal in the Balokole Revival of Uganda' (PhD thesis, Columbia University, 1975), 140–42.

of public confession.[76] Recently, the work of Derek Peterson on revivalism and dissent has concentrated on the controversy between revivalists and their opponents – the 'patriotic critics' – to explore the processes of building political communities and the social history of dissent in East Africa. For Peterson, revivalists viewed conversion as a form of 'political and cultural criticism', emphasizing new ways of living, refusing to act as members of the political communities, and calling for 'moral and social reform'.[77]

Conversely, patriotic critics endeavoured to build political communities, encouraged people to be bound to their communities, and insisted on polygamy to strengthen communities. Divergent viewpoints between revivalists and patriotic critics on community building aroused controversy in their societies, with dissenters marking revivalists as 'anti-social' and 'destroyers of civil communities'.[78] Notwithstanding the wide range of studies about the East African revival, there has been no effort to delve into the experience of Christians who challenged the movement within established churches.

This book adds to the existing scholarship by examining the religious experience of formerly enslaved people in nineteenth- and twentieth-century Tabora in western Tanzania. It shows how slaves with diverse linguistic and cultural backgrounds from various parts of the East African interior came together to create mission communities, adapted to the Christian culture, and integrated their own culture and experiences of slavery into Christianity. Because they had laboured in the region as slaves, they learned the Kinyamwezi language and the regional culture. The interaction with Nyamwezi residents inspired them to move away from missionaries' understanding and translation of the language and culture, shaping the interpretation of texts in the Kinyamwezi language. In the end, the translation of Nyamwezi texts became an act of 'cultural mediation' and a 'conversation' between Christian and Nyamwezi concepts.[79] Translators, mostly formerly enslaved people and porters working

---

[76] See Kevin Ward and Emma Wild-Wood (eds), *The East African Revival: History and Legacies* (Farnham: Ashgate, 2012); Jason S. Bruner, 'The Politics of Public Confession in the East African Revival in Uganda, ca. 1930–1950' (PhD thesis, Princeton University, 2013); Jason S. Bruner, 'Contesting Confession in the East African Revival', *Anglican and Episcopal History*, Vol. 84, No. 3 (2015), 253–78; Jason S. Bruner, *Living Salvation in the East African Revival in Uganda* (Rochester, NY: University of Rochester Press, 2017), 46–59; and Daewon Moon, 'The Conversion of Yosiya Kinuka and the Beginning of the East African Revival', *International Bulletin of Mission Research*, Vol. 41, No. 3 (2017), 204–14.

[77] Peterson, *Ethnic Patriotism*, 3–6, 127, and 173.

[78] Ibid., 128 and 150–51.

[79] I use Jean and John Comaroff's idea of 'long conversation' to describe the encounter between missionaries and the Nyamwezi. See Jean and John Comaroff,

in missions as resident catechists and teachers, sometimes changed concepts intentionally as they determined the words from Kinyamwezi to be used in translation. Thus, translation became an independent interpretation, and translators acted as independent intellectuals in shaping an African interpretation of Christianity.[80] This book situates the study of slavery and Christianity within the context of the multiple language communities in western Tanzania to understand how the translation process produced first-generation African teachers and catechists who laid the basis for the growth of African Christianity in villages.

This book also delves into the range of missionary sources to show the experience of lay Christians who opposed religious authority in Catholic and Moravian missions. The formerly enslaved people who initially worked in missions as resident catechists and teachers shaped the new ethos of Christianity in the villages beyond the missions in the second decade of the twentieth century in Tanzania. Nevertheless, catechists mounted a rebellion against Catholic Church authorities because they did not accept the clergy's reluctance to remunerate and recognize catechists' work in the villages. They alluded to them as 'examples of successful mission work' in villages.[81] Mission diaries and reports of the Moravian mission help us to reconstruct the experiences of Christians who opposed the revival movement and prevented born-again pastors and evangelists from holding church services. For the first time in the history of the East African revival, Christians challenged the doctrines of salvation, sin, and public confession embedded in the movement and broke away from the mainstream Moravian church in missions and villages to form an independent church that drew dissatisfied Christians who had expressed dissent in churches.

Translations as Sources of Christianity in Post-Abolition Tanzania

To tell the story of the religious experiences of formerly enslaved people in post-abolition Tanzania, I use as sources translations that reproduce the source text or transfer meaning from the source or donor language to the target or receiving language.[82] Using translations as a source on the history

---

Of Revelation and Revolution: Christianity, Colonialism and Consciousness in South Africa, Vol. 1 (Chicago, IL: University of Chicago Press, 1991), 243.

[80] Susan Bassnett, 'The Translator as Cross-Cultural Mediator', in Kirsten Malmkjær and Kevin Windle (eds), The Oxford Handbook of Translation Studies (Oxford: Oxford University Press, 2011), 91–107.

[81] Richard Hölzl, 'Educating Missions: Teachers and Catechists in Southern Tanganyika, 1890s–1940s', Itenerario, Vol. 40, No. 3 (2016), 405.

[82] Daniel P. Kunene, introduction to Thomas Mofolo, Chaka, trans. Daniel P.

of Christianity remains, for the most part, a new approach, with few works looking at missionary translations as evidence.[83] For decades, the topic has attracted attention in literary studies, with scholars using translations to understand culture, societies, and history from fiction.[84] In East Africa, however, translation has until recently attracted few historians to examine religious texts and works of fiction. The limited number of historical studies that have used texts, record books, and imaginative works as sources of African history draw connections between translations and political innovation and suggest that translated texts can form the basis for explaining changing social relations.[85] Studies of this sort demonstrate that the disparities arising from divergent meanings of words should not be regarded as 'mistakes' but rather as 'evidence of the complex ontological and political debates [that] provoked early evangelistic activity'.[86] Some studies on missionary translations of texts and colonial registers of vernacular Christianity provide historians with avenues to probe into the salient features of evangelical entanglements and authority embedded in the texts.[87]

For almost two decades of evangelization (between 1878 and 1900), the Moravian and Church Missionary Society (CMS) missionaries in Unyamwezi relied on the translated works of Edward Steere, who had been working as bishop of the Universities Mission to Central Africa (UMCA) in Zanzibar, including his Kiswahili New Testament Bible, stories, and texts about the Kiswahili and Kinyamwezi languages as a basis for their missionary work in Unyamwezi. By the mid-1880s, children who received instruction at the mission and domestic servants could read the texts.[88] By the turn of the twentieth century, many Africans living in the missions had attended mission schools

---

Kunene (London: Heinemann, 1981), xix; Beatrix Heintze, 'Translations as Sources for African History', *History in Africa*, Vol. 11 (1984), 131–32; Willis Barnstone, *The Poetics of Translation: History, Theory, Practice* (New Haven, CT: Yale University Press, 1993), 22; Bible Society of Tanzania, *150 Years of Kiswahili Bible Translations* (Dodoma: Bible Society of Tanzania, 1994), 3.

[83] Peel, *Religious Encounter*, 11.

[84] Kunene, introduction to Mofolo, *Chaka*, xiv–xix.

[85] Peterson, *Creative Writing*, xi and 3.

[86] Peterson, 'Translating the Word', 31.

[87] Dube, 'Conversion to Translation', 161; Emma Hunter, 'Language, Empire and the World: Karl Roehl and the History of the Swahili Bible in East Africa', *Journal of Imperial and Commonwealth History*, Vol. 41, No. 4 (2013), 600.

[88] CMS Uyui, Central Africa, 23 February 1883, CMS/B/OMS/G3 A6/O/64/23; CMS Uyui, June 1885, CMS/B/OMS/G3 A6/O/102/24; Edward Steere, *The Kinyamwezi Language as spoken in the Chiefdom of Unyanyembe* (London: Society for the Promotion of Christian Knowledge, 1882), 13.

INTRODUCTION 21

and could read, write, and become involved in translation.[89] European missionaries and Africans relied on Kiswahili source texts for translating religious texts into Kinyamwezi. The meanings of words and expressions underwent significant changes as translators sought suitable translations. Translation into Kinyamwezi was crucial to the development of Christianity in western Tanzania because it made religious texts and songs available in various editions.[90]

Translation of religious texts and songs was one of the preoccupations of early missionaries and the Nyamwezi first-generation Christians in western Tanzania. Kinyamwezi translations of religious texts appeared in the first two decades of the twentieth century, with the first complete edition of the Kinyamwezi Gospel of Matthew appearing in 1907. The translation of the Gospel of Matthew was followed by the revised Gospel of Matthew in 1909, the Old Testament stories in 1910, the Kinyamwezi reading primer of 1911, the Kinyamwezi hymn book in 1912, and Kinyamwezi sermons of 1912 and 1913. Revised editions of some texts and new works gained momentum in missions and villages in the second decade of the twentieth century.[91] The prominence of Kinyamwezi texts was mainly attributable to the increasing number of Nyamwezi teachers (*vahembeki*) who had attended mission schools. Translations, as John Peel notes, were the first works of the modern Nyamwezi 'intelligentsia' because they are 'sources of information about the world which produced them and the narratives which are of intrinsic interests' for historians of the Christianization of Unyamwezi.[92] By employing linguistic skills and some rudimentary training from the mission schools, catechists and teachers 'crossed linguistic and cultural boundaries', preaching and teaching to spread the faith in villages beyond missions.[93] The mastery

---

[89] Kisanji, *Historia Fupi*, 76.

[90] For details about the idea of language as an important factor in the translation of the texts, see Heintze, 'Translations as Sources', 131–32.

[91] Kisanji, *Historia Fupi* 76, 256–59; *Matthäus-Evangelium auf Kinyamwezi (Deutsch-Ost-Afrika)* (Herrnhut: Missionsanstalt der Envagelischen Brüder-Unität, 1907); *Muhola ja Tjelu ja Ilagano Lipya Jakundulwa Mugati na Mupizya Wiswe Jesu Klisto Jatonilwe Mukijombele Tja Kinyamwezi*, trans. L.R. Stern (London and Herrnhut, 1909); *Fibula ja Kinyamwezi/Fibel der Nyamwezisprache* (Herrnhut: Missionsanstalt der Envagelischen Brüder-Unität, 1911); and *Ibuku lya nimbo zya mukanisa/Kleines Gesangbuch für Unyamwezi* (Herrnhut: Missionsanstalt der Envagelischen Brüder-Unität, 1912); and see Nis H. Gaarde, 'A Brief Report of Unyamwezi for the Year 1921', *Periodical Accounts Relating to Moravian Missions*, Vol. 11, No. 3 (June 1922), 136–37.

[92] Peel, *Religious Encounter*, 11.

[93] Paul Kollman and Cynthia Toms Smedley, *Understanding World Christianity: Eastern Africa* (Minneapolis, MN: Fortress Press, 2018), 41.

of culture and language enabled catechists and evangelists in the villages of western Tanzania to form 'the basis for the modern intelligentsia' by becoming 'scripture readers' and translators.[94] Changes made by translators in wording and expressions provide glimpses into the aspirations of early Christians in building Christian communities based on kinship relations and patronage.[95]

Texts reveal African adaptation and agency in making Christianity in nineteenth- and twentieth-century western Tanzania. They also suggest translation as a form of dissent and the influence of Nyamwezi culture, social relations, and chiefly authority on translating religious texts. Traces of Nyamwezi culture in the translations shed light on the daily interactions between the Nyamwezi porters, friends, converts, and residents in missions and missionaries, laying the groundwork for a complex back-and-forth translation process.[96] Thus, writes Emily Callaci, texts become 'active components of social change in which they were produced' and can 'reveal change and continuity over time'.[97]

Unyamwezi in Western Tanzania: Communities, Geography, and Missions

This book centres on communities in the Unyamwezi region of western Tanzania. Today, the largest part of Unyamwezi is within the Tabora administrative region, with its headquarters in Tabora town. The Tabora region has six administrative districts: Igunga, Kaliua, Nzega, Sikonge, Tabora Municipal, and Uyui. The population in Tabora town grew from 30,000 residents in 1903 to 2,539,715 in 2012.[98] In the nineteenth century, the town was strategically located at the junction where the central trade route from Bagamoyo on the Indian Ocean coast split into two branches. The first route led to Ujiji, and the second to the north around the western shores of Lake Victoria to present Uganda. The town became an important trade centre, a junction of major trade routes.[99] The Nyamwezi people emerged as leading caravan porters travelling

---

[94] Peel, *Religious Encounter*, 156–61.

[95] See, for instance, Brauer's Sermons, 1913, 53 and 56, KFC.

[96] For the daily interactions between the Nyamwezi people and missionaries in missions, see Kisanji, *Historia Fupi*, 30–47 and 76.

[97] Emily Callaci, *Street Archives and City Life: Popular Intellectuals in Postcolonial Tanzania* (Durham, NC: Duke University Press, 2017), 11–12.

[98] Karin Pallaver, 'A Triangle: Spatial Processes of Urbanization and Political Power in 19th-Century Tabora, Tanzania', *Afriques*, Vol. 11 (2020), https://doi.org/10.4000/afriques.2871; URT, *Population and Housing Census* (Dar es Salaam: Ministry of East African Cooperation, 2012), 2.

[99] David C. Sperling and Jose H. Kagabo, 'The Coast Hinterland and the Interior

INTRODUCTION   23

between the coast and the interior, transporting salt, dried fish, cattle, iron hoes, tobacco, ivory, and forest products to the coast and exchanging these for foodstuffs, cloth, and other trade goods. This involvement of the Nyamwezi people resulted in socioeconomic and political changes in Unyamwezi.[100]

In 1880, Ebenezer John Southon, the first resident medical doctor of the London Missionary Society (LMS) at the mission of Urambo Kilimani, described the linguistic and cultural diversity of the communities he encountered in Unyamwezi. Of all communities inhabiting the region, wrote Southon, the Nyamwezi were the largest. In the northeast, the Sukuma inhabited a large part of the country, extending from the south end of Lake Victoria. The Nyamwezi and Sukuma shared language and culture with a few noticeable dialectical differences. The Kisukuma language differed widely from other languages of the region, such as Kiha, Kitaturu, and Kikalaganza, but it was akin to Kigalagala, Kinyamwezi, and Kikimbu.[101] The Watuta or Wangoni lived in a small district about sixty miles northwest of Urambo, having moved into the region during the great migration of Nguni-speaking communities from southern Africa in the nineteenth century. The Wakalaganza occupied Uyango, Unzali, Usunga, and Unyanyembe. The Wagala inhabited the central parts of Unyamwezi. Other ethnic communities inhabiting the region included

---

of East Africa', in Nehemia Levtzion and Randall L. Pouwels (eds), *The History of Islam in Africa* (Athens: Ohio University Press, 2000), 288–90; Stephen J. Rockel, *Carriers of Culture: Labor on the Road in Nineteenth-Century East Africa* (Portsmouth, NH: Heinemann, 2006), 135; Andrew Roberts, 'Political Change in the Nineteenth Century', in Isaria N. Kimambo and Arnold J. Temu (eds), *A History of Tanzania* (Nairobi: East African Publishing House, 1969), 73.

[100] Roberts, 'Political Change', 73; Andrew Roberts, 'Nyamwezi Trade', in Richard Gray and David Birmingham (eds), *Pre-Colonial African Trade: Essays on Trade in Central and Eastern Africa before 1900* (London: Oxford University Press, 1970), 39–74; Andrew Roberts, 'The Nyamwezi', in A. Roberts (ed.), *Tanzania before 1900* (Nairobi: East African Publishing House, 1968), 122–39; Jan-Georg Deutsch, *Emancipation without Abolition in German East Africa c. 1884–1914* (Oxford: James Currey, 2006), 20–22; Rockel, *Carriers of Culture*, 47 and 231; Stephan J. Rockel, 'Caravan Porters of the Nyika: Labor, Culture, and Society in Nineteenth-Century Tanzania' (PhD thesis, University of Toronto, 1997), 18; Alfred C. Unomah, 'Economic Expansion and Political Change in Unyanyembe, c.1840–1900' (PhD thesis, University of Ibadan, 1972), 75.

[101] Raphael G. Abrahams, *The Political Organization of Unyamwezi* (Cambridge: Cambridge University Press, 1967), 5; Southon, 'The History, Boundary and People of Unyamwezi IV', Urambo, 16 September 1880, CWM/LMS Central Africa/Incoming Correspondence, Box 3/Folder 4/No. 3.

the Wakama, whose language, said Southon, was like that of the Wakalaganza, Waha, Wasumbwa, Wakonongo, and Wakimbu.[102]

Southon described the region's physical features, describing it as a large plateau between 3,800 and 4,200 feet above sea level. The region had a gentle slope, he said, from northeast to southeast. He found the trend was more perceptible in central Unyamwezi, while the north and northeast had ridges rising suddenly, forming large plains with isolated mountains. These added to the picturesque character of the country with their bold and rugged appearance. In his description, these ridges were of no great height and comprised granite rocks. Vast rocks of varying shapes and sizes of granite were found in profusion across a level plain. Gneiss, quartz, and schist were also scattered over the surface of some parts of the region. Some plains and occasionally chains of mountains were mostly covered with forests, forming one of the characteristic features of northern Unyamwezi.[103] The plains in the north of Unyamwezi contained different types of soil which as a result determined population distribution and agricultural activities: grasslands with fertile soil and abundant water supply were thickly populated because they supported agriculture and human settlement, while areas such as Usumbwa and its adjoining parts of northern Unyamwezi (in the present-day Kahama and Nzega district) had a low population because its poor-quality soil made it unfavourable for the establishment of settlements and crops.[104]

Southon further described the central part of Unyamwezi as consisting of undulating ridges and hills and considered the country's most fertile portion. This area had scattered hills and a few mountain ranges in the western part of Uyui. A series of undulating hills converged beyond Urambo with plains, elevations, and depressions, making them appear like rolling hills of igneous and schistose rocks. The valleys were suitable for cultivation during the rainy season because of the rich humus soil between the hills that allowed for the growth of various crops. As a result, a dense population of Nyamwezi people established permanent settlements and cultivated their crops. The southern part of Unyamwezi had well-watered plains, some of which were wooded, with numerous streams intersecting the plains. Most of the streams were

---

[102] Southon, 'The History, Boundary and People', 16 September 1880, CWM/LMS/Box 3/Folder 4/No. 3.

[103] Southon, 'The History, Boundary and People of Unyamwezi II', Urambo, 24 July 1880, CWM/LMS/Box 3/Folder 4/No. 3; Raphael G. Abrahams, *The Peoples of Greater Unyamwezi, Tanzania (Nyamwezi, Sukuma, Sumbwa, Kimbu, Konongo)* (London: International African Institute, 1967), 29; Abrahams, *Political Organization*, 8.

[104] Abrahams, *The Peoples*, 31.

perennial, making the region one with dense forests and scattered populations.[105] Notwithstanding dense forests, some parts of southern Unyamwezi attracted human settlements because the fertile soil supported a variety of crops, including maize, bananas, and rice.[106]

Southon concluded his description of the drainage pattern of Unyamwezi by saying that it consisted of perennial rivers, including the Igombe in the western Tabora district, commencing at about sixty miles (ninety-six kilometres) north of the headquarters of the chiefdom of Mirambo; the Ugalla and Ruangwa in the southwest; and the Manonga and the Isanga in central Unyamwezi. Other rivers included the Wembere on the eastern borders of the Nzega district and the Moyowosi on the western borders of the Kahama and Tabora districts. He also noted that some rivers flowed only intermittently during the rainy season, affecting the drainage patterns of Unyamwezi.[107] The country had two seasons: the dry season between July and August and the rainy season between November and April. The region contained three major vegetation zones: the lowest level of open grasslands, in some places with thorn bushes commonly known as *mbuga*; the sparsely populated upper levels dominated by woodland; and forests called *miombo* (known scientifically as Brachystegia). Woodlands (*miombo*) dominated much of the area of Ukimbu and Ukonongo, and were unsuitable for settlement and cultivation because the poor soil did not yield groundwater. Consequently, Ukimbu and Ukonongo remained, for the most part, sparsely populated.[108] All of these topographical factors would influence the choices made by European evangelists and Christian converts in locating their missions and communities.

Notwithstanding cultural and ecological diversity, wars, insecurity, and slavery dominated the region throughout the nineteenth century. Prolonged periods of drought weakened the legitimacy of some chiefs, and frequently people deserted their compounds and villages in search of food, leading to some enslavement.[109] Wars between chiefdoms increased insecurity in

---

[105] Ibid.

[106] Kisanji, *Historia Fupi*, 40.

[107] Southon, 'The History, Boundary and People of Unyamwezi II', Urambo, 24 July 1880, CWM/LMS/Box 3/Folder 4/No. 3.

[108] Abrahams, *The Peoples*, 30–31; Abrahams, *Political Organization*, 8.

[109] Rev. Blackburn to Mr Lang, Uyui, January 1884, CMS/B/OMS/G3 A6/0/26; Rev. Blackburn to Mr Lang, CMS Uyui, 14 January 1884, CMS/B/OMS/G3 A6/0/26; Blackburn, Rev. J., Uyui, 14/1/1884, G3 A6/O/1884 [Missing], Nyanza Mission Precis; Aylward Shorter, *Chiefship in Western Tanzania: A Political History of the Kimbu* (Oxford: Clarendon Press, 1972), 249. See also, Juhani Koponen, *People and Production in Late Precolonial Tanzania: History and Structures* (Helsinki: Finnish Society for Development Studies, 1988), 129; and Juhani

Unyamwezi, as people were taken as captives and prisoners of war. As a result, throughout the second half of the nineteenth century, the chiefdoms' headquarters remained occupied by many people living as unfree dependents, some working as domestic servants and others as concubines and soldiers.[110] The development of long-distance trade in ivory and slaves between the coast and Unyamwezi exacerbated insecurity in the second half of the nineteenth century. Chiefs sought to control trade routes, and with guns obtained from coastal traders, they raided villages, taking men and women as captives and slaves.[111]

Location of Catholic and Protestant Missions in Unyamwezi

Because Unyamwezi witnessed intensive slave trading in the late nineteenth century, it attracted numerous European missionaries who focused on the abolition of slavery. The first Christian mission in Unyamwezi was established at Uyui in 1878 by the CMS. Their mission was near the chiefdom's headquarters (*ikulu*) at Isenegezya. The same year, the Congregational LMS established a mission at Urambo Kilimani. That mission was located a few miles from Mirambo's headquarters at Iselamagazi.[112] These CMS and LMS missions were located far from the central caravan route running from the coast to Tabora and Ujiji in the interior. They concentrated on Christianizing, educating, and administering medical aid without challenging the dependent status of the people and the practices of chiefs like Mirambo respecting slavery.

Koponen, 'War, Famine, and Pestilence in Late Precolonial Tanzania: A Case for Heightened Mortality', *International Journal of African Historical Studies*, Vol. 21, No. 4 (1988), 641.

[110] Urambo, 8 September 1879, CWM/LMS/Box 2/Folder 2; John B. Kabeya, *Mtemi Mirambo: Mtawala shujaa wa Kinyamwezi* (Nairobi: East African Literature Bureau, 1971), 20–23.

[111] Rockel, *Carriers of Culture*, 47; Rockel, 'Caravan Porters of the *Nyika*', 18; Roberts, 'The Nyamwezi', 121–31. See also A. Mackay to Mr Hutchinson, Uyui, 11 June 1880, CMS/B/OMS/C A6/O/109.

[112] C.J. Wilson to Mr Wright, Uyui, 18 February1878, CMS/B/OMS/C A6/O 3/67; Edward Hore, Kwikuru, Urambo, 4 August 1878, CWM/LMS Central Africa/ Incoming Correspondence, Box 1; John H. Speke, *Journal of the Discovery of the Source of the Nile* (New York, 1864), 92 and 119; Norman R. Bennett, 'The London Missionary Society at Urambo, 1878–1898', *Tanzania Notes and Records*, No. 65 (March 1966), 43; Kabeya, *Mtemi Mirambo*, 20; Nolan, 'Christianity in Unyamwezi', 77.

INTRODUCTION   27

Nonetheless, their slow progress led to the closure of their missions in 1887 and 1898. The CMS closed the mission of Uyui in 1887 without leaving it to another mission society. They lost interest in Unyamwezi when they opened a short route to Uganda through the Maasailand.[113] Conversely, the LMS invited the Moravian missionaries to take over the Urambo mission. Southern Unyamwezi, taken over by the Moravians after the failure of the LMS at Urambo in 1898, was even more peripheral to the centres of the trade routes.[114]

The Catholic White Fathers joined the LMS and CMS missionaries in Unyamwezi and founded their missions at Kipalapala, Ngaya, Ushirombo, and Ndala in 1881, 1893, 1894, and 1896. Tabora and Bulungwa missions followed in 1900 and 1902. The missions were close to the headquarters of the chiefdoms of Unyanyembe, Msalala, Ushirombo, Lunzewe, Utambala, Ndala, and Bulungwa (Map 1).[115] The Catholic missions of Tabora, Kipalapala, Ndala, and Ushirombo were located on the trade routes traversed by caravans and slaves making their way from the interior to the coast. The White Fathers established their missions on the trade routes because they understood these places could be easily reached by slaves seeking refuge and orphans whose parents had been taken into slavery. Consequently, missions and orphanage centres attracted marginalized people, including orphans and runaway slaves, to the mission communities. Because of the strategic locations of their missions, the Catholics were less responsive to the chiefs and, accordingly, less useful as a source of chiefly legitimacy.[116] Like the CMS and LMS missions, the Catholic missions of Kipalapala, Ngaya, and Bulungwa soon closed. The White Fathers abandoned Kipalapala and closed the orphanage centre in

---

[113] Nolan, 'Christianity in Unyamwezi', 87; Salvatory S. Nyanto 'Society, Conversion, and Frustrations in the CMS and LMS Missions of Unyamwezi, Western Tanzania, 1878–1898', *Tanzania Journal of Sociology*, Vol. 4 (June 2018), 75.

[114] W. Draper to Rev. R. Wardlaw Thompson, Urambo, 24 April 1895, CWM/ LMS/Box 9/Folder 3/No. 9, 11 April 1896, CWM/LMS/Box 9/Folder 4/No. 9, and 5 December 1896, CWM/LMS/Box 9/Folder 4/No. 9; W. Draper to Rev. G. Bousins, Urambo, 18 April 1897, CWM/LMS/Box 9/Folder 5/No. 9; W. Draper to Rev. G. Bousins, Urambo, 24 January 1898, CWM/LMS/Box 10/Folder 1/No. 9, and 9 March 1898, CWM/LMS/Box 10/Folder 1/No. 9; Nolan, 'Christianity in Unyamwezi', 87; interview with Oscar E. Kisanji, Tabora-Kaze Hill, 31 November 2016. Until the year 1885, the CMS had baptized seven people. They were mostly members of Rev. Blackburn's household from various parts of the East African interior. The situation was worse for the LMS missionaries who left Urambo in 1898 without having baptized anyone.

[115] Ushirombo Diary, 5 February 1891, WFA 01.43; Ndala Diary, 8–9 January 1896, WFA 01.43; Nolan, 'Christianity in Unyamwezi', 157 and 196.

[116] F. van Vlijmen, 'The Origins of the Archdiocese of Tabora', unpublished MS, Ndala, 1990, p. 39, AAT 23.01; Hastings, *The Church in Africa*, 213.

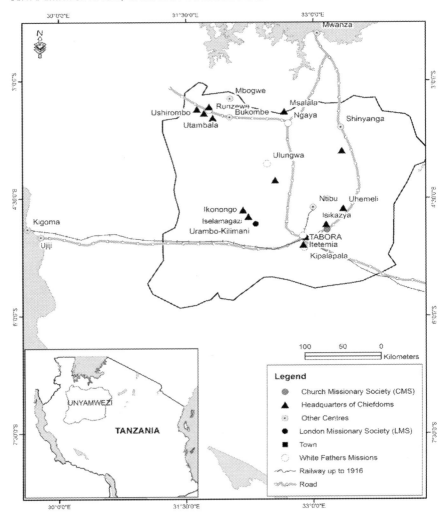

Map 1 Location of Missions in Unyamwezi in the Nineteenth Century, 1878–98.

1888. Ngaya and Bulungwa missions followed in subsequent decades.[117] The missions of Kipalapala, Ngaya, and Bulungwa failed to attract the residents to Christianity despite decades of evangelization. Nearly all the people who

[117] F. van Vlijmen, 'The Origins of the Archdiocese of Tabora', p. 5, AAT 23.01; Nolan, 'Christianity in Unyamwezi', 159, 176, 185–86, and 194. The White Fathers closed the Ngaya and Bulungwa missions in 1922. In 1910 the mission of Msalala (Ngaya) had only four catechumens.

INTRODUCTION   29

lived in the mission communities were formerly enslaved people who had been the property of travelling merchants or Nyamwezi owners.[118]

Evangelization succeeded in some parts of Unyamwezi and failed in others because different chiefs chose different ways of managing their relations with missions. In some places, chiefs, headmen, and others were interested in becoming Christians and offered their children instruction. In other parts of Unyamwezi, chiefs and headmen invited missionaries for private gain and created dependent relations with missionaries: they made decisions to accept the missionaries and allocated places for them to build mission stations. Since insecurity and unrest dominated the second half of the nineteenth century in Unyamwezi, chiefs placed missionaries in strategic areas, such as along the trade routes and near the headquarters of their chiefdoms. These chiefs offered protection to missionaries against the robbers on the road and against possible invasion from the Nguni and other neighbouring chiefdoms.[119] Chiefs thus hoped to gain benefits from missionaries through control of their activities and movements and access to imported items, including guns, to strengthen their chiefdoms against invasion.[120]

Mtemi Mirambo sponsored the LMS missionaries at Urambo Kilimani and recommended to Southon that he build a mission at Urambo Kilimani. He offered Southon materials and workers to build the mission. Mirambo also offered him armed escorts when the missionary wished to travel because the trade route between the coast and the interior was unsafe.[121] Mirambo also encouraged other chiefs from the neighbouring chiefdoms to supply Southon with various provisions. The chiefs of Kirira and Masukia, along with Chief Makabacha and Chief Manuguruguru, offered Southon vegetables and banana trees.

[118] Nolan, 'Christianity in Unyamwezi', 182 and 185.

[119] See for instance, J.B. Thomson to Dr Mullens, Unyanguru [Ulyankulu], Urambo, 4 August 1878, CWM/LMS/Box 1; J.B. Thomson to Dr Mullens, Ujiji, Tanganyika, 25 August 1878, CWM/LMS/Box 1; Southon to Rev. Whitehouse, Urambo, 1 November 1879, CWM/LMS/Box 2/Folder 3; Rockel, *Carriers of Culture*, 132–33.

[120] The symbiotic relationship between chiefs and missionaries was common in sub-Saharan Africa. See, for instance, Aldrin T. Magaya, 'Christianity, Culture, and the African Experience in Bocha, Zimbabwe, c. 1905–1960s' (PhD thesis, University of Iowa, 2018), 31–36.

[121] J.B. Thomson, Unyanguru Rev. Dr Joseph Mullens, Urambo, 4 August 1878, CWM/LMS/Box 1; Southon to Rev. Whitehouse, Urambo, 2 December 1879, CWM/LMS/Box 2/Folder 2; Bennett, 'The London Missionary Society'.

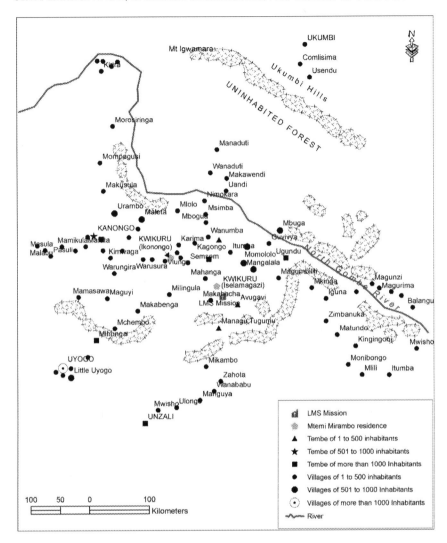

Map 2 Location of the LMS Mission and Milambo's Ikulu.

Chief Kasabula offered the missionaries a site to establish a new mission at Usene.[122] One factor influenced the strategic location of the mission at Urambo Kilimani: the station was close to Mirambo's headquarters at

[122] E. Southon MD to Rev. Whitehouse, Balton Hill, Urambo, 4 May 1880, CMW/LMS/Box 3/Folder 1; E. Southon MD to Rev. Whitehouse, Urambo-Central Africa, 29 November 1880, CMW/LMS/Box 3/Folder 3; Edward Hore, Church Mission Station (CMS), Uyui, 30 November 1880, CMW/LMS/Box 3/Folder 4.

INTRODUCTION   31

Iselamagazi, and Mirambo placed the missionaries under his protection in times of invasion. His wars against neighbouring chiefdoms made him 'in every way dangerous' and created a state of dependence among the LMS missionaries (see Map 2).[123]

In 1878, chief Majembi Gana (meaning one hundred spades) of Uyui invited the CMS missionaries to his territory. He gave them a place near his *ikulu* at Isenegezya to establish a mission and plots of land for rice farming. He was determined to keep peace and, perhaps for fear of Mirambo's intimidation, never asked for 'guns and gunpowder' from missionaries.[124] Similarly, at Ngaya, in 1891, Hwami, the area's village headman (*mnangwa*), invited the White Fathers to establish a mission near his *ikulu*. With the *mtemi* of Msalala, Gagi pledged to provide the White Fathers with physical protection during the invasion. In Ushirombo, in 1894, the chiefs of the adjoining chiefdoms of Lunzewe, Ushirombo, and Utambala invited the White Fathers to extend their work in the area.[125]

By the end of 1896, Mtemi Ntabo or Matolu had allowed the White Fathers to establish a mission station in Ntabo's chiefdom of Ndala. The chiefdom had a concentration of eighty communities occupying about a hundred square kilometres of farmland, densely grouped around Uhemeli, about four kilometres to the south of Ntabo's *ikulu* (see Map 3).[126] Ntabo wished to keep missionaries under her control. Some of her subordinate leaders, too, preferred having the missions close to Ntabo's *ikulu*. But the White Fathers proposed setting up the mission of Ndala at Uhemeli because it was the most densely populated village in the chiefdom.[127] Ndala and Uyui chiefdoms were contiguous territories in northern Unyamwezi, and soon the news of the missionaries' presence at Uhemeli spread to the Uyui villages. Having heard about the White Fathers' presence at Uhemeli, the *mtemi* of Uyui invited the missionaries to work in his territory. Thirteen villages ruled by the chief of Uyui were located within walking distance of the Ndala mission. The many villages of both Ndala and Uyui increased the population of what would later form the Christian community

---

[123] (Ulyankulu), Urambo, 4 August 1878, CWM/LMS/Box 1; J.B. Thomson to Dr Mullens, Ujiji, Tanganyika, 25 August 1878, CWM/LMS/Box 1; Southon to Rev. Whitehouse, Urambo, 1 November 1879, CWM/LMS/Box 2/Folder 3; Dr Kirk to Earl Granville, Zanzibar, 14 November 1880, CMS/B/OMS/G3 A6/O/18.

[124] Charlies Stokes to Mr Wright, Uyui, 17 November 1879, CMS/B/OMS/C A6/O 24; Alfred Copplestone to W. Wright, Uyui, 21 April 1880, CMS/B/OMS/C A6/O 9/46; Nolan, 'Christianity in Unyamwezi', 88.

[125] Ushirombo Diary, 5 February 1891, WFA 01.43; Nolan, 'Christianity in Unyamwezi', 157.

[126] Nolan, 'Christianity in Unyamwezi', 198.

[127] Ndala Diary, 9 January and 20 April 1896, WFA 01.43.

Map 3 Location of the White Fathers' Mission and Ntabo's Ikulu.

in the mission and beyond. In about a four- to five-kilometre circuit, there were more than fifty homesteads in the territory of Uhemeli (Ndala). At the same time, about twenty-five villages of the chiefdom of Uyui were close to the mission.[128]

Organization of the Book

The book is organized into six chapters. In Chapter 1, I show that the history of authority, adaptation, and dissent was part of the social life of communities in nineteenth-century Unyamwezi. The development of long-distance trade between Unyamwezi and the Indian Ocean coast from 1840 intensified slavery as chiefs acquired slaves by raiding and capturing people from neighbouring

---

[128] Ndala Diary, 20–21 January and 9 April 1896, WFA 01.43.

chiefdoms. Wars resulting from the migrations of Nguni communities from southern Africa also increased insecurity, as bands of raiders ravaged the land, killing men and women and carrying off cattle and property. In the end, I demonstrate that notwithstanding the turbulent moments, slaves from various parts of the East African interior who laboured in the region as domestic and field slaves had adapted themselves to the Nyamwezi culture, and utilized the limited opportunities to move away from the bondage of slavery to new positions in society. Nevertheless, by the second half of the nineteenth century, as social and economic opportunities offered slaves avenues to freedom, Nyamwezi people questioned their existing loyalties, especially the legitimacy of chiefs.

The increasing dependence on trade in ivory, slaves, and forest products in nineteenth-century Unyamwezi created a moral and spiritual legitimacy vacuum that could be filled out by Christianity. In Chapter 2, I show that as chiefs sought to enhance their legitimacy by making missionaries their dependents, they caused intergenerational tensions between themselves and young people who desired mission schooling and healing. Increasingly, men, women, and children joined newly established Christian missions because they offered them breathing spaces, free from the oppression of domestic servitude and ruthless chiefs. Because the downtrodden who joined mission communities originated from different parts of the East African interior and had diverse sociocultural and linguistic backgrounds, they adopted Kinyamwezi as the lingua franca. In due course, mission stations became centres of everyday life that involved many kinds of social relationships, including fictive kinship, friendship, and marriage.

The multilingual context of those early Christians made it important to translate the Bible, religious texts, and songs into Kinyamwezi because that language was widely spoken in the region among the Nyamwezi people and formerly enslaved people who had been living in the region. In Chapter 3, I show that unlike the coast, where Kiswahili (with 'Ajamī or Ajamiyya) gained prominence, formerly enslaved people and porters living in missions moved away from Kiswahili toward Kinyamwezi as the medium of translation. In so doing, they departed from the 'Ajamī script of Kiswahili, and as a consequence influenced missionaries' inclination to the Kinyamwezi as the language of translation and evangelization in missions and villages. Translation in Unyamwezi occurred in the daily interactions between missionaries, the Nyamwezi missions' residents, and those who regularly attended Sunday services. Translation, too, involved cooks and workers at the missions, friends, and mission porters, whose knowledge of the cultures and the language made it possible to converse with missionaries about the Kinyamwezi language and related cultural topics. Mastery of the Kinyamwezi language and their knowledge of reading and writing inspired residents of the missions to translate the New Testament, religious texts, and songs into the Kinyamwezi language.

The ongoing interaction between porters, slaves, teachers, catechists, and European missionaries inspired the adaptation of the Christian culture in villages beyond the confines of Catholic mission stations. In Chapter 4, I show that teachers and catechists working in villages encountered diverse linguistic and practical challenges. The difficulties, nevertheless, did not diminish their courage. Instead, they demonstrated their intellectual and cultural ingenuity through their efforts to mediate between their still-evolving use of Kinyamwezi as the language of Christianity and the multiple linguistic traditions present in the villages. In villages beyond missions, teachers took on many additional tasks in teaching and administration and saw themselves as independent agents rather than followers of missionaries' instructions. Their families became exemplary Christian families in villages and laid the foundation for African Christianity as children were baptized, attended mission schools, and became teachers, catechists, and in some cases nuns and priests. The task of administering village outstations eventually led to conflicts and divisions within the Catholic mission stations, as teachers and catechists demanded higher salaries and greater recognition.

For the village outstations of the Moravians and Swedish Free Mission, the development of Christianity in twentieth-century western Tanzania took a new shape. In Chapter 5, I show that the administration of the village outstations under the auspices of African teachers (*vahembeki*) was pursued in tandem with the tireless efforts of lay women, whose work among women was instrumental in fashioning a new Christian identity and creating spiritual connections. Like men, lay women taught children in Sunday schools, while others accompanied village teachers and launched home-visit campaigns to attract more Nyamwezi women to Christianity. Teachers and Nyamwezi women relied on knowledge of scripture and the Protestant tradition of reading and personal interpretation of religious texts in shaping the course of Christianity in western Tanzania. Ultimately, the administration of village outstations and the tradition of reading and interpreting texts in twentieth-century Unyamwezi inspired African teachers and women not only to mount a rebellion against the influence of revivalism but also to develop ideas of self-governance (*kujitawala*) of the church that had impact on the nationwide movement for independence.

The Moravian Christians' experience in the revival movement was somewhat different from that of the rest of East Africa. In Chapter 6, I demonstrate that while many born-again pastors in western Tanzania worked from within the established church, Christians critical of them seceded to form their own 'independent' churches, installing their pastors and recruiting adherents from the established churches. Divergent interpretations of the teachings on salvation, sin, and the public confession of sins divided revivalists and their born-again pastors on the one hand and the dissenters on the other, and both mission stations and village outstations became the sites of such dissent. The aftermath of dissent in Unyamwezi coincided with the wave of Africanization and nationalism in Tanganyika, whose influence also filtered into village and mission churches. The influence of the Second World War in placing the Moravian church in Rungwe – bordering the Moravian Church in western Tanzania to the north – under the control of Africans was felt in Unyamwezi. By the 1950s, complaints that Africans were denied complete authority had become common in churches, and in education and healthcare institutions. The push for Africanization of the church dominated the congregations until 1962 when the church assumed complete authority over its own synodal proceedings, constitution, and provincial board.

CHAPTER 1

Authority, Adaptation, and Dissent in Nineteenth-Century Unyamwezi, 1840–77

The history of authority, adaptation, and dissent dominated the social life of communities inhabiting Unyamwezi during the nineteenth century. In particular, the development of long-distance trade between Unyamwezi and the Indian Ocean coast from 1840 onwards brought an intensification in the practice of slavery as chiefs acquired slaves by raiding and capturing people from neighbouring chiefdoms. At the same time, wars resulting from the migrations of Nguni communities from southern Africa also increased insecurity, as bands of raiders ravaged the land, killing men and women and carrying off cattle and property. In response, a new type of leader arose in Unyamwezi, one who embraced new opportunities to accumulate wealth through long-distance trade but who, by providing captives for the Indian Ocean slave trade, also contributed to the increase in war and insecurity. Despite turbulent moments in Unyamwezi, slaves from various parts of the East African interior who laboured in the region as domestic and field slaves had adapted themselves to the Nyamwezi culture. While a significant number of slaves remained tied to their owners, some ran away from the throes of enslavement and found a marronage village. Others utilized the limited opportunities to move away from the bondage of slavery to new positions in society. By the second half of the nineteenth century, as social and economic opportunities offered slaves avenues to freedom, Nyamwezi people questioned their existing loyalties and especially the legitimacy of chiefs.

This chapter draws examples from nineteenth-century accounts of European travellers and explorers who passed through Unyamwezi. Their reports about wars, insecurity, instability, enslavement, and porterage serve as a prism to explore authority, adaptation, and dissent in Unyamwezi society in the late precolonial era before Christian missionaries ventured into the region. These reports provide glimpses into the origins and development of the trade in ivory and slaves in Unyamwezi and the place of Nyamwezi caravan porters and chiefs in the trade. The reports also help establish a link between the development of long-distance trade and the emergence of chiefdoms in the interior that controlled the trade routes and increased instability and turbulence in the interior.[1] I supplement information from nineteenth-century accounts with works by ethnographers and historians of Unyamwezi that offer insights into the development of political systems and the nature and organization of porterage in the nineteenth century. They also shed light on the trade in ivory and slaves before the arrival of missionaries in western Tanzania.[2] In the end, the chapter seeks to show that the socioeconomic and political changes taking place in nineteenth-century Unyamwezi and the resultant adaptation and dissenting characters of slaves were to have an impact on the development of Christianity.

Ritual Authority, Conflicts, and Dissent in Unyamwezi, 1840–77

Ritual authority, conflicts, and dissent dominated Unyamwezi social life before communities encountered missionaries. Ritual authority, or 'ritual chieftainship' as John Iliffe calls it, entailed knowledge about the conduct of ritual, and more importantly, it involved the control of knowledge of the ritual of the chiefs, which allowed chiefs in Unyamwezi to assert political and ritual authority. Before 1840, ritual authority was rooted in kinship and knowledge of the spiritual world. The connection between authority and knowledge was expressed through the veneration of ancestors. Families built shrines that offered liminal spaces for ancestral veneration in times of misfortune and other problems facing members of the family and the clan at large (Figure 1).[3] Ritual offerings ranged from libations of sorghum flour mixed with water

[1] For details about increased elephant hunting, see for instance Stephen J. Rockel, *Carriers of Culture: Labor on the Road in the Nineteenth-Century East Africa* (Portsmouth, NH: Heinemann, 2006), 52.

[2] See, for instance, Rockel, *Carriers of Culture*; Stephen J. Rockel, 'Slavery and Freedom in Nineteenth-Century East Africa: The Case of Waungwana Caravan Porters', *African Studies*, Vol. 68, No. 1 (April 2009), 87–109; Andrew Roberts, 'The Nyamwezi', in A. Roberts (ed.), *Tanzania Before 1900* (Nairobi: East African Publishing House, 1968), 117–50; Aylward Shorter, *Chiefship in Western Tanzania: A Political History of the Kimbu* (Oxford: Clarendon Press, 1972); Juhani Koponen, *People and Production in Late Precolonial Tanzania: History and Structures* (Helsinki: Finnish Study for Development Studies, 1988); and Raphael G. Abrahams, *The Peoples of Greater Unyamwezi, Tanzania (Nyamwezi, Sukuma, Sumbwa, Kimbu, Konongo)* (London: International African Institute, 1967).

[3] For details about concepts of liminality in ritual studies, see, for instance, Victor W. Turner, *The Ritual Process: Structure and Anti-Structure* (1969; repr. New Brunswick, NJ: Aldine Transaction, 2008), 95; and Victor W. Turner, 'Liminality

Figure 1 Ancestral Veneration in Unyamwezi (Undated Image).

(*lwanga* in Kinyamwezi), beer, or porridge to the blood sacrifice of a sheep or goat.[4]

The caption of Figure 1 raises issues about ritual authority and conflicts in the social change of Unyamwezi. Ancestors (*wahenga*) had the authority to control household members' affairs. Family members venerated them to ensure the family's prosperity, cattle, and harvests. That authority was conspicuous during farming, with members consulting *wahenga* before they planted seeds and after the harvest when they offered new seeds to ancestors.

---

and Communitas', in Ronald L. Grimes (ed.), *Readings in Ritual Studies* (Upper Saddle River, NJ: Prentice Hall, 1996), 512.

[4] Raphael G. Abrahams, *The Nyamwezi Today: A Tanzanian People in the 1970s* (Cambridge: Cambridge University Press, 1981), 20–21.

In Unyamwezi, travellers, especially porters, made ritual offerings to ancestors at the beginning and end of their journeys to safeguard them from robbers and other dangers on the road. Richard Burton and John Speke, passing through Unyamwezi in 1860 and 1864 respectively, noted that diviners, or *waganga*, were among the Nyamwezi caravan porters. Ritual experts brought 'medicine for the road', providing advice and ritual protection for the entire caravan on their way to the coast and their return to Unyamwezi.[5] Family members built shrines for ancestral veneration to maintain the relations between the living and the dead, and displeasing ancestors could lead to conflicts, diseases, misfortunes, and death among households.[6]

The Nyamwezi conceived witchcraft as 'an alternative explanation to misfortune', and witchcraft accusations 'were especially common where men [and women] lived in villages, stressed neighbourly and egalitarian virtues, and favoured explanations in personal terms'.[7] Because people of Ukimbu in southern Unyamwezi were a 'forest people', they saw witchcraft as a 'village activity', whereas the Shambaa 'associated witchcraft with the forest; dangerous medicines had to be kept in the horns of wild animals and hidden in the bush'.[8] The practice of magic dominated the social world of Unyamwezi and caused serious misfortunes including sickness and death.[9] To remedy the problem, the Nyamwezi consulted the diviner, *mfumu* or *mganga*, who was 'a key figure in the magico-religious system' of the society. For Raphael Abrahams, the *mfumu* interpreted the problem for an individual or group and decided which forces were impinging on their lives and informed people whether a particular illness or other misfortunes stemmed from ancestral anger, sorcery (*bulogi*) or spirits. Once the *mfumu* identified the influence of the forces, he or she went on 'to tell them how to deal with them, giving detailed instructions about the form of ritual which [was] necessary'.[10]

---

[5] Richard F. Burton, *The Lake Regions of Central Africa: A Picture of Exploration*, 2 vols (London: Longman, Green, Longman, and Roberts, 1860), Vol. 1, 347–48; John H. Speke, *Journal of the Discovery of the Source of the Nile* (Edinburgh and London: William Blackwood and Sons, 1863), 117. See also Rockel, *Carriers of Culture*, 73.

[6] Ancestral spirits could possess members of the household, causing the above-mentioned problems. For details of spirit possession and consequent implications in Unyamwezi, see Aylward Shorter, *East African Societies* (London: Routledge & Kegan Paul, 1974), 97–100.

[7] John Iliffe, *A Modern History of Tanganyika* (Cambridge: Cambridge University Press, 1979), 27.

[8] Ibid.

[9] Raphael G. Abrahams, *The Peoples*, 78.

[10] Abrahams, *The Peoples*, 79.

40 SLAVE EMANCIPATION, CHRISTIAN COMMUNITIES, AND DISSENT IN TANZANIA

Rituals could also involve the slaughtering of cattle, most often by the chief himself, in response to the threats of invasions, epidemics, drought, and other natural disasters. Appeasing the chiefs' ancestors required regular sacrifices at ancestral graves to address such communal misfortunes and ensure the welfare of the territory over which the living chiefs ruled.[11] Ritual sacrifices of cattle epitomized the authority of the living chief over the subjects in his territory and demonstrated the ability of the chief to mediate between the living people and the ancestors.[12] Thus, rituals functioned as an 'arena where [subjects in the chiefdom] assembled to seek life, peace, and collective good fortune'.[13] In nineteenth-century Ukimbu, for instance, 'life-crisis rituals' and 'rituals of redress' dominated chieftainship.[14] In other parts of Unyamwezi, chiefs consulted ancestral spirits to maintain stability and authority in the face of war and natural disasters. Iliffe, citing Wilhelm Blohm, offers a case in Unyamwezi where a nineteenth-century chief poured beer on his predecessors' grave to provide rain to save the chiefdom from drought:

> Here is your water!
> Give me rain! Let it rain!
> Why have you abandoned me? [Are you not still] my master?
> I inherited the office from you. It was not stolen.
> [Yet] you have abandoned me.
> If you [continue to] abandon me so that there is no rain in the
> land, the people will depart.
> See, here is your goat, and this is your sheep![15]

Before 1840, then, subjects gave their allegiance to chiefs who could support them in the most trying moments. After 1840, authority was increasingly based on a leader's wealth in property, slaves, and control over armed forces. The new chiefs ruled by coercion and therefore did not command the same moral authority as the old chiefs, whose power and status depended on ritual powers and the security they offered via the ancestors. Chiefly authority and status became a matter of accumulating wealth from the trade in ivory, slaves,

---

[11] Abrahams, *The Nyamwezi Today*, 20–21; Wilhelm Blohm, *Die Nyamwezi*, 2 vols (Hamburg, 1931–1932), cited in Iliffe, *Modern History*, 28.

[12] James L. Giblin, *The Politics of Environmental Control in Northeastern Tanzania, 1840–1940* (Philadelphia: University of Pennsylvania Press, 1992), 37.

[13] Neil Kodesh, *Beyond the Royal Gaze: Clanship and Public Healing in Buganda* (Charlottesville: University of Virginia Press, 2010), 5.

[14] Aylward Shorter, 'Symbolism, Ritual, and History: An Examination of the work of Victor Turner', in Terence O. Ranger and Isaria N. Kimambo (eds), *The Historical Study of African Religion* (Berkley: University of California Press, 1972), 139.

[15] Iliffe, *Modern History*, 28.

weapons, and other products.[16] The chief of Uyui, Suwarora, controlled the trade route passing through his territory and bought firearms from coastal traders. With the influx of weapons into his territory, the road to Karagwe became unsafe for travellers. Thus, on their way to Karagwe, Speke and his colleagues could not pass through Uyui for fear of the chief, who 'would tear [them] to pieces'. Ukulima, the chief of Nunda, advised Speke to remain at Nunda for a while before embarking on the *safari kuu* (grand march) until the situation in Uyui returned to normal.[17] Speke's fear of the chief indicates that the road between Uyui and Karagwe had become unsafe for travellers because of Suwarora's constant wars against the Swahili merchants of Tabora, who also struggled to control the trade route.

Besides Suwarora, Mirambo, who initially worked as a caravan porter, also offers an example of a chief in Unyamwezi whose importation of guns from Zanzibar enabled him to organize raids for plunder and to establish a stronger polity that could resist Nguni and slave raiding. Mirambo was born between 1830 and 1840 and ascended to the throne in the 1860s. Villages were abandoned out of fear of Mirambo's raids, and his war against the resident merchants of Unyanyembe temporarily blocked communication between the coast and the interior.[18] Another traveller and explorer, Henry Morton Stanley, arriving at Unyanyembe on his way to Congo in 1871, reported on Mirambo's war against the coastal resident merchants of Tabora over control of the trade route; the war made the route between Tabora and Ujiji impassable for travellers.[19] In due course, the conflict between chiefs and merchants over increasing tolls became one of the major causes of regional insecurity.

Mirambo died on 2 December 1884, while at war against his rivals. His death diminished the power of the chiefdom following the ascendancy of a drunkard and weak successor, Mpandashalo (Figure 2).[20] Subchiefs of Ussongo and Msalala revolted against Mpandashalo and demanded

---

[16] Rockel, *Carriers of Culture*, 60.

[17] Speke, *Journal of the Discovery of the Source of the Nile (1863)*, 92 and 119.

[18] J.B. Thomson to Dr Mullens, Unyanguru [Ulyankulu], Urambo, 4 August 1878, CWM/LMS Central Africa/Incoming Correspondence, Box 1; J.B. Thomson to Dr Mullens, Ujiji, Tanganyika, 25 August 1878, CWM/LMS/Box 1; Southon to Rev. Whitehouse, Urambo, 1 November 1879, CWM/LMS/Box 2/Folder 3.

[19] John B. Kabeya, *Mtemi Mirambo: Mtawala shujaa wa Kinyamwezi* (Nairobi: East African Literature Bureau, 1971), 27.

[20] T.T. Shaw to R.W. Thompson [Foreign Secretary, LMS], Urambo, 3 March 1885, CWM/LMS/Box 6/Folder 2/No. 6; Charlie Stokes to Mr Lang, Uyui Station, CMS, 23 September 1885, CMS/B/OMS/G3 A6/O/160. See also Kabeya, *Mtemi Mirambo*, 1; Raphael G. Abrahams, *The Political Organization of Unyamwezi* (Cambridge: Cambridge University Press, 1967), 40–41.

Figure 2 Mtemi Mpandashalo, Successor of Mirambo, c.1890.

independence from Mirambo's former chiefdom. At Msalala, two headmen, Hwimi and Sundi, waged war after Mirambo's death, as they wanted to readjust their territorial boundaries to become independent. The two joined together to force out Chasama from Msalala Ndogo because he was too weak to challenge Mirambo's successor. They then divided the territory among themselves, making the subchiefdom independent from Mirambo's successor. The revolts of the subchiefs of Msalala and Ussongo weakened Mirambo's former chiefdom. They blocked the road to and from the coast, making it difficult for porters to cross through Mirambo's country. Continual uprisings of subchiefs shifted power from Mirambo's chiefdom to chief (*mtemi*) Mtinginya of Ussongo in eastern Unyamwezi, who emerged as a 'big man'. Likewise, Hwami established his authority and brought together former rivals of Mirambo, including *mtemi* Kapela of Bukune.[21] The revolts against Mpandashalo and the ascendancy of Mtinginya and Hwami show how conflict between different rivals remained crucial in Unyamwezi between the 1840s and the 1870s (see Figure 3).

[21] Charles Wise [CMS Msalala] to Mr Lang, Urambo, Central Africa, 9 January 1885, CMS/B/OMS/G3 A6/O/37; Blackburn to Mr Lang, CMS Uyui, 16 January 1885, CMS/B/OMS/G3 A6/O/41; Charlie Stokes to Mr Lang, Uyui Station, CMS, 23 September 1885, CMS/B/OMS/G3 A6/O/160; Francis P. Nolan, 'Christianity in Unyamwezi, 1878–1928' (PhD thesis, Cambridge University, 1977), 162 and 165.

Figure 3 Mtemi Hwami of Msalala and His People, c.1880s.

Porterage, Adaptation, and Conflicts in Unyamwezi, 1840–77

Nyamwezi long-distance caravan porterage occupied a prominent position as the major means of carrying ivory and other goods, and linked communities in the interior with those along the East African coast throughout the nineteenth century (see Map 4). Henry Morton Stanley described the porters as 'the camel, the horse, the mule, the ass, the train, the wagon and the cart of East and Central Africa'. The Nyamwezi porters, added Stanley, 'traveled regions where the camel could not enter and where the horse and the ass could not live'.[22] Long-distance caravans began to form in Unyamwezi in the 1840s, carrying ivory to coastal towns such as Pangani, Saadani, Kunduchi, Mbuamaji, and Kilwa.[23] When the Nyamwezi began to carry ivory to the coast, they

---

[22] Norman R. Bennett (ed.), *Stanley's Despatches to the New York Herald, 1871–1873, 1874–1877* (Boston, MA: Boston University Press, 1970), 10. Because of the prominence of the Nyamwezi caravan porters in the nineteenth century, today the Kiswahili saying 'mzigo mzito mpe mnyamwezi' ('Let heavy loads be given to the Nyamwezi') has become common in normal conversation and politics. See, for instance, 'Msemo wa "mzigo mzito mpe mnyamwezi" una maana gani?' JamiiForums, 25 April 2018, https://www.jamiiforums.com/threads/msemo-wa-mzigo-mzito-mpe-mnyamwezi-una-maana-gani.1434561/ (accessed 1 May 2019); and Milard Ayo, 'Swali la "Mzigo mzito mpe Mnyamwezi" limejibiwa na Naibu Waziri Kilimo Dr Mwanjelwa', blog, 22 June 2018, http://millardayo.com/2wwddd/ (accessed 1 May 2019).

[23] Rockel, *Carriers of Culture*, 47; Stephan J. Rockel, 'Caravan Porters of the

Map 4 Trade Routes from the Interior to the Coast, c.1890.

demanded six to nine dollars per journey. Still, the rate of porterage (*upagazi*) increased to ten dollars in 1857 and afterwards to twelve dollars. With that quite good income, Nyamwezi porters could buy domestic items to carry back home, such as coloured cloth, brass wire, and pigeon's-egg beads.[24]

Nyika: Labor, Culture, and Society in Nineteenth-Century Tanzania' (PhD thesis, University of Toronto, 1997), 18.

[24] Burton, *Lake Regions*, Vol. 1, 340; O.F. Raum, 'German East Africa: Changes in African Life under German Administration, 1892–1914', in Vincent Harlow and E.M. Chilver (eds), *History of East Africa*, Vol. 2 (Oxford: Clarendon Press, 1965), 169. For a detailed explanation of the rates for Nyamwezi porters per journey between 1850 and 1900, see Rockel, *Carriers of Culture*, 223; and Southon to Rev. Whitehouse, Urambo, 2 December 1879, CWM/LMS/Box 2/Folder 2/No. 2. For other payment rates to porters, see S.C. Lamden, 'Some Aspects of Porterage in East Africa', *Tanganyika Notes and Records*, Vol. 61 (1963), 158–59.

The Nyamwezi economy adapted to the seasonal needs of long-distance caravans and trade. The most favourable season for coastward-bound travel fell between June and September. The caravans set out in all seasons except the rainy season (*masika*) between October and May because, as Burton reported, 'it was difficult to persuade the people of Unyanyembe to leave their fields'.[25] Many porters (*wapagazi*) preferred to remain in Unyamwezi, mostly working in the fields along with other members of the households. The few Nyamwezi who did march with their ivory during the rainy season demanded exorbitant wages from merchants, since it meant that they could not contribute to farming; they used their earnings to hire replacement labour to help their women and children with the work while they were away.[26] Consequently, as Raum observed, Nyamwezi porters 'learned to live in two economies – the subsistence economy at home and the wage economy on the march'.[27]

There were three kinds of caravans in East Africa. The first consisted of the Nyamwezi, whom Burton called 'the most novel and characteristic [of all porters] in East Africa'.[28] The reliability of the Nyamwezi porters, noted Karl Weule, made them 'for the whole [nineteenth] century, the mainstay of the caravan trade between the coast and the heart of the continent'.[29] In the 1870s, about six thousand Nyamwezi porters travelled to the coast every year. In the 1880s, the French Catholic missionary François Coulbois estimated the number of Nyamwezi porters yearly to the coast at fifteen to twenty thousand.[30] In the second category, patrons commissioned Swahili freemen from the coast to direct and escort the caravans to the coast and back to the interior.

---

[25] Burton, *Lake Regions*, Vol. 1, 339; Richard F. Burton, 'The Lake Regions of Central Equatorial Africa, with Notices of the Luna Mountains and the Sources of the Nile; Being the Results of an Expedition Undertaken under the Patronage of Her Majesty's Government and the Royal Geographical Society of London, in the Years 1857–1859', *Journal of the Royal Geographical Society of London*, Vol. 29 (1859), 16–17.

[26] Rockel, *Carriers of Culture*, 49; Burton, *Lake Regions*, Vol. 1, 339; Richard F. Burton, *Zanzibar: City, Island, and Coast*, 2 vols (London: Tinsley Brothers, 1872), Vol. 2, 298; Roberts, 'The Nyamwezi', 129.

[27] Raum, 'German East Africa', 169; Andrew Roberts, 'Nyamwezi Trade', in Richard Gray and David Birmingham (eds), *Pre-Colonial African Trade: Essays on Trade in Central and Eastern Africa before 1900* (London: Oxford University Press, 1970), 66.

[28] Burton, *Lake Regions*, Vol. 1, 341.

[29] Karl Weule, *Native Life in East Africa: The Results of an Ethnological Research Expedition*, trans. Alice Werner (1909; repr. Westport, CT: Negro University Press, 1970), 418.

[30] François Coulbois, *Dix Années au Tanganyika* (Limoges, 1901), 41; Koponen, *People and Production*, 113.

46 SLAVE EMANCIPATION, CHRISTIAN COMMUNITIES, AND DISSENT IN TANZANIA

In the third category were caravans organized by wealthy Arab merchants, mostly residents of Tabora and Kazeh, who paid the Nyamwezi to lead parties to and from the coast. The Nyamwezi caravans consisted of large parties of men, with a few carrying their goods to the coast, and others hired by wealthy merchants. The number of annual visits of Nyamwezi merchants travelling to the coast was greater than those of the caravans engaged by the coastal merchants and comprised of other groups, and the Nyamwezi porters were the most trusted in East Africa. In their caravans, Burton noted, 'there is no desertion, no discontent, and, except in certain spots, little delay ... They work with a will ...'.[31]

The growth of long-distance trade, led by Nyamwezi porters, created various new occupations and interest groups. Nyamwezi chiefs, including Mirambo, Nyungu ya Mawe, Mnwasele, and Suwarora, competed for control of trade routes by demanding heavy tolls and consequently accumulated wealth that was used to strengthen their chiefdoms and armies.[32] With the importation of guns from Zanzibar, roads in the interior became 'unsafe for travelers': chiefs raided villages and took men and women as captives and slaves, thereby increasing insecurity in the region.[33]

Sons of chiefs also joined the ranks of porters taking ivory from Unyamwezi to the coast. At the time of his visit to Unyamwezi in 1857 and 1858, Burton reported that Chief Fundikira, son of Swetu of Unyanyembe, had become powerful because of his experience as a porter.[34] Trade in ivory and porterage earned respect in Unyamwezi, and young men and sons of chiefs could not command respect, writes Roberts, unless 'they had seen the sea'. Edward Steere insists that those who could not reach the coast were considered 'milksops'.[35] For Nyamwezi, young men travelling to the coast with heavy goods on their shoulders became a symbol of social status in the nineteenth century. A young man who had been to the coast became a wealthy trader (*nkwabi*, pl. *bakwabi*), gained high respect (as *mundeva*), and proved himself worthy of marrying because he had attained wealth and the status of manhood by demonstrating 'householder honour', 'heroic honour', 'civic honour', and

---

[31] Burton, *Lake Regions*, Vol. 1, 341.

[32] Roberts, 'The Nyamwezi', 121–31; Aylward Shorter, 'Nyungu-Ya-Mawe and the "Empire of the Ruga-Rugas"', *Journal of African History*, Vol. 9, No. 2 (1968), 238.

[33] A. Mackay to Mr Hutchinson, Uyui, Unyamwezi, 11 June 1880, CMS/B/OMS/C A6/O/109.

[34] Burton, *Lake Regions*, Vol. 2, 31; Roberts, 'The Nyamwezi', 128.

[35] Roberts, 'The Nyamwezi', 128; Edward Steere, 'On East African Tribes and Languages', *Journal of the Anthropological Institute of Great Britain and Ireland*, Vol. 1 (1871), cl.

'cosmopolitan masculinity'.[36] Such Nyamwezi ambition fulfilled the desire of chiefs and their sons to gain wealth and respect, yet it became a source of insecurity as chiefs competed to break the merchants' caravan monopoly.

The wealth from porterage furthered the development of chiefdoms in Unyamwezi. By the second half of the nineteenth century, there were eleven chiefdoms in present-day Tabora, Urambo, Sikonge, and Uyui districts: Kiwere, Ngulu, Ugunda, Unyanyembe, Karunde, Uyui, Ibili, Busagari, Bukumbi, Ulyanhulu, and Uyowa.[37] And there were eight chiefdoms in the present-day Nzega and Igunga districts: Ndala, Puge, Unyambiyu, Nyawa, Bussongo, Karitu, Mwakarunde, and Mwangoye. Of all these chiefdoms, Unyanyembe emerged as the largest and most populous chiefdom in Unyamwezi in the first half of the nineteenth century, having established regular contact with the coastal traders doing business in ivory and other forest products. Its growth, however, came to a grinding halt in the 1860s and 1870s when Mtemi Mirambo challenged it.[38]

Regular trade contacts between Unyamwezi and the coast increased social mobility, leading to the emergence of an occupational group that accumulated wealth from porterage, the *bandeba* (sing. *mundeba*), consisting of indigenous and resident coastal traders. This new professional group also accumulated wealth through cattle herding and farming. The *bandeba*, or *vandeva*, relied on slaves imported from the Manyema country in eastern Congo to produce food on their extensive farms that was then sold to caravans passing through Unyamwezi.[39] Besides cooperation with coastal traders, the *bandeba*, writes Rockel, 'were able to employ wage laborers as well as attract clients and buy slaves'.[40] Rockel suggests that the new group could buy and own slaves for commercial and domestic purposes. Many *bandeba* were then able to challenge the well-established authority of chiefs in Unyamwezi.[41]

---

[36] 'Slave Trade in East Africa', 30 November 1974, 5–6, AAT 526.502; John Iliffe, *Honour in African History* (Cambridge: Cambridge University Press, 2005), 100–118; Rachel J. Taylor, 'Crafting Cosmopolitanism: Nyamwezi Male Labor, Acquisition of Honor, c. 1750–1914' (PhD thesis, Northwestern University, 2018), 33–34.

[37] Abrahams, *Political Organization*, 28–36.

[38] Ibid., 29; John Salaita, 'Colonialism and Underdevelopment in Unyanyembe, 1900–1960' (MA thesis, University of Dar es Salaam, 1975), ii; Kabeya, *Mtemi Mirambo*, 27–31; Alfred C. Unomah, 'Economic Expansion and Political Change in Unyanyembe, c. 1840–1900' (PhD thesis, University of Ibadan, 1972), 75–125.

[39] Unomah, 'Economic Expansion', iv and 75.

[40] Rockel, *Carriers of Culture*, 231.

[41] 'Slave Trade', 6, AAT 526.502.

Commoners – cattle owners, farmers, hunters, medical experts – and merchants at Tabora also gained substantially from porterage; their newfound wealth brought them power and influence. Alfred Unomah referred to the resident Arabs and coastal traders of Tabora and Ku'ihara as a 'new agri-commercial bourgeoisie' who, besides doing trade, possessed political power, commanded great respect among the people, and became the essential instruments of social and political transformation in Unyanyembe.[42] Nonetheless, Unomah's lumping together of commoners, hunters, and medical experts as the 'bourgeoisie' negates the crucial elements of social conflict that developed from the interaction of different groups engaged in this new commercial activity. The wealth accumulated from cattle herding and farming was also a source of conflict and instability. More importantly, slave hunting across Unyamwezi and other parts of the East African interior intensified to meet the growing demand from merchants for domestic and field slaves and slaves to be sold to coastal traders,[43] thus increasing conflict and instability.

Porterage emerged as an organized profession and a crucial way of obtaining wealth, power, and influence for men in Unyamwezi between the 1840s and 1877. By 1857, Nyamwezi porters dominated the trade route through Ugogo in central Tanganyika.[44] Regional economies with neighbouring communities inspired the development of long-distance trade, which formed the basis for the integration of the Nyamwezi porters into the global economic system. The Nyamwezi porters emerged as 'actors in the same international economy of production, consumption and desires as were sailors of the Western Indian Ocean and beyond'.[45] With increasing demand for ivory, slaves, and forest products, porterage became 'a full-time activity for many of the professional *pagazi*', who worked in gangs employed by Arab and Nyamwezi traders'.[46] As porterage came to dominate the activities of the Nyamwezi and the caravan system expanded to meet the increased demands of the global economy, 'remote populations were brought into the market system, either by choice

---

[42] Unomah, 'Economic Expansion', iv and 75; Abdul Sheriff, *Slaves, Spices, and Ivory in Zanzibar: Integration of an East African Commercial Empire into the World Economy, 1770–1873* (1987; repr. Oxford: James Currey, 2000), 181.

[43] Rockel, *Carriers of Culture*, 54 and 231.

[44] Roberts, 'The Nyamwezi', 128; Rockel, *Carriers of Culture*, 54 and 177.

[45] Stephen J. Rockel, 'Between *Pori, Pwani* and *Kisiwani*: Overlapping Labour Cultures in the Caravans, Ports and Dhows of the Western Indian Ocean', in Abdul Sheriff and Engseng Ho (eds), *The Indian Ocean: Oceanic Connections and the Creation of New Societies* (London: Hurst, 2014), 96.

[46] Abdul Sheriff, *Slaves, Spices and Ivory in Zanzibar: Integration of an East African Commercial Empire into the World Economy, 1770–1873* (1987; repr. Oxford: James Currey, 2000), 182.

or force'.[47] In the end, the 'mobile labour culture' and 'crew culture' of the Nyamwezi caravan porters helped them to develop '*utani* [joking] relationships that spread into the world of long-distance caravans and commerce to facilitate intertribal economic and cultural interactions' and 'provide survival strategies to the caravan towns and ports of the Swahili coast'.[48]

The development of porterage also corresponded to increased professional elephant hunting in Unyamwezi and Ukimbu. This change became noticeable from the 1860s onwards when their accumulated wealth enabled these professional elephant hunters (*vayaga*, *vamakoba*) to access guns brought to the interior by porters. The hunters organized hunting parties under the auspices of chiefs and sold elephant tusks to the coastal merchants.[49] With available firearms and the demand for more ivory tusks along the coast of East Africa, elephant hunting increased, leading to a shortage of ivory in the region. In addition to the professional elephant hunters, elephant hunting and ivory firms emerged and cooperated with some members of the merchant class, the *bandeba*, in organizing hunting expeditions and collecting ivory and other goods to bring to the coast.[50]

Apart from enriching merchants, the importation of guns into Unyamwezi enabled the territorial chiefs (*batemi*) who controlled the trade routes to organize hunting expeditions and wars of territorial expansion, causing further conflict between chiefdoms in Unyamwezi. The cooperation between Nyamwezi porters and coastal traders eventually led to commercial competition and hostilities. Conflicts erupted between the Nyamwezi chiefs, including Mirambo and Nyungu ya Mawe, and the coastal traders because they were determined to restrict traders from exerting influence in Unyamwezi. An instance of this was reported in 1875 when Nyungu ya Mawe attacked Kirurumo's chiefdom of Uyanzi in northeastern Ukimbu to prevent his caravans from passing through the chiefdom, which also resulted in tensions with coastal traders.[51]

---

[47] Stephen J. Rockel, 'Slavery and Freedom in Nineteenth-Century East Africa: The Case of Waungwana Caravan Porters', *African Studies*, Vol. 68, No. 1 (April 2009), 89.

[48] Rockel, 'Between Pori, Pwani and Kisiwani', 97; Abdul Sheriff, 'Introduction: Globalisation with a Difference: An Overview', in Sheriff and Ho (eds), *The Indian Ocean*, 4.

[49] Rockel, *Carriers of Culture*, 56; 'Slave Trade', 6, AAT 526.502; Alfred C. Unomah and J.B. Webster, 'East Africa: The Expansion of Commerce', in John E. Flint (ed.), *The Cambridge History of Africa*, Vol. 5, *From c.1790 to c.1870* (Cambridge: Cambridge University Press, 1977), 282.

[50] Rockel, *Carriers of Culture*, 57.

[51] Shorter, 'Nyungu-Ya-Mawe', 243–44.

The trade growth increased the demand for crops to feed the passing caravans. The increasing demand for crops made labour scarcer and more valuable, and this, in turn, contributed to increased slave hunting to meet the needs of agricultural production. Red rice flourished mainly in eastern Unyamwezi. Crops such as millet, maize, and cassava were also plentiful in the region. The farmers obtained new seed for planting from the neighbouring regions of Lake Tanganyika and Ugogo.[52] Other crops grown in the region included tobacco, sorghum, tomatoes, pepper, and sweet potatoes, grown mainly for domestic consumption and for feeding the caravans. There was also a bountiful supply of milk, honey, and poultry in Unyamwezi, cheap enough for caravans to afford.[53] Wealthy Swahili merchants living at Unyanyembe had gardens and fields cultivating mainly wheat, onions, cucumbers, and fruits introduced from the coast. Their constant communication with the coast through trade enabled them to obtain imported manufactured goods including various types of clothes, beads, copper wire, hats, and firearms and gunpowder. According to Alfred Unomah, 'the imported manufactured goods were novelties in the interior and the Africans did not spare any local possessions in their attempt to acquire them'.[54]

Collecting forest products also required labour to meet the demand for fruits, honey, and other products to feed the communities and passing caravans. Most of the region had dense forests with plenty of wild fruit trees. Communities collected honey, made baskets, wooden utensils, and bark cloth, and hunted wild animals.[55] Despite the range of agricultural and forest products the Nyamwezi could produce and exploit, they lacked high-quality salt. Their source for salt was Uvinza in western Tanzania, so men carried agricultural and forest products there to exchange for salt.[56] The Nyamwezi also needed men to carry agricultural and forest products to exchange for cattle and hides with the Gogo, Sukuma, and Ha herders in the neighbouring regions.[57]

---

[52] Burton, *Lake Regions*, Vol. 1, 397–98; Koponen, *People and Production*, 104.

[53] Burton, *Lake Regions*, Vol. 1, 397–98.

[54] Unomah, 'Economic Expansion', 76.

[55] Burton, *Lake Regions*, Vol. 1, 397–98.

[56] Stephan J. Rockel, '"A Nation of Porters": The Nyamwezi and the Labour Market in Nineteenth-Century Tanzania', *Journal of African History*, Vol. 41, No. 2 (2000), 177; Rockel, 'Caravan Porters', 80–81; John E.G. Sutton and Andrew Roberts, 'Uvinza and its Salt Industry', *Azania*, Vol. 3 (1968), 45–86.

[57] Rockel, '"A Nation of Porters"', 177; Rockel, 'Caravan Porters', 81; Peter Rigby, *Cattle and Kinship among the Gogo: A Semi-Pastoral Society of Central Tanzania* (Ithaca, NY: Cornell University Press, 1969).

AUTHORITY, ADAPTATION, AND DISSENT IN NINETEENTH-CENTURY UNYAMWEZI 51

Apart from agriculture and forest produce, iron ore was found in a few parts of Unyamwezi, enabling the Nyamwezi to forge a variety of implements for domestic use and firearms used in raiding and wars, as well as hunting. There were ironworks at Isanga, in Muhunze chiefdom, at Igwisi in Busangi, and in central Unyamwezi.[58] Phillipe Broyon reported on ironworking in the south and west of Mirambo's headquarters, where people made iron tools of various qualities. Iron was also forged in Ukonongo and the Kimbu chiefdom of Ipito.[59] The ironworking exacerbated conflicts between traders and chiefs because it amplified the supply of firearms.

In the 1850s and 1860s, the migrations of the Nguni from southern Africa further increased the insecurity in Unyamwezi. While escaping the Shaka of the Zulu in South Africa, the Nguni ravaged the land, killing men and women, invading chiefdoms, and stealing cattle and property. In northern Unyamwezi, for example, they destroyed several villages in Magangati, claiming many lives and taking some as prisoners and slaves.[60] Again in 1850, shortly after the death of Zwangendaba, the Nguni under Mpagalala invaded Ukimbu and Runzewe, leaving what Ebner and Shorter described as 'a trail of destruction'.[61] Besides wreaking havoc and increasing tensions among the communities they encountered, the Nguni stimulated changes in political and military organization in Unyamwezi. Chiefdoms copied Nguni fighting techniques and formed a stable military contingent, the *varugaruga* or *barugaruga*. In Kinyamwezi, the term meant young, unmarried, professional soldiers. The army was a collection of war captives, deserters from caravans, runaway slaves, and many other young men.[62] The armies of Mirambo and Nyungu ya Mawe emerged as effective military forces because of the esprit de corps and discipline they

---

[58] Roberts, 'Nyamwezi Trade', 44; Koponen, *People and Production*, 260.

[59] Phillipe Broyon, 'Description of Unyamwesi, the Territory of King Mirambo, and the Best Route Thither from the East Coast', *Proceedings of the Royal Geographical Society*, Vol. 22, No. 1 (1877–1878), 36; Henry Morton Stanley, *How I Found Livingstone: Travels, Adventures, and Discoveries in Central Africa, Including an Account of Four Month's Residence with Dr. Livingstone* (New York: Scribner, Armstrong & Co., 1872), 533; Ernst Diesing, 'Eine Reise in Ukonongo', *Globus*, Vol. 95 (1909), 327; Aylward Shorter, 'Ukimbu and the Kimbu Chiefdoms of Southern Unyamwezi' (PhD thesis, Oxford University, 1968), 372 and 434, as cited in Roberts, 'Nyamwezi Trade', 44.

[60] CWM/LMS Central Africa/Incoming Correspondence, Box 2/Folder 3; Southon to Rev. Whitehouse, Urambo, 1 November 1879.

[61] Shorter, 'Nyungu-Ya-Mawe', 238; Elzear Ebner, *The History of the Wangoni and their Origin in South African Bantu Tribes* (Ndanda and Peramiho: Benedictine Publications, 1987), 69.

[62] Shorter, 'Nyungu-Ya-Mawe', 241.

SLAVE EMANCIPATION, CHRISTIAN COMMUNITIES, AND DISSENT IN TANZANIA

learned from the Nguni. This allowed the *barugaruga* to intensify their wars of conquest, plunder, and acquisition of new territories in Unyamwezi.[63]

Slavery, Conflicts, and Marronage in Unyamwezi, 1840s–1877

Although the Nyamwezi were leading long-distance caravan porters, the persistence of conflicts and turbulence in the interior meant that the perpetrators could also become victims of enslavement. Slavery was part of the social life in Unyamwezi, which increased insecurity and conflict in the area before the arrival of missionaries. Among the circumstances that forced men, women, and children into slavery was hunger and poverty. They prompted some men and women, of their own volition, to offer themselves as slaves to other families in return for food and protection.[64] By living at other homesteads, individual men and women could be incorporated into the new family as homestead members and become *umsese wahenaho* (the slave belonging to that family). Individuals who spent their lives in the master's household could marry with the consent of the master, but as a rule, children became part of the slave owner's family. While some slaves who relocated to other families owing to food shortages lived permanently as *basese*, others broke the bondage of slavery to form marronages. In contrast, others could, at some point, rejoin their own families. People who broke the chain of enslavement were widely known in Unyamwezi as *basugwa* or *mwizahongo* (voluntary slaves who had returned to their families).[65]

Stephen Rockel relates James Augustus Grant's 24 January 1861 observations of domestic slaves in the households of Indian and Arab residents of Tabora while passing through the town. In the house of an Indian trader, Moossah Mzuri, Grant noticed 'lots of clean slave women all about the house' and that his house was 'an immense establishment … being surrounded by a circle of small … servants' houses'. Grant's account shows that Arab, Indian, and Swahili traders who were living in Tabora had established themselves with 'large homesteads centered on their *tembes*, with associated villages of *Waungwana* retainers as well as slaves and servants of varying origins' who always 'tended gardens and managed herds of cattle'. In addition to Arab,

---

[63] Roberts, 'The Nyamwezi', 133, E. Southon MD to Rev. Whitehouse, Urambo, Central Africa, 1 November 1879, CWM/LMS/Box 2 Folder 3.

[64] See, for instance, James L. Giblin, 'Famine, Authority, and the Impact of Foreign Capital in Handeni District, Tanzania, 1840–1940' (PhD thesis, University of Wisconsin-Madison, 1986), 53.

[65] Interviews with Januari Italange and Anna Wande, Ussongo, 16 November 2016, Merkiori Maganga Filipo, Magreti Machibya and Filipo Milembe, Ussongo, 16 November 2016, and Peter Kadama Kafuku, 22 November 2016.

Indian, and Swahili residents, writes Rockel, the villages of the Nyamwezi people in the Unyanyembe chiefdom were comprised of households with 'free and servile inhabitants' from various parts of Unyamwezi and the East African interior who also 'worked their gardens and fields and managed their livestock'.[66] That slaves and servants were of varying origins shows the diversity of slaves (both domestic and field slaves) who laboured for their owners (Arab, Indian, and Nyamwezi) in the region. These accounts suggest that most domestic slaves in Unyamawezi were women who shouldered domestic responsibilities in the households of wealthy and influential individuals in Tabora town and villages. Most domestic slaves were children of adolescent age, and Grant commended them for their hard work and efficiency in carrying out the daily routine of households.[67]

Accounts of domestic slavery recorded in nineteenth-century journals correspond with Salome Benjamini Kasofi's recollection of her grandfather's wife, whose story offers an example of a voluntary slave who married her master and became part of the family. Although Salome's recollection does not explicitly offer the reasons for domestic slavery, it is evident that her grandmother resorted to domestic servitude as an alternative to her family's problems, which may have included hunger and impoverishment. She only recalls that her grandmother voluntarily went to her grandfather for domestic work. She initially lived as a dependent of her grandmother and later as a wife. She recalled, 'Babu alikuwa na msese wa kike. Msese alikuja kutafuta kazi akawa kama mtoto wa nyumbani. Baadaye babu alimpenda, akampa mimba, akazaa mtoto. Tulikuwa tunamwita bibi' ('My grandfather owned a slave woman. She came looking for domestic work and became part of the family. Later, my grandfather loved her, and they had a baby. We called her our grandmother').[68]

Men, women, and children could be subjected to domestic slavery as compensation for the failure to repay a debt or, in some cases, to resolve conflict between families, clans, and chiefdoms. Oscar E. Kisanji recalled that his grandmother was taken into domestic slavery as compensation for

---

[66] James Augustus Grant, journal entry, 24 January 1861, as cited in Stephen J. Rockel, 'The Home and the World: Slavery and Domestic Labor in a Nineteenth-Century East African Caravan Town', in James Williams and Felicitas Hentschke (eds), *To Be at Home: House, Work, and Self in the Modern World* (Berlin and Boston: De Gruyter, 2018), 126.

[67] Ibid., 129.

[68] Interview with Salome Benjamini Kasofi, Tabora, 30 November 2016. For details on the incorporation of female slaves into the owner's family, see 'Chisi-Ndjurisiye-Sichyajunga', in Marcia Wright, *Strategies of Slaves and Women: Life-Stories from East/Central Africa* (London: James Currey, 1993), 83–90.

her guardian's failure to pay cows as a debt. The guardian offered her to the debtor, who, in due course, took her as his wife. He recalled: 'Bibi mzaa mama – Kiluvi Malunga – alilelewa na mzee ambaye hakuwa baba yake. Mzee huyo alimtoa bibi kama fidia kwa mzee wa familia nyingine baada ya kushindwa kumlipa deni la ng'ombe. Mzee alimchukua bibi kama fidia na mwishowe akamwoa' ('My grandmother – Kiluvi Malunga – was brought up by one old man who was not her father. The guardian offered her as compensation to another family because he could not pay cows as a debt. The debtor took her and finally married her').[69]

Kisanji's recollection of his grandmother's experience shows how pawnship, debt bondage, and debt slavery were part of African life in the nineteenth century. Pawnship was a form of dependency that involved using people as collateral to secure debt payment. Pawns, writes Steven Feierman, 'held the hope of being redeemed by kinsmen'.[70] Nonetheless, Kinsanji's grandmother never returned to her old household and was incorporated into the new family as a wife. Kisanji's recollection of his grandmother shows that it was not always the case that pawns were reclaimed by kinsmen. Pawnship, thus, subjected freeborn men, women, and children to domestic servitude when family members failed to pay their debts, making it another source of enslavement.[71]

The need for slaves increased conflicts in Unyamwezi from the 1840s onwards. Chiefs like Mirambo and Nyungu ya Mawe acquired some of their slaves by raiding and capturing the people of neighbouring chiefdoms. Mirambo's constant raids against the chiefdom of Unyanyembe blocked the trade route from Tabora, made it dangerous for caravans passing through Unyanyembe, and forced the people to desert their villages for fear of being taken as war captives and slaves. Both Mirambo and Nyungu ya Mawe waged raiding wars against neighbouring chiefdoms and increased the number of

---

[69] Interview with Oscar E. Kisanji, Tabora, 30 November 2016 and 12 June 2017.

[70] Steven Feierman, *Peasant Intellectuals: Anthropology and History in Tanzania* (Madison: University of Wisconsin Press, 1990), 55. For more detail on pawnship as a form of dependency in African societies, see also Sean Stilwell, *Slavery and Slaving in African History: New Approaches to African History* (Cambridge: Cambridge University Press, 2014), 15; Koponen, *People and Production*, 335.

[71] Koponen, *People and Production*, 337; Giblin, 'Famine, Authority, and Capital', 51 and 53. See also James L. Giblin, 'Pawning, Politics and Matriliny in Northeastern Tanzania', in Toyin Falola and Paul Lovejoy (eds), *Pawnship in Africa: Debt Bondage in Historical Perspective* (Boulder, CO: Westview Press, 1994), 43–54; and James L. Giblin, 'Pre-Colonial Politics of Disease Control in the Lowlands of Northeastern Tanzania', in Gregory Maddox, James Giblin, and Isaria N. Kimambo (eds), *Custodians of the Land: Ecology and Culture in the History of Tanzania* (London: James Currey; 1996), 134.

captives and slaves at their chiefly headquarters and military contingents, *barugaruga*.[72] The *barugaruga* whom Henry Morton Stanley referred to as 'the forest thieves of Mirambo', wreaked havoc as they raided neighbouring villages, taking men and women as captives and seizing loads of caravans passing through Unyamwezi.[73] Passing through Unyamwezi in the second half of the nineteenth century, Stanely reported, Mirambo's army burned three or four villages of the Wakamba, taking people as captives and slaves. Some people abandoned their villages, emigrating to western Ugala for fear of Mirambo's army.[74] The Wangoni from southern Africa, whose methods of enslavement and warfare were adopted by regional leaders such as Mirambo and Nyungu ya Mawe, also enslaved Nyamwezi men and women through wars and raids.[75]

A common practice among chiefs during this period was to offer slaves as gifts when they paid visits to other chiefs. As a way of establishing a relationship of kinship, a visiting chief offered slaves and other tribute. In this way, some slaves offered to the chief would be incorporated into the chief's family and become members of the chiefdom. Like other chiefs in Unyamwezi, Mirambo acquired slaves not only through trade, wars, and raids but also as tribute offered by other African chiefs. The visit of Mtemi Ruhaga of Buha to Mirambo's headquarters brought slaves who were integrated into Mirambo's *barugaruga*. Others served as officials (*banyikuru*) and monitored the daily undertakings at the headquarters of the chiefdom.[76] Offering slaves as gifts increased control over dependents and was an important sign of the power and status of Mirambo and other new chiefs who lacked the ritual authority of older chiefs.

---

[72] Southon to Rev. Whitehouse, Urambo, 1 November 1879, CWM/LMS/Box 2/ Folder 3; Shorter, 'Nyung-Ya-Mawe', 241; Richard Reid, 'Mutesa and Mirambo: Thoughts on East African Warfare and Diplomacy in Nineteenth Century' *International Journal of African Historical Studies*, Vol. 31, No. 1 (1998), 78; Richard Reid, *War in Pre-Colonial Eastern Africa: The Patterns and Meanings of State-Level Conflict in the Nineteenth Century* (Oxford: James Currey, 2007), 64–65; Edward Hore, *Missionary to Tanganyika 1877–1888: The Writings of Edward Coode Hore, Master Mariner* (London: Frank Cass, 1971), 78–79.

[73] Stanley, *How I Found Livingstone*, 404; Taylor, 'Crafting Cosmopolitanism', 91–94.

[74] Stanley, *How I Found Livingstone*, 353.

[75] See, for instance, E. Southon MD to Rev. Whitehouse, Urambo, Central Africa, 1 November 1879, CWM/LMS/Box 2 Folder 3; Rev. Blackburn to Mr Lang, Uyui, 10 February 1885, CMS/B/OMS/G3 A6/O/40.

[76] Southon to Rev. Whitehouse, Balton Hill-Urambo, 4 May 1880, CWM/LMS/ Box 3/Folder 1.

Figure 4 Sirboko's Slaves (Men and Women) Carrying Wood Fuel and Harvesting Rice in Unyamwezi, c.1860s.

Merchants also bought and owned slaves for domestic and commercial purposes. Sirboko, whom Burton described as 'a broken-down ivory merchant', was one of the merchants in Unyamwezi who accumulated wealth that enabled him to buy and own slaves for commercial and domestic purposes. He traded ivory to Zanzibar for years but settled in Uyui in the second half of the nineteenth century. Sirboko had settled in Uyui in the 1860s when Speke was on his way to Uganda. He offered Speke and his porters a place to stay in Uyui because the Watuta, a Nguni group, had destroyed villages. Sirboko, afraid of returning to Zanzibar for fear of being apprehended for debt, forged an alliance with the chiefs of Uyui against the Watuta and established himself in Unyamwezi following their defeat. He increased his family, owned slaves, and farmed rice, relying mainly on slave labour (Figure 4).[77]

Agricultural prosperity in Unyamwezi – which mostly relied on servile dependents – led Richard Burton, while passing through Unyanyembe, to describe it a 'land of promise', the 'great *bandari* [harbour]' or 'meeting-place of merchants', the 'far-farmed land of the moon', and the 'rice-lands'.[78] Burton's observations indicate the predominance of agriculture in Unyamwezi, which communities and wealthy merchants relied upon for their own consumption and to feed the caravans going to and from the interior and the coast. Juhani Koponen noted the high proportion of women involved

---

[77] Speke, *Journal*, 101–2.
[78] Burton, *The Lake Regions*, Vol. 1, 313–14 and 321–25.

in farming, arguing that they 'predominated among domestic and agricultural *shamba* (plantation) slaves'.[79] With agricultural prosperity, Unyamwezi became one of the more densely populated regions in the interior of East Africa in the second half of the nineteenth century. While passing through Unyamwezi in the 1850s and seeing the increasing population – including slaves working in the fields – Burton was prompted to call it the 'Garden of Central Intertropical Africa'.[80]

With the increase in the slave population and commercial expansion of Unyamwezi in the 1870s, there was an increase in slaves working on the farms of wealthy merchants and residents. As a result, many slaves were incorporated into their owners' households, including the households of chiefs.[81] These changes widened the disparity between male and female slaves in the second half of the nineteenth century, with male slaves having more social and economic opportunities open to them than female slaves. For instance, male slaves recruited into the chiefs' military contingents could accumulate enough wealth to assert some measure of independence from chiefs. Such opportunities were denied to female slaves. Instead, women were increasingly sold to slave traders, and some were exchanged or pawned to big men, headmen, and chiefs.[82]

Because of the limited avenues through which slaves could become free in Unyamwezi, desertion to marronage offered many slaves the opportunity to break away from the yoke of slavery. Msogoti, a slave from southern Unyamwezi (in the present-day Inyonga), along with other slaves, ran away from slave owners to establish a settlement that came to be known as Mbugani.[83] The village's proximity to the caravan route inspired more desertions of slaves from the interior who could not make the long march to the coast. In due course, the village of Mbugani grew to include fugitive slaves of diverse backgrounds whose experience in slavery and the afterlives of slavery bound them to 'independent', 'organized, self-governing communities that expanded through agriculture, trade and fresh intake of *watoro*' from

---

[79] Jan-Georg Deutsch, 'Notes on the Rise of Slavery and Social Change in Unyamwezi, c.1860–1900', in Henri Médard and Shane Doyle (eds), *Slavery in the Great Lakes Region of East Africa* (Athens: Ohio University Press, 2007), 78; Koponen, *Development for Exploitation: German Colonial Policies in Mainland Tanzania, 1884–1914* (Helsinki: Finnish Historical Society, 1994), 335.

[80] Burton, *Lake Regions*, Vol. 2, 7.

[81] Deutsch, 'Notes on the Rise of Slavery', 97–98.

[82] Ibid., 98.

[83] Interview with Issa Mrisho Msogoti and Jumanne Madole Ezekiel, Maungulu village, 27 July 2021.

Unyamwezi and other parts of central Tanganyika.[84] As the founders of the village were formerly enslaved people, it gained fame among residents as a 'village of run-away slaves' (*kijiji cha watumwa waliotoroka*). This discourse remains evident among village elders.

With increasing famine and drought in the nineteenth and twentieth centuries that ravaged parts of central and western Tanzania, more people were forced to seek refuge in Mbugani because it was endowed with fertile soil and abundant crops. Because many immigrants sought refuge in the village, they became residents of Mbugani kwa Msogoti. Msogoti and the members of his kin became the new patrons of the immigrants who had attached themselves to his family and worked for him in return for food and protection. He also allocated land for settlement and farming to the newcomers and settled disputes over land in the village.[85]

That Msogoti and Nyamwezi fugitive slaves were custodians of the Mbugani village and acted as patrons to the newcomers there has a dominant place in the memories of slavery in the village. It has also shaped how stories are told about the village's history, slavery, and social life. Descendants of Msogoti still take a collective pride as founders of the village, expressing that 'we are the founders of this village' (*sisi ndiyo waanzilishi wa kijiji hiki*).[86] The collective pride of the clan reveals descendants' 'ownership' of the story of the creation of the village, and residents who are not members of kin openly and broadly share this view. Residents in the twentieth century who identified themselves as inhabitants of 'Kijiji cha Mbugani kwa Msogoti' implied that the ownership of the village was granted to Msogoti and the members of his kin.[87] Halima, a descendant of Msogoti, openly remarked that 'nilikuwa najisikia raha na sifa' ('I was thrilled and proud'), which shows how Msogoti's clan has maintained its identity and place in the village in twentieth-century western Tanzania.[88] Halima and Issa are among the descendants of Msogoti whose claims reveal how individual and collective memory shape the discourses of post-slavery experiences in Mbugani village. The pride that some formerly enslaved people and their descendants attach to their experience and

---

[84] Fred Morton, *Children of Ham: Freed Slaves and Fugitive Slaves on the Kenya Coast, 1873 to 1907* (Boulder, CO: Westview Press, 1990), xvi.

[85] Interview with Halima Msogoti, 31 December 2021. For details on impact of famine, see, for instance, E.G. Hampel, 'A Short Narrative of the Work and Growth in the First 25 Years of Kilimatinde Hospital 1928–1953', 1954, CMS/ACC 212/F 8.

[86] Interview with Issa Msogoti, Maungulu village, 27 July 2021.

[87] Interview with Evan Eliud Lumambo and Vaileth Paulo Chalula, Kilimatinde village, 31 December 2021.

[88] Interview with Halima Saidi Msogoti, Mbugani village, 31 December 2021.

collective memory of the village is indicative of the agency they asserted in reshaping the narratives of enslavement in twentieth-century central and western Tanzania.

Conclusion

In his magisterial work *A Modern History of Tanganyika*, John Iliffe proposed the concept of enlargement of scale in studying the long nineteenth century. He argued that while people were integrated into the outside world through a long-distance trading system based on Zanzibar, societies 'experienced enlargement of scale most unevenly'.[89] Iliffe contended that some participated in the trading system while 'others resisted' it; some created new political systems using profits accumulated from the trading system, but others 'defended their old polities or saw them shattered by change', and some 'adopted elements of coastal culture', while others 'inherited ideas and customs'. These mixed reactions, Iliffe observed, 'formed a spectrum comparable to the later spectrum of responses to colonial rule'.[90] Iliffe's concept of enlargement of scale allows us to appreciate the spectrum of adaptation and dissent in nineteenth-century Unyamwezi regarding the development of long-distance trade, slavery, and authority. The development of long-distance trade between Unyamwezi and the coast from 1840 onwards brought uneven development in the region. As chiefs and wealthy individuals increasingly acquired some of their slaves by raiding and capturing the people of neighbouring chiefdoms, the development of the caravan trade also fuelled insecurity and turbulence in the region. With guns accumulated from the trade, wars between chiefdoms became common as chiefs competed to control the trade routes between the coast and the interior. As chiefs raided villages, taking men, women, and children as war captives and slaves, the trade routes that linked Unyamwezi, parts of the interior, and the coast were, on several occasions, gridlocked, making them impenetrable for traders, explorers, and missionaries in the last quarter of the nineteenth century.[91]

Increased unrest in the second half of the nineteenth century inspired slaves to devise coping mechanisms to break the chains of enslavement in Unyamwezi. Indeed, a significant number of enslaved men and women who lived in families due to food shortages adapted themselves to the new mode of life as unfree dependents; others broke the bondage of slavery to form

---

[89] Iliffe, *A Modern History*, 40.

[90] Ibid.

[91] See, for instance, Charles Wise [CMS Msalala] to Mr Lang, Urambo, Central Africa, 9 January 1885, CMS/B/OMS/G3 A6/O/37.

marronages, and still others rejoined their own families in villages.[92] The village of Mbugani along the central caravan route in western Tanzania is one of many villages not recorded in the literature that slaves ran away to in pursuit of their freedom. By breaking away from the control of owners, slave exhibited their agency in forming independent communities beyond slavery. Villages of runaway slaves attracted slaves from various parts of Unyamwezi and western Tanzania and bound them together through the ideals of belonging, patronage, and post-slavery experiences. Adaptation and dissent characterized the social lives of slaves who joined missions in the second half of the nineteenth century and continued to dominate everyday life as formerly enslaved people integrated into mission communities and Unyamwezi society.

[92] Issa Msogoti, Maungulu village, 27 July 2021.

CHAPTER 2

Slave Emancipation, the Beginnings of Mission Communities, and Everyday Life in Missions, 1878–1914

By the second half of the nineteenth century, new chiefs had emerged in Unyamwezi, relying on trade in ivory, slaves, and forest products as sources of wealth and legitimacy. Overdependence on trade to the detriment of ritual knowledge created a moral and spiritual legitimacy vacuum that Christianity could fill. Men, women, and children found newly established Christian missions to be breathing spaces where they might escape domestic servitude and ruthless chiefs. CMS and LMS Missionaries in rural locations first sought to attract Nyamwezi villagers by offering medical care and education, but gained no converts. By contrast, the White Fathers' missions near the caravan routes attracted formerly enslaved people and displaced persons who settled as permanent residents. The downtrodden in these stations came from various areas of the East African interior and had diverse linguistic and cultural backgrounds. Still, many had lived in Unyamwezi as slaves for long periods before joining mission communities and had learned the Kinyamwezi language. With Kinyamwezi as the lingua franca, the mission stations became centres of everyday life. Life around the mission stations involved many kinds of social relationships, including fictive kinship, friendship, and marriage. A similar process occurred around the stations of the Moravian missionaries who had replaced the CMS and LMS. In effect, the early Christian communities of western Tanzania operated in a language that the European missionaries officially in charge spoke only imperfectly.

One of the major categories of the disadvantaged that joined the missions was slaves. Thus this chapter is also about how slave emancipation and the adoption of Christianity contributed to the creation of new forms of legitimacy in the region. Chiefs sought to enhance their legitimacy by making missionaries their dependents, which meant they had to control access to missionary healing and Western education, causing intergenerational tensions between

62 SLAVE EMANCIPATION, CHRISTIAN COMMUNITIES, AND DISSENT IN TANZANIA

themselves and young people who desired mission schooling and healing.[1] Chiefs also controlled missionaries in their territories by offering gifts of various kinds and providing protection on the road and in times of invasion. This chapter covers the period between 1878, when the first Christian missions were established, and 1914, when German colonial rule experienced a crisis with the beginning of the First World War. The key events of this period involved slave emancipation, the creation of mission communities, and everyday life in the missions.

Chiefs, Missionaries, and Legitimacy in Unyamwezi, 1878–90s

Chiefs wished to be perceived by their subjects as controlling the missionaries. One way to demonstrate authority over the missionaries was to control access to their healing.[2] Healers in Unyamwezi were accustomed to deriving ideas and methods from various sources, making them and their patients open to new medicines and therapies. The Nyamwezi adoption of missionary biomedicine was based not on the view that European healing was superior but rather on the eclecticism in healing that had long existed in western Tanzania. Patients moved from one healer or secret society to another in a quest for alternative therapies and medicines.[3]

Several diseases were common in Unyamwezi in the second half of the nineteenth century as communities encountered European travellers, explorers, and missionaries. Missionaries identified sleeping sickness, fever, pneumonia, laryngitis, gonorrhoea, elephantiasis, and smallpox.[4] Smallpox was particularly dangerous in villages and other areas where the population was

---

[1] See for instance, Rev. Blackburn to Mr Lang, Uyui, 8 September 1882, CMS/B/ OMS/G3 A6/O/65.

[2] See for instance CWM/LMS Central Africa/Incoming Correspondence, Box 3/ Folder 2, E. Southon M.D. to Rev. Whitehouse [General Secretary of the LMS], Urambo, 21 June 1880.

[3] Tabora Regional Book (Western Province), 1929, 5, TNA. John Janzen calls such a process the 'therapy group', in which members of the household move patients from one healer to another. See John M. Janzen, *The Quest for Therapy in Lower Zaïre* (Berkley: University of California Press, 1978), 129; and Steven Feierman, 'Explanation of Uncertainty in the Medical World of Ghaambo', *Bulletin of the History of Medicine*, Vol. 74, No. 2 (2000), 330.

[4] J.B. Thomson to Rev. Joseph Mullens, DD, Unyanguru, 4 August 1878, CWM/ LMS/Box 1, and 9 September 1878, CWM/LMS Box 2/Folder 2; Southon, MD to Rev. Whitehouse, Urambo, 1 November 1879, CWM/LMS/Box 2/Folder 3; E. Southon, MD to Mr Whitehouse, Urambo, 31 December 1880, CWM/LMS/Box 3/Folder 4; George Litchfield to Mr Hutchinson, Uyui, 26 October 1880, CMS/B/ OMS/G3 A6/O/4.

concentrated. While passing through Unyamwezi in 1871, Henry Morton Stanley reported on the impact of the disease, calling it 'the great and terrible scourge of East and Central Africa'.[5] Tabora and many other towns in the nineteenth century offered opportunities for the disease to spread through caravan porters. Congestion in the town and other large communities increased person-to-person virus transmission through inhalation. Richard Burton, passing through Unyamwezi in the second half of the nineteenth century, reported on the devastating impact of smallpox on slaves and caravan porters at Kazeh (Tabora). He also noted the prevalence of malaria in Unyamwezi and several other parts of the central plateau.[6] On his mission to find Livingstone, Stanley also reported that smallpox killed porters between Mgunda Mkali and Unyanyembe. He reported seeing skulls along the caravan road, indicating the havoc the disease caused among the caravan porters.[7] Smallpox affected several villages in Unyamwezi as well. In 1884, smallpox devastated the chief's village in Uyui. In only one month, January 1884, an average of five to twenty-five people died daily.[8] The eruption of smallpox in Uyui forced men and women to abandon their homes and move to the Uyui mission in search of food, medicine for several diseases, and supposedly a smallpox vaccine.[9]

Besides smallpox, elephantiasis affected chiefs, headmen, and ordinary people in Unyamwezi in the second half of the nineteenth century. The

[5] Henry Morton Stanley, *How I found Livingstone: Travels, Adventures, and Discoveries in Central Africa, Including an Account of Four Month's Residence with Dr. Livingstone* (New York: Scribner, Armstrong & Co., 1872), 533; Helge Kjekshus, *Ecology Control and Economic Development in East African History: The Case of Tanganyika, 1850–1950* (Berkley: University of California Press, 1977), 132.

[6] Richard F. Burton, *The Lake Regions of Central Africa: A Picture of Explorations*, 2 vols (London; 1860), Vol. 2, 318; Juhani Koponen, *People and Production in Late Precolonial Tanzania: History and Structures* (Helsinki: Finnish Society for Development Studies, 1988), 154. See also James L. Giblin, *The Politics of Environmental Control in Northeastern Tanzania, 1840–1940* (Philadelphia: University of Pennsylvania Press, 1992), 127, for the link between congested centres and smallpox epidemic.

[7] Stanley, *How I found Livingstone,* 178 and 533–34; see also Koponen, *People and Production,* 166.

[8] Rev. J. Blackburn to Mr Lang, CMS Uyui, 14 January 1884, CMS/B/OMS/G3 A6/O/39; Rev. J. Blackburn, Uyui, 9/2/1884, G3 A6/O/1884 [Missing], Nyanza Mission Precis.

[9] Alfred Copplestone, Uyui, 26 February 1881, CMS/B/OMS/G3 A6/O/40; Blackburn, to Mr Lang, CMS Uyui, 10 February 1885, CMS/B/OMS/G3 A6/O/40, and 14 January 1884, CMS/B/OMS/G3 A6/O/26; Rev. J. Blackburn, Uyui, 2 September 1884, G3 A6/O/[Missing] Nyanza Mission Precis.

disease was reported in the territory of Mirambo; it inspired experimentation with indigenous and missionary therapies.[10] The disease was characterized by the abnormal enlargement of the limbs and external genitals in males and females, severe pain, disability, and social stigma. The disease occurred when filarial parasites were transmitted to human beings through mosquitoes.[11] Mirambo's headmen and the people from distant villages went to the mission for treatment and advice and, upon returning, carried with them knowledge about healing to other villages. Other patients were drawn to the mission because the missionaries invited neighbours to bring sick persons for treatment.[12] Treatment of elephantiasis was an important factor in making missionary medicine popular in Unyamwezi, as people wanted to experiment with alternative therapies besides indigenous medicine.

Despite the popularity of the medical services at Urambo, Africans never became Christians during the ten-year presence of the LMS. Therefore, the missionary work ended in frustration.[13] While chiefs and subjects encountered a new source of healing, they did not commit to becoming Christians. After the death of Dr Southon on 26 July 1882, Mirambo requested help from the missionary society, asking for two men to be sent out to Urambo: a missionary and a medical doctor. This reveals Mirambo's priorities in responding to the activities of missionaries in his territory, particularly the LMS missionaries at Urambo Kilimani (see Figure 5).[14] Evangelization failed in this area

[10] E. Southon, MD to Rev. Whitehouse [General Secretary of the LMS], Urambo, 21 June 1880, CWM/LMS/Box 3/Folder 2.

[11] 'Lymphatic filariasis (Elephantiasis)', World Health Organization, https://www. who.int/health-topics/lymphatic-filariasis#tab=tab_1 (accessed 7 November 2023).

[12] [History of Case: In-Patient, 'Maganga' chief, about 69 years old, admitted 18 May 1880, Register No. 3/File No. 3], Urambo, 21 June 1880, CWM/LMS/Box 3/Folder 2; E. Southon, MD to Rev. J.O. Whitehouse, Urambo, 14 September 1880, CWM/LMS/Box 3/Folder 3; E. Southon, MD to Rev. Whitehouse, Urambo [Medical Report], 31 December 1880, CWM/LMS/Box 3/Folder 4; W. Draper to Rev. R. Wardlaw Thompson, Urambo, 18 February 1891, CWM/LMS/Box 8/ Folder 3 /No. 8.

[13] W. Draper to Rev. R. Wardlaw Thompson, 11 April 1896, CWM/LMS/Box 9/No. 4; W. Draper to Rev. R. Wardlaw Thompson, 5 December 1896, CWM/LMS/ Box 9/Folder 4 /No. 9.

[14] W.C. Willoughby to Mr Whitehouse [Acting for Secretary, LMS], Urambo, 11 May 1883, CWM/LMS/Box 5/Folder 2 /No. 5; W. Draper to Rev. R. Wardlaw Thompson, Urambo, 11 April 1896, CWM/LMS/Box 9/Folder 4 /No. 9; W. Draper to Rev. R. Wardlaw Thompson, Urambo, 5 December 1896, CWM/LMS/ Box 9/Folder 4 /No. 9. Terence O. Ranger outlines four claims about the purpose of medical work among missionaries. First, missionary medicine carried on

Figure 5 LMS Mission at Urambo Kilimani in 1883.

because Mirambo and his people chose different ways of managing their relations with the missions. The need for guns and medical assistance appeared to be the main concern for Mirambo, his headmen, and ordinary people in Uyowa. They were less interested in becoming Christians.

As people became increasingly interested in the missionaries' medical work, chiefs became concerned that these missionaries would undermine their authority, particularly because it was closely associated with healing. The 'social process', as Janzen calls it, in diagnosis and healing enabled the Nyamwezi people to remain eclectic, deriving ideas and methods of healing from a broad range of sources. This made healers and diviners (*bafumu*) and patients open to missionary medicine and indigenous therapies.[15] They estab-

---

the work of Christ, and missionaries were true successors of Christ the Healer; second, medicine had the power to penetrate heathen societies that were resistant to evangelization; third, medicine was considered a weapon against heathenism and African superstition; and finally, the hospital instilled a sense of time, work discipline, and sobriety. See Terence O. Ranger, 'Godly Medicine: The Ambiguities of Medical Mission in Southeastern Tanzania, 1900–1945', in Steven Feierman and John M. Janzen (eds), *The Social Basis of Health and Healing in Africa* (Berkely: University of California Press, 1992), 257–59.

[15] Janzen, *The Quest for Therapy*, 129, 219–220; Steven Feierman, 'Explanation of Uncertainty', 330. For healing among the Nyamwezi and Sukuma, see Colby R. Hatfield, 'The Nfumu in Tradition and Change: A Study of the Position of Religious Practitioners among the Sukuma of Tanzania, East Africa' (PhD thesis, Catholic University of America, 1968).

lished different categories of therapeutic approaches in the quest for healing, including divination and secret societies (*buswezi* and *migawo*) which dominated Nyamwezi therapeutic practices throughout the nineteenth century.[16]

Most chiefs offered missionaries gifts of various kinds and provided protection on the road and in times of invasion. Mirambo, Matolu, and *mnangwa* (headman) of Matolu, Kipaya, invariably provided the LMS and the White Fathers at Urambo Kilimani and Ndala with food and cattle. They also mobilized men to bring them building materials.[17] Mirambo expressed his determination to serve the missionaries, saying that because 'he invited the *mzungu* (the white person) to settle here [at Urambo Kilimani], he feels bound to supply him'.[18] Mirambo used the daily supply of cattle, food, protection, and human labour to control missionaries' activities at Urambo. Missionaries were expected to demonstrate their loyalty by providing him with firearms.[19]

Mirambo's demand that missionaries visit his *ikulu* as often as three times per day slowed the missionaries' progress. For example, Southon complained, 'Mirambo takes up so much of my time that I have little left for writing. He insists [on visiting] me three times daily, and I have to meet him in return'.[20] Mirambo demanded guns from the missionaries to control subjects in his territory, including missionaries, and protect his people against invasions from neighbouring chiefdoms. He gave his headmen 'instructions to accept nothing but a gun' from missionaries.[21] Indeed, some headmen demanded firearms for use in raids and conflicts beyond the boundaries of their chiefdoms.[22] The LMS missionaries were thus directly involved in encouraging violence in the region. With guns obtained from the missionaries and some that were locally

---

[16] Hans Cory, 'The Buswezi', *American Anthropologist*, Vol. 57, No. 5 (1955), 925.

[17] J.B. Thomson to Dr Mullens, Unyanguru [Ulyankulu], Urambo, 4 August 1878, CWM/LMS/Box 3/Folder 1; E. Southon MD to Rev. J.O. Whitehouse, Urambo, 21 January 1880, CWM/LMS/Box 3/Folder 1; E. Southon to Mr Whitehouse, Urambo, 1 June 1880, CWM/LMS/Box 3/Folder 2; Ndala Diary, 8 and 25 January, 20 February, 7 March, and 8 April 1896, WFA 01.43.

[18] E. Southon, MD to Rev. Whitehouse, Balton Hill, Urambo, 4 May 1880, CWM/LMS/Box 3/Folder 1.

[19] E. Southon, MD to Rev. Joseph Mullens, DD, Unyanguru, Urambo, 4 August 1878, CWM/LMS/Box 3/Folder 1, and Unyanyembe, 2 December 1879, CWM/LMS/Box 2/Folder 2.

[20] E. Southon, MD to Rev. Joseph Mullens, DD, 4 August 1878, CWM/LMS/Box 3/Folder 1.

[21] J.B. Thomson to Dr Mullens, Unyanguru [Ulyankulu], Urambo, 4 August 1878, CWM/LMS/Box 1; E. Southon, MD to Mr Whitehouse, Urambo, 31 December 1880, CWM/LMS/Box 3/Folder 4.

[22] Southon, MD to Mr Whitehouse, Urambo, 31 December 1880, CWM/LMS/Box 3/Folder 4.

EMANCIPATION, THE BEGINNINGS OF MISSION COMMUNITIES, AND EVERYDAY LIFE 67

made, Mirambo raided communities of the neighbouring chiefdoms, taking men and women as captives and slaves.[23]

Besides healing, mission schools attracted the young, and in most cases, chiefs made decisions over how many children should attend mission schools. They allowed the children of their subjects to attend mission schools after finishing their daily work for the chiefs. In Unyamwezi, following the rise of trade-based chiefdoms, nearly all the people, including children, were claimed by the chief, and were engaged during the day in tending his cattle and other work.[24] Recruiting young boys for schools became a source of tension between chiefs and commoner households. Chiefs thought that when parents sent the boys to school, they were defying chiefly authority by reasserting authority over them. For example, Chief Majembi Gana refused to allow anyone into the mission for instruction, asserting that children in his village were engaged in tending his cattle and were not to be distracted. Later, the chief allowed children in his territory to spend a few hours of their day attending the mission school, after their work for him was done. But some of his subordinate headmen refused to let children attend missionary instruction and demanded payment from missionaries.[25] Majembi Gana's refusal and that of his subordinates to let children attend the mission school demonstrates how chiefs acted in 'the defence of [their own] interests' against that of missionaries.[26]

In 1883, Majembi Gana promised to send one or two boys to be taught reading, writing, and carpentry, agreeing not to interfere with the villagers and others who wished to attend the school.[27] However, in 1884, the chief

[23] J.B. Thomson to Rev. Joseph Mullens, DD, Unyanguru, Urambo, 4 August 1878, CWM/LMS/Box 1; Dr Kirk to Earl Granville, Zanzibar, 14 November 1880, CMS/B/OMS/G3 A6/O/18; Andrew Roberts, 'Nyamwezi Trade', in Richard Gray and David Birmingham (eds), *Pre-Colonial African Trade: Essays on Trade in Central and Eastern Africa before 1900* (London: Oxford University Press, 1970), 44; Phillipe Broyon, 'Description of Unyamwesi, the Territory of King Mirambo, and the Best Route Thither from the East Coast', *Proceedings of the Royal Geographical Society*, Vol. 22, No. 1 (1877–78), 36.

[24] Rev. Blackburn to Mr Lang, CMS Uyui, 3 December 1883, CMS/B/OMS/G3 A6/O/8.

[25] Rev. Blackburn to Mr Lang, Uyui, 8 September 1882, CMS/B/OMS/G3 A6/O/65; Rev. Blackburn to Mr Lang, Uyui, 23 February 1883, CMS/B/OMS/G3 A6/O/64; Rev. Blackburn to Mr Lang, CMS Uyui, 3 December 1883, CMS/B/OMS/G3 A6/O/8. Majembi Gana, chief of Uyui, died in January 1885 and was subsequently succeeded by Mtani, referred to as Kanoni in the CMS correspondence.

[26] David Maxwell, *Christians and Chiefs in Zimbabwe: A Social History of the Hwesa People* (Westport, CT: Praeger, 1999), 5.

[27] Rev. J. Blackburn, Uyui, 3.12.1883 [compiled by Miss. G.E. Belcher, 1952], G3

changed his mind. He offered Rev. Blackburn two boys but refused to grant his subjects 'liberty to send their boys'. The chief was by now making sure that his kin monopolized the opportunities for schooling that were denied to others. Thus, in the conflict between the chief and the people over control of the young, missionaries only gained his conditional support if educational opportunities were restricted to youths of his own choosing. When drought and famine struck the region in 1884, the chief's prohibition against sending children to school broke down. Men, women, and children sought refuge in the mission, hoping the missionaries 'had the power to make medicine to cause rain to come'.

Furthermore, the recurring famine and drought in 1884 forced men and women from the territory of Mihama in northeastern Unyamwezi to move to Uyui. Wells and springs dried up, and cattle died of thirst and lack of pasture. The move to the Uyui mission made 'the people [of Uyui] very difficult', perhaps because the newcomers were thought to bring both insecurity and smallpox.[28] Indeed, smallpox erupted in the entire district, claiming the lives of many people in the chief's village and undermining confidence in the chief's ability to address his people's needs.

Following the outbreak of famine and smallpox, and the influx of people into the Uyui mission in 1884, the chief allowed children and their parents to interact with the missions. He asked Rev. Blackburn if he wanted another boy whose parents had died of smallpox in addition to the two boys the chief had already given him. That the chief was willing to give Blackburn another child demonstrates the extent to which the drought and the outbreak of smallpox undermined confidence in the chief's ability to address the needs of his people, even if it only resulted in him allowing a few children to attend mission schools.[29] The altered relations between the chief and missionaries enabled the CMS to obtain children for instruction. The decision of village parents to take their children to the mission enabled them to reaffirm their authority over their young.

A6/O/1883 [Missing], Nyanza Mission Precis.

[28] Rev. Blackburn to Mr Lang, CMS Uyui, 14 January 1884, CMS/B/OMS/G3 A6/O/26. See also Rev. J. Blackburn, Uyui 14 January 1884, G3 A6/O/ [Missing], Nyanza Mission Precis.

[29] Rev. J. Blackburn, Uyui, 9.2.1884, G3 A6/O/1884 [Missing], Nyanza Mission Precis; Rev. Blackburn to Mr Lang, Uyui, 9 February 1884, CMS/B/OMS/G3 A6/O/39.

Abolition of Slavery, Public Declarations, and Certification of Freedom, 1897–1914

The abolition of slavery in Catholic missions and the beginnings of mission communities involved flight to the missions, public declarations, and certification of emancipation. Many slaves ran away to the mission because they thought that missions offered a refuge from the abuse of slave owners. Between 1909 and 1910, about forty-six adult women sought refuge in the White Sisters' convent in Tabora, while the number of girls and children in the orphanage reached fifty-one.[30] The list of names of former slave women and orphan girls who sought refuge in the White Sisters' convent at Tabora between 1909 and 1910 shows the diversity of the community. They had Nyamwezi, Christian, and Swahili names such as 'Nyamizi', 'Kalundi[e]', 'Kalekwa', 'Sumuni', 'Vumilia', and 'Sesilia'. While the document does not tell us how they became free, it seems to suggest that they, too, worked for the White Sisters to earn cash to buy their freedom.[31] It was not uncommon for runaway slaves to buy their freedom from their masters to get into mission communities. In 1900, the military officers in Tabora recognized the sum of seven rupees or two cows as equivalent to the price for which slaves could buy freedom from their owners. The price of freedom increased after 1907 to twenty or thirty rupees, and at the time of the First World War in 1914, the price of emancipation had increased to forty rupees.[32]

Some enslaved men and women persuaded missionaries to let them join mission communities by paying half the price required by owners to earn their freedom, while relying on the missions to pay the balance. For instance, in 1905, the slave Luangalla and his wife Kashindye joined the community at the Ushirombo mission. Still, their owner, Mlasso, complained to the mission that they had left without his consent. Luangalla paid thirty rupees for himself and twenty rupees for Kashindye to buy their freedom.[33] Maria Wantiho also wanted to buy her freedom because her owner, named Mtagwa, denied her permission to join the mission community at Tabora. She paid fifteen rupees out of the required forty rupees. Maria's determination to join the mission community encouraged the mission to pay the remaining amount.[34] The fact that missionaries paid some of the money required for slaves to be released

---

[30] 'Notre Dame de Tabora', 1 July 1909–1 July 1910, AAT 350.002.

[31] Noms des femmes, filles et enfants à Notre Dame 1909–1910, 1 July 1910, AAT 350.002; Noms des autres réfugiées à Notre Dame, 1909–1910, AAT 350.002.

[32] Francis P. Nolan, 'Christianity in Unyamwezi, 1878–1928' (PhD thesis, University of Cambridge, 1977), 266–67; John Iliffe, *A Modern History of Tanganyika* (Cambridge: Cambridge University Press, 1979), 131.

[33] Tabora Military Station, No. 1297, 16 September 1905, AAT 526.503.

[34] P. Grünn to Mr Bauer, Magistrate of Tabora, 2 December 1913, AAT 526.503.

70 SLAVE EMANCIPATION, CHRISTIAN COMMUNITIES, AND DISSENT IN TANZANIA

from the bonds of slavery often acted to limit the freedom they enjoyed in mission communities. That the missionaries kept their certificates of freedom suggests the formerly enslaved residents lacked freedom of movement in mission communities.

Throughout German colonization of German East Africa (*Deutsch-Ostafrika*), from 1890 to 1914, the German Parliament (*Reichstag*) engaged in heated debate about the abolition of slavery in their colonial territory. The debate centred on three German African colonies: Togo, Cameroon, and German East Africa. The debate in the Reichstag did not concentrate on Namibia (*Deutsch-Südwestafrika* or German Southwest Africa) because there were no slaves in the colony. German East Africa drew considerable attention because it had not only the largest number of slaves in the German empire but also the greatest economic potential.[35] The debates in the Reichstag developed alongside the anti-slavery campaigns in Catholic and Protestant churches in Europe in the 1880s. Driven by the quest to make the interior of Africa a 'specialized ministry', Cardinal Charles Allemand Lavigerie, bishop of Algiers and founder of the society of the White Fathers (today, Missionaries of Africa), held meetings in Germany, Belgium, France, and Britain that called for anti-slavery campaigns in Africa. The anti-slavery movement in Germany reached a climax in 1888, when Catholic and Protestant churches organized a meeting in Cologne, calling for state intervention over slavery in German East Africa.[36] In 1895, in response to the Parliamentary debate and the growing anti-slavery movements in Germany, Kaiser Wilhelm II signed the Parliamentary act prohibiting slave dealing in the empire. Nevertheless, the act only applied to German officials in the colonies, leaving unaddressed the people in colonies – including subjects in German East Africa.[37]

---

[35] Jan-Georg Deutsch, *Emancipation without Abolition in German East Africa, 1884–1914* (Oxford: James Currey, 2006), 99. Debates continued into the 1920s, when the League of Nations Committee on Slavery asked the British government whether slavery still existed in German East Africa, Togo, and Cameroon. See Report on Tanganyika Territory, Covering the period from the conclusion of the Armistice to the end of 1920, UKNA CO 1071/366 [Cmd. 1428]; Report on Tanganyika Territory for the year 1922, UKNA CO 1071/366; and Slavery in Tanganyika by Sir George Maxwell, KBE, CMG, 31 March 1934, UKNA CO 323/1257/9.

[36] Jean-Claude Ceillier and François Richard, *Cardinal Charles Lavigerie and the Anti-Slavery Campaign* (Rome: Society of the Missionaries of Africa, 2012); François Renault, *Lavigerie: L'Esclavage Africain et L'Europe, 1868–1892*, Vol. 2, *Campagne Antiesclavagiste* (Paris: Éditions E. De Boccard, 1971), 258–94, 337–63.

[37] Deutsch, *Emancipation*, 99.

EMANCIPATION, THE BEGINNINGS OF MISSION COMMUNITIES, AND EVERYDAY LIFE 71

Although the 1895 Parliamentary act prevented German colonial officials from owning slaves, in German East Africa, slaves were bought and sold 'under the watchful eyes of local administrative officers'. In most instances, 'these transactions were even taxed'.[38] The reluctance of the German colonial officials to ban slavery stemmed from their political and economic interests in the colony, and thus they sought ways to cooperate with slave traders. In Tabora, for instance, Arabs and coastal Swahili traders constituted the propertied class that offered Germans the strongest political alliances. Furthermore, Nyamwezi men and women still owned many slaves because slavery was entrenched as an integral part of the social system. Thus, colonial officials had to approach the issue of abolition with caution.[39]

While political and economic interests made German colonial officials look the other way on slave dealing, they were nevertheless empowered to free slaves who complained of maltreatment and who wanted to join mission communities of their own volition. In 1901, Bernhard Heinrich von Bülow, Germany's imperial chancellor, issued a decree mandating that slaves had the right to work for themselves two days a week, to be cared for in their old age and sickness, and to be sold with their consent. Though the law empowered slaves with the right to be sold only with their consent, slave masters continued selling slaves against their will, and of course, the fear of threats from owners lingered for many slaves if they refused to be sold.[40] Bülow issued another decree at the end of 1904 that declared all children of slaves free, especially those born after 1905.[41] After the enactment of the decrees, the report about slavery in Ndala mission shows that there were several instances in which the German colonial state sent soldiers to collect fugitive slaves who had run to the mission seeking protection. The Ndala report does not specify what the soldiers did with the runaway slaves, nor do we learn of the possible reprisals of slave owners against the runaways. But the flight of slaves to the mission demonstrates their determination to emancipate themselves from slavery.[42]

Some slaves who had bought their freedom and joined the mission community influenced other slaves to leave their owners. Paulo is an example of a

[38] Ibid., 97.

[39] Ibid.; Juhani Koponen, *Development for Exploitation: German Colonial Policies in Mainland Tanzania, 1884–1914* (Helsinki: Finnish Historical Society, 1995), 200, 332.

[40] Père Slegers, 'Ndala: rapport sur l'esclavage', 15 June 1913, AAT 355.108; Nolan, 'Christianity in Unyamwezi', 266; Deutsch, *Emancipation*, 168 and 247. See also Report on the Tanganyika Territory, covering the period from the conclusion of the Armistice to the end of 1920, UKNA CO 1071/366 [Cmd. 1428].

[41] Nolan, 'Christianity in Unyamwezi', 266; Deutsch, *Emancipation*, 168.

[42] Slegers, 'Ndala'.

formerly enslaved person whose owner, Maganga bin Mzigawe, accused him of encouraging his remaining slaves to leave for the mission without his permission. Paulo obtained his certificate of freedom, attended mission school, and later on worked as a teacher at Isenga mission school. The determination of the remaining slaves of Maganga to join the mission community as free persons encouraged missionaries to buy their freedom to avoid tensions between Paulo, runaway slaves, and Maganga. Yet as part of the manumission process, Maganga's slaves declared before witnesses that they left the owner of their own will: they had desired to become free, and Paulo could not be held accountable.[43]

Between 1891 and 1914, the German colonial state recognized public declaration as a precondition for obtaining a certificate of freedom (*Freibrief*, pl. *Freibriefe*) from the colonial office. Formerly enslaved people declared before groups of witnesses that they had joined the mission community voluntarily. The list of slave 'redemptions' (*rachats d'esclaves*) between 1908 and 1909 (see Table 1) indicates that slaves who declared before witnesses in Tabora originated from various parts of the East African interior, including Rwanda, Burundi, Uganda, Karagwe, and the eastern Congo. They were both male and female slaves between the ages of fifteen and sixty, indicating that the majority were in their most productive years. Witnesses were formerly enslaved people living in the mission community whose names suggest that some were Nyamwezi from Tabora, while others came from elsewhere in the East African interior. Some witnesses were relatives of slaves living near the mission who could testify to the slaves' desire to join the mission community or live with their relatives as free persons. Christians and non-Christians could bear witness on behalf of slaves declaring their desire to become free.[44]

The practice of public declarations in German East Africa continued after the outbreak of the First World War, which implies that it had already become a part of the social system. For instance, at the Tabora mission, men and women who formerly belonged to slave owners declared in the presence of witnesses that they would no longer be slaves and refused to return to their owners. While some slaves who had gone to live at the Tabora mission without their owners' consent never returned to their owners and declared before witnesses that they would live at the mission, others went instead to live with their relatives. Similarly, at Isenga mission school, some slaves testified that they would never return to their owners, while others chose to live with their

---

[43] Political Office Tabora to Rev. Fr F. van Aken, the Catholic Mission Tabora, 3 August 1922, AAT 526.502; Senior Commissioner to Rev. Father Superior, White Fathers' Mission, Tabora, 5 January 1923, AAT 526.502/Ref. No. 88/1/4/2.

[44] Rachats d'esclaves, 1908–1909, AAT 322.399.

Table 1 Slaves, Owners, and Their Witnesses, 1908–09.

	Name of Slave	Age	Gender	Origin	Owner	Witnesses	Date of Freedom
1.	Bakafwa-Buna	-	F	Mnyarwa-Nda	Kafalebe	Kito Kizozo, Jacques Trebe?	1 January 1908
2.	Nsabo	-	-	Mbembe	Msanzya of Ushirombo	Kato Kizozo, Marino Kashinga	5 February 1908
3.	Batakushi-manga	-	F	Mbembe	Brikeshi of Usambiro	Bito Kizozo	26 March 1908
4.	Baruti	18	F	Mbembe	Musoka of Ulungwa	Fransisko Matwana, Andrea Kwikizya	22 April 1908
5.	Herman Kautu and his mother	25	M	Mrundi	Muwena Lukanka	-	27 April 1908
6.	Henriette Nyamisi	25	F	Mugera-Urundi	Muwena Lukanka of Igalula	Bito Kizozo, Athanasa Mukamwa	27 April 1908
7.	Merikani Muganda	25	-	Muganda	Biyoya of Msalala kwa Kayombo	Kito Kizozo, Andrea Giti	23 June 1908
8.	Bangaire	24	F	Mrundi	Lwakikono of Thaka	Kito Kizozo, Kwihamuka	21 October 1908
9.	Antonia Nangaiza	30	F	Mrundi	Lusamo of Masumbwe	Kito Kizozo, Antonio Magarwa	27 October 1908
10.	Kipili	60	F	-	Lutora of Igalula	Kito Kizozo, Albert Kabona	7 December 1908
11.	Ihyahya	-	-	-	Paulo Nyanzala	Eugenie Kaduma, Caroli Katunga	28 December 1908
12.	Mugembe	-	M	-	Kabilya of Bulebe	Mikaeli Kruka Mayango	4 January 1909
13.	Nakuga-iwa	-	-	-	Kigimbi of Mgarule	Kito Kizozo, Raphael Mvuno	12 February 1909
14.	Philipo Mabruki	-	M	-	Kahinze of Ihema	Kizozo, Kaduma	18 February 1909
15.	Shiniga	-	-	Ufipa	Magango of Bahuha, Ushirombo	Kito Kizozo, Madika of Igalula	26 April 1909

No.	Name	Age	Sex				Date
16.	Paulina Mwandaki	30	F	Mbembe	Nturunguni of Msalala	Kizozo, Kaduma, Gabriel Malembeka	4 May 1909
17.	Kati	-	-	Nyambolela	-	-	10 May 1909
18.	Kazuyaye	-	M	-	Burerero of Usambiro	Kizozo, Liborio Muhozya	June 1909
19.	Mukaboga-nda	20	M	-	Lunako of Usambiro	Casmir Bwamurungu, Kaduma	28 June 1909
20.	Makamfu	-	M	-	Makaya	-	26 July 1909
21.	Agnes Lihoho	15	F	-	Michael Kitikiti	Kaduma, Antoine Katoto	9/8/1909
22.	Gertude Muturu-twa	-	F	Kwezi	Kitokowa of Rwanda	Baruabe Kabyuzya, Caroli Mpera, Kaduma	13 August 1909
23.	Monika Kwigema	-	F	-	Magoma of Wangoni	Kizozo, Henri Maganga, Fabie Kangulu	22 September 1909
24.	Antonia Kwigoya	-	F	-	Zolo d/o Mwene Mpagalala	Kizozo, Maganga, Kangulu	22 September 1909
25.	Virginie Mkulizya-bi	35	F	Karaggwe	Kauze (Mwalo)	Caroli Mpera Simoni Mdaraka	23 October 1909
26.	Justin Barakubu-Nga	-	M	-	Mihambo of Utambala	Victor Kabwika, Beda Kafiki	29 October 1909
27.	Mukoyya	14	F	Nyandanyi Buyenze	Rwandagazya of Uyovu	Kizozo, Kafiki	12 November 1909
28.	Naboha	25	F	-	Muhekera of Ulungwa	Kafiki, Costantino Kutunga	13 November 1909
29.	Chomkera	-	F	Mbembe of Ulungwa	-	Kizozo, Philipo Mukiza	30 November 1909
30.	Kalekwa Kutanwa	40	F	Mbembe	Kigimbi of Ulungwa	Kizozo, Louis Mabala	1 December 1909
31.	Mutoshi-ma	16	-	Mrundi	Muhozya of Ulungwa	Kizozo, Jeay Mugunda	27 December 1909

Source: Compiled from Rachats d'esclaves, 1908–09, AAT 322.399 (27 December 1919).

EMANCIPATION, THE BEGINNINGS OF MISSION COMMUNITIES, AND EVERYDAY LIFE   75

relatives near the mission.[45] Formerly enslaved people living at the Tabora mission used witness statements as a platform to declare publicly their desire to become free. These statements also avoided conflicts between slaves and their owners, between the slave owners and the mission, and between missions and the colonial state before the three parties could negotiate about the certification of freedom.[46]

With support from the German colonial state in ending slavery, public declarations resulted in an increase in the number of *Freibriefe* of slaves who entered the mission community in Tabora: from 150 in 1900 to 591 in 1912.[47] Out of the 591 certificates, only 121 *Freibriefe* of formerly enslaved people who joined mission communities in Unyamwezi remain in the archives of the Archdiocese of Tabora, which seems to suggest that the majority of slaves left mission communities after marriage to raise families in the town and surrounding villages but maintained their ties with the mission as Christians. Nonetheless, existing certificates of freedom provide several clues about those formerly enslaved people. Some who moved to the missions came from female slave owners, indicating that economic opportunities such as agriculture enabled women to own slaves in Unyamwezi. For instance, an enslaved woman, Ysalu, originated from Iramba but settled at Ndala in the household of a female slave owner, Mwanamiso.[48] Other enslaved women, such as Nyamisi, Limi, Kagori Msukuma, and Kuilwa Msukuma, lived in the households of Nyamizi Msumbwa and Bibi Msau at Tabora and Ndala. The three slaves originated from Urambo and Ukune in the Lake Victoria region of Tanzania, denoting the diversity of slaves who formed early mission communities in the region.[49]

Some certificates list places in central Tanzania as the origins of former slaves who joined mission communities. This can be seen in the certificates of Kaunga, a male slave from Unyaturu, and a female slave named Nyarusi, from Ugogo. The reasons behind their move to Ndala and Tabora remain unclear from the certificates. But nineteenth-century travellers described central Tanzania as prone to famine and drought; John Hanning Speke, for instance, passing through Ugogo, described the region as 'the greater famine

---

[45] F. van Aken to the Senior Commissioner, 6 January 1923, AAT 526.502.

[46] For details on slaves and their witnesses at Tabora mission, see Rachats d'esclaves, 1908–1909, AAT 322.399.

[47] Nolan, 'Christianity in Unyamwezi', 267.

[48] Freibrief no. 3, 29 January 1904, AAT 526.503.

[49] Freibrief no. 152, 29 October 1897, AAT 526.503; Freibrief no. 133, 27 July 1907, AAT 526.503; Freibrief no. 134, 27 July 1907, AAT 526.503; Freibrief no. 135, 27 July 1907, AAT 526.503.

lands'.[50] Indeed, famine forced people into enslavement as they could not feed themselves, and many slaves found their way into missions to make ends meet.[51] The two certificates corroborate accounts of elders who revealed that people were enslaved in Ukimbu and other parts of Unyamwezi because of famine, which claimed many lives. As Oscar Kisanji recalled, 'Hata njaa za Wagogo zilileta watu katika nchi ya Kiwele' ('Even severe famines in Ugogo brought many Gogo people into the territory of Kiwere'), revealing the extent to which famine drove enslavement in the region.[52]

From the *Freibriefe*, we learn that slaves who received these certificates at Ushirombo, Tabora, and Ndala missions were between four and forty years of age, suggesting that many slaves were taken in their (re)productive years.[53] Women and girls constituted most of the slaves receiving certificates of freedom. The many women who received emancipation certificates in Unyamwezi demonstrate the strategies employed in their quest for freedom. Evidence shows that between the late 1890s and the 1900s, enslaved women in Unyamwezi sought their autonomy from owners as they fled to the missions, while others used the courts to reclaim their freedom.[54] Nevertheless, by 1912, only 3,276 slaves out of an estimated total of 233,000 in 1890 had received certificates of freedom. By 1914, however, the number of slaves living in the district of Tabora fell from 233,000 in 1890 to 70,000. Notwithstanding the decline in the number of slaves in the district, exchanges of domestic slaves

---

[50] John H. Speke, *Journal of the Discovery of the Source of the Nile* (Edinburgh and London: William Blackwood and Sons, 1863), 56. See also Gregory H. Maddox 'Leave Wagogo, You Have no Food: Famine and Survival in Ugogo, Tanzania, 1916–1961' (PhD thesis, Northwestern University, 1988), 78–123, 352–93.

[51] Freibrief no. 102, 11 December 1903, AAT 526.503; Freibrief no. 275, 26 October 1909, AAT 526.503.

[52] Interview with Oscar E. Kisanji, Tabora–Kazeh Hill, 30 November 2016.

[53] See for instance Tabora, 2 December 1913, AAT 526.503; Freibrief no. 152, 29 October 1897, AAT 526.503; Freibrief no. 133, 27 July 1907, AAT 526.503; Freibrief no. 135, 27 July 1907, AAT 526.503; Freibrief no. 110, 16 December 1903, AAT 526.503; Freibrief no. 111, 16 December 1903, AAT 526.503; Freibrief no. 203, 1909, AAT 526.503; Freibrief no. 62, 31 July 1903, AAT 526.503; and Freibrief no. 83, 25 March 1911, AAT 526.503.

[54] Jan-Georg Deutsch, 'Prices for Female Slaves and Changes in their Life Cycle: Evidence from German East Africa', in Gwyn Campbell, Suzanne Miers, and Joseph C. Miller (eds), *Women and Slavery*, Vol. 1, *Africa and the Western Indian Ocean Islands* (Athens: Ohio University Press, 2007), 140; Claire Robertson, 'Slavery and Women in Africa: Changing Definitions, Continuing Problems', in William H. Worger, Charles Ambler, and Nwando Achebe (eds), *A Companion to African History* (Hoboken, NJ: Wiley, 2019), 151.

EMANCIPATION, THE BEGINNINGS OF MISSION COMMUNITIES, AND EVERYDAY LIFE   77

were still reported in some parts of Tabora and other parts of Uyamwezi as German colonial rule in German East Africa ended.[55]

After the war, in 1918, the certification of emancipation for slaves in Tabora continued under the auspices of the British colonial officials who took over the administration of German East Africa (which became Tanganyika). Nonetheless, the practice of issuing certificates lasted for three years, between 1919 and 1922. The colonial government ran short of certificates of freedom to be offered to slaves in the territory and subsequently stopped the practice.[56] In 1922, one week after the shortage of these certificates was announced, the British colonial government enacted the Involuntary Servitude (Abolition) Ordinance, which declared slave dealing a punishable offence. Slaves could now go wherever they wished or remain with their former masters.[57] Even though the ordinance declared slave dealing a punishable offence, cases of slavery were still reported in some parts of the Tabora region, as the Nyamwezi slave owners took advantage of the 'unsettled state of the district' and forcibly enslaved men, women, and children.[58] The decline of slavery in Unyamwezi, therefore, writes Deutsch, was due to 'the prolonged struggles between owners and slaves, in which slaves tried to make the best of the limited choices and opportunities available to them'.[59]

Female Slaves, Orphanages, and the Beginnings of Mission Communities, 1897–1914

Women and girls in nineteenth- and twentieth-century Unyamwezi constituted most of the slaves who joined mission communities. Evidence from archives and documentary sources show that most runaway slaves were women (adult

---

[55] Jan-Georg Deutsch, 'Notes on the Rise of Slavery and Social Change in Unyamwezi, c. 1860–1900', in Henri Médard and Shane Doyle (eds), *Slavery in the Great Lakes Region of East Africa* (Athens: Ohio University Press, 2007), 76; Deutsch, *Emancipation*, 165–66 and 183; Koponen, *Development for Exploitation*, 200, 612.

[56] Letter from Senior Commissioner (Political Office Tabora), to Rev. F. van Aken, Tabora Catholic Mission, 3 August 1922, AAT 526.502 B, 1922; Memo from the Administrative Office to Rev. F. van Aken, Tabora Territory, 14 August 1922, AAT 526.502.

[57] *Tanganyika Territory Gazette*, Vol III, 1922 [The Involuntary Servitude (Abolition) Ordinance, No. 13 of 1922], 317, TNA; Memo from the Administrative Office to Rev. F. van Aken, 14 August 1922, AAT 526.502; Report on Tanganyika Territory for the year 1926, UKNA CO 1071/366 [Colonial No. 18].

[58] Report on Tanganyika Territory for the year 1922, UKNA CO 1071/366.

[59] Deutsch, *Emancipation*, 242.

girls and children) who joined the missions of Tabora in the hope of finding refuge from the abuses of slavery (see Tables 1, 2, and 3). Between 1909 and 1910, about eighty-six female slaves joined the mission communities of the White Sisters in Tabora, Ndala, and Ushirombo.[60] The list contains names of former slave women and orphan girls between four and forty years of age. The certification of freedom from 1900 to 1914 and lists of slave women and girls who joined the mission community of Tabora between 1909 and 1910 show names of children, including Msurikwao, Faida, Sifa, Sijana, Mambo, Mua, and Tschura, aged between five and thirteen years. They originated from, among other places, Manyema, Ukimbu, Urundi, and Uganda.[61] The names of the owners of these female slaves, 'Mashaka', 'Msuaheli Juma', 'Musuaheli Mabruki', and 'Msuaheli Fataki', suggest that they were enslaved to Nyamwezi and Swahili residents of Tabora. While circumstances leading to their enslavement remain unknown from the primary sources, we can suggest, as argued by Edward Alpers, that 'being female made one especially vulnerable to enslavement' in nineteenth-century East Africa.[62] The suffix 'ndogo' (used in this context to mean younger), as in the names 'Kalekwa ndogo' and 'Karunde ndogo', is indicative of the early ages at which girls found themselves in the bonds of enslavement. The etymology of the names 'Kalunde' (a female child born during the rainy season) and 'Kalekwa' (an orphan or abandoned child) are names from Unyamwezi or Usukuma. It is reasonable to suggest that various circumstances, including hunger, poverty, and vulnerability, accounted for their enslavement. But since they were young children, as their names suggest, their mothers or guardians likely sold themselves into slavery because children could not withstand the long march carrying tusks of ivory along the trade route to the coast.[63]

These female slave children lived entirely dependent on what the missions could provide to maintain their precarious existence and meet basic needs, including food and shelter. In the end, missionaries became 'patrons and protectors' of slave women whose susceptibility made them 'construe relationships as familial to impute kinship [and] to forge relationships' that bound

---

[60] See, for instance, Notre Dame de Tabora, 1 July 1909–1 July 1910, AAT 350.002; Noms des femmes, filles et enfants à Notre Dame 1909–1910, 1 July 1910, AAT 350.002; Noms des autres réfugiées à Notre Dame, 1909–1910, AAT 350.002.

[61] Freibrief no. 63, 7 July 1902, AAT 526.503; Freibrief no. 35, 11 December 1902, AAT 526.503; Freibrief no. 62, 31 July 1903, AAT 526.503; Freibrief no. 44, 2 July 1903, AAT 526.503.

[62] Edward A. Alpers, 'The Story of Swema: Female Vulnerability in Nineteenth-Century East Africa', in Claire C. Robertson and Martin Klein (eds), *Women and Slavery in Africa* (Madison: University of Wisconsin Press, 1983), 186.

[63] 'Notre Dame de Tabora', 1 July 1909–1 July 1910, AAT 350.002.

them into closer relationships with their patrons in the missions.[64] In 1898, Fr Van der Burgt reported in the mission journal that fifteen women and girls who had joined the White Sisters' convent at Ushirombo were 'small, weak, and poor young women'.[65] At Ndala, missionaries offered similar portrayals of slaves, often marking them as 'poor', 'unfortunate', and 'victims'.[66] By seeking refuge in missions, missionaries hoped that the slave girls would be 'called back to health' and receive the benefits of European 'civilization' – that is, the educational, healthcare, and other opportunities offered by converting to Christianity.[67] It is no wonder, therefore, that the slave children who sought refuge in the mission communities and orphanage centres and lived as totally dependent at Tabora, Ushirombo, and Ndala in the Vicariate Apostolic of Unyanyembe would convert to Christianity, becoming part of the first generation of Christians in the region.[68]

In addition to those of younger ages, adult female slaves joined mission communities in large numbers. We learn from the list of female slaves (see Tables 2 and 3) who joined the mission community of the White Sisters in Tabora that adult female slaves included Twinambene from the Manyema region in eastern Congo, who joined the Tabora mission at the age of forty; Karunde from Usukuma or Unyamwezi, who joined the mission of Tabora at the same age; and Nyamizi Mbembe, who joined the mission of Uyui (the German official who provided her with the *Freibrief*, possibly referred to the Ndala mission).[69] Other slaves, including Njanzara from Shirira, joined the mission at age fifty and joined the mission community of Tabora for protection.

---

[64] Andreana C. Prichard, *Sisters in Spirit: Christianity, Affect, and Community Building in East Africa, 1860–1970* (East Lansing: Michigan State University Press, 2017), 59; Michelle Liebst, *Labour and Christianity in the Mission: African Workers in Tanganyika and Zanzibar, 1864–1926* (Woodbridge: James Currey, 2021), 44.

[65] MSOLA Diary, 1898, 216, quoted in Ceillier and Richard, *Cardinal Charles Lavigerie*, 157; Salvatory S. Nyanto, 'Waliletwa na Kengele ya Kanisa: Discourses of Slave Emancipation and Conversion at Ndala Catholic Mission in Western Tanzania, 1896–1913', *Tanzania Journal of Sociology*, Vol. 2/3 (2017), 77.

[66] Ndala Diary, April 1897, Nyanto, 'Waliletwa na Kengele ya Kanisa', 77.

[67] Ndala Diary, June 1897 and January 1898.

[68] See, for instance, Noms des femmes, filles et enfants à Notre Dame 1909–1910, 1 July 1910, AAT 350.002; Noms des autres réfugiées à Notre Dame, 1909–1910, AAT 350.002. See also Ceillier and Richard, *Cardinal Charles Lavigerie*, 156–60.

[69] Freibrief no. 65, 4 August 1903, AAT 526.503; Freibrief no. 557, 8 January 1913, AAT 526.503; Freibrief no. 166, 10 August 1910, AAT 526.503; Freibrief no. 732, 5 May 1912, AAT 526.503.

Table 2 Certificates of Freedom (*Freibriefe*) Granted to Slaves Living at Tabora and Ushirombo, 1900–14.

	Slave	Age	Gender	Cert #	Origin	Residence	Slave up to	Owner
1.	Ndayaundi	20	F	290	Urundi	Ushirombo	2 August 1900	Kazinga
2.	Kamhura	12	F	350	Uganda	Tabora	10 July 1901	Bibi Mama Salima
3.	Selimani	5	M	311	Uvinza	Tabora	13 April 1901	Sualeh Ramadhan
4.	Serasi	25	F	15	Wahehe?	Tabora	12 June 1902	Mtusi Ugoie of Uyui
5.	Msurikwao	7	F	20	-	Tabora	7 July 1902	Mashaka
6.	Sijana	9	F	35	Kisalibuko	Tabora	11 December 1902	Msuaheli Juma
7.	Mkwana	20	F	34	-	-	29 November 1902	MnyamweziMakwaya
8.	Malisila	35	M	110	Sukuma	Tabora	16 December 1903	Bibi Fatuma
9.	Missossie	5	M	111	Sukuma	Tabora	16 December 1903	Bibi Fatuma
10.	Kaunga	24	M	102	Unyaturu	Tabora	11 December 1903	Mkimbu Nyao
11.	Faida	9	F	95	Uganda	Tabora	16 September 1903	Mganda Asumani
12.	Twinambe-ne	40	F	65	Manyema	Tabora	4 August 1903	Mtusi Kahera
13.	Msurikwao	10	F	63	Ruanda	Tabora	4 August 1903	Mtusi Mkonongo
14.	Mambo	9	F	62	Manyema	Tabora	31 July 1903	Msuaheli Mabruki
15.	Tschura	7	F	44	Urundi	Tabora	2 July 1903	Msuaheli Fataki
16.	Majengo	5	M	12	Unyamwesi	Tabora	18 April 1903	Msuaheli Malipo
17.	Faida	7	F	85	Ukimbu	Tabora	19 November 1904	Mbembe Majuti
18.	Mkawie	24	F	20	-	Tabora	8 February 1905	Mpiri Sangallo
19.	Hamisi	10	M	27	-	Tabora	22 February 1905	Myao Kiribolo
20.	Juma	7	M	33	Mwemba	Tabora	18 March 1905	Mniamwezi Feruzi

21.	Basao	24	F	49	-	Tabora	3 May 1905	Mnyassa Songoro
22.	Kashindye	-	F	-		Tabora	16 September 1905	Mlasso
23.	Lusugua	17	F	69	Ruanda	Tabora	20 June 1906	Ndagaja
24.	Mungwasos-cha	16	F	95	Ruanda	Tabora	18 August 1906	Mtusi Hamisi
25.	Sawo Mbita	22	F	34	Urundi	Tabora	4 April 1907	Kapera
26.	Kuilwa Msukuma	12	M	135	Urambo	Tabora	20 July 1907	Nyamizi Msumbwa
27.	Kagori Msukuma	10	F	134	Urambo	Taboa	20 July 1907	Nyamizi Msumbwa
28.	Limi	30	F	133	Ukune	Tabora	20 July 1907	Nyamizi Msumbwa
29.	Mwemba	30	M	203	-	Tabora?	1909	Seleman bin Rajabu
30.	Mapokero?	7	F	211	Ruranyuru	Tabora	13 November 1909	Not specified
31.	Jarugire?	5	F	213	-	Tabora	13 November 1909	Not specified
32.	Runanzari	9	M	48	Tabora	Tabora	13 February 1911	Uledi-Tabora
33.	Munde	30	F	91	Uwembe	Tabora	27 March 1911	Mary Kapeta
34.	Kolorinda	25	F	550	Ruanda	Tabora	3 January 1912	Maganga
35.	Adubera Mbemba	28	M	1089	Mbembe	Tabora	2 December 1912	Myege Msumbwa
36.	Njanzara	50	F	557	Shirira	Mission	8 January 1913	Msambiro Rukina
37.	Schihanire	25	F	558	-	Mission	8 January 1913	Msambiro Rukina
38.	Munjofu	35	M	556	Ngaruka	Mission	8 January 1913	Msambiro Rukina
39.	Maria Wantiho	-	F	-	-	Tabora	2 December 1913	Mutagwa
40.	Nyansila	35	F	588	Ruanda	Sokoni Tabora	16 January 1914	Mamajalala Mkongala
41.	Mua	20	F	13	-	Tabora	n.d.	Bibi Namapany

Source: Archdiocese of Tabora Archives, Freibriefe, AAT 526.50.

Table 3 Certificates of Freedom (*Freibriefe*) Granted to Slaves Living at Ndala and Uyui, 1897–1914.

	Slave	Age	Gender	Cert #	Origin	Residence	Slave up to	Owner
1.	Nyamisi	27	F	152	Ushirombo	Ndala	29 October 1897	Bibi Msau of Ndala
2.	Kissasi	25	M	161	-	Ndala	2 December 1897	Kabaza
4.	Shekanawa	28	F	163	Manyema	Ndala	2 December 1897	Suaheli Ali
5.	Njamisi	18	F	147	Ubembe	Ndala	29 October 1897	Bibi Mtau
6.	Njuwake	7	F		Ndala	Ndala	17 June 1898	Not specified
7.	Mugroa	10	F	6	Mkimbu	Ndala	29 January 1904	Mwana Misso
8.	Mugroa	10	F	6	Mkimbu	Ndala	29 January 1904	Mwana Misso
9.	Sifa	4	F	7	Mkimbu	Ndala	29 January 1904	Mwana Misso
10.	Kimbulu	8	M	4	Ukimbu	Ndala	29 January 1904	Mwana Misso
11.	Nyamizi		F	46	-	Ndala	22 May 1904	Mwana Misso
12.	Tsorro	6	M	33/02	Ussuwi	-	15 October 1905	Mnyamwesi Mussabida
13.	Mukwaha	10	M	53	Ruanda	Ndala	9 May 1905	Mshimiha
14.	Kalekwa	13	F	104	Uyuwi	Ndala	8 June 1907	Mtussi Mhasi
15.	Syawari?	35	F	103	-	Ndala	8 June 1907	Mtussi Mhasi
16.	Turogowane	35	F	129	Unyamwesi	Ndala	20 July 1907	Mkomate of Ndala
17.	Kalimundzia	10	M	130	Unyamwesi	Ndala	20 July 1907	Mkomate of Ndala
18.	Athanasi Mtaki	17	M	157	Mhussi	Ndala	7 September 1907	Kilasso
19.	Mtaki	14	M	158	Usandani	Sungwisi	7 September 1907	Nhonoli
20.	Maria Magdalena Sizya	30	F	181	Ubembe	Mwasu-ngu Uyuwi	30 October 1907	Mayengo of Uyui
21.	Magdalena Dotto	35	F	58	Ubembe	Mission Ndala	13 April 1908	Wadeki of Ndala
22.	Arashasia Kwangu	25	F	202	Ussonge	Ndala	2 October 1908	Kashina Nkolozi

23.	Daria Kubanga	-	F	277	Usukuma	Ndala	26 October 1909	Shesoma
24.	Sabina Kalunde	-	F	276	Marango	Ndala	26 October 1909	Kagambo
25.	Maliyabo	-	F	278	Unyema	Ndala	26 October 1909	Lugenzi
26.	Nyarusi	-	F	275	Ugogo	Ndala	26 October 1909	Masali
27.	Bugumba	20	M	157	-	Ndala	1 September 1910	Matayiri ya Ushetu?
28.	Kapembe	25	M	168	-	Makene-nya	10 August 1910	Mwana Msandwa of Ndala
29.	Mwalu	30	M	167	-	Makene-nya	18 August 1910	Mwana Msandwa of Ndala
30.	Nyamizi	30	F	95	-	Makene-nya	10 August 1910	Mwana Msadwa of Ndala
31.	Karunde	40	F	166	-	Makene-nya	10 August 1910	Mwana Msandwa of Ndala
32.	Kalunde	35	F	244	Bungombe	Ndala	21 November 1910	Ijeke Mnyamwesi
33.	Nyamisi	30	F	83	Kawende	Ndala	25 March 1911	Kalunda[e] Myamwesi of Unyanye-mbe
34.	Kabula	12	F	200	Ndala	Ndala	5 July 1911	Mrumwe Kayumbo
35.	Liangano	25	F	199	Congo	Ndala	5 July 1911	Mrumwe Kayumbo
36.	Nyangano Yulia	30	F	204	Uwembe	Ndala	6 July 1911	Kayumbo of Ndala
37.	Kahula	11	F	205	Ndala	Ndala	6 July 1911	Kayumbo of Ndala
38.	Mruaja	20	F	218	Unyika	Ndala	20 July 1911	Mtussi Kanala
39.	Nyabulwa	35	F	574	Mbembe	Ndala	24 January 1912	Mbisa Selemani
40.	Nyamizi Mbembe	40	F	732	Ubembe	Uyui	7 May 1912	Kilunga Mbembe
41.	Turimbembe	12	F	733		Uyui	7 May 1912	Kilunga Mbembe
42.	Upande	30	M	866	Manyema	Ndala	24 June 1914	Mwinyi-mvua of Ndala
43.	Subule	30	F	1067	Mniaturu	Ndala	20 November 1914	Mogi? Mnyamwezi
44.	Ndikumwa-mi	30	M	813	Uganda	Ndala	25 June 1914	Not specified

Source: Archdiocese of Tabora Archives, Freibriefe, AAT 526.50.

Reports of adult female slaves who sought protection in the missions abound in the mission journal of Ndala in December 1897, suggesting that many adult females frequented the missions of Unyamwezi to form Christian communities in the second half of the nineteenth century.[70] Moreover, the Kiswahili suffix 'mkubwa' (elder) in the names 'Paulina mkubwa' and 'Namamsumna mkubwa' recorded in the list of slave women and children who sought refuge at the White Sister's community of Tabora between 1909 and 1910 suggests that they sought refuge at the mission because they wanted to protect their children against the experiences of enslavement and the long march from the interior to Unyamwezi and the coast.[71]

That some female slaves joined mission communities as adults seems to suggest that they were mothers of younger female slaves and that they sought freedom to protect their daughters, who were sold to slave dealers and passing caravans. In this regard, most women in Unyamwezi and the East African interior put themselves in precarious positions as they attempted to negotiate their vulnerability as the slave trade expanded with the trade in ivory and firearms. The experience of these female slaves is akin to the story of Swema, whose mother provides a sense of the selfless motives of enslaved women, as she sold herself into slavery to protect her daughter, who 'was still young and able to carry a tusk of ivory to the coast'.[72] While adult and young female slaves and children were not necessarily tied by blood relations, the diverse residents in the mission communities of Tabora, Ushirombo, and Ndala forged ties of kinship based on post-slavery experiences in the missions, which in turn impacted the nature and character of the communities that they helped to create.[73]

Adult and young female slaves who joined early mission communities of the White Sisters of Tabora, Ndala, and Ushirombo originated not only from Unyamwezi but also from Congo, Uganda, Rwanda, Burundi, and central and western Tanzania. They had learned the Kinyamwezi language and used it as a lingua franca while living in the region as slaves. Thus, they were conversant in the language when they joined the mission communities. For example, Kaunga and Nyarusi from central Tanzania joined Ndala and Tabora missions.[74] Turimbembe and Nyamizi Mbembe came from Uyui. Turimbembe

---

[70] Ndala Diary, 1, 2, and 8 December 1897.

[71] Noms des femmes et enfants, Notre Dame, 1909–1910, AAT 350.002; Noms des autres réfugiées a Notre Dame, 1909–1910, AAT 350.002.

[72] Alpers, 'The Story of Swema', 192.

[73] We learn from the certificates of freedom between 1897 and 1919 that former slaves in the missions of Tabora, Ushirombo, and Ndala originated from Unyamwezi, Usukuma, eastern Congo, Rwanda, Burundi, and Uganda.

[74] Freibrief no. 102, 11 December 1903, AAT 526.503; Freibrief no. 275, 26 October

EMANCIPATION, THE BEGINNINGS OF MISSION COMMUNITIES, AND EVERYDAY LIFE   85

was twelve years of age when she received her certificate of freedom, and Nyamizi Mbembe was forty when she became a member of the mission of Ndala mission community. As these two instances attest, the shared experience of escaping slavery and finding refuge inspired the formation of new communities of adults and children from diverse backgrounds in the missions. The name Mbembe suggests that the two slaves might have originated from Ubembe in the present DRC. While the reasons for the granting of freedom remain unclear from the *Freibriefe*, they might have moved to a mission community to escape mistreatment by their owners.[75]

Married female slaves from different owners also joined mission communities after receiving their certification of freedom. Kiweba and his wife Nyansolo, who belonged to different owners from Usambiro, received their certificates of freedom and joined the mission community of Ndala. Ruduri from Isambi-Kivu (Congo) and Namukuru from Burundi also belonged to the owners of Rusabira and Kadsjokadsjo. The experience of these two slaves, who came from different areas in the Great Lakes region, demonstrates that, given the linguistic and cultural diversity of slaves who joined the mission communities, building communities was undoubtedly challenging. Nevertheless, the Kinyamwezi language they had learned while living in Unyamwezi as slaves helped overcome their cultural and linguistic differences and allowed them to communicate in mission communities.[76]

The names provide further clues about how these culturally diverse people formed a new community in Unyamwezi by adopting the language and names of the Wanyamwezi. Nyamizi Mbembe and Njamisi Ubembe, both living at Ndala, declared Ubembe along the shores of Lake Tanganyika in Congo as their country of origin. But on their certificates, they used Nyamwezi names, implying that they had adopted the Nyamwezi name Njamisi, or Nyamizi, after arriving at Ndala mission and desired to be integrated into the culture of the community at Ndala. Njamisi is a different rendering of the same name, Nyamizi, implying that two different people adopted the same name.[77] The fact that most of the inhabitants of Ndala lived at the mission following formal manumission and later changed their names to incorporate themselves into the mission community was emphasized by Maria Nyamizi Leo Kalenga, the daughter of a formerly enslaved person from Congo who moved to Ndala

---

1909, AAT 526.503.

[75] Freibrief no. 733, 7 May 1912, AAT 526.503.

[76] Freibrief no. 512, 29 July 1909, AAT 526.503; Freibrief no. 513, 29 July 1909, AAT 526.503.

[77] Tabora, Freibrief no. 147, 29 October 1897, AAT 526.503; Tabora, Freibrief no. 732, 7 May 1912, AAT 526.503.

SLAVE EMANCIPATION, CHRISTIAN COMMUNITIES, AND DISSENT IN TANZANIA

mission and formed one of the earliest mission communities in the area.[78] Her name, Maria Nyamizi Leo Kalenga, contains the traces of three heritages: her father's, the Christian, and the Nyamwezi in which she was raised. She adopted a Nyamwezi name to be fully incorporated into the Nyamwezi community. Maria Nyamizi Leo Kalenga further insisted that although formerly enslaved people became assimilated into the Nyamwezi society by adopting Nyamwezi names and culture, they still remembered their ancestral origins. She explained that 'slaves from different areas established Ndala village. Although they call themselves Wanyamwezi and speak Kinyamwezi, even today, during wedding ceremonies, they call themselves Wamanyema, Warundi and Waha.'[79]

We also learn from the names of formerly enslaved people the various circumstances leading to their enslavement and emancipation. The name Nyansila or Nyanzila is assigned to girls to suggest a person who makes a path on the road with her steps during long walks – a vivid illustration of the impact of long-distance trade that dominated Nyamwezi and other interior communities in the nineteenth century. It is reasonable to assume that Nyansila entered the mission community in Tabora after she was abandoned along the way as caravans marched to the coast.[80] The slave Njanzara (Nyanzara), whose name signifies drought, suggests someone who became enslaved due to famine and destitution. Kalekwa (masculine, Mlekwa) means a slave orphan and suggests a person who joined a mission community because her parents had been enslaved. The name Upande or Lupande denotes a piece of cloth and must refer to a slave purchased in exchange for a piece (*lupande*) of cloth.[81]

Community Building and Everyday Life in the Missions, 1897–1914

Attendance at daily and Sunday services became mandatory for those in the Ushirombo, Tabora, and Ndala mission communities. Anastazia Maturino Mulindwa, whose father originally came from Uganda to join the mission community at Ushirombo, said that attendance at Sunday services was

---

[78] Interview with Maria Leo Kalenga, Ndala, 7 January 2016.

[79] Interview with Maria Nyamizi Leo Kalenga, Ndala, 6 September 2016. In Kiswahili, 'Kijiji cha Ndala kimeanzishwa na mchanganyiko wa watumwa. Ingawa wanajiita Wanyamwezi na kuzungumza Kinyamwezi hadi sasa wakati wa ndoa hupiga vigelegele wakitaja Kongo Manyema, Burudi, Rwanda na Buha'.

[80] Freibrief no. 588, 16 January 1914, AAT 526.503; 'Slave Trade in East Africa', 30 November 1974, 2, AAT 526.502.

[81] Freibrief no. 557, 8 January 1913, AAT 526.503; Freibrief no. 104, 8 June 1907, AAT 526.503; Freibrief no. 866, 24 June 1914, AAT 526.503. See also 'Slave Trade in East Africa', 2, AAT 526.502.

EMANCIPATION, THE BEGINNINGS OF MISSION COMMUNITIES, AND EVERYDAY LIFE   87

compulsory, asking rhetorically, 'Utakaa misheni bila kusali?' ('Can you live at a parish without attending church services?').[82] Children also became part of the communities through baptism, and parents who left the community after marriage to build their own houses maintained their place in the communities by bringing their children to the mission church for baptism.[83]

Besides attending services in the church, orphans carried out other responsibilities under the missionaries' supervision. Girls in the orphanage performed work in the fields under the supervision of the White Sisters in the Ushirombo and Ndala missions. They also learned domestic skills such as sewing, washing, ironing, mending, and cooking. Men worked as carpenters and brickmakers.[84] Maria Kalenga, a daughter of the runaway slave Leo Kalenga and Eliasi Matoja, a former catechist, described the kinds of work at the Ndala mission. Maria recalled how 'People living in mission compounds planted food crops for themselves, made bricks to build the church, and learned how to pray and read and write', Eliasi remarked that 'they worked as usual'.[85] The impression from the testimonies of Maria and Eliasi is that the missions attracted orphans, slaves, and other men and women who worked to sustain themselves and their new communities.

Residents of the mission communities sought to control their lives and make the missions places where they could pursue their interests and activities, but they were not always successful. Children and orphans who exhibited what the missionaries called 'intolerable behaviour' lived under close supervision until they reached the age of marriage. They could leave the community and live in the village near the Ushirombo mission.[86] At Lububu mission, recalls Melkior Mpila, girls in the White Sisters' convent had 'freedom coupled with order and special regulations' ('walikuwa na uhuru wenye amri na utaratibu maalumu') and that children displaying unacceptable behaviour

---

[82] Interview with Anastazia Maturino Mulindwa and Telesfora Amosi Mwakyembe, Ushirombo, 5 December 2016. The Holy Ghost Fathers (Spiritans) also made attendance at religious instruction and observances mandatory to the redeemed slaves living in Bagamoyo mission. For details see Giblin, *Politics of Environmental Control*, 61.

[83] Interviews with Tekla Herman, Ushirombo, 5 December 2016, and Felista Lonjini Namna, Uhemeli (Isakala), Ndala, 6 September 2016.

[84] Translated German Documents [Annual Report about the Development of German East Africa, 1905–1906], 51, UDSM/History Resources Room.

[85] Interviews with Maria Nyamizi Leo Kalenga, Ndala, 6 September 2016, and Eliasi Matoja Kilunga, Chamihwa, 9 September 2016. In Kiswahili, Maria: 'watu wa kwenye makambi walilima chakula chao wenyewe, walichoma matofali ya kujenga kanisa, walifundishwa kusali pamoja na kusoma na kuandika', and Eliasi: 'walikuwa wanafanya kazi kama kawaida'.

[86] Interview with Tekla Herman, Ushirombo, 5 December 2016.

were told to leave 'so that they would not disrupt the mission's regulations' ('ili wasivuruge utaratibu wa misheni').[87] As a result, close supervision, with a strict timetable for the range of activities in the mission, isolated boys and girls from the wider village life and culture, as well as village friends. At mission schools, writes Kathleen Symthe about the Ufipa region of southwestern Tanzania, 'missionaries rarely allowed children out of the Fathers' or Sisters' walled compounds and then only under supervision'.[88]

Despite the strict supervision, mission communities provided avenues through which Christian men and women could interact and extend networks of friendship and kinship among the residents. The appeal of the mission was widespread, as village children came to play with the children of the mission, and adults from distant villages joined the communities.[89] Adults tried to integrate the orphans, children, and older people who joined the community by creating kinship relations that were not based on blood ties or marriage but amounted to 'fictive' or 'networked' kinship based on the shared experience of enslavement and mission experience.[90] Adult residents in Tabora, Ushirombo, and Ndala missions may have adopted the orphans and treated them as their children, leading to the growth of a mission community for those missions that attracted and enabled former slaves, orphans, and older people to extend their social relationships beyond members of their households (see Figure 6). In 1906, about fifteen boys and ten girls lived in the orphanage at Tabora mission, while fifty people lived in the mission village. At Ushirombo mission, 58 boys and 65 girls lived in the orphanage, 40 older women lived in one house, and about 489 people lived in three villages around Ushirombo mission. Between 1905 and 1906, one Christian village at Ushirombo consisted of 192 homesteads and 22 new families originating from the two orphanages of the mission.[91] At the Ndala mission, there was one orphanage with 20 boys and 9 families living in the mission village. And in 1909, there was one orphanage centre with 28 boys at Ngaya (Msalala) mission and about 178 people living in the village near the mission.[92] These accommodations for orphans and older

---

[87] Interview with Melkior Mpila, Ndala village, 22 July 2021.

[88] Kathleen R. Smythe, *Fipa Families: Reproduction and Catholic Evangelization in Nkasi, Ufipa, 1880–1960* (Portsmouth; NH: Heinemann, 2006), 80.

[89] Adrian Hastings, *The Church in Africa, 1450–1950* (Oxford: Clarendon Press, 1996), 213; interview with Getruda Mateo, Emmanuel Ndekanilo, Ushirombo, 5 December 2016.

[90] Elisabeth McMahon, *Slavery and Emancipation in Islamic East Africa: From Honor to Respectability* (Cambridge: Cambridge University Press, 2013), 196.

[91] Aylward Shorter, *Cross and Flag: The 'White Fathers' during the Colonial Scramble (1892–1914)* (Maryknoll, NY: Orbis Books), 74.

[92] Annual Report, 1905–1906, 51–52, UDSM/History; Hastings, *The Church*, 213.

Figure 6 The Orphanage Centre at Kipalapala Mission in 1889.

people attracted more men, women, and children from surrounding villages to the mission.

Between 1900 and 1914, festivals, gatherings, and communal meals were opportunities for extending social relationships for both men and women who lived temporarily or permanently at the mission compounds of Ndala and Ushirombo.[93] Mission festivals featured the culture of neighbourhood food sharing. It was customary for Nyamwezi to eat communally outside the homestead, where everyone, family members and strangers, was welcome to eat. These customs strengthened friendships inside as well as outside the mission communities.[94] In later decades, neighbourhood gatherings and food sharing became evident in the *lusangi* open-air meetings and revival movements that invariably functioned as an arena for expanding friendship networks among Christians and non-Christians in Unyamwezi's Moravian missions. These festivals lasted several days, with events consisting of preaching the Word, baptism of new converts, and confirmation.[95]

At Ndala, weekly festivals and dances attracted men, women, and children within and outside the mission. Every Saturday evening, those in the

---

[93] See, for instance, Ndala Diary, 2 December 1903, and 16 September 1904, WFA 01.43.

[94] Rev. Blackburn to Mr Lang, CMS Uyui, 24 June 1884, CMS/B/OMS/G3 A6/O/113.

[95] Teofilo H. Kisanji, *Historia Fupi ya Kanisa la Kimoravian Tanganyika Magharibi* (Kipalapala: TMP, 1983), 171 and 251; interview with Esta Isaya Nkomabantu, Rev. Mathias Aron Kiligito, Rev. Charles Jeremiah Kinyonga, and Rev. Edson Nhomba, Sikonge, 27 November 2016.

90   SLAVE EMANCIPATION, CHRISTIAN COMMUNITIES, AND DISSENT IN TANZANIA

mission village and some from outside the mission gathered at the mission for dances. In 1909, eleven boys lived in the orphanage, while the mission village included twenty-four adults and fourteen children (apparently boys and girls) who also attended the dances and festivals.[96] The weekly dances and festivals grew in the later decades due to the increasing population around the mission. Recalling those weekly dances at the Ndala mission, Maria Kalenga and Eliasi Matoja said, 'Every ethnic group had to show its dance'. Each week featured a dance of the people from a particular region, such as Congo, Rwanda, Burundi, and the Lake Region of Tanzania.[97] As a child, Maria Kalenga attended these gatherings almost every weekend to see the dances of each ethnic group. She said, 'I went to watch the dances every weekend', emphasizing that she never missed these weekly events.[98]

Weekly festivals and dances in missions created a new space to negotiate social relationships for married and unmarried men, women, and orphans, who could meet to be entertained and interact with new and old friends. Some of the bonds did not last and easily faded away, but many relationships grew stronger, with some even leading to marriage. The traditional conflict between the young and their elders over the choice of partners continued in the mission. Still, residents eventually persuaded the missionaries to allow them to choose their spouses, and the dances became occasions for men and women to find marital partners. At Ushirombo, a Kisumbwa song, 'Askofu nakomeye ngomba ukuswela nansasuye' ('Bishop, I am grown up, I need to marry this one'), was common among those living in the mission community.[99] Getruda Mateo further stressed that when men married women of the mission, they were not required to pay bridewealth. However, this situation caused conflict between parents and the young, especially girls who wished to join missions because their parents would likely be unable to pay bridewealth.[100] Getruda Mateo recalled the experience of her grandparents at the Ushirombo mission:

[96] Nolan, 'Christianity in Unyamwezi', 223.

[97] Interview with Maria Nyamizi Leo Kalenga, 6 September 2016, and Eliasi Matoja Kilunga, Chamihwa, 9 September 2016. In Kiswahili, 'kila mmoja alikuwa anaonesha ngoma yake'.

[98] Maria Nyamizi Leo Kalenga, 6 September 2016. In Kiswahili, 'nilikuwa nakwenda kutazama ngoma'.

[99] Interview with Anastazia Maturino Mulindwa and Telesfora Mwakyembe, Ushirombo, 5 December 2016.

[100] Interview with Getruda Mateo, Ushirombo, 5 December 2016. For more on the importance of bridewealth in African families and clans, see James L. Giblin, 'Divided Patriarchs in a Labour Migration Economy: Contextualizing Debate about Family and Gender in Colonial Njombe', in Colin Creighton and C.K.

EMANCIPATION, THE BEGINNINGS OF MISSION COMMUNITIES, AND EVERYDAY LIFE   91

Babu na Bibi walitoka magharibi wakaoana humo kwenye ngome. Babu alikuwa kwenye ngome [ya kina baba] na bibi alikuwa kwenye ngome [ya kina
mama] wakapendana wakafunga ndoa wakapewa eneo wakajenga wakazaa
watoto na sisi wajukuu tukazaliwa. Kila aliyekuwa anaoa anapewa eneo la
kujenga.

My grandfather and grandmother came from the West and married in mission
houses. My grandfather lived in a separate house [for men], and my grandmother in one for women. They loved each other and got married. The mission
offered them a piece of land to build themselves a house.[101]

As at Ushirombo, the weekly festivals and dances at the Ndala mission led
men and women to marriage. Maria Kalenga recalled that her maternal grandmother, Antonia, married a formerly enslaved person from Congo, Adofu
Nyamiti. Likewise, in 1913, Leo Kalenga from Congo married Maria's mother,
Marina Sitta, a runaway slave from Iramba in central Tanzania. Reminiscing
about her parents' marriage, Maria Kalenga explains, 'as my father had grown
enough to marry, priests told him to choose himself a wife'.[102] After marriage,
the Ndala and Ushirombo missions granted new couples land in the village
surrounding the mission to build houses and raise Christian families. The couples maintained strong ties to the missions by attending church services. They
also took their children to the missions for instruction and Sunday services
and participated in other activities that demanded the parents' presence in the
missions. Parents ensured that their children were baptized and raised according to Christian doctrines.[103] The number of children in the orphanage at the
Ushirombo mission declined between 1900 and 1914, as many female orphans
married at an early age. At the Ndala mission, the number of boys declined
from twenty in 1906 to fifteen in 1908 and eleven in 1909. By 1914, the orphanage population at Ndala and Ushirombo was diminishing, with few residents
in the buildings, because they grew up and moved into the nearby villages.
Sunday services, weekly dances, and festivals contributed to the declining
population in mission communities as they led to marriage through increased
social interactions between unmarried men and women. The married couples

---

Omari (eds), *Gender, Family and Work in Tanzania* (Aldershot: Ashgate, 2000),
191.

[101] Interview with Getruda Mateo, Ushirombo, 5 December 2016.

[102] Ndala Diary, 20 April 1913, WFA 01.43; interview with Maria Nyamizi Leo
Kalenga, Ndala, 6 September 2016. In Kaswahili, 'baada ya baba kukua, mapadri walimwambia achague mke wa kuoa'.

[103] Interview with Maria Nyamizi Kalenga, Ndala, 6 September 2016; Hastings,
The Church, 215.

Regulations, Work, and the Ambiguities of Freedom in Mission Communities, 1905–14

Mission regulations and the range of manual labour that characterized the lives of formerly enslaved people in the missions of Tabora, Ndala, and Ushirombo challenged the kind of freedom they had sought in joining mission communities. Nearly all residents in the mission communities of the Catholic mission stations were formerly enslaved people who had been the property of travelling merchants or Nyamwezi owners. Mission communities varied in size, composition of inhabitants, degree of discipline, and the social context in which they came into being. Notwithstanding the diversity in the languages and cultures of residents, all mission communities were places where European culture, rather than the culture of African occupants, controlled their day-to-day undertakings. The daily activities in missions included regular working hours and attendance at religious services that were mandatory for all residents.[105]

In addition to several fugitive slaves who moved into mission communities, the White Fathers established mission villages for ransomed slaves and orphanages at Tabora, Kipalapala, and Ushirombo.[106] Between 1905 and 1914, they bought many formerly enslaved people outright in the slave markets to keep them in the mission communities. They recorded their names in the mission's register of redemption (*registre des rachats*). We learn that at the Ushirombo mission, the White Fathers made annual shopping expeditions, so to speak, to the slave market of Ujiji. They bought children to emancipate, who were to be Christianized as part of the assimilation process in mission villages. Others tied to the mission villages included adults who were not Christians but who joined seeking protection.[107] The White Sisters, too, established mission communities at Tabora, Ndala, and Ushirombo mission stations. The report on the activities of the White Sisters at Tabora for 1909

---

[104] Ushirombo Diary, 24 August 1914, WFA 01.43; Annual Report, 1905–06, 51–52, UDSM/History, mission statistiques [Ndala], année 1907–08, AAT 350.002; Nolan, 'Christianity in Unyamwezi', 150; interview with Maria Nyamizi Leo Kalenga, Ndala, 6 September 2016, and Emanueli Ndekanilo, Getruda Mateo, and Maria Maliseli, Ushirombo, 5 December 2016.

[105] Hastings, *The Church*, 214.

[106] F. van Vlijmen, 'The Origins of the Archdiocese of Tabora' (unpublished manuscript, Ndala, 1990), 39; Nolan, 'Christianity in Unyamwezi', 182, 185.

[107] Hastings, *The Church*, 213.

EMANCIPATION, THE BEGINNINGS OF MISSION COMMUNITIES, AND EVERYDAY LIFE 93

and 1910 shows that seventy women, girls and children were redeemed by the White Sisters at Tabora. As mentioned above, the report also indicates that forty-five women and children had sought refuge, and forty-nine girls and young children were living in the orphanage centre.[108]

Missionaries' financial contribution to the ransoming of slaves also underpinned their claims on the loyalty of formerly enslaved people. Since slaves could not foot the bill for redemption, missionaries paid part of the required amount for slaves to become free and enter mission communities. For instance, in 1905, the slave Luangalla and his wife Kashindye moved into the mission community at Ushirombo. Still, their owner, Mlasso, complained to the mission that they had gone without his consent. Luangalla paid thirty rupees for himself and twenty rupees for Kashindye to redeem them all from slavery.[109] Maria Wantiho also requested that her freedom be bought because her owner Mtagwa was unwilling to let her move into the mission community. Maria Wantiho paid fifteen rupees out of the required forty to buy her freedom. Maria's determination to join the mission community encouraged the White Sisters at Tabora to pay the remaining amount.[110]

Because missionaries contributed to the cost of emancipation, the life choices of the formerly enslaved were largely limited, within the confines of the missions. In principle, the certificates stated the day that redemption was granted to the freed slaves themselves, but in practice, colonial administrators often handed the documents directly to missionaries who kept them in their houses. The 130 *Freibriefe* from various mission stations deposited in the archive of the Archdiocese of Tabora indicates the limitations placed on the freedom of former slaves in mission communities. While some slaves who bought their freedom joined their relatives in the villages, a significant number of slaves whose liberation the mission had contributed to financially were compelled to live in the mission communities.[111] In addition to mandatory attendance of church services, residents in Christian villages performed different activities that bound them together.

Missionaries also owned large tracts of land near mission stations. They employed residents of nearby village communities as part of the 'mission workforce' to grow various crops for consumption and partly for sale.[112]

---

[108] Noms des autres Réfugiées a Notre Dame, 1909–1910, AAT 350.002; Noms des femmes, filles et enfants à Notre Dame, 1909–1910, AAT 350.002; Notre Dame de Tabora, 1 July 1910, AAT 350.002.

[109] Tabora Military Station, No. 1297, 16 September 1905, AAT 526.503.

[110] Tabora, 2 December 1913, AAT 526.503.

[111] The *Freibriefe* are still held in the archives, implying that they remained property of the missionaries.

[112] On the mission 'work force', see Michelle Liebst, 'African Workers and the

Missionaries' dependence on formerly enslaved people as part of the mission labour force resulted in the growth of mission villages, which depended on missionaries for protection and survival. At Ushirombo, since missionaries kept their certificates of freedom, formerly enslaved people depended on what missions could provide in exchange for living and working within the confines of the mission. It is no wonder that by 1900 the village community in Ushirombo had concentrated right outside the White Sisters' convent, with its residents living and working on mission plots.[113] A sketch map of 1908 in the Kisanji Family archive shows the Catholic mission in Tabora surrounded by large plots on which the formerly enslaved residents invariably worked. Similarly, the earliest missions of Ndala and Ushirombo had large mission plots where residents in village communities worked, producing various crops to sustain the missionaries and for their own consumption.[114]

All this said, and despite their limited mobility and dependence on missionaries, the formerly enslaved people in the missions' sphere of influence had the means to shape aspects of their everyday lives through the new relationships that became possible within the missions. Some of these bonds were ephemeral, but other relationships grew stronger, with some even leading to marriage.[115] As we have seen, marriage among mission dependents became a means to greater independence from the mission in exchange for domestic interdependence. After marriage, Ndala and Ushirombo missions granted new couples land in the villages surrounding the mission to build houses and raise Christian families.[116] Although many residents left village communities to establish their households after marriage, parents ensured their children were baptized and raised in the Christian faith.[117] In this way, weekly dances, marriage, church attendance, and parenting according to mission expectations all formed part of the process whereby people freed through the missions' legal, financial, and public mediation negotiated their ongoing relationship with the

---

Universities' Mission to Central Africa in Zanzibar, 1864–1900', *Journal of Eastern African Studies*, Vol. 8, No. 3 (2014), 307.

[113] Interview with Anastazia Maturino Mulindwa and Telesfora Mwakyembe, Ushirombo, 5 December 2016; translated German documents [Annual Report about the Development of German East Africa, 1905–06], 51, UDSM/History.

[114] Map of Tabora showing ground ownership in 1908, compiled by Rev. Herrmann with compass and tape measure, KFC.

[115] Interview with Anastazia Maturino Mulindwa and Telesfora Mwakyembe, Ushirombo, 5 December 2016.

[116] Interview with Tekla Herman, Ushirombo, 5 December 2016, Felista Lonjini Namna, Uhemeli (Isakala), Ndala, 6 September 2016.

[117] Interview with Maria Nyamizi Kalenga, Ndala, 6 September 2016; Hastings, *The Church*, 215.

Figure 7   The Mission Community near the White Sisters Convent in Ushirombo, c.1900.

missions and exercised a degree of agency in determining the direction of their post-slavery lives (Figure 7).

Conclusion

The use of public declarations of intent by slaves to leave their current owners for missions suggests the determination, initiative, and creativity of the enslaved people seeking freedom in Western Tanzania. The persistent use of declarations shaped the German and British legal systems because administrators relied on public statements and witnesses as preconditions to certify the free status of slaves who desired to leave their owners of their own volition. Accordingly, the British colonial state, which took over the colony's administration (now Tanganyika) after the war, applied the Indian Evidence Act and the Oaths Act retroactively from 1 April 1919. Adopting these two laws was also intended to provide a uniform legal framework across the British Empire. Hence, witnesses and oaths of affirmation, which had become common practice among slaves, became embedded in the British legal system in Tanganyika.[118] The legal recognition of slaves' public declarations in western Tanzania implied the new government's recognition of *Freibriefe* as evidence in the legal processes for certification of freedom. Nevertheless, as slavery regimes disintegrated in the early twentieth century and were finally outlawed

---

[118] Applied Indian Acts, Cap. 2, 1 December 1920, in Alison Russell, *The Laws of Tanganyika Territory*, Vol. 1 (London: Waterlow & Sons, 1929), 10.

in 1922, the character of these dependencies changed, and *Freibriefe* became less significant as the prerequisite for freedom.[119]

For slaves who joined the mission communities, public declarations before witnesses seemed an ideal means of negotiating the unwanted tensions that would often arise between slave owners and missions and between missions and government authorities. While slaves flocked to mission communities in the hope of finding refuge from the oppressive institution of slavery, their ability to create a new mental landscape was limited by missionaries' expectations and work discipline within the mission walls, especially while the institution of slavery continued beyond them. The ties that bound formerly enslaved people within the milieu of missions turned into what historians and anthropologists have described as 'emancipation without abolition' and as a condition which, much like slavery, often involved 'marginality and integration' because 'the workload combined with the need to adapt cultural norms and practices set by missionaries constituted a new kind of unfreedom'. It is unsurprising, therefore, 'that slaves ransomed by missionaries at times thought of the mission as yet another owner'.[120] Nevertheless, the adoption of the Kinyamwezi language helped former slaves in forging the new communities because they used the language in the translation of the Bible and church songs that laid the basis for the growth of African Christianity in western Tanzania.

[119] Letter from Senior Commissioner (Political Office Tabora) to Rev. F. van Aken, Tabora Catholic Mission, 3 August 1922, AAT 526.502 B; Memo from the Administrative Office to Rev. F. van Aken, Tabora Territory, 14 August 1922, AAT 526.502.

[120] Salvatory S. Nyanto and Felicitas M. Becker, 'In Pursuit of Freedom: Oaths, Slave Agency, and the Abolition of Slavery in Western Tanzania, 1905–1930', *Law and History Review*, Vol. 24, Special issue 1: 'African Legal Abolitions' (February 2024), 140. See Deustch, *Emancipation without Abolition*. On the notion of 'marginality and integration', see Igor Kopytoff and Suzanne Miers, 'African "Slavery" as an Institution of Marginality', in Suzanne Miers and Igor Kopytoff (eds), *Slavery in Africa: Historical and Anthropological Perspectives* (Madison: University of Wisconsin Press, 1979), 16.

CHAPTER 3

Translation as Dissent: Language, Society, and Christianity in Unyamwezi, 1906–20s

Members of the early Christian communities in Unyamwezi came from different parts of the East African interior and spoke different languages. The multilingual context of those early Christians made it important to translate the Bible, religious texts, and songs into Kinyamwezi because that language was widely spoken in the region among the Nyamwezi people and formerly enslaved people who had been living in the region. Unlike the coast, where Kiswahili (with ʿAjamī or Ajamiyya) gained prominence in the nineteenth and twentieth centuries as both 'a religious language' and 'the main language for the administration of the natives',[1] formerly enslaved people and porters living in missions moved away from Kiswahili toward Kinyamwezi as the medium of translation. In so doing, they departed from the ʿAjamī script of Kiswahili. They influenced missionaries' inclination to the Kinyamwezi as the language of translation and evangelization in missions and villages.[2] Translation occurred in the daily interactions between missionaries, the Nyamwezi missions' residents, and those who regularly attended Sunday

---

[1] Farouk M. Topan, 'Swahili as a Religious Language', *Journal of Religion in Africa*, Vol. 22, Fasc. 4 (Nov. 1992), 331–49; Jörg Haustein, *Islam in German East Africa, 1885–1918: A Genealogy of Colonial Religion* (London: Palgrave Macmillan, 2023), 51.

[2] Examples of these texts include Yohanes Rebman, *Engili ya Lukasi Iliofasirika Kua Maneno ya Kisuaheli* (St Chrishona, 1876); Edward Steere, *Anjili kwa Yohana: Kiswahili* (London: British and Foreign Bible Society, 1875); Edward Steere, *Anjili ya Bwana na Mwokozi Wetu Isa Masiya kwa Mattayo: Maneno ya Kiswahili* (London: British and Foreign Bible Society, 1876); Edward Steere, *Anjili kwa Marko: Kiswahili* (London: British and Foreign Bible Society, 1879); and Edward Steere, *Kitabu cha Agano Jipya la Bwana na Mwokozi wetu Isa Masiya Kimefasirika katika Maneno ya Kwanza ya Kiyonani* (London: Kimepigwa Chapa kwa British and Foreign Bible Society, 1883).

98 SLAVE EMANCIPATION, CHRISTIAN COMMUNITIES, AND DISSENT IN TANZANIA

services. Such interaction also involved cooks and workers at the missions, friends, and porters, whose knowledge of the cultures and the language made it possible to converse with missionaries about the Kinyamwezi language and related cultural topics. It also involved the Nyamwezi young men living on the missions' premises who attended mission schools and worked as teachers. Conversant in the Kinyamwezi language and with their knowledge of reading and writing, formerly enslaved people and mission porters who formed the first generation of Christians in the region translated the New Testament, religious texts, and songs into the language.

This chapter looks at translation as a form of dissent in western Tanzania, centring on the texts translated into Kinyamwezi and how language and culture influenced the interactions of formerly enslaved people, porters, residents, and missionaries. It covers the period from 1906, when Nyamwezi Christian catechists and teachers began translating the New Testament and other religious texts into the Kinyamwezi language, to the 1920s, when many Nyamwezi teachers and catechists, who were by then working in villages, expanded translation to other religious texts. The chapter centres on the Moravians to examine the earliest editions of the Kinyamwezi New Testament of 1907 and 1909, the Kinyamwezi reading primer of 1911, Rev. Max Brauer's sermons, which were written and delivered in Kinyamwezi between 1912 and 1916, and finally, Kinyamwezi songs and the Kinyamwezi version of the Lord's Prayer, written between 1912 and the 1920s.[3] The chapter situates translations of religious texts within the context of the multiple language communities found in western Tanzania to show how the influence of the Kinyamwezi language, widely spoken by mission porters and formerly enslaved people from various parts of the East African interior, influenced the translation of texts. The move to the Kinyamwezi language in the translation of religious texts laid the basis for a modern 'intelligentsia' in the region because it produced first-generation African teachers and catechists who worked as 'translators' and ' scripture readers' in the village, leading to the growth of African Christianity in twentieth-century Unyamwezi.[4]

---

[3] Unfortunately, the language barrier constrained me from using sources written in the German language, which would have provided me with insights into the historical context of German East Africa. They include Klaus J. Bade, 'Antisklavereibewegung in Deutschland und Kolonialkrieg in Deutsch-Ostafrika 1888–1890: Bismarck und Friedrich Fabri', *Geschichte und Gesellschaft*, Vol. 3, No. 1 (1977), 31–58; and Klaus J. Bade, *Friedrich Fabri und der Imperialismus in der Bismarckzeit: Revolution, Depression, Expansion (Beiträge zur Kolonial- und Überseegeschichte)* (Freiburg: Atlantis, 1975).

[4] J.D.Y. Peel, *Religious Encounter and the Making of the Yoruba* (Bloomington: Indiana University Press, 2000), 11 and 156–61.

The Roots of Dissent: Language, Society, and Christianity in Unyamwezi

Catholic and Protestant missionary societies established their first missions in different parts of Unyamwezi in the second half of the nineteenth century. With the establishment of German rule in the 1880s, Kiswahili became both a 'language of rule and a language of education', and in no time, it was 'the lingua franca of the colony' and 'the primary language of the German administration'.[5] Of course, the Germans capitalized on the language because it had spread into the East African interior through long-distance caravans. Individuals who effectively communicated in the language earned positions in the administration as tax collectors, soldiers (*askaris*), and rulers (*liwalis*) and subsequently acted as intermediaries between the Germans and colonial subjects.[6] No sooner had Kiswahili become the primary language for the administration of German East Africa than a debate about language policy dominated religious and political spheres. While the German administration shifted the use of Kiswahili from 'a language of commerce and diplomacy' to the language of education and administration, Protestant missionaries deemed it a 'Muslim language' or an 'Islamic language'. At the same time, the Arab elite perceived it as a 'slave language'. It turned their attention to the vernacularization of religious texts to 'Christianize and de-Islamicize' or 'de-Arabize' the ʿAjamī script with Roman script.[7]

Therefore, the departure from the ʿAjamī script to the Kinyamwezi language as the primary translation language in the early twentieth century was part of the larger discourse on language in German East Africa. The move to Kinyamwezi began in Zanzibar with Bishop Edward Steere of the UMCA, who was also inspired to work on the grammar of Kinyamwezi as spoken in the chiefdom of Unyanyembe. His translation of the Kinyamwezi language was probably his last work.[8] Steere never visited Unyamwezi, but his discussions with a Nyamwezi porter, 'who without forgetting his tongue, had learnt

---

[5] Haustein, *Islam in German East Africa*, 51; Emma Hunter, 'Language, Empire and the World: Karl Roehl and the History of the Swahili Bible in East Africa', *Journal of Imperial and Commonwealth History*, Vol. 41, No. 4 (2013), 603.

[6] John M. Mugane, *The Story of Swahili* (Athens: Ohio University Press, 2015), 198.

[7] Haustein, *Islam in German East Africa*, 53; Mugane, *Story of Swahili*, 202; Caitlyn Bolton, 'Making Africa Legible: Kiswahili Arabic and Orthographic Romanization in Colonial Zanzibar', *American Journal of Islamic Social Sciences*, Vol. 33, No. 3 (2016), 68.

[8] Steere's other works on languages included *Collections for a Handbook of the Shambala Language* of 1867, *A Handbook of the Swahili Language as Spoken at Zanzibar* of 1870, *Swahili Tales* of 1870, *Collections for a Handbook of the Makonde Language* of 1876, *Collections for a Handbook of the Yao Language* of

100   SLAVE EMANCIPATION, CHRISTIAN COMMUNITIES, AND DISSENT IN TANZANIA

to speak Swahili', and his 'native friends' are characteristic of the context in which translation of the Kinyamwezi was rooted.[9] Steere frequently talked to the Nyamwezi porters who arrived in Zanzibar. He noted that many Nyamwezi men aspired to make their journey to the coast and regarded their countrymen at home who could not make it to the coast as 'milksops', implying that they lacked courage. Steere's conversations with the Nyamwezi porters exposed them to knowledge of the Bible, and upon their return to Unyamwezi, they formed the basis for translating texts into their tongue.[10]

Steere's translation, as he states, relied on the Kinyamwezi dialect spoken at Unyanyembe because the central caravan route from the coast to the interior of East Africa passed through the chiefdom – an area that today extends between Tabora town and Ussoke. Regular contact between the coast and the interior was one reason Unyanyembe's chiefdom population increased until the second half of the nineteenth century, when Mtemi Mirambo of Uyowa chiefdom challenged its hegemony. Because Steere encountered porters and slaves at Zanzibar who originated from Unyanyembe, he adopted that language as the 'standard' dialect of Kinyamwezi in working on the handbook.[11] Steere also benefited from the support of formerly enslaved people with whom he interacted daily in the mission community of Zanzibar. Juma, a formerly enslaved person from Unyamwezi, was one resident who helped Steere translate the Kinyamwezi language. He had made many journeys between Unyanyembe and Zanzibar before joining the mission community at Zanzibar. He was undoubtedly a Nyamwezi from Unyanyembe who was enslaved in Zanzibar, as he was conversant in the Kinyamwezi dialect of Unyanyembe. It was, therefore, from Juma that Steere's notes 'were derived'.[12] Steere's reliance on Juma as his source suggests that he did not make journeys to Unyamwezi, nor was he conversant in the language. Steere's exposure to the dialect of Unyanyembe through Juma prompted him to embark on this task. His lack of information about the language, which was 'as yet of necessity far from perfect', led him to call the work 'collections for a handbook'.[13]

1871, and *Swahili Exercises: Compiled for the Universities' Mission to Central Africa* of 1878.

[9] Edward Steere, *The Kinyamwezi Language as spoken in the Chiefdom of Unyanyembe* (London: Society for the Promotion of Christian Knowledge, 1882), 5.

[10] Edward Steere, 'On East African Tribes and Languages', *Journal of the Anthropological Institute of Great Britain and Ireland*, Vol. 1 (1871), cl.

[11] Alfred Chukwudi Unomah, 'Economic Expansion and Political Change in Unyanyembe, c. 1840–1900' (PhD thesis, University of Ibadan, 1972), 75–125.

[12] Steere, *The Kinyamwezi Language*, 6.

[13] Ibid., 3.

The influence of porters in translating Steere's Kinyamwezi handbook encouraged them to push for translating religious texts into the Kinyamwezi language as they joined the Moravian missions in the region. The demand for indigenous-language translations encouraged Christians in Unyamwezi to read the Bible and religious texts and sing songs in the Kinyamwezi language, making it 'the book language of the [Moravian] mission'.[14] As we have seen, the ever-reliable Nyamwezi porters not only carried missionaries' loads from the coast to Unyamwezi and back but also ensured the missionaries' safety against the dangers of the road. They interacted with missionaries, and some converted to Christianity. At the Urambo Moravian mission, a mission porter named Yohanesi Kipamila and his wife, Kitambi, became the first Nyamwezi individuals to convert to Christianity in 1903.[15]

The daily activities of the domestic workers and cooks in the Moravian and CMS missions also allowed workers to discuss various issues with missionaries. At Uyui, Saburi, who worked as a cook in the mission, together with one domestic servant, had daily conversations with Rev. Blackburn of the CMS that provided them the opportunity to learn the 'Divine things' and become two of the first converts in the mission. Saburi's conversion was a 'genuine conversion' because he was among the boys who had attended mission school and could read the religious texts and write 'in [his] own tongue'.[16] Similarly, cooks and domestic servants working in the Moravian missions of Urambo Kilimani, Kitunda, Sikonge, and Ipole interacted with missionaries, establishing friendships with ministers. In the process, they taught the missionaries the Kinyamwezi language and culture. Their interactions with missionaries allowed them to learn to read and write, leading some to become teachers (*vahembeki*) in villages.[17]

The Nyamwezi also used the existing custom of communal meetings (called *baraza*) in shaping the course of translation. At the Urambo Moravian mission, porters from the coast and people in the villages talked with the

---

[14] Nis H. Gaarde, 'A Brief Report of Unyamwezi for the Year 1921', *Periodical Accounts Relating to Moravian Missions*, Vol. 11, No. 3 (June 1922), 142.

[15] Edward C. Hore, Kwikuru-Urambo, 4 August 1878, CWM/LMS Central Africa/Incoming Correspondence/Box 1; J.B. Thomson to Rev. Joseph Mullens, DD, Unyanguru, Urambo, 4 August 1878, CWM/LMS/Box 1; Teofilo H. Kisanji, *Historia Fupi ya Kanisa la Kimoravian Tanganyika Magharibi* (Kipalapala: TMP, 1980), 45–47.

[16] George Litchfield to Mr Fenn, Uyui, 23 July 1881, CMS/B/OMS/G3 A6/O/53; Rev. Blackburn to Mr Lang, CMS Uyui, 24 June 1884, CMS/B/OMS/G3 A6/O/113; Charlie Stokes to Mr Lang, Uyui, 24 June 1885, CMS/B/OMS/G3 A6/O/102.

[17] E. Southon to Rev. J.O. Whitehouse, Urambo, 21 January 1880, CWM/LMS/Box 3/Folder 1; Kisanji, *Historia Fupi*, 30–44.

102   SLAVE EMANCIPATION, CHRISTIAN COMMUNITIES, AND DISSENT IN TANZANIA

missionaries on their veranda, exchanging questions and answers about all kinds of subjects, including Christianity and Islam. These talks extended to the villages of the adjoining chiefdoms of Kirira and Msene, where children held evening meetings for up to five days with missionaries.[18] People often visited the Uyui mission, and their curiosity about the many things they saw at the mission led them to take part in these discussions on the veranda.[19] Thus, the varied interactions of the Nyamwezi with missionaries in missions and villages provided the basis for early translations of the New Testament, religious texts, and songs.

Translation from Below: The New Testament and Religious Texts, 1906–12

The move to the Kinyamwezi language in the translation of religious texts in Unyamwezi began in 1906 when three young men (*vijana watatu*) made the first translation of the New Testament into Kinyamwezi. These unidentified boys were among the 264 students living in the Moravian mission of Urambo Kilimani. While their origins remain obscure from mission sources, it seems plausible to argue that the 264 students were sons and daughters of Nyamwezi Christians, formerly enslaved people and porters who were living at the Urambo Kilimani mission. Ludorf R. Stern, a Moravian missionary at the Urambo mission station, reported in 1906 that the boys 'had finished copying the New Testament into Kinyamwezi'.[20] As Kisanji reported, it is unclear whether Stern's original text meant the young men were 'copying' (*kunakili*) the New Testament. The expression would imply that the boys were trying to be faithful to the text without changing the meaning of the words. But the work of the *vijana* transcended the mere activity of copying, as they exercised their intellectual skills and rendered an independent translation of the New Testament into the Kinyamwezi language.

It is quite clear that Bishop Edward Steere's Kiswahili New Testament Bible of 1883 was the original text from which the young men worked as translators. Steere's Old Testament stories of the Bible and his separate Gospels of John (1875), Matthew (1876), and Mark (1879) had already been in use in the

---

[18] Ebenezer Southon, MD to Mr Whitehouse, Urambo, 31 December 1880 [medical report], CWM/LMS/Box 3/Folder 4; Arthur Brooks to Rev. R. Wadlaw Thompson, Urambo, 24 April 1888, CWM/LMS/Box 7/Folder 3 /No. 7.

[19] Rev. Blackburn to Mr Lang, Uyui, 23 February 1883, CMS/B/OMS/G3 A6/O/64.

[20] Kisanji, *Historia Fupi*, 76. Kisanji translated Ludolf Stern's report into Kiswahili as 'vijana watatu, wanafunzi wa Bwana Hartmann, walikuwa wakimaliza kunakili Agano Jipya katika Kinyamwezi. Unajua kuwa hata hii kazi ya kuandika kwa asili ni kitu kipya kwao.'

LANGUAGE, SOCIETY, AND CHRISTIANITY IN UNYAMWEZI 103

Moravian missions of Urambo, Sikonge, and Ipole, and the CMS mission of Uyui. The three Gospels were used with Johannes Rebmann's Gospel of Luke of 1876. Steere completed a full translation of the New Testament in 1883.[21] There are natural similarities in the organizational structure, wording, and content of Steere's Kiswahili New Testament and the Kinyamwezi New Testament. There seem to have been a few words and expressions left out when the boys translated the Kinyamwezi New Testament from the Kiswahili Bible. However, the young translators exercised some autonomy in rendering the source text in words that could be understood in Unyamwezi. For instance, names appearing in Steere's Kiswahili New Testament, such as Muungu (God), Isa (Jesus), Maryamu (Mary), Roho (Spirit), and Mattayo, were changed to Mulungu, Jesu, Malija, Loho, and Matajo as the translators strove to render the source into Kinyamwezi.[22]

Of course, the influence of ʿAjamī script was obvious in Steere's translation of the Kiswahili New Testament. In addition to using Arabic names (Isa and Maryamu), Rebmann's translation of the Gospel of Luke employed ʿAjamī script. This meant that the letter 'q' was written instead of the letter 'k' in words and expressions like *haqiqa* (of course, certainly), *rafiqi yangu* (my friend), and *haqi zote za Buana* (all rights belong to God).[23] Thus, the young men grappled with both Kinyamwezi and the Arabic influence in the Kiswahili New Testament to find adequate translations of the words. As the young men translated the first New Testament into Kinyamwezi, they pushed away Arabic concepts in favour of the Kinyamwezi concepts. The involvement of the three young men in translating the New Testament shows how the students in Urambo, Kitunda, and Ipole missions exercised a formative intellectual role in interpreting religious texts. Their stay on the mission grounds allowed them to interact and talk with missionaries about religious texts, the Kinyamwezi language, and their culture. The talks enabled the Nyamwezi

---

[21] February 1883, CMS/B/OMS/G3 A6/O/64/23; 'Central Africa: Letter from the Late Mrs. Stokes', *Church Missionary Gleaner*, Vol. 11, No. 126 (June 1884), 70; Rebman, *Engili ya Lukasi*; Steere, *Anjili kwa Yohana*; Steere, *Anjili ya Bwana*; Steere, *Anjili kwa Marko*; Steere, *Kitabu cha Agano Jipya*; *Migani ja vutemi vwa Mulungu: Geschichten aus dem Reiche Gottes* (Herrnhut: Missionsanstalt der Envagelischen Brüder-Unität, 1910).

[22] Steere, *Anjili ya Bwana* (1876); Steere, *Kitabu cha Agano Jipya* (1883); *Matthäus-Evangelium auf Kinyamwezi (Deutsch-Ost-Afrika)* (Herrnhut: Missionsanstalt der Envagelischen Brüder-Unität, 1907); *Muhola ja Tjelu ja Ilagano Lipya Jakundulwa Mugati na Mupizya Wiswe Jesu Klisto Jatonilwe Mukijombele Tja Kinyamwezi*, trans. L.R. Sterne (London and Herrnhut, 1909).

[23] Rebman, *Engili ya Lukasi*, 1876, KFC.

104   SLAVE EMANCIPATION, CHRISTIAN COMMUNITIES, AND DISSENT IN TANZANIA

students to familiarize the missionaries with ideas and concepts in their language and the use of expressions that their people could readily understand.

In 1907, one year after the translation of the New Testament, Ludorf R. Stern translated the Gospel of Matthew into Kinyamwezi in sixty-four pages. But he did not explain his method of translation.[24] In 1909, the full text of the Kinyamwezi New Testament with all the books (the four Gospels, the Book of Acts, Letters of Paul, and the Book of Revelation) was printed with a total of 534 pages. Like the separate Gospel of Matthew of 1907, the Kinyamwezi New Testament edition never provided any information about the translation process. It is most likely that Stern published the young men's translation of the New Testament.[25] In 1910, the Old Testament stories were translated into Kinyamwezi (*migani ja vutemi vwa Mulungu*). They became one of the texts the Nyamwezi people used in the Moravian missions, covering the stories in the Book of Genesis and Old Testament prophets (*vapilofeti*) and kings (*vatemi*). Like other translated texts, it had no guide to accompany the translation.[26] The Kinyamwezi Gospel of Matthew of 1907, the complete New Testament of 1909, and the Old Testament stories of 1910 came out after the work of the young Nyamwezi translators, indicating their influence in shaping the translated texts. Based on their original translations, they were all printed in Herrnhut, Germany, and London in the United Kingdom.

In addition to the three *vijana*, teachers (*vahembeki*), primarily former porters and slaves, exercised their intellectual creativity by assisting with the translation work. While working in the parish outstations (*sinagogo*), teachers were involved in creating the translations that would enable people to read the New Testament and other religious texts, sing the songs, and learn the catechism in their language.[27] By the end of 1912, teachers circulated Kinyamwezi religious texts in villages for lay Christians and students. They included *Fibula ja Kinyamwezi* (Kinyamwezi Reader), *Migani ya vutemi wa mulungu* (stories about God's kingdom), and *Mhola ja tjelu* (the Good News, commonly called the New Testament). Others included *Mamigani ga kuswana kupya* ('Stories about the Life and Work of Jesus as told in the Gospels'), *Ibuku lya vuhembeki mu mihayo ja mulungu* (teacher's book/guide about God, commonly called the Catechism), and *Ibuku lya nimbo zya mukanisa* (the Hymn Book).[28]

---

[24] *Matthäus-Evangelium* (1907).

[25] *Muhola ja Tjelu* (1909).

[26] *Migani ja vutemi vwa Mulungu* (1910).

[27] Kisanji, *Historia Fupi*, 76.

[28] *Ibuku lya nimbo zya mukanisa/Kleines Gesangbuch für Unyamwezi* (Herrnhut: Missionsanstalt der Envagelischen Brüder-Unität, 1912); *Fibula ja Kinyamwezi/ Fibel der Nyamwezisprache* (Herrnhut: Missionsanstalt der Envagelischen

The influence of the Kinyamwezi language was evident in the translated versions of the source texts, and the Nyamwezi young men and teachers altered some words as they tried to find workable translations. For instance, the translators changed the word *vapilofeti* or *mupilofeti* for prophets to *vafumbuzi* (in Kinyamwezi) to mean 'wise men'. They changed the word *mupilofeti* or *vapilofeti* in later versions to *valola masonda* to mean 'messengers'. In this way, the Nyamwezi translators offered both 'wise men' and 'messengers' as alternative ways of understanding what the European missionaries meant by 'prophet'.[29] Similarly, the translators rendered the word 'angel' as 'messenger' (*mukombe*). Translators used the term *mukombe* to highlight the importance of continuous revelation through the agency of individual messengers. The Nyamwezi *vakombe* or *bakombe* carried messages for the chief about war, drought, invasions, chiefly meetings, or other events that needed immediate attention in the society. Thus, assigning the role of the Christian 'angels' to the Nyamwezi *vakombe* was a way of indigenizing the faith.[30] Therefore, by substituting 'messengers', or in Kinyamwezi, *vakombe*, for 'angels', Nyamwezi Christians seemed to be opening up to the possibility that such messengers could transmit divine revelation.[31] Thus, as messengers, the Nyamwezi *vakombe* were the transmitters of continuous revelations (in this case, the messages of the chief about war, drought, invasions, and chiefly meetings) in a manner that was not found in European ideas about the roles of angels.[32]

The translators also moved away from political authority to divine authority as they used the Kinyamwezi term *mwanangwa* (chief) to convey the idea of Jesus as a powerful political force with authority like that of the Nyamwezi

---

Brüder-Unität, 1911); *Ibuku lya vuhembeki mu mihajo ja Mulungu: Buch der Lehre in den Worten Gottes* (Herrnhut: Missionsanstalt der Envagelischen Brüder-Unität, 1900); *Migani ja vutemi* (1910). See also Kisanji, *Historia Fupi*, 94.

[29] Brauer's Sermons, 1912, 17–18, KFC; Mateho 1:20, in *Mhola ja tšelu* (1907), and Matajo Ifungu 2:4, in *Mhola ja tjelu* (1909).

[30] Interview with Oscar E. Kisanji, Tabora, 19 June 2017.

[31] John K. Thornton, *Africa and Africans in the Making of the Atlantic World, 1400–1800* (Cambridge: Cambridge University Press, 1998), 236 and 239.

[32] Brauer's Sermons, 1912, 17–18, KFC; P.J.L. Frankl and Yahya Ali Omar, 'The Idea of "The Holy" in Swahili', *Journal of Religion in Africa*, Vol. 29, Fasc. 1 (February 1999), 110. For the changing of words such as *fitabu* or *kitabu* in place of *ibuku* or *mabuku* and *vamalaika* or *malaika* in place of *mukombe*, see Mateo 1:1, 1:17, 20, 24, 2:3, 13; Vukundukule wamwa Yohana, 21:9, in *Ilagano Ipya: Mhola ya Chelu yamwa Guku na Mupizya Wiswe Yesu Kristo* (Dodoma: The Bible Society of Tanzania, 1951).

chiefs who commanded respect from all the Nyamwezi.[33] *Banangwa* were headmen of small chiefdoms and villages in Unyamwezi who claimed descent from a chiefly lineage and represented the chief. Originally, the word *mwanangwa* meant the son of a chief who could also rule parts of the chiefdom.[34] Thus, the expression *mwanangwa wa Davidi, mwana wa Abrahamu* as a reference to Jesus, made Christ appear to be the chief in the chiefly lineage of David and Abraham (see Table 4). In so doing, he became identified with a ruling clan's founding figure and leader. In Unyamwezi, the founders of the homesteads or clans were literally 'builders' of homesteads and clans, which combined families under one founder or leader. Leaders or founders of the clans frequently claimed to be related to each other.[35]

The concept of an angel with wings flying in heaven was also difficult for the Nyamwezi Christians and translators. They found it rather absurd and associated angels with witches who could fly. They tried to find an accurate term to replace a fanciful term, so in both versions of the Gospel of Matthew, they used *mukombe wa guku* (literally, the messenger of our grandfather) to mean 'messenger of God' (see Table 4). As we have seen, *mukombe* was widely used in Unyamwezi to mean a person who carried messages to distant villages about wars, chiefly meetings, drought, famine, and death, to mention just a few examples. Using the Kinyamwezi word transformed the European conception of angels into ordinary individual 'messengers' to the people in Unyamwezi societies. Furthermore, Kinyamwezi word *guku* (grandfather) changed the meaning of God to that of an elder in the family or society, reinforcing the idea of kinship prevalent in Unyamwezi, in which elders had a close relationship with ancestral spirits and were thus intermediaries between the deities and the people.[36] Table 4 on the first and second chapters of the Gospel of Matthew in the two versions of 1907 and 1909 summarizes the translation process to show how teachers and students strove to find workable translations.

---

[33] Mateho 1:1, in *Matthäus-Evangelium* (1907); Matajo 1:1, in *Muhola ja Tjelu* (1909).

[34] Raphael G. Abrahams, *The Political Organization of Unyamwezi* (Cambridge: Cambridge University Press, 1967), 63; Raphael G. Abrahams, *The Peoples of Greater Unyamwezi, Tanzania (Nyamwezi, Sukuma, Sumbwa, Kimbu, Konongo)* (London: International African Institute, 1967), 55.

[35] Mateho 1:1, Matajo Ifungu 1:1; Abrahams, *The Peoples*, 41; Abrahams, *The Political Organization*, 13. The Nyamwezi expression changed later to '*mwana wamwa Davidi, mwana wamwa Abrahamu*' to mean, the Son of David [and] the son of Abraham. See 'Mhola ya Chelu Kitisi Yatonilwe na Mateo' 1:1, in *Ilagano Ipya* (1951).

[36] Mateho 1:13; Matajo Ifungu 1:13; Mateo 1:13; interview with Oscar E. Kisanji, Kaze-Hill, Tabora, 19 June 2017.

Table 4 Changing Concepts and Meanings of Words in the Kinyamwezi New Testament.

Section	*Mhola ja tšelu,* 1907	*Mhola ja tjelu,* 1909	Changing Words, Concepts, and Meanings
Chapter 1 Verse 1	Lwenulu lupapulo lwa vuvyalwa vwa Jesu Klisto mwanangwa wa Davidi, mwana wa Abalahamu.	Lwenulu lupapulo lwa vuvyalwa vwa Jesu Klisto mwanangwa wa Davidi, mwana wa Abalahamu.	No change; the two versions regard Jesus as *mwanangwa* (chief) to liken his authority to that of chiefs in Unyamwezi. But the term changes the meaning as Jesus becomes the political chief, the chief in the lineage of David and Abraham, and not the son of David and Abraham. He becomes the founding figure, the founder of a clan.
Chapter 2 Verse 13	Mukombe wa guku upelage munsi ja Egipiti.	Mukombe wa Guku upelageko mu nsi ja Egipiti.	Retains the words *mukombe wa guku*, which literally means 'the messenger of our grandfather', but it is used in this context to mean 'the messenger of God'. The Kinyamwezi word is used as a substitute for the word 'angel'. The Kinyamwezi term transforms the European understanding of angels to that of ordinary individual 'messengers' who could convey the message to societies. The word *guku* transforms the meaning of God into an elder in the family and society. The term reinforces the idea of kinship in a context where elders are closer to spirits than the young.
Chapter 4 Verse 17	Vukumbu na lusiku lwenulu Jesu wavukizadja, kutanizya mhola na kuhaja: Mupilulage mojo, kwiši vutemi vwa mumalunde vwegelile bihi.	Vukumbu na lusiku lwenulu Jesu wavikizadja, kutanizya mhola na kuhaja: Mupilukage isala kwiši vutemi vwa ilunde vwegelileho bihi.	The word *vutemi* (chiefdom), changes the meaning from the unseen heavenly chiefdom (*vwa ilunde or mumalunde*) to the chiefdom present in Unyamwezi (*vwegelile[ho] bihi*). The expression *mupilulage mojo* (change your heart) transforms into *mupilukage isala* (change your mind). The word *mojo* is borrowed from the Kiswahili word *moyo* but written in different orthographies. In a later edition, the translators adopt the Kiswahili word *moyo*.

Table 4 *continued*

Section	*Mhola ja tšelu*, 1907	*Mhola ja tjelu*, 1909	Changing Words, Concepts, and Meanings
Verse 22	Ališi nene ndi-wavwila inwe, munhu wikuva na muduguje, akute-melwa kitanga hivanza. Ališi homwene akumu-vwila muduguje: veve muhumbu, mwenuju akute-melwa kitanga …	Ališi nene ndi-vavwila inwe, vose valikuva na mudu-guvo, vakutemelwa kitanga. Ališi homwene akumu-vwila muduguje: weve muhumbu, mwenuju akute-melwa kitanga …	The 1907 edition centres on one person in their relation to kin. The 1909 edition centres on more than one person and their kin relations' *inwe vose valikumwa na muduguvo.* In the 1907 edition, the word *hivanza* (council) is used to draw imagery of the Nyamwezi council of elders (*ivanza lya chalo*, pl. *mavanza ga chalo*). The word is omitted in the 1909 edition. *Muduguvo,* meaning 'their relatives', shows the limitations of translators' vocabularies in their attempt to explain kinship relations among the Nyamwezi in their language. It could have been *vadugu vavo.* Limited vocabulary prompted translators to rely on the Kiswahili source text for the word mudugu to mean ndugu, as they found a workable translation solution.
Chapter 21 Verse 9	Ališi vanhu vose, vamutongelaga na vamulondezadja, vitanaga na kilaka vuhaja: Hozyana kumwanangwa wa Davidi, adošiwe luvango, homwene aliza mulina lya Guku, Hozyana kušika kwigulwa mno mno.	Ališi vanhu vose, vamutongelaga na vamulondezadja, vitanaga na kilaka vuhaja: Hosana kumwanangwa wa Davidi, adošiwe luvango, homwene alizaho mulina lya Guku! Hosana kušika kwigulwa muno muno!	Jesus retains the mwanangwa (chief) title of Unyamwezi chiefs. He becomes the chief in the lineage of David and Abraham. The word *Guku* (grandfather) puts Jesus in the line-age of the clans in Unyamwezi as an elderly family member, reinforcing kinship relations.

The Influence of Kinyamwezi on Translations: Rev. Max Brauer's Sermons, 1912–16

The works of the young men, porters, and teachers in translating texts into the Kinyamwezi language influenced Moravian missionaries working in Unyamwezi to follow suit. Because these translated texts had filtered into villages, Rev. Max Brauer and many other missionaries were encouraged to translate their Sunday homilies into Kinyamwezi. Rev. Brauer and his wife arrived in Unyamwezi from Germany in 1900, two years after the LMS missionaries invited the Moravians to take charge of the mission work in Unyamwezi.[37] Brauer was both a missionary and a construction technician. He built the mission houses at Kitunda to the west of the Rungwa River in 1901; at Sikonge to the South of Tabora in 1902; and at Ipole, about twenty kilometres south of Sikonge, in 1903. Brauer worked at the Ipole mission until the First World War reached Unyamwezi in 1916.[38]

Brauer had one cook, two domestic servants, and one Nyamwezi builder (*fundi mwenyeji*) who helped him construct the mission houses. On one occasion, Brauer had about 130 porters to carry his belongings as he travelled from one mission to another.[39] The missions also attracted Nyamwezi converts to mission villages. Boys lived in one dormitory, *changilo*, which was an extension of the practice of the Nyamwezi chiefs accommodating young men at the chiefdoms' headquarters. The young men in the mission's *changilo* attended mission schools and later became teachers (*vahembeki*).[40] As was the case with earlier missionaries' efforts, Brauer relied on converts, workers, porters, and the boys living in the Sikonge and Ipole missions to assist him; his interactions with these friends, students, and workers influenced the translation of Brauer's sermons into Kinyamwezi. Brauer's daily interactions with the Nyamwezi Christians suggest that he may have had discussions with Nyamwezi-speaking residents in his mission village before he attempted to translate his sermons into Kinyamwezi. The written sermons indicate Brauer's lack of fluency in Kinyamwezi, which forced him to write down his sermons before delivering them. It is reasonable to believe that he wrote the sermons in consultation with the Nyamwezi Christians, mission residents, porters, and friends a few days before Sunday services.[41]

The multiple expressions for the divinity among the Nyamwezi influenced Brauer's translation of the unseen God (*mulungu*) as the grandfather of the

---

[37] W. Draper to Rev. G. Bousins, Urambo, 18 April 1897, CWM/LMS/Box 9/Folder 5/No. 9; W. Draper to Rev. G. Bousins, Urambo, 24 January 1898, CWM/LMS/Box 10/Folder 1/No. 9, and 9 March 1898, CWM/LMS/Box 10/Folder 1/No. 9.

[38] Ndala Diary, 22 and 25 September and 11 October 1916, WFA 01. 43; Kisanji, *Historia Fupi*, 107; John T. Hamilton and Kenneth G. Hamilton, *History of the Moravian Church: The Renewed Unitas Fratrum 1722–1957*, 2nd edn (Bethlehem, PA: Interprovincial Board of Christian Education, Moravian Church of America, 1983), 615; Gaarde, 'A Brief Report', 129–31; Nolan, 'Christianity in Unyamwezi, 1878–1928' (PhD thesis, University of Cambridge, 1977), 299–300.

[39] Kisanji, *Historia Fupi*, 37–38, 41, 43, and 79.

[40] Ibid., 76.

[41] Ibid., 43.

110 SLAVE EMANCIPATION, CHRISTIAN COMMUNITIES, AND DISSENT IN TANZANIA

Nyamwezi (*guku wiswe*). Brauer learned of that concept from his daily conversations with Nyamwezi cooks, converts, workers, and friends at the Ipole mission.[42] For the Nyamwezi, elders and chiefs earned respect in Unyamwezi societies by functioning as intermediaries between the living and the ancestors, particularly in times of trouble. Brauer's translation of 'God' as *guku wiswe* (our grandfather) reveals his reliance on Nyamwezi friends who taught him their understanding of God as an elder kinsman, building a sense of kinship that includes God. The other word for God was *data wiswe*, meaning 'the father of all Nyamwezi', a term that strengthened kinship relations in the Christian family.[43]

On some occasions, Brauer seemed to have translated parts of the homilies alone, and his diction caused confusion among the village congregants. For example, in the sermons, the translation of a reference in the Gospel of Matthew to the Three Wise Men described them as *vasenzi* (barbarians) and *vafumu* (fortune tellers). The word *vasenzi* shows the extent to which Brauer had trouble finding alternative translations for words that would express the meaning he wished to convey to the Nyamwezi. His chosen words are likely to have conveyed a meaning quite different from what he intended. Because Kiswahili was widely known by this time in Unyamwezi, Brauer's Nyamwezi listeners were well acquainted with terms such as those for barbarism (*ushenzi*) and civilization (*ustaarabu*). Thus, they must have been puzzled as to why Brauer referred to the three gift-bearing wise men as barbarians.[44] Even worse, the word *vafumu* implied that the wise men were fortune tellers like the Nyamwezi witches (*valogi*), who used their power for malicious ends. However, the word may have also suggested that the *vafumu* visited newborn babies to prophesy their destiny and place in Unyamwezi societies.[45]

Translating the word *vasomi* (literate people) as a cognate of the Kiswahili word *wasomi* to refer to the Nyamwezi again indicated that many Christians

---

[42] Brauer's Sermons, 1912, 16, KFC. For details of Brauer's interactions with converts, cooks, and mission workers, see Kisanji, *Historia Fupi*, 40–43.

[43] *Fibula ja Kinyamwezi*, 46, KFC.

[44] See for instance, Unomah, 'Economic Expansion', 75; Stephan J. Rockel, 'Slavery and Freedom in Nineteenth-Century East Africa: The Case of Waungwana Caravan Porters', *African Studies*, Vol. 68, No. 1 (2009)', 88; John Iliffe, *A Modern History of Tanganyika* (Cambridge: Cambridge University Press, 1979), 64–74.

[45] Brauer's Sermons, 18, KFC; 'Two Nyamwezi Texts', 10, AAT 361.000; Colby R. Hartfield, 'The Nfumu in Tradition and Change: A Study of the Position of Religious Practitioners among the Sukuma of Tanzania, East Africa' (PhD thesis, Catholic University of America, 1968), 91–92. For details about the wise men from the East, see Matthew 2:1–12 RSV.

could read and write. When Brauer used the term *vasomi* during the sermons, he encouraged others to learn. Brauer likely used *vasomi* to distinguish between Christians and non-Christian residents of Unyamwezi. *Vasomi* mostly lived in the mission villages, including the boys who lived in the mission's dormitories (*changilo*) while preparing to teach in villages. The word could be understood to reinforce the identity of the Nyamwezi Christians who had been formerly marginalized.[46] The expression in Brauer's sermons that 'we can read from the Scripture on our own' (tulikuvala kusoma mwibuku) suggests that the majority who attended the sermons could read the scripture. Their mastery of the of the language undoubtedly helped Brauer translate his sermons into Kinyamwezi. Thus, his use of this expression shows how Brauer's emphasis on the individual reading the Bible in the vernacular became the basis of a new community identity among Nyamwezi Christians in the Moravian missions and village outstations.[47] The creation of a new Unyamwezi identity further suggests that the Nyamwezi had an 'invented tradition' of reading and translating text and that 'tradition' had already been 'constructed and formally instituted' within the realm of Christianity.[48]

Brauer's message in his homilies on the Sunday of Advent, 12 December 1912, centred on Matthew 11: 2–6. He called upon the congregants to prepare the way for the coming of Jesus Christ: 'Mujisesage nzila imwa Guku … mwanangwa wa Mulungu, homwene vapilofeti vose vamulaganaja' (literally: 'prepare the way for our grandfather … chief of God, whom Prophets spoke about'). Brauer's statement invoked Jesus as an elder (*guku*) to demonstrate kinship with the Nyamwezi as a blood relative and as *guku wiswe* (our grandfather). Jesus could thus settle disputes and maintain peace among the people. He also became the chief (*mwanangwa*) in the chiefly lineage of the Nyamwezi. In Unyamwezi, *vanangwa* were headmen who could rule parts of the chiefdom. Brauer's choice of the word *vapilofeti* – from his native German, *Propheten* – to mean 'prophets' showed the reciprocal translation process between Brauer and the Nyamwezi in translating his homilies.[49]

The character of Chief Mweta of Ugunda, who ruled the territory in which the mission of Ipole was located, influenced Brauer's translation of Jesus as the 'new chief of the world' (*mutemi wa liwelelo*) and the chief of the Nyamwezi (*mutemi*).[50] Chief Mweta accumulated wealth from selling

---

[46] Brauer's Sermons, 1913, 21, KFC.

[47] Brauer's Sermons, 1913, 17 and 48, KFC.

[48] Eric Hobsbawm, 'Introduction: Inventing Traditions', in Eric Hobsbawm and Terence Ranger (eds), *The Invention of Tradition* (Cambridge: Cambridge University Press, 2012), 1.

[49] Brauer's Sermons, 1912, 1–10, KFC.

[50] Ibid., 1913, 52–55, and 62–64, KFC.

cattle and ivory tusks and did not take advice from the people but was said to practise bribery and favouritism. A few days before the Sunday service of 16 March 1913, the chief visited the village of Ipole, and the chief's assistants ordered the people to clear the roads for him and refurbish their houses. Every person was required to meet him; people were called to sing and clap their hands while women sang with loud ululations.[51]

The visit of Chief Mweta influenced Brauer's sermon of 16 March 1913 about the coming of Jesus as the new chief of the Nyamwezi people. Brauer declared, '[O]ur chief is coming' ('mutemi wiswe aliza, mutemi aliza'). Thus, Jesus became the new chief of Ugunda. He was humble before the people (*Jesu mutemi wiswe mufula/mudekanu*) and provided patronage in the face of Chief Mweta, who had enriched himself and taken bribes.[52] The coming of the new chief (Jesus) was also meant to save the people from disease and bring equality and love to all the people at Ipole. Brauer offered a contrast between what a chief should do and what Chief Mweta had done. In this way, Brauer's teaching about the coming of Jesus as the new chief reflects the aspirations of the Nyamwezi people to build a community of kin under a just ruler. This community would become politically strong and dependent on Jesus as the new patron.[53]

Brauer concluded his sermon by saying: 'Hosana, blessed is the chief who is coming in the name of our grandfather. Hosana in the highest – Amen' (Hozana, adošiwe luvango mutemi, homwene alizaho mulina lya guku; Hozana kušika kwigulya munogwene – Amini).[54] This quote was, of course, drawn from the Gospel of Matthew, in which the triumphant entry of Jesus into Jerusalem as 'the new king' occurred amid Rome's persistent religiopolitical threat to Israel. The Roman occupation of Judea affected Jewish religious, social, political, and economic life. The entry of Jesus as the 'new king' implied the arrival of a leader who would save the people from a context of sociopolitical and economic crisis.[55] Brauer drew upon the story in the gospel to present the analogous situation in the territory of Ugunda, which was also

---

[51] Ibid., 1913, 53, and 56, KFC.

[52] Ibid., 1913, 52–53, 56–57, and 59, KFC.

[53] Brauer's Sermons, 1913, 56, and 58, KFC. For more details about patronage in the face of famine, see James L. Giblin, *The Politics of Environmental Control in Northeastern Tanzania, 1840–1940* (Philadelphia: University of Pennsylvania Press, 1992), 124–27.

[54] Brauer's Sermons, 1913, 59, KFC.

[55] Marcus J. Borg, *Conflict, Holiness and Politics in the Teachings of Jesus* (New York: Edwin Mellen, 1984), 1–4, and 27–29; Mateho 21: 9; Matajo, Ifungu 21: 9; Matthew 21: 9 (RSV). In both the 1907 and 1909 editions of the Kinyamwezi gospel of Matthew, the quote reads: 'Hozyana/Hosana, kumwanangwa

in the throes of political unrest caused by Chief Mweta. The conclusion of this sermon suggests that Brauer was conveying a subversive message toward Chief Mweta and that he was thereby expressing the aspirations of his congregants for a change of leadership in Unyamwezi.

The message about Jesus as the new chief of the Unyamwezi continued in Brauer's homilies of Wednesday, 19 March 1913. This time, his message was adapted for the few Christians who attended the service on Wednesday, compared to the many non-Christians who had also participated in the previous Sunday's service. He referred to these non-Christians as *vašenzi vingi* (many heathens/barbarians), indicating that his homilies also attracted unconverted Nyamwezi people whom he distinguished from Christians. Brauer regarded conversion to Christianity as a mark of 'civilization' (*ustaarabu/uungwana*) that removed people from the 'barbarism' (*ushenzi*) he attributed to non-Christians.[56] As 'civilized Christians', Brauer expected them to acknowledge their wrongdoings, which every 'civilized' person must do. As we discussed in Chapter 1, such distinctions had spread in Unyamwezi society through the professional porterage (*upagazi*) network, in which those Nyamwezi men who had accumulated wealth and social prestige (*vandeva*) were distinguished from those who had not made it to the coast.[57]

Language and Culture in the Translation of Songs and the Lord's Prayer, 1912–20s

Singing was deeply embedded in Nyamwezi culture in almost all activities, including marriages, funerals, rituals, communal gatherings, cultivation, harvesting, and hunting. The drum was used in all the ceremonies as an accompaniment for dancing.[58] Nevertheless, singing as part of social life was not confined to the Nyamwezi alone. Instead, it dominated the social world of the Sukuma, where songs were ideally 'manifestations of power and marginality in marriage practices'.[59] Beyond marriage, writes Gunderson, Sukuma songs also functioned as 'labor songs' because they drew 'attention to context and

---

wa Davidi, adošiwe luvango, homwene aliza [ho] mulina lya Guku! Hozyana/ Hosana kušika kwigulya muno.'

[56] Brauer's Sermons, 1913, 60, KFC.

[57] Michelle R. Moyd, *Violent Intermediaries: African Soldiers, Conquest, and Everyday Colonialism in German East Africa* (Athens: Ohio University Press, 2014), 65.

[58] Interview with Oscar E. Kisanji, Kaze-Hill, 19 June 2017. See also Abrahams, *The Peoples*, 37.

[59] Esther J. Masele and Venkatachalam Lakshmanan, 'Manifestations of Power and Marginality in Marriage Practices: A Qualitative Analysis of Sukuma

processes of those activities surrounding labor activity where music is present, which include composition, performance, transmission, as well as the song and the text itself'.[60]

However, the new Kinyamwezi songs in missions and villages did not use drums or other musical accompaniment. Missionaries discouraged the use of drums claiming they were 'sinful', 'devilish', and 'forms of paganism'.[61] By lacking drums, the new hymns attracted relatively few Africans compared to traditional festivals and gatherings where drums served as important accompaniments. Singing without musical accompaniment at Christian gatherings made the services seem monotonous. Most likely, people stayed away from church services because they did not enjoy the music, and even the congregants who attended the services might have found the music and services boring. Likewise, unclear concepts and unfamiliar melodies in the Kinyamwezi songs alienated many Nyamwezi. Oscar Kisanji, a descendant of first-generation Moravian Christians in Unyamwezi, recalled that the people 'could not draw distinctions between the songs of joy and sorrow'.[62] Later, however, drums were included in the services and used in place of bells to adapt to the expectations of the Nyamwezi people. The inclusion of drums made the songs 'dynamic and interactive' and attracted the people to the Sunday services. The Nyamwezi had traditionally used drums to call people together for chiefly messages and communal events, and this practice undoubtedly influenced the missions adopting them in place of bells.[63]

As with the translation of Christian texts, the teachers and early Christians took the lead in translating songs into Kinyamwezi. Because of this, church music saw not only changes in instrumental accompaniment but also in lyrics. The discussions centred on the choice of words as the Nyamwezi people tried to widen the missionaries' limited vocabularies to convey the intended meaning more accurately and in a form that was attractive to more people. For instance, the early Kinyamwezi songs translated the word 'trumpet' as

---

Songs in Tanzania,' *Journal of International Women's Studies*, Vol. 22, No. 1 (2021), 386.

[60] Frank Gunderson, *Sukuma Labor Songs from Western Tanzania: 'We Never Sleep, We Dream of Farming'* (Leiden and Boston: Brill, 2010), 10.

[61] See, for instance, Anna Maria Busse Berger, *The Search for Medieval Music in Africa and Germany, 1891–1961: Scholars, Singers, Missionaries* (Chicago, IL: University of Chicago Press, 2021), 140–42.

[62] Interview with Oscar E. Kisanji, Kaze-Hill, 19 June 2017.

[63] Ibid.; interview with Samweli Saimoni Mhoja, Nhazengwa, Nzega, 22 November 2016; Fergus J. King, 'Nyimbo za Vijana: Biblical Interpretation in Contemporary Hymns from Tanzania', in Gerald O. West and Musa W. Dube (eds), *The Bible in Africa: Transactions, Trajectories, and Trends* (Leiden: Brill, 2000), 367.

kalumbete, from the Kiswahili word *tarumbeta*. However, the appropriate word in Kinyamwezi is *milangale*, the word for an instrument used to convey chiefly messages about drought, the death of a chief, and invasion, to mention just a few examples.[64]

The influence of the Kinyamwezi language and culture in the translation of songs was also evident in the two stanzas of *Nimbo* no. 13 of 1912, which depicted Jesus as the chief (*mutemi*) of the Nyamwezi, suggesting he had the status of one who could settle differences and maintain peace between families and the society at large. The depiction of Jesus as their chief with powers analogous to those of Nyamwezi chiefs shows the aspirations of the Nyamwezi Christians to build an independent community of kin alongside that of the other chiefs of Unyamwezi. Thus, the Nyamwezi Christians desired a leader who could act as patron to the largely marginalized people who made up the early Christian communities. Yet the song also described Jesus as the 'lonely chief' or the 'poor chief' (*mpina*).[65] The translation of the word *mpina* as the 'lonely chief' reinforced the sense of belonging to a community for the Nyamwezi Christians who had formerly been marginalized in Unyamwezi.

The word *mpina* rendered the European concept of the poverty of Christ, portraying Christ as humble to distinguish him from the old Nyamwezi chiefs. This translation likely reflected the missionaries' preference for leadership that renounced worldly wealth over leadership that promised followers access to such wealth. While European missionaries would have found the idea of a poor chief who would renounce his desire for worldly wealth attractive, the Nyamwezi chiefs were not at all poor. Their religious and political authority enabled them to accumulate wealth and command respect from their subjects and dependents.[66] Furthermore, Nyamwezi Christians may have understood the word 'poor' to mean someone who lacked social connections.

Most importantly, as Brauer noted in one of his sermons, most Christians thought that the possession of wealth meant better lives. Thus, Christians in Unyamwezi did not want a poor leader. Instead, they wanted a leader who was wealthy and strong to provide patronage in times of misfortune.[67] In the later editions of the Kinyamwezi songs, the word *mpina* was replaced by

---

[64] *Nimbo zya Kikristo*, No. 246, 1938; *Nyimbo za Kikristo*, No. 11, 1988, KFC; Vukundukule 4:1, Moravian Church of Western Tanganyika (hereafter referred to as MCWT); *Nimbo zya Kikristo*, 1958.

[65] *Ibuku lya Nimbo zya mukanisa* (1912). In *Nimbo* No. 31, the authority of Jesus is extended to become the chief of the whole world (*mtemi wa liwelelo lyose*).

[66] *Nimbo*, No. 13, 1912. In the culture of the Nyamwezi, all people belonged to the chief. This claim was made in Uyui when the CMS requested children to attend instruction at the mission. For details, see Rev. Blackburn to Mr Lang, CMS Uyui, 3 December 1883, CMS/B/OMS/G3 A6/O/8.

[67] See Brauer Sermons, January 1913, 14, KFC.

116 SLAVE EMANCIPATION, CHRISTIAN COMMUNITIES, AND DISSENT IN TANZANIA

the Kinyamwezi *mtemi* as the title of Jesus. The shift from *mpina* to *mtemi* signified the increasing influence of the Kinyamwezi culture and language on Christian concepts, as Christians succeeded in returning to their conception of leadership, which involved the accumulation and redistribution of wealth by patrons.[68] In subsequent editions of the Kinyamwezi songs, the word *mpina* was replaced by the Kinyamwezi *mtemi* as the title of Jesus and changed later to the Kiswahili title *mfalme*. The shift from *mpina* to *mtemi* and *mfalme* signified the increasing influence of Nyamwezi Christians, as they succeeded in returning to their conception of leadership and patronage. It may well have indicated the increasing influence of the Kiswahili language among the Nyamwezi-speaking translators. The title also demonstrates that the Nyamwezi were moving away from the European depiction of Jesus as disinterested in worldly wealth.[69]

The translation of some songs reflected the daily interactions of the people. It demonstrated the influence of the Nyamwezi in choosing words that would make the songs meaningful and attractive to lay Christians in the Sunday services. Nyamwezi song no. 10 of 1912, for example, used the word 'curse' (*kumšyolo* or *mšyolo*) as equivalent to the Christian understanding of sin.[70] That use changed the Christian understanding of sin as an 'offence against God' to a form of harm done to others and kin. Members of kinship groups and society at large endeavoured to maintain relations among kin to avoid being harmed by curses. Thus, the change from sin against God to harm against others is an example of the extent to which the Nyamwezi reinterpreted Christianity – not within the context of individual salvation, but within the context of reciprocal obligations among members of families and communities.[71]

Furthermore, song no. 10 described Jesus as 'resembling our relatives' ('watwikola mdugu wiswe') and as 'liking to be tied to our blood' ('watogwa kutungwa na magazi giswe'), indicating the kinship ties binding Christians together to create their Christian identity. The two expressions changed the image of Jesus from the chief of the Nyamwezi (*mtemi*) to an elder who could interact with and relate to the people in the society.[72] In this way, the translators claimed kinship with Jesus, just as they would have claimed kinship with chiefs. Of course, Jesus was still a chief, but he became the chief of Christians in Unyamwezi and was related to them by kinship. The idea of

---

[68] *Nimbo zya Kikristo*, No. 16, 1938, KFC.
[69] *Nimbo zya Kikristo*, No. 16, 1938, KFC.
[70] *Nimbo*, No. 10, 1912. The Kinyamwezi word, *mšyolo* or *kumšyolo* is also used in *Nimbo*, No. 5, 1912, KFC.
[71] *Nimbo*, No. 10, 1912, Brauer's Sermons, 1913, 46, KFC; Kisanji, *Historia Fupi*, 26.
[72] *Nimbo*, No. 10, 1912, KFC.

Jesus as a blood relative also depicted him as the clan's founder and implied that the community of converts should be reimagined as a clan. The image of Jesus as a blood relative also shows how translation reflected the needs of the Nyamwezi who, having lost their kinship ties in slavery, sought to build an 'affective spiritual community' based on spiritual connection.[73]

With the influence of the Kinyamwezi language and culture, the translation of songs gained momentum in the 1920s owing to the increasing number of teachers (*vahembeki*) who had attended mission schools. They composed new songs with African melodies that appealed to the Nyamwezi people and were sung in all the Moravian missions. In missions and villages, teachers like Isai Mgunda played an essential role in this transformation as he composed numerous songs the Nyamwezi could sing easily with indigenous rhythms. Similarly, Abele Kasanga Kanola, a teacher at Usoke after the First World War, became a 'brilliant singer with an attractive voice' and composed songs in Kinyamwezi. Furthermore, Lukasi Masamalo, Daniel Kugayiwa, and Matia Kasumali of the Ipole and Sikonge missions held 'singing meetings' on Saturdays with men and women in preparation for Sunday services.[74]

In addition to songs, the influence of the Kinyamwezi language and culture in translating the Lord's Prayer (*data wiswe*) in 1911 was inevitable. The use of *data* (father/parent) in the title suggested that God had become the parent of the Nyamwezi people. This interpretation reinforced the role of parents in strengthening families and building communities. In the prayer, the phrase 'obscene words' (*mihajo ja mavi/mabi*) was used to translate the Christian concept of sin as a curse meant to harm others through the instrument of speech. The expression 'do not put our minds into temptation' (*ukatutege masala*) was a translation of 'lead us not into temptation'. The word *masala* originally meant 'mind'. In this prayer, the mind, not an individual, became the subject of temptation. The expression changed the meaning, implying that God was the one who caused the Nyamwezi people to err against one another in society. This parallels the *swezi* and *migabo* spirits in Unyamwezi culture that were thought to possess people, causing them to harm each other.[75] The expression 'may you save us from punishment' (*utukomole iswe kuluduko*) was substituted for the expression 'but deliver us from evil'. The translation

---

[73] Andreana C. Prichard, *Sisters in Spirit: Christianity, Affect, and Community Building in East Africa, 1860–1970* (East Lansing: Michigan State University, 2017), 4.

[74] Kisanji, *Historia Fupi*, 256 and 259; Gaarde, 'A Brief Report', 136–37.

[75] See, for instance, Abrahams, *The Peoples*, 78; Raphael G. Abrahams, *The Nyamwezi Today: A Tanzanian People in the 1970s* (Cambridge: Cambridge University Press, 1981), 21; and Aylward Shorter, 'The Migawo: Peripheral Spirit Possession and Christian Healing', *Anthropos*, Vol. 1/2 (1970), 110–26.

SLAVE EMANCIPATION, CHRISTIAN COMMUNITIES, AND DISSENT IN TANZANIA

of 'obscene words' and 'deliver us from evil' shows how the Nyamwezi transformed the concept of 'sin' and punishment to reflect their social relations.[76] These terms demonstrate how the Nyamwezi Christians needed to emphasize the value of protection against human acts of evil, rather than deliverance from abstract evil, in a context where colonialism and slavery under chiefs threatened them. While colonialism introduced new threats, the greatest fear in Unyamwezi remained that of being reduced to slavery under the chiefs. Table 5 below provides examples showing how the reciprocal process in the translation of songs and the Lord's Prayer changed words, concepts, and sounds of words.

Table 5 Translation of Kinyamwezi Songs and the Lord's Prayer.

Ibuku lya Nimbo zya Mukanisa, 1912, Hymn No. 13, verses 1 and 2	Concepts, Meaning, and Changes
1. Ii mutwe na magazi, howeve gokala: Vakutungila ngala kumutwe ya minhwa, O Jesu, weve mutemi, lukumo uli na; hamavupina gako nakakugisya! 2. Ka! Vanhu va vudaki, vagukomelile Muvili kumšigiti, vakuvulagile! Howeve wadekana, kuduko wavutja Na sele weve ufwa, Jesu Mupizya	Jesus becomes the chief, assuming the title of the Nyamwezi chief, mutemi. As the mutemi, Jesus became powerful, with authority like that of the Nyamwezi chiefs, who commanded respect from the Nyamwezi people. The Nyamwezi are called to respect the poor or the lonely chief (mpina), Jesus. First, the word mpina, meaning that Jesus is the 'lonely chief', reinforces the sense of belonging to a community for the Nyamwezi Christians who had formerly been marginalized. Second, using the word mpina to mean Jesus as the 'poor chief' renders Christ humble, one who renounces worldly wealth. It changed the meaning and authority of the Nyamwezi chiefs, who accumulated wealth and commanded respect from everyone, including those who lived at the headquarters as unfree dependents. In subsequent editions, Jesus earns the Kiswahili title (mfalme). The title mfalme changes meaning as it renders more prestige and conveys a stronger sense of a Nyamwezi chiefly power.

---

[76] *Fibula ja Kinyamwezi*, 46, KFC.

Nimbo, No. 10, 1912, Verses 1 and 2	Concepts, Meaning, and Changes
1. Munda yane ndišinya Kwigulya nigagwa valimbila vose Vakombe valitanya Lingaga! Lingaga! Mupizya wawyalwa. 2. Jesu alifuma leo, kwilunde Wiza kutwinja mšyolo, Watwikola, mdugu wiswe, Watogwa kutungwa na magazi giswe.	The word *vakombe* for 'angels' is used to mean messengers. The word changes the meaning from unseen beings to ordinary people who could communicate with the Nyamwezi people. The term also demonstrates the importance of continuous revelation of the individual 'messengers' in society, thus indigenizing the faith within the Unyamwezi culture. The word *mšyolo* for 'curse' changes the meaning of the Christian understanding of sin as an 'offence against God' to harm done to other people. Jesus becomes the relative of the Nyamwezi (*mdugu wiswe*). The word *mdugu* is borrowed from the Kiswahili word *ndugu*. It changes the authority of Jesus as the chief of the Nyamwezi (*mtemi*) to the leader who is also a member of a kinship group. The change reinforces the role of Christianity in strengthening the bonds of family and community.
The Lord's Prayer: *Data Wiswe*, 1911	Concepts, Meaning, and Changes
Data wiswe, uli mwilunde. Lina Lyako likuziwe! Nsi jako ize! Kikova tšako tšakwile haliwelelo, kitiši tšakwila mwilunde! Utupage lelo Kiliwa kiswe! Uleke kuva na mihajo ja mavi giswe, kitiši iswe twaleka kuva na mihajo kwa vakenaguzi viswe! Ukatutege masala, ališi utukomole iswe kuluduko! kwisi nsi na ngunzu na lukumo zili zyako zya kalekale na myaka de. Amini.	The translation of 'obscene words' (*mihajo ja mihajo ja mabi*) becomes a cognate of sin to mean curse; that is, the harm is done to others through the instrument of speech. The expression 'do not put our minds to the test' (*ukatutege masala*) changes the meaning, implying that God influences the Nyamwezi to commit mistakes. The translation of 'deliver us from evil' (*utukomole iswe kuluduko*) is equivalent to 'may you deliver us from evil'. It transforms the meaning of evil into punishment as a human act instead of the abstraction of evil.

Conclusion

The publication of the Kinyamwezi New Testament in 1907, translated with the guidance of the three young men who were living in the mission dormitories of the Urambo Kilimani, embodied a radical departure from the translation of religious texts and songs from European and Kiswahili languages into the Kinyamwezi language.[77] The publication of the New Testament completed one year of the boys' painstaking work of making religious texts available in the language spoken in Unyamwezi and their process of choosing good words for concepts associated with religion, culture, and authority.[78] Although the task of translating the New Testament into the Kinyamwezi language 'was a new thing to them', the young men's agency in 'translating the message' was crucial to 'domesticating a religious import' because they rendered an independent translation of the New Testament that reflected Kinyamwezi cultural values and the social context of marginalized groups. In doing so, they showed 'the efforts of African Christians to shed the European influences of an imported Christianity [and] transform[ed] it into an African religious experience'.[79] The need for the three young men to translate the New Testament into the Kinyamwezi language was rooted in the experience of multiethnic communities, including porters and slaves who learned the language and used it as a lingua franca. Because formerly enslaved people and porters were well versed in the Kinyamwezi language and culture, they formed the first generation of the literate Christian community (*vasomi*) in the region with their knowledge of reading and writing. They challenged the idioms of 'paganism' and 'heathenism' (*ushenzi*), which were widely used as part of the European civilizing mission.[80] As *vasomi*, the knowledge of reading and writing enabled the Nyamwezi to translate the texts into Kinyamwezi and enhanced their ability to read the scriptures and religious texts independently. They also reworked religious songs from the vantage point of the Nyamwezi culture, adding new African melodies that departed from the missionaries' versions, which sounded unappealing to the ears of the people. In addition to literacy and knowledge of the Kinyamwezi language and aspects of culture, early translators capitalized on their daily interactions with missionaries, Nyamwezi residents of the missions, and those who regularly attended

---

[77] Kisanji, *Historia Fupi*, 76.

[78] Peel, *Religious Encounter*, 156–61; Derek R. Peterson, 'Translating the Word: Dialogism and Debate in Two Gikuyu Dictionaries', *Journal of Religious History*, Vol. 23, No. 1 (1999), 31; Derek R. Peterson, *Creative Writing: Translation, Bookkeeping, and the Work of Imagination in Colonial Kenya* (Portsmouth, NH: Heinemann, 2004), 118.

[79] Nicholas M. Creary, *Domesticating a Religious Import: The Jesuits and the Inculturation of the Catholic Church in Zimbabwe, 1879–1980* (New York: Fordham University Press, 2011), 619.

[80] Brauer's Sermons, 1913, 21, KFC; Listi ya Vakristo Vahanya, Kanisa ya Ulilwansimba, Sikonge, No. 3, 1944, KFC.

LANGUAGE, SOCIETY, AND CHRISTIANITY IN UNYAMWEZI   121

Sunday services as a basis for making Kinyamwezi 'the book language' for the texts used in the Moravian missions and village outstations.[81]

Their departure from Kiswahili and European languages influenced missionaries to take an interest in the Kinyamwezi language as the medium of translating texts and Sunday sermons. Use of the language was instrumental in Christianizing the people in Unyamwezi and encouraged Christians to read and interpret the Bible and religious texts and sing songs independently. The Nyamwezi expression in Brauer's Kinyamwezi sermons that 'we can read from the Scripture on our own' ('tulikuvala kusoma mwibuku') shows how the many Christians in twentieth-century Unyamwezi who attended the sermons and could read the scripture formed the basis for a new community identity among Nyamwezi Christians in the Moravian missions and village outstations.[82] Further, the influence of African Christians in translating texts resulted in changes in some of the meanings conveyed by the words and concepts in the Bible, religious texts, and songs. The concepts used embodied the Nyamwezi understanding of kinship and how they were related to one another in the new spiritual communities. They also epitomize how translation reified the aspirations of the early generation of Christians who had lost their kinship ties through slavery to build a new sense of belonging based on spiritual connection. In addition to translation, most of the young Nyamwezi men who attended mission schools worked in villages as teachers and pastors. They composed songs in Kinyamwezi, administered the churches in villages, taught catechism, and prepared the young and adults for baptism and confirmation, leading to the growth of Christianity in areas that had only marginal missionary influence.

[81] Gaarde, 'A Brief Report', 142.
[82] Brauer's Sermons, 1913, 17 and 48, KFC.

CHAPTER 4

Catechists, Women, and Dissent in Villages beyond the Catholic Missions, 1930–50s

The ongoing interaction between porters, slaves, teachers, catechists, and European missionaries inspired the adaptation of the Christian culture in villages beyond the confines of Catholic mission stations. While mission stations formed 'melting-pot' communities for the growth of Christianity in villages, teachers, and catechists working in villages demonstrated their intellectual and cultural creativity by reimagining the Christian ethos apart from the European culture in the missions.[1] Their families became exemplary Christian families and laid the foundation for African Christianity as children were baptized, attended mission schools, and became teachers, catechists, and in some cases nuns and priests. Among the areas where teachers and catechists exercised creativity was translation. In addition to translation, teachers and catechists administered the churches in villages, taught catechism, and prepared the young and adults for baptism and confirmation. Ultimately, they became intellectuals who influenced congregants' interpretation of Christianity as they appropriated Christianity within the realm of Unyamwezi culture.[2]

This chapter turns from exchanges within the mission stations to examine how linguistic and cultural translation played out in the further growth of Christian communities in the villages beyond missionaries' reach between 1930 and the 1950s. The ongoing interaction between teachers, catechists, and European missionaries in missions, the prime mover for adaptation of the Christian culture, fed into broader social and cultural change among Christian villagers. Although the mission stations had worked effectively as centres

---

[1] Norman Etherington, 'Mission Station Melting Pots as a Factor in the Rise of South African Black Nationalism', *International Journal of African Historical Studies*, Vol. 9, No. 4 (1976), 592–605.

[2] Salvatory S. Nyanto, 'Priests without Ordination: Catechists and their Wives in Villages beyond Missions, 1948–1978', *Catholic Historical Review*, Vol. 108, No. 3 (Summer 2022), 569.

where a new Christian identity and church language were forged from multiple influences, the villages in which catechists and teachers worked presented diverse linguistic and practical challenges. In these settings, teachers and catechists demonstrated intellectual and cultural ingenuity in mediating between their still-evolving use of Kinyamwezi as the language of Christianity and the multiple linguistic traditions present in the villages. They took on many additional tasks in teaching and administration, and saw themselves as independent agents rather than followers of missionaries' instructions.

For example, in addition to their duties teaching catechism, some volunteer catechists designed a simple method of reading and writing alphabets on the writing tables that helped village children learn to read and write. Despite the many challenges, including lack of remuneration for their work, volunteer catechists bought books with their own money, established classrooms, designed teaching aids, and accompanied their pupils to the missions for regular examinations. Their resourcefulness and creativity encouraged literacy among children in villages and actively helped to shape the experience of Christianity more generally.[3] The works of catechists in villages eventually led to conflicts and divisions within the Catholic mission stations, as teachers and catechists demanded higher salaries and greater recognition. The complexity of the conflicting loyalties involved was evident in the way European missionaries sometimes supported catechists' demands for greater recognition, while African priests objected, arguing that catechists needed to learn to support themselves.

Building Village Outstations Beyond Catholic Missions, 1930–50

Catechists strategically established village churches to reach as many people as possible. Because people lived in villages and engaged in agriculture as their principal occupation, choosing a place that would attract villagers for Sunday services was imperative. For this reason, catechists in villages surrounding the Ndala mission established village churches in valleys where soil fertility attracted people from far and wide to grow various crops.[4] The soil fertility of Uhemeli territory, of which Ndala was a part, supported permanent settlement to such a degree that there were more than fifty homesteads in roughly a four-to-five-kilometre circuit. Most importantly, most people lived within an hour and a half's walking distance of the villages of Uhemeli and Uyui territories. These facts imply that many villages were 'within walking distance of the mission'. In contrast, in the adjoining territory of Uyui, about

[3] Francis P. Nolan, 'Christianity in Unyamwezi, 1878–1928' (PhD thesis, University of Cambridge, 1977), 315.
[4] Ndala Diary, 9 January 1896, WFA 01.43.

124   SLAVE EMANCIPATION, CHRISTIAN COMMUNITIES, AND DISSENT IN TANZANIA

twenty-five villages could be found between one and two hours from the Ndala mission.[5]

Nonetheless, many village outstations were far from the Ndala mission station. The peripheral location of villages at longer distances from Ndala made it difficult for European missionaries to reach the people there and hold Sunday services. Therefore, these villages needed African catechists to work as substitutes for priests. For instance, the village outstations of Kaloleni and Mwisi were about twenty-seven and thirty kilometres, respectively, from the Ndala mission, which meant that villagers depended entirely on resident African catechists to shoulder the mission work because European missionaries rarely visited them.[6]

In addition to soil fertility, the Nyamwezi established settlements along roads and railways just as in the precolonial period settlements had been built along the major caravan route.[7] In the same way, a considerable number of villages in the region of the Catholic missions of Ndala, Ndono, Itaga, and Kipalapala were located along the main roads, making it easy for resident catechists who lived in these villages to deliver services and maintain communication between the villages, the missions, and Tabora town.[8] However, some Catholic missions had so many outstations that the European missionaries could not handle them all, regardless of distance.

The development of village outstations coincided with the problem of disease-carrying tsetse flies affecting parts of the Unyamwezi region. In Tabora district alone, reported the district officer, there were 'tse tse flies, except in the clearings'.[9] The district's most serious concentrations of sleeping sickness were found in Usinge, Kaliua, Usoke, Ngulu, Ugunda, Urambo, Ushetu, Ilunde, Urwira, and Nyonga. Other sleeping sickness-ridden areas in Unyamwezi included Ulyankulu, Ibiri, Kwihara, Ushetu, Uyowa, Katunda-Ntankwa, Ndono, and Ussoke.[10] Besides human mortality, the outbreak of sleeping sickness decimated the cattle population, which increased the

---

[5] Ndala Diary, 20–21 January and 9 April 1896, WFA 01.43; *Les Missions d'Afrique des Pères blancs* (MdA), no. 130, July–August 1898, 356, AGMAfr.

[6] See Ndala Diary, Map, 1896–1978, WFA 01.43.

[7] Juhani Koponen, *Development for Exploitation: German Colonial Policies in Mainland Tanzania, 1884–1914* (Helsinki: Finnish Historical Society, 1995), 297–302. Report by His Britannic Majesty's Government to the Council of the League of Nations on the Administration of Tanganyika Territory for the year 1927, UKNA CO 1071/367 [Colonial No. 32].

[8] Ndala Diary, 9 January 1896, WFA 01.43.

[9] Tabora District Book, Tanganyika Territory, 1928 [Center for Research Libraries, film 27852, reel no. 20], TNA; Koponen, *Development for Exploitation*, 644.

[10] Tabora District Book, 1928, TNA; Settlement Officer to Provincial Commissioner,

CATECHISTS, WOMEN, AND DISSENT IN VILLAGES BEYOND THE CATHOLIC MISSIONS   125

price of meat in Unyamwezi. The glaring shortage of cattle became evident between the 1930s and 1950s in Ussoke, Ndono, Tabora, Kahama, and Nzega. In Ussoke and Ndono alone, the number of cattle declined from 6,689 to 2,093 between 1952 and 1954 due to the rising tide of sleeping sickness in the area.[11] In the Nzega district, the areas of Mambali, Wembere in the southeast, parts of the north and west along the Iborogero-Igurubi road up to the Manonga river, and west of Bukene had become clear of the tsetse fly and people could settle in villages.[12]

The persistence of tsetse flies in various parts of Unyamwezi discouraged settlement and agricultural development. Areas such as Ilalangulu, Kaliua, Urambo, Ndono, Ussoke, Mabama, Loya, Ntankwa, and Ussangu II remained mostly uninhabited and uncultivated.[13] In the Tabora district, the population was concentrated between forty miles west of Tabora and twenty miles east and about twenty miles north and south of the central railway line. People had evacuated the areas from Usoke to Usinge south of the central railway line to the Ugala River, resulting in a decrease in agricultural production that caused food shortages in Unyamwezi. For instance, between 1923 and 1933, the average price of groundnuts in Tabora fell from 4.5 shillings per kilogram to 1.5 shillings per kilogram. Following the decline in production, the colonial authority restricted the Nyamwezi from exporting foodstuffs, such as millet,

---

11 December 1950, TNA 63/P4/66/Vol.III/535; Settlement Officer to Provincial Commissioner, 15 January 1951, TNA 63/P4/66/Vol.III/543.

[11] Report on Ndono-Ussoke Sleeping Sickness Settlement, 30 September 1955, TNA 63/P4/66/Vol. IV/708–13; District Commissioner's Safari Report: Ussoke/ Ndono Settlement Area, 12–15 October 1955, TNA 47/M1/5D/19. See also W.F. Harrington, Esq., MC, Acting Provincial Commissioner, Tabora Province/Tanganyika Territory, Annual Reports for the Provincial Commissioners on Native Administration for the Year 1930, 73, UDSM EAF.

[12] Tabora Provincial Book, 19 November 1955 [film 27852, reel no. 19], TNA; Nzega District Book, Vol. I, 28 February 1946, TNA.

[13] Minutes of a meeting held in the Provincial Office, 22 January 1952, TNA 47/ T5/5; D.W. Freeman to the District Commissioner, 10 February 1953, TNA 63/ P4/66/Vol. III/595; Settlement Officer to the District Commissioner, Nguruka, 9 August 1954, TNA 63/P4/66/Vol. III/656; District Commissioner to the Provincial Commissioner, 13 December 1954, TNA 47/T5/50; Colin Maher to the District Commissioner, 12 July 1954, TNA 47/T5/40; A.T.P. Seabrook, General Manager, Overseas Food Corporation to the District Commissioner, 25 October 1954, TNA 47/T5/47; Barua ya Mtemi Nguruwe bin Kalele wa Usangi Igwisi kwenda kwa Bwana Provincial Commissioner, 21 August 1953, TNA 63/P4/66/ Vol. III/613.

SLAVE EMANCIPATION, CHRISTIAN COMMUNITIES, AND DISSENT IN TANZANIA

sorghum, maize, beans, cassava, sweet potatoes, and rice, due to the food shortage in various areas of the Tabora district.[14]

Ndala Catechists' School: Former Slaves, Catechists, and Women in Villages, 1930–50

Catechists in the Catholic missions of Unyamwezi were usually men and women who stayed in Catholic missions or village outstations after they had received special instruction. These catechists visited Christians in villages and taught the Catholic Church's fundamental doctrines. In areas with chiefs who opposed Christianity, the visits of catechists 'would make friendly relations [between chiefs and missionaries] possible'.[15] The principal task of catechists in Catholic missions and villages was to teach the young and the adult in preparation for baptism. They taught the answers from the catechism to be memorized before pupils could take an entry examination required for baptism. Catechists thought up simple tunes to help the students remember the answers to the catechism exam.[16] Catechists fulfilled these tasks because they were eager to get the training and opportunities to take up leadership positions in the church and its missions and village outstations.

Before the institutionalization of catechists in the Catholic missions of Unyamwezi, formerly enslaved people worked as 'resident catechists' in the Catholic missions. At Ndala, Leo Kalenga, a formerly enslaved person from the Congo, taught catechumens in preparation for baptism and confirmation.[17] At the Ushirombo mission, formerly enslaved people Gerado Kazoza and Matorino Mulindwa worked as catechists in the villages of Ilyambamgongo and Namabuye.[18] The 'resident catechists' had no formal training. They were few, and were mostly confined to the missions and nearby villages. More importantly, although resident catechists were integrated into the culture of the Nyamwezi and Christianity, their previous status thwarted their work, as formerly enslaved people found it difficult to command respect from other Christians.[19] Notwithstanding the challenges of overcoming the stigma

---

[14] 'Trade and Industry', Tabora District Book, 1928, TNA; Mr F.H. Jones, Acting District Officer, 'Extract from the Tour Report No. 3/33, January 27, 1933', 31, TNA.

[15] Francis P. Nolan, 'The Changing Role of the Catechist in the Archdiocese of Tabora, 1879–1967', 31 August 1967, 5, AAT 325.297.

[16] Ibid., 11.

[17] Interview with Maria Nyamizi Kalenga, Ndala, 7 January 2016.

[18] Interviews with Emmanuel Ndekanilo, Ushirombo, 5 December 2016, and Anastazia Maturino Mulindwa, Ushirombo, 5 December 2016.

[19] Ndala Diary, 1 December 1906, WFA 01.43; Ndala Diary, 4 April 1897, WFA

Figure 8 Ndala Catechists' School (*Misongeni*).

attached to slavery, early resident catechists were still regarded as 'masters of the new ways' because they had attended mission schools, which enabled them to read, write, and prepare children and adults for baptism.[20]

To cater to the needs of the increasing number of Christians in villages, the Catholic White Fathers established a school (famously called *misongeni*) for training catechists at Ndala in 1928 (Figure 8). The school was closed for a while before the Second World War but was reopened after the war in 1948. The school admitted those who had worked as catechists but needed further training. Catechists were trained to serve mostly in villages far from the missions. There was neither an age limit nor an entrance fee; married men with families, unmarried men, and those who volunteered to work as catechists could attend the school. The only criterion was a standard of education sufficient to teach children in the village outstations and to teach religion classes in primary and secondary schools.[21] The course lasted two years, and Kiswahili

---

01.43; interview with Fr Arnold Malambwa, Bussondo, 24 November 2016.

[20] 'The Origins and Role of Catechists in the Archdiocese of Tabora, 1879–1967' [31 August 1967], 12–13, AAT 325.297.

[21] C. Michaud, Tabora, 13 October 1928, AAT 325.299; Liste des Catéchistes [1 March–31 May 1928], AAT 325.299; Les Catéchistes, 10 April 1930, AAT 325.299; Rapport de l'école des Catéchistes (Ndala), 10 August 1949, AAT 325.299; School for Catechists at Ndala, July 1962, AAT 325.299; Archbishop Marcus Mihayo, Tabora, 'Application for Assistance to Swiss Catholic Lenten Appeal', 4 April 1963, AAT 325.299; Marcus Mihayo to Rt Rev. Msgr H. Goertz,

was the medium of instruction. But in villages, catechists used Kiswahili and Kinyamwezi to teach children about baptism and to lead prayers. To limit costs, the school capped the maximum number of student catechists to twenty-eight per intake. Student catechists earned a salary, though it remained below twenty shillings per month. Finding the salary insufficient, catechists made frequent requests for raises.[22]

Student catechists attended thirty classes per week. Eight weekly classes were devoted to learning about catechism, while other classes focused on the Bible, church history, mathematics, liturgy, hygiene, music, and the Kiswahili language. Students took written examinations in all subjects at the end of each month.[23] In addition, catechists performed an hour of manual labour each day after classes, working in the fields and growing various crops. Every Thursday afternoon, they went to the bush to collect firewood. Every Saturday afternoon, catechists were occupied with hygiene and rehearsal of songs for Sunday masses. They spent their leisure hours listening to the radio, playing cards, and playing football matches with the villagers of Ndala.[24] The range of mission activities helped catechists extend networks of friendship. Catechists maintained these networks among themselves and with the villagers of Ndala through football matches, and extended these into villages after the two-year course at the Ndala mission. Nonetheless, the requirement of constant manual labour on a tight schedule made many catechists feel they lacked freedom and were treated like schoolboys.[25]

The wives of the student catechists attended three catechism classes each week and courses on home crafts, cooking, and handicrafts. Women who had never been to school also attended reading and writing classes. In this way, women shaped the new identity of the literate Christian community. Missionaries referred to Christians as *basomi* or *vasomi* (literate people)

Tabora, 27 March 1963, AAT 325.299; 'The Pastoral Institute of Ndala, Archdiocese of Tabora', 28 January 1964, AAT 325.299.

[22] Barua toka kwa Walimu Wote wa Ndala kwenda kwa Arkiaskofu C. Bronsveld, 7 February 1954, AAT 325.299; School for Catechists at Ndala, July 1962, AAT 325.299; The Pastoral Institute, 28 January 1964, AAT 325.299. The archdiocese stopped paying salaries to student catechists in 1960 because it could no longer shoulder the financial burden.

[23] Kawaida ya Shule ya Walimu-Ndala, 8 November 1948, AAT 325.299; 'School for Catechists at Ndala', July 1962, AAT 325.299; Kawaida ya Walimu, 19 November 1949, AAT 325.299; Ndala Walimu-School, Timetable, 19 November 1949, AAT 325.299.

[24] The Pastoral Institute, 28 January 1964, AAT 325.299; Kawaida ya Walimu, 19 November 1949, AAT 325.299.

[25] See, for instance, Ndala Diary, 31 July 1960, AAT 325.299.

around the school and in their sermons because community members could read religious texts and write. Wives of student catechists spent most of their free time on handicrafts.[26] These activities offered opportunities to establish friendships with other women in the mission and those living in the village of Ndala who were not part of the mission community. They also rehearsed songs with the men on Saturday evenings in preparation for Sunday masses. In addition to studying, wives of student catechists bore the responsibility for childcare.

The classes for women were not meant to train them to work as village catechists. Instead, European missionaries intended to prepare women to serve as a model of the traditional Christian family, in which wives and daughters were to manage their domestic responsibilities, prepare food for the family, and care for children.[27] Yet at the same time, the range of activities performed by catechists and their wives in the mission helped them extend their fictive kinship networks beyond their blood relations in the villages where they worked after the two-year course at Ndala.[28] Mission experience further enabled women to build an 'affective community' of Christians in villages that were based not on family but on spiritual connections.[29]

The two-year stay at the Ndala catechists' school and their mission experience prepared catechists and their wives to form village communities that inspired the growth of Christianity. At the end of the two-year course, catechists and their families returned to the village outstations to take up their duties. The catechists taught the rudiments of religion to beginners, prepared the catechumens for baptism, and gave instruction to all Christians. Other responsibilities included leading prayers on Sundays and at festivals, visiting families in villages at least once a week, holding a period of instruction every evening, and teaching religious classes in nearby schools. All catechists earned a minimum salary. However, most catechists farmed to improve their financial situation or occasionally left their outstations and villages for temporary jobs or to collect wild honey in the forests.[30]

---

[26] 'School for Catechists at Ndala', July 1962, AAT 325.299.

[27] Ibid.; 'The Pastoral Institute', 28 January 1964, AAT 325.299; Marcus Mihayo to Rt Rev. Msgr H. Goertz, Tabora, 27 March 1963, AAT 325.299.

[28] Elisabeth McMahon, *Slavery and Emancipation in Islamic East Africa: From Honor to Respectability* (Cambridge: Cambridge University Press, 2013), 196.

[29] Adreana C. Prichard, *Sisters in Spirit: Christianity, Affect, and Community Building in East Africa, 1860–1970* (East Lansing: Michigan State University, 2017), 4.

[30] 'School for Catechists at Ndala', July 1962, AAT 325.299; 'The Pastoral Institute', 28 January 1964, AAT 325.299.

The first catechists who joined the school in 1928 completed the course in 1930 and, together with their families, returned to their parishes to be assigned villages to work. They included Yosefu Matuzya (from Igalula), Yulius Mwabira (from Kahama), Mikaeli Lubinga (from Bulungwa), Marco Kismi and Marco Kapaya (from Itaga), Simoni Kulwa and Francisko Mihambo (from Ndala), and Gervasi Poriki and Petro Munyanganande (from Kaniha). Others were Stanslaus Muyega and Atanasi Mugansa (from Ndono), Mikaeli Mkisiwa and Lonjini Hanga (from Busongo), and Agustino Kasu (from Lukula).[31] Catechists from Ndala who began the course in 1937 and completed it in 1939 went to work in different villages of the Ndala mission. Recalling these catechists, Paulina Mwanamihayo said that 'they all began working as catechists during the British period'.[32] The archival report about catechist Benedikto Inega indicates that he began working at the Ipazi outstation on the mission of Kitangiri in 1939. Other catechists who went to different villages included Joseph Nsubi, who went to work at Chabutwa, Paskali Maganga, who went to Puge; and Paskali Machibya and Bernard Mapalala, who worked at Izimba in Usongo (see Map 5).[33]

Some catechists returned to work in their home villages that still had no catechists. For instance, Tito Nsimbila returned to his village, Kaguwa, to work as a catechist, and Philipo Manyelo from Iyombo also returned as a catechist. Similarly, Gaspali Sunhwa returned to work at Puge after he completed the course.[34] The catechists used the knowledge they had acquired from Ndala School to teach and lead congregants in the village outstations. Prayers and liturgy, in general, were in Latin and Kinyamwezi. Although catechists were unfamiliar with Latin, they relied on the catechism written in Kinyamwezi. They occasionally used Kiswahili, as it was well-known in the region. The commitment of catechists and lay Christians to learning and spreading literacy were to have an impact on the development of Christianity in the villages of twentieth-century western Tanzania. Their mastery of Kinyamwezi enabled them to interpret texts (hymnodies, the Bible, prayer books, and songs) in their own ways, adapt Christianity into the existing Unyamwezi culture, and become literate 'masters of new ways' among the Nyamwezi.[35] By employing their linguistic skills and some rudimentary training from the mission schools,

---

[31] Liste des Catéchistes [1 March–31 May 1928], AAT 325.299.

[32] Interview with Paulina Mwanamihayo, Ndala (Uhemeli), 7 January 2016. In Kaswhaili, 'wote walianza kazi wakati wa mwingereza'.

[33] 'Catechist Benedicto Inega-Kitangiri Mission', 25 October 1956, AAT 325.297; interviews with Paulina Mwanamihayo, Ndala (Uhemeli), 7 January 2016, and Maria Nyamizi Kalenga, Ndala, 6 September 2016.

[34] Interview with Felista Lonjini, Ndala, 6 September 2016.

[35] J.D.Y. Peel, *Religious Encounter and the Making of the Yoruba* (Bloomington:

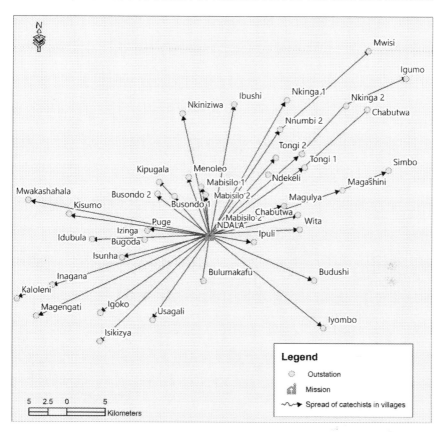

Map 5 The Spread of Catechists in Villages of the Ndala Catholic Mission, 1930–60s.

catechists 'crossed linguistic and cultural boundaries to [preach, teach,] and spread the faith' using the Kinyamwezi language.[36] Thus, village catechists worked as 'priests without ordination', and their wives worked as 'substitutes for sisters'.[37]

Indiana University Press, 2000), 156–61, Nyanto, 'Priests without Ordination' 564.

[36] Paul Kollman and Cynthia Toms Smedley, *Understanding World Christianity: Eastern Africa* (Minneapolis: Fortress Press, 2018), 34 and 41.

[37] Msgr Goertz, Päpstliches Werk der Glaubensverbreitung [The Pontifical Society for the Propagation of Faith], to Archbishop Marc Mihayo, 4 July 1962, AAT 325.299; interviews with Joakimu Soteri Lusalago, Mabisilo, 6 September 2016, and Merkiori Maganga, Magreti Machibya, and Magdalena Filipo Milembe, Usongo, 16 November 2016. See also Nyanto, 'Priests without Ordination'.

A sizeable number of volunteer catechists and lay Christians bought books to learn to read, and some catechists in villages established their schools, refined teaching methods, and developed ways of obtaining pupils for instruction. Others volunteered to teach catechism in the mission and outstations without pay. Around Tabora, some people who wanted to learn to read and write bought books from the mission, studying them on their own. Some succeeded in teaching themselves how to read and write and established schools to teach children and adults in villages.[38] One representative case was that of Mlewa, a catechist who established a village school at Usunga. He had attended the Usoke Moravian mission school, where he acquired the knowledge that enabled him to set up his school. He went to the Catholic mission at Tabora to obtain books and then enrolled groups of pupils at Usungu village.[39] In 1929, at his own expense, Mlewa built a classroom for pupils in the village (see Figure 9). In 1931, catechist Mlewa of Usungu completed his first year as an instructor with 150 pupils. One visiting priest reported that Mlewa's class was 'in progress … [and] most [pupils] knew the first part of catechism and had learnt the prayers too'.[40]

The schools of volunteer catechists preserved an informality that permitted some adaptation to the indigenous culture. The village schools run by volunteer catechists like Mlewa grew in number and fitted quickly into the missions' school system. Volunteer catechists built classrooms at their own expense with their pupils' assistance, and designed writing tables to facilitate learning to read and write. We learn of a group of catechists from Ndala who, in addition to teaching catechism, designed a simple method of reading and writing alphabets on the writing tables. Francis Nolan states they 'designed their alphabet by means of which they corresponded in a quite original script'.[41] However, having no records of the writings of these catechists makes it challenging to dig deeper into their teaching methods and what Nolan regards as 'new alphabets'. Through such initiatives, these catechists fit into the category of 'peasant intellectuals' or 'local intellectuals'.[42]

---

[38] Nolan, 'Changing Role', 1968, 12–13, AAT 325.297.

[39] Nolan, 'Christianity in Unyamwezi', 1977, 315.

[40] Nolan, 'Changing Role', 1968, 12, AAT 325.297.

[41] Nolan, 'Christianity in Unayamwezi', 315.

[42] Ibid. For details about 'peasant intellectuals' (used in this context to mean Nyamwezi Christian intellectuals), see Steven Feierman, *Peasant Intellectuals: Anthropology and History in Tanzania* (Madison: University of Wisconsin Press, 1990) and Emma Hunter, *Political Thought and the Public Sphere in Tanzania: Freedom, Democracy and Citizenship in the Era of Decolonization* (Cambridge: Cambridge University Press, 2015).

Figure 9 Undated Image of a Catechist Teaching Children in the Village Outstation.

Like employed catechists, volunteer catechists in villages offered their pupils regular examinations at the mission and tried to place them on the same footing as the students of employed catechists. Volunteer catechists invited bishops and priests for visits, built chapels, and organized the construction of paths to facilitate communication between villages and missions. After working for a considerable period, some volunteer catechists came to be considered 'official mission catechists'. Still, most continued to work without pay to 'save the honour of being a *mwalimu* [teacher]'. At Mwale village outstation, some twenty miles south of Tabora, no missionary visited the outstation for four years. Yet the volunteer catechist continued his classes with many catechumens. At Igalula, east of Tabora, five volunteer catechists organized classes with catechumens from the village outstation.[43]

The work of catechists (both volunteer and employed) in the villages and the schools they created played an increasingly important role in attracting children and catechumens to Christianity. At Ushirombo, the diarist commented, 'The wind is blowing towards the school; [Nyamwezi] people speak only of schools; there is no salvation outside school'.[44] With the growing inter-

[43] Nolan, 'Christianity in Unyamwezi', 314–16.
[44] Ushirombo Diary, 11 January 1928, WFA 01.43.

est in schooling, catechists gradually became figures of considerable prestige and influence in Unyamwezi. Their influence began to undermine the authority of chiefs in Unyamwezi, and so became a source of contention between chiefs and catechists. Occasionally, chiefs complained that catechists used their position to prevent pupils from working for them.[45] Catechist Anthony Nkisa challenged the authority of chiefs in Unyamwezi. At Ndala, he led the Christians in rebellion against the chief's imposition of thirty days of forced labour instead of the customary one or two days a month.[46] The movement against the chief of Ndala demonstrates the declining authority and influence of chiefs over the people as some missions and outstations grew to become centres of dissent in the region.

With the increasing number of Christians working in villages, including volunteer and 'official' catechists, dependent outstations were now becoming independent parishes in areas beyond Ndala parish. The Catholic parish of Usongo was founded in 1930, while Kitangiri, Mwisi, and Puge became parishes in 1949.[47] By 1952, catechists completing training at Ndala worked in villages of many parishes in Unyamwezi, including Ushirombo, Lububu, Ndala, Tabora, Kaniha, and Ngaya parishes. Other parishes included Kitangiri, Bulungwa, Kahama, and Usongo.[48] The catechists' work influenced other men to join the school at Ndala to work as catechists after completion. Joakimu Soteri, for example, was motivated by catechists, including his brother-in-law, to join the school and become a catechist himself. Soteri's first outstation was at Chapela in Uyui between 1952 and 1957, after which he relocated to Mabisilo. He used Kinyamwezi in worship and daily communication, which enabled the Nyamwezi Christians to understand the liturgy better than they could in Latin.[49] Similarly, the wives of catechists influenced women in villages where their husbands worked since village women learned from them the skills the wives had acquired during their stay at the Ndala mission.[50]

Apart from attracting Nyamwezi villagers to Christianity, catechists encouraged some of their sons and daughters to become teachers, nuns, and

[45] Nolan, 'Christianity in Unyamwezi', 317.

[46] Nolan, 'Changing Role', 1968, 12–13, AAT 325.297.

[47] Annual Report, Nzega District, 1930–1931, TNA 967.823; Annual Report on Native Affairs, Nzega District, 1949, TNA 967.823; Jubilee Usongo na Igumo, Matukio ya Kila Siku, 1980, WFA Rel 74.

[48] Catéchistes, November, 12 August 1952, AAT 325.299.

[49] Interview with Joakimu Soteri Lusalago, Mabisilo, 6 September 2016. In Kaswahili, 'nilitumia Kinyamwezi kuanzia mwanzo hadi mwisho wa ibada'.

[50] 'School for Catechists', July 1962, AAT 325.299, 'The Pastoral Institute of Ndala', 28 January 1964, AAT 325.299, Marcus Mihayo to Rt Rev. Msgr H. Goertz, Tabora, 27 March 1963, AAT 325.299.

CATECHISTS, WOMEN, AND DISSENT IN VILLAGES BEYOND THE CATHOLIC MISSIONS 135

priests. For example, catechist Adelado Nkunde was the brother of another catechist, and his sons became priests. He worked at the Catholic mission of Ndala, while his brother, Benedicto Inega, served in the parishes of Lububu and Kitangiri.[51] Adelado's sons, John Kabeya and Ambrose Mhaliga, were ordained priests and played important roles in Catholic life in Unyamwezi. Father Kabeya wrote a well-known history of Mirambo.[52] At the same time, Father Mhaliga composed Kinyamwezi songs that were widely used in the liturgy in Unyamwezi because they departed from Latin and used Kinyamwezi idioms and references to Nyamwezi culture. Moreover, several daughters of catechists attended mission schools and worked as teachers, while others became some of the first indigenous nuns in Unyamwezi.[53]

Catechists and Christians in Mission Statistics, 1928–56: A Synthesis

Indeed, the contribution of catechists to the consolidation of Christianity in villages beyond the mission station is indisputable. The parish statistics collected from various mission stations in Tabora provide a glimpse into the number of catechists working in villages, their impact on the growth of Christianity in Unyamwezi, and the growth of Christianity in Unyamwezi between 1928 and 1956. First, the number of catechists in the Catholic missions of Unyamwezi increased with the establishment of the catechists' training college in 1928, from 154 in 1928 to 263 in 1939 (see Table 6).[54] Second, the increase in the number of catechists permitted an increase in village outstations. The proliferation of new village outstations had a bearing on the number of baptized Catholics, whose numbers increased from 10,000 in 1930 to 18,111 in 1937 and 27,250 in 1956 (see Table 7).[55] As the Catholic population of Unyamwezi grew, the church also opened new missions. The Catholic mission of Usongo was opened in 1931, followed by Busondo in 1933, Itamuka in 1936, and Kaniha in 1938. The Bulungwa mission, which had closed in 1922, was reopened in 1937 with ten village catechists.[56]

---

[51] Catechist Benedicto Inega, Kitangili Mission, 25 October 1956, AAT 325.297.

[52] John B. Kabeya, *Mtemi Mirambo: Mtawala shujaa wa Kinyamwezi* (Nairobi: East African Literature Bureau, 1971).

[53] Interviews with Theodori Kulinduka, Gaspali Bundala, and Mikaeli Katabi, Ndala, 8 September 2016, Theodori Kulinduka, Ndala, 7 January 2016, and Felista Lonjini Namna, Uhemeli, 6 September 2016.

[54] Nolan, 'Changing Role', 31 August 1967, AAT 325.297.

[55] Statistics, Tabora Archdiocese, 1930–50, AAT 322.399.

[56] F. van Vlijmen, 'The Origins of the Archdiocese of Tabora', 5, AAT 23. 01.

Table 6 Number of Catechists in Catholic Missions, 1928–46.

	1928	1929	1930	1931	1932	1933	1934	1935	1936	1937	1938	1939	1940	1941	1942	1943	1944	1945	1946
Ushirombo	8	20	16	18	18	18	21	21	20	22	16	16	14	13	13	13	13	13	13
Mbulu (Iraku)	26	26	23	21	20	20	20	18	18	26	26	26	25	20	19		-	-	-
Ndala	29	32	29	20	20	20	20	21	20	21	23	23	23	25	28	28	28	29	30
Tabora	8	15	18	25	24	24	24	23	23	23	29	32	15	20	21	21	12	14	12
Itaga	14	12	13	12	13	13	16	16	15	19	22	21	15	15	15	15	21	21	24
Mbulu (Kahama)	29	29	28	28	28	17	22	26	25	32	29	24	21	29	29	29	31	31	30
Lububu	15	16	16	22	22	22	23	17	20	20	20	22	26	26	30	30	32	42	42
Ndonno	25	13	21	15	18	18	18	18	14	16	12	12	22	22	22	22	15	20	22
Ussongo					12	14	14	20	17	16	16	16	18	19	19	20	20	25	25
Bussanda						11	17	17	26	33	37	36	13	13	13	13	13	13	13
Itamuka									12	12	12	12	15	15	16	16	26	26	26
Bulungwa										10	11	13	15	7	9	9	11	11	11
Kaniha											6	8					8	8	8
Igalula													12	12	12	12	12	12	12
Makiungu													21	21					
TOTAL	154	163	164	173	177	181	201	194	209	250	259	263	256	257	247	228	242	265	268

Source: Compiled from Francis P. Nolan, 'The Changing Role of the Catechist in the Archdiocese of Tabora, 1879–1967' (AAT 325. 297), 31 August 1967, and *Statistiques des missions 1937–1948* (AAT 350.002).

Table 7 Number of Baptized Christians in Catholic Missions, 1937–56.

	1937	1938	1939	1940	1941	1942	1943	1944	1945	1946
Tabora	2100	2351	2401	1242	1760	1800	1962	1800	1109	1253
Itaga	1398	1480	1506	1557	1683	1688	1714	1876	1684	2248
Ndonno	1130	1200	1270	1324	1385	1400	1400	1400	1420	1450
Ndala	3697	3984	4199	4382	4720	4974	5173	5351	5294	4209
Ussongo	1080	1153	1184	1396	1455	1542	1600	2050	2117	2180
Lububu	1464	1533	1587	1600	1685	1740	1800	1840	1276	1292
Ushirombo	1534	1152	1152	1238	1242	1046	1091	960	985	-
Bulungwa	300	354	403	486	528	564	672	680	762	735
Itamuka	94	107	107	188	288	290	-	-	-	-
Mbulu-Kahama	1765	1845	1860	1820	1884	1947	1957	2009	1323	1425
Mbulu-Iraku	1480	1622	1760	1850	1945	2000	-	-	-	-
Makiungu	1328	1485	1541	1679		2114	-	-	-	-
Ngaya	-	-	-	-	-	-	-	-	700	-
Kipalapala	-	-	-	-	-	-	-	-	-	-
Kaniha	-	-	406	-	434	525	581	591	604	-
Bussanda	741	911	1082	787	916	1026	1152	1213	1322	-
Lukula	-	-	-	751	776	830	913	973	1146	1216
Mwamagembe	-	-	-	-	246	300	295	319	347	-
Igalula	-	-	-	-	-	-	-	374	410	410
Kitangili	-	-	-	-	-	-	-	-	-	-
Urambo	-	-	-	-	-	-	-	-	-	-
Igumo	-	-	-	-	-	-	-	-	-	-
TOTAL	**18,111**	**19,177**	**20,458**	**20,300**	**20,947**	**23,786**	**20,310**	**21,436**	**20,499**	**16,418**

Table 7 *continued*

	1947	1948	1949	1950	1951	1952	1953	1954	1955	1956
Tabora	1260	1251	1283	1451	1300	1345	1424	1554	2179	2137
Itaga	1987	2797	1500	1800	2217	2285	2290	2137	2213	2374
Ndonno	-	-	3500	-	1600	600	675	1007	856	917
Ndala	4415	4661	4864	4900	4500	4728	6023	6208	6468	6943
Ussongo	2000	1600	1625	1352	1380	2150	2400	1705	1799	752
Lububu	1300	1320	1700	942	973	1021	1057	968	1060	1096
Ushirombo	1015	1089	1141	1141	1224	1306	1414	15241	1619	1470
Bulungwa	766	870	785	821	958	1006	1093	1057	1127	1248
Itamuka	-	-	-	-	-	-	-	-	-	-
Mbulu-Kahama	1537	1614	1806	1888	1952	2025	2100	2450	2500	2500
Mbulu-Iraku	-	-	-	-	-	-	-	-	-	-
Makiungu	-	-	-	-	-	-	-	-	-	-
Ngaya	790	800	840	774	800	880	998	1250	950	985
Kipalapala	-	-	420	420	403	400	400	368	392	402
Kaniha	724	810	934	1007	1158	1061	1135	1505	1555	1549
Bussanda	-	-	-	-	-	-	-	-	-	-
Lukula	1259	1346	1337	1385	1418	1527	1513	1453	1508	1680
Mwamagembe	-	-	-	-	-	-	-	-	-	-
Igalula	295	409	409	450	450	445	465	465	442	480
Kitangili	-	-	-	817	905	919	874	926	853	864
Urambo	-	-	-	-	-	4050	2160	1363	1245	1388
Igumo	-	-	-	-	-	-	-	-	-	1015
TOTAL	**17,348**	**18,567**	**22,144**	**19,148**	**21,238**	**25,748**	**26,021**	**39,657**	**26,766**	**27,250**

Compiled from *Statistiques des missions 1937–1948*, *Statistiques annuelles 1938–1957*, and *Statistiques de Mbulu (Kahama) 1921–1943* (AAT 350.002), and *Statistiques* (AAT 335.207).

CATECHISTS, WOMEN, AND DISSENT IN VILLAGES BEYOND THE CATHOLIC MISSIONS   **139**

The increasing number of catechists working in villages, as indicated in the mission statistics, corresponded to the steady increase in the number of Christians in some mission stations, including Mbulu (Kahama), Lukula, Bulungwa, Ndala, Tabora, and Itaga. The Christian population grew in the Tabora mission because Tabora town's market and strategic location at the central railway junction attracted people from villages and travelling traders into the town. Nevertheless, the Second World War halted the progress in Tabora, leading to a decline in the number of Christians in the town as fear of the war caused many people to evacuate. The population had increased from 2,100 in 1937 to 2,400 in 1939 but sharply declined during the war.[57] The war did not seriously affect growth in some missions, such as Itaga and Ndala. Their peripheral locations and the wide range of activities at the Ndala catechist school, including socializing through weekly dances, attracted the villagers to Christianity. The increasing number of baptized Christians between the years 1937 and 1956, from 3,697 to 6,943 in Ndala and from 1,398 to 2,374 in Itaga, is indicative of the progress of Christianity, notwithstanding the war.[58]

Despite its proximity to Tabora town, the Christian population at Kipalapala mission station remained relatively small. Parish statistics show that the Christian population dropped from 420 in 1949 to 402 in 1956.[59] Of course, the construction of the central railway prompted people to abandon Kazeh in 1912 in favour of Tabora town, leaving only a few people at Kipalapala.[60] Mtemi Saidi Fundikira of Unyanyembe's conversion to Islam in 1917 influenced his subordinates, formerly enslaved people, orphans, and dependents living in the chiefly compound (*ngomeni*) at Itetemia to follow suit, causing the area to become predominantly Muslim.[61] There was also a relative decline in the Christian population at Urambo mission, from 4,020 in 1952 to 1,388 in 1956. The loss was attributable to the persistence of sleeping sickness, which ravaged communities and the cattle population, leading people to abandon their settlements and relocate to new areas designated by the government.[62]

---

[57] *Statistiques annuelles*, Tabora 1937–1956, AAT 350.002.

[58] *Statistiques annuelles*, Ndala, Itaga, 1937–1956, AAT 350.002.

[59] *Statistiques annuelles*, Kipalapala, 1949–1956, AAT 350.002.

[60] See, for instance, Karin Pallaver, 'A Triangle: Spatial Processes of Urbanization and Political Power in 19th-Century Tabora, Tanzania', *Afrique: Débats, méthodes et terrains d'histoire*, Vol. 11 (2020), https://doi.org/10.4000/afriques.2871 (accessed 10 June 2024).

[61] Interviews with Saidi Ramadhani Fundikira, Tabora, 6 March 2020, and Issa Ndima Kapakila, Kipalapala, 12 March 2020.

[62] 'Sleeping Sickness-Tabora (including Kitunda)', Tabora District Book, 1927 and 1929, TNA; Nolan 'Christianity in Unyamwezi', 306–8.

140   SLAVE EMANCIPATION, CHRISTIAN COMMUNITIES, AND DISSENT IN TANZANIA

Farming by people in Ngaya, Igalula, and Kitangiri accounted for the few Christians in the missions. It is no wonder that the overall number of recorded Christians in the three mission stations mostly remained below nine hundred between 1950 and 1956.[63]

Nevertheless, the missing reports on the number of Christians in some missions presents a more formidable challenge in gauging the growth of Christianity in twentieth-century western Tanzania. In 1943, the Pallotine Fathers took over the administration of the Makiungu and Mbulu (Iraku) missions following the division of the Vicariate Apostolic of Tabora. Consequently, the two mission stations ceased to be part of Tabora,[64] and the Pallotine priests reported the annual progress of the two missions to their superior, not to the White Fathers in Tabora. The division of the vicariate apostolic of Tabora leaves us with no reports about the growth of Christianity in the two missions between 1943 and 1956.

Indeed, filling out the parish register was a daunting task for many new African priests, who, with little experience of keeping records, could not account for missing information. Lack of training in the handling of parish registers halted progress, as some annual reports could not be filled out as scheduled. Some new priests learned the task from their peers, adding to their workload. Because new priests received no training from the White Fathers, the task was intimidating, laborious, and unattractive to most African priests at the mission stations in the diocese of Tabora (which in 1960 became the archdiocese). Father Mirambo, sent to administer the Ngaya mission station, spent almost a year getting used to the rigour of keeping the parish register. His experience was common for the many priests who left their parish registers unattended.[65]

The cases of the Ndonno and Ngaya mission stations reveal the challenges faced by African priests in keeping mission statistics. We learn that upon submitting the annual report of Ndonno mission to the vicar apostolic Rev. Cornelius Bronsveld, Father Alexander Kabapere complained that his inexperience caused the report to fall short of expected standards. He said: '[N] itazileta karatasi hizo lakini ufahamu kuwa kazi hiyo siijui ... hivyo utaona nimekosea mambo mengi' ('I will submit my report, but you should know that I am not aware of this task ... you will notice so many flaws'). He also insisted that 'it would be certainly be [sic] better if such problems should be explained beforehand'.[66] The priest in charge of Ngaya mission, Father Peter

---

[63] *Statistiques annuelles*, Ngaya, Kitangiri, and Igalula, 1950–1956, AAT 350.002

[64] *Statistiques annuelles*, Makiungu and Mbulu (Iraku), 1942, AAT 350.002.

[65] Fr Mirambo to Bronsveld, 1951, AAT 350.002.

[66] Fr Alexander Kabepele to Rev. Fr C. Bronsveld, Vicar Apostolic, Ndonno, 2 July 1950, AAT 350.002.

Mirambo, encountered similar difficulties in his annual report of 1950, and his remarks – 'I have done what I know' and 'I know not the exact number of them [Christians]' – are symptomatic of the extent to which lack of knowledge about the parish halted the missions' progress.[67]

Sustaining Catechists: Contestations, Ruptures, and Dissent in Villages, 1950s–60s

By the mid-twentieth century, despite the many challenges, Christianity in Unyamwezi had a firm foothold in villages beyond the mission stations. The phenomenal expansion of Christianity and enormous increase in Christians were largely attributable to the zealous efforts of village catechists.[68] While their work became an important force to be reckoned with, life in villages presented a more formidable challenge. Teaching postulants, catechumens, and children, leading believers in Sunday prayers and services, and visiting sick Christians in villages added to the day-to-day workload of catechists on top of their other familial responsibilities.[69]

While catechists performed similar tasks (teaching, singing, and leading congregants on Sundays), differences in monthly salaries and remunerations (*posho*) reveal evidence of unequal treatment, divisions, and decreased morale. In some mission stations and village outstations, catechists earned 100 shillings, whereas others received 70, 20, and 12 shillings per month, and still others earned 30, 20, and 12 shillings, respectively.[70] Church authorities attributed the differences in catechists' salaries and remunerations to 'hard work and zealous efforts' and increased numbers of students attending religious instruction.[71] Nevertheless, these discrepancies sowed discord between catechists and church authorities, significantly discouraging much of the catechists' work. Differences in pay further increased discontent and grudges

---

[67] Fr Mirambo to Bronsveld, 1951, AAT 350.002.

[68] See, for instance, Nolan, 'Christianity in Unyamwezi', 316.

[69] Catechist Salary, Circular no. 3, 25 May 1957, AAT 325.298.

[70] Catechist Salary, 25 May 1957AAT 325.298; Fr Peter Mirambo, Ushetu mission, to Fr Anthony Nyambwe, 2 January 1958, AAT 325.298; Urambo Catholic mission, 2 January 1958, AAT 325.298; Fr Peter Mirambo to Archbishop Cornelius Bronsveld, Ushetu, 6 January 1958, AAT 325.298; Urambo Catholic Mission, 22 January 1958, AAT 325.298; Catechists Salaries: Tabora Parish, 6 March 1958, AAT 325.298.

[71] Catechist Salary, 1957, AAT 325.298, Fr Mirambo to Fr Nyambwe, 1958, AAT 325.298; Fr Mirambo to Archbishop Bronsveld, 1958, AAT 325.298.

142 SLAVE EMANCIPATION, CHRISTIAN COMMUNITIES, AND DISSENT IN TANZANIA

among catechists who could not see a 'clear cut between their responsibilities and hard work'.[72]

Persistent grudges over unfair treatment and the challenges of village life encouraged Tabora, Upuge, and Ndonno catechists to demand salary rises and *posho* from church authorities. Catechists from nearly all the village outstations of the three missions met at Ndonno to discuss their work as catechists and the 'real situation' in villages that 'put their lives at risk'. The culture of friendship, collegiality, and support at the Ndala catechist school helped these catechists to unite to share the common experiences of their village lives and express their resentment with church authorities. Networks of friendship and support continued after their time at Ndala School, whose graduates maintained regular communication, visited one another, and shared personal experiences working in the village outstations.[73] In no time, catechists working in the outstations of Tabora, Upuge, and Ndonno missions joined in solidarity to provide a platform for their 'subaltern voices'; the letter of complaint became a 'weapon of the weak' deployed against the dominant discourse of discipline and hard work and the wage policies imposed on them by church authorities.[74]

The range of networks created at the Ndala School inspired catechists in other mission stations to mount a collective rebellion against the clergy. After the disgruntled catechists met at Ndala mission to discuss their lives in the villages, they submitted their resolutions to the archbishop, condemning the bishop for having 'forsaken them' and stating that '[catechists] were no longer servants of the bishop nor priests ... they were free to live without interference'.[75] Catechists further emphasized that 'the priest would take his food to the village outstation' and that 'no woman would be allowed to cook for the priest unless he paid 5 shillings for each day'. As for salary adjustments, catechists defiantly informed the bishop that 'they would assess the amount they want to be paid' ('tutapima kiasi tunachotaka kulipwa').[76]

---

[72] Fr Mirambo to Fr Nyambwe, 2 January 1958, AAT 325.298.

[73] Letter from catechists of Tabora, Ndonno, and Upuge to Achbishop Mihayo, 21 February 1961, AAT 325.298.

[74] Ibid. In formulating these arguments about 'subaltern voices' and 'weapons of the weak', I am indebted to the work of Ranajit Guha and Gayatri C. Spivak (eds), *Selected Subaltern Studies* (New York: Oxford University Press, 1988), and James C. Scott, *Weapons of the Weak: Everyday Forms of Peasant Resistance* (New Haven, CT: Yale University Press, 1985).

[75] Mgomo wa Makatekista dhidi ya Askofu na Mapadri, Ndala, 20 February 1961, AAT 325.298. In Kiswahili, 'Arkiaskofu ametutupa ... hatuko watumishi wake wala mapadri ... kumbe tuko huru kufanya tutakavyo'.

[76] Mgomo wa Makatekista, 20 February 1961, AAT 325.298.

CATECHISTS, WOMEN, AND DISSENT IN VILLAGES BEYOND THE CATHOLIC MISSIONS 143

Dissent crystalized in the village outstations of Kahama mission as cat-echists expressed their opposition to the policies of the church authorities. They called for priests to gather and teach congregants 'without assistance from village catechists'. At the Igalula outstation, the catechist-in-chief called for 'democracy' and freedom for catechists to make decisions and act in the best interests of their congregations, without priestly meddling.[77] Catechists' demands reflect the asymmetrical relationship they had with priests and church authorities and their marginal position within the church hierarchy. Despite being the primary agents for spreading Christian culture beyond the missions, catechists remained duty-bound to abide by church authority in undertaking pastoral work in their villages. Relations of this sort, coupled with a demanding schedule, work discipline, and manual labour in missions and village outstations, culminated in catechists' complaints that 'they were being treated like schoolboys' and 'slaves'.[78]

Many catechists felt offended by their mistreatment and abandoned their pastoral work. They joined with labourers migrating into towns, mining cen-tres, and coastal plantations of Unyamwezi, where there was the potential to earn cash and regain respectability.[79] At the Ushetu mission, three catechists gave up their jobs. At the Ndala mission, one catechist working in the out-station permanently abandoned his work and left for the Mwadui gold mine (Williamson's gold mine) in search of decent wages to provide for his family. Another catechist at Sikonge lost his passion for the job, and no one volun-teered to replace him.[80] The fact that there was no replacement suggests that the villagers understood the plight of the catechists and that no younger mem-bers would consider taking the job. Although the available primary sources do not relate to the fate of the catechist at Sikonge, the problem clearly persisted for quite some time. It also suggests that the networks catechists created at Ndala helped communicate their discontent to the villagers, who found it nec-essary to prevent the young from becoming catechists.[81]

---

[77] Ibid.

[78] Ndala, 31 July 1960, AAT 325.298; Fr Anthony Nyambwe, Results of the Parish Priests Meeting, 8–9 February 1968, AAT 325.298.

[79] For discussion of honour in Unyamwezi, see Michelle R. Moyd, *Violent Inter-mediaries: African Soldiers, Conquest, and Everyday Colonialism in German East Africa* (Athens: Ohio University Press, 2014), 65; and John Iliffe, *Honour in African History* (Cambridge: Cambridge University Press, 2005), 281.

[80] Fr Mirambo to Fr Nyambwe, 2 January 1958, AAT 325.298; letter of catechists, 21 February 1961, AAT 325.298; Fr Peter Dalali, Lukula Parish, 16 July 1962, AAT 325.298.

[81] Fr Peter Dalali, Lukula Parish, 16 July 1962, AAT 325.298.

144 SLAVE EMANCIPATION, CHRISTIAN COMMUNITIES, AND DISSENT IN TANZANIA

Catechists' withdrawal from pastoral work had a noticeable impact on the growth of Christianity in Unyamwezi; in their absence, village believers, children, and catechumens attending religious instruction remained at a standstill. At Ndala, dissenting catechists significantly affected the catechist school's turnover because they discouraged aspiring young men from joining the school. J.B. Cuivrier, working at the Ndala catechist school, complained that problems began to surface only five days after his appointment. The main problem, grumbled Cuivrier, was that '[he] had no students ... only seven had applied'.[82] He toured other parishes looking for students but hardly got one. The young men Cuivrier approached to join the school aspired to live a decent life and demanded a salary. He resorted to travelling to Kahama – an area peripheral to Ndala – hoping to get pupils, but his efforts yielded no substantial results. Catechists' dissenting voices against church authority in Kahama accounted for the declining interest among the young in joining the catechists' school. It is also plausible to suggest that the catechists' resolutions against inequality and unfair treatment made at the meeting of Kahama had an impact on Cuivrier's disappointing results in the area.[83]

The diminishing number of student catechists at Ndala School and the catechists' abandonment of villages forced the clergy to reconsider monthly salaries as a strategy for retaining catechists in the villages. Nevertheless, the decision to remunerate catechists aroused controversy between the White Fathers and Nyamwezi clergy. The White Fathers thought that catechists should be paid a salary and receive other remunerations through donations from Europe, arguing that catechists' busy work schedules rendered them incapable of cultivating the land like other villagers. The White Fathers' insistence on subsidizing catechists encouraged a few mission stations, Ndala, Itaga, Tabora, and Mbulu (Kahama), to pay catechists a salary.[84] Conversely, Nyamwezi priests held to the principle of self-reliance. They held a strong conviction that catechists should not be overworked like 'slaves', but instead, 'they should be taught to become self-reliant' by cultivating the fields allocated to them.[85] Nyamwezi priests, therefore, objected to the idea of offering benefits to some catechists, as such favouritism 'aroused terrific envy among

---

[82] Fr J.B. Cuivrier to Archbishop Mihayo, Ndala, 22 October 1967, AAT 325.298.

[83] Ibid.; Mgomo wa Makatekista, 20 February 1961, AAT 325.298.

[84] Fr J.B. Cuivrier to Fr Maguire, Ndala mission, 26 August 1970, AAT 325.298; letter to Archbishop Mihayo, Ndala, 20 October 1969, AAT 325.298; Fr Anthony Nyambwe to Archbishop Mihayo, 19 March 1968, AAT 325.298.

[85] Fr Anthony Nyambwe: Results of the Parish Priests Meeting, 8–9 February 1968, AAT 325.298; Fr Anthony Nyambwe to Archbishop Mihayo, 19 March 1968, AAT 325.298.

CATECHISTS, WOMEN, AND DISSENT IN VILLAGES BEYOND THE CATHOLIC MISSIONS   145

the rest … [and would] cause harm to the parish[es]'.[86] The Nyamwezi priests' emphasis on self-reliance corresponded to the ideals of *ujamaa*, villagization, and rural development initiatives that filtered into rural Unyamwezi in the 1960s and called for people to 'stop begging' and instead work hard to build a 'socialist Tanzania through [their] own sweat'.[87]

Divisions were evident in 1960s Unyamwezi and Tanzania at large because the Catholic Church did not support *ujamaa* wholeheartedly, and in some parts of the country, Catholics were hostile to *ujamaa*. The basis for Catholic opposition to Nyerere's *ujamaa* policy after 1970 was three-fold: first, it threatened the missionaries' privileges; second, it inspired fear of losing their ideological influence; and third, *ujamaa* could open the doors for Marxism and Communism to penetrate the country.[88] At the same time, Julius Kambarage Nyerere and Tanganyika National Union (TANU) national-ist leaders envisioned Tanzania as a secular state in which, under *ujamaa*, citizens were bound to fulfil their obligations to the society. Under secularism, the government attached no importance to the numerical strength of any sect or religious community, nor did it submit to religious communities' demands irrespective of their influence.[89]

Although the state and the ruling party did not favour any religion, they fully guaranteed and respected the right and freedom of people to follow the religion that best fit their aspirations.[90] In his speech to the interreligious seminar held in Tabora, Nyerere recognized that while neither the country nor TANU had a religion, many people were undoubtedly religious. He said, 'our country does not have religion [but] our people have religion. Some do have, and others do not have [religion] … I am Catholic, but it neither belongs to Tanzanians nor the government nor CCM [Chama Cha Mapinduzi]'.[91] The result of the declaration of Tanzania as a secular state is that it relegated reli-gion to the margins of the preoccupations of government and party leaders.

---

[86] Fr Peter Dalali, Lukula Parish, 16 July 1962, AAT 325.298.

[87] For typical expressions of these ideals, see 'Socialism Depends on Workers', *The Nationalist*, 24 July 1967; 'Sweat Will Build Tanzania: Nyerere Analyses Workers' Role and Responsibility', *The Nationalist*, 28 July 1967.

[88] Issa G. Shivji, *Development as Rebellion: A Biography of Julius Nyerere*, Vol. 3, *Rebellion without Rebels* (Dar es Salaam: Mkuki na Nyota Publishers, 2020), 65–67.

[89] Ibid., 54.

[90] Ibid.

[91] Julius K. Nyerere, 'Nyufa: Mazungumzo ya Mwalimu Julius K. Nyerere Kwenye Klabu ya Waandishi wa Habari wa Tanzania, Hoteli ya Kilimanjaro', Dar es Salaam, 13 March 1995, in Mwalimu Julius Kambarage Nyrere, *Chemchemi ya Fikra za Kimapinduzi* (Dar es Salaam: Mkuki na Nyota, 2022), 401–24.

SLAVE EMANCIPATION, CHRISTIAN COMMUNITIES, AND DISSENT IN TANZANIA

Instead, they were only obliged to tell the people about *ujamaa* and social relations in the country.[92] The government used religious festivals like maulid, eid alFitr, Christmas, and interreligious meetings as integral podia to clarify its attitudes towards religion in the society, to make policy statements, and to seek Muslim and Christian support for its socialist programmes.[93]

Nevertheless, the divisions between the White Fathers and Nyamwezi clergy over support for the catechists resulted in no lasting solution to the problem. Catechists quit for good, leaving village outstations unattended. The increasing number of catechists leaving for towns and elsewhere concerned church authorities enough to address the problem. Ultimately, the archbishop of Tabora, Marko Mihayo, suggested that priests adopt the Moravian model of monthly remunerations (*posho*) for evangelists drawn from monthly tithes (*zaka*) and other contributions. Although the Moravian model appealed to the archbishop as a strategy to deal with the dissenting catechists, he admitted that Catholics would not succeed in using tithes and other contributions because 'paying tithe was not an obligation followed by punishment (*luduko*) to those who failed to pay. It was paid of a person's own volition'.[94]

Furthermore, the agricultural economy depended on reliable rainfall, which made tithe contributions irregular. Thus, making tithe contribution a monthly obligation, the archbishop observed, 'would cause apathy, dissidence, and tension among Catholics'. Eventually, the archbishop preferred ad hoc remunerations – instead of monthly salaries – for catechists who had demonstrated initiative in their work and 'presents' for those the archbishop referred to as 'ordinary catechists'.[95] The archbishop's categorizing of catechists in this way reignited divisions among them and hatred of the clergy. Moreover, the archbishop's policies did little to encourage or assist the work of catechists in the villages, as most catechists occasionally received presents that had little impact on their lives.

Conclusion

Throughout the process of evangelization in western Tanzania, missionaries invariably depicted catechists simply as 'examples of successful mission work' and as 'filial adjunct[s]', which suggested that catechists could not

---

[92] Julius K. Nyerere, 'Ujamaa Tanzania na Dini: Hotuba aliyotoa Rais Julius K. Nyerere siku ya Kufungua Semina ya Viongozi wa Madhehebu mbalimbali ya Dini huko Tabora', Jumatatu, 27 July 1970.

[93] Imtyaz Yusuf, 'Islam and African Socialism: A Study of the Interactions between Islam and Ujamaa Socialism in Tanzania' (PhD thesis, Temple University, 1990).

[94] Archbishop Mihayo to Fr Anthony Nyambwe, 12 March 1968, AAT 325.298.

[95] Ibid.

work as 'self-reliant missionary activists'.[96] These claims about self-reliance, however, were built on false promises and should be regarded with scepticism in scholarly work. The everyday experience of catechists presents a much different picture than the official view that, as Msgr H. Goertz, secretary general of the Pontifical Society for the Propagation of the Faith, argued, the two-year training at Ndala encouraged catechists to become 'priests without ordination'. At the same time, their wives and women at large were said to have acted as 'substitutes for sisters'.[97] Goertz's claims did not develop in a vacuum. Instead, it was in response to the agency that catechists and women exhibited in shaping the development of Christianity in rural Unyamwezi. Thus, the mastery of the local culture and language enabled catechists in the villages of western Tanzania to form 'the basis for the modern intelligentsia'; by becoming 'scripture readers' and translators, they offered religious instruction to the young and adults and presided over Sunday services in the Kinyamwezi language, for which they developed novel expressions, sayings, and proverbs.[98] These methods of evangelization were grounded in Kinyamwezi language and culture and made catechists an important part of the new identity of the literate Christian community (*vasomi*).[99]

In addition to the culturally embedded methods of evangelization, catechists' training inspired them to become 'masters of new ways' because they could read and write and were well versed in their own culture.[100] While mission stations functioned as centres of Christian civilization and cultural 'melting pots', the limited number of missionaries left many villages isolated from missionary work. Thus, catechists filled that void as carriers of culture by administering catechesis, leading believers in Sunday services, and translating religious texts into the Kinyamwezi language. As 'substitutes for sisters', women and wives of catechists demonstrated exemplary leadership and 'attract[ed] more people [in villages] to the Christian faith'.[101] Some women who had never been to school also attended classes in reading and writing to form part of the new identity of the literate Christian community.[102]

---

[96] Richard Hölzl, 'Educating Missions: Teachers and Catechists in Southern Tanganyika, 1890s–1940s', *Itenerario*, Vol. 40, No. 3 (2016), 405; Anita de Luna, 'Evangelizadoras del Barrio: The Rise of the Missionary Catechists of Divine Providence', *U.S. Catholic Historian*, Vol. 21, No. 1 (Winter 2003), 53.

[97] Rt Rev. Msgr H. Goertz, Society for the Propagation of the Faith, to Archbishop Marko Mihayo, 4 July 1962, AAT 325.299.

[98] Peel, *Religious Encounter*, 156–61.

[99] Rt Rev. Msgr H. Goertz to Archbishop Marko Mihayo, 4 July 1962, AAT 325.299.

[100] Nolan, 'Christianity in Unyamwezi', 316.

[101] Mafungo ya Wakatekista, Tabora, 18 February 1979, AAT 325.297.

[102] Nyanto, 'Priests without Ordination', 564.

The growing number of Christians in villages increased the demand for teachers and catechists, and thus some village outstations expanded to become full-fledged mission stations. Continuing grudges over unfair treatment coupled with untenable life in villages and the refusal to pay salaries and other remuneration encouraged catechists to rebel against the church authorities because catechists thought they were being treated like 'slaves'.[103] Indeed, catechists' opposition to unequal treatment affected the progress of Christianity in villages because they abandoned their pastoral work in favour of new opportunities. In no time, villagers in the many outstations found no reason to encourage their sons and daughters to pursue a two-year course at Ndala School. That they persuaded their sons and daughters to refrain from becoming catechists suggests what Jonathon Glassman has referred to as 'consciousness fashioned out of fragments of the hegemonic ideologies which [catechists] had found at hand'.[104]

[103] Fr Anthony Nyambwe, Results of the Parish Priests Meeting, 8–9 February 1968, AAT 325.298.
[104] Jonathan Glassman, 'The Bondsman's New Clothes: The Contradictory Consciousness of Slave Resistance on the Swahili Coast', *Journal of African History*, Vol. 32, No. 2 (1991), 277.

CHAPTER 5

Teachers, Women, and Kinship Networks in Villages beyond the Moravian and Swedish Free Missions, 1930–50s

The development of Christianity in twentieth-century western Tanzania took a new shape under the patronage of Africans working in villages as teachers (*vahembeki*). In the village outstations of the Moravians and Swedish Free Mission, the contribution of African teachers (formerly enslaved people, mission porters, and Nyamwezi men and women) remained evident because of the relatively few European missionaries available to shoulder the mission work in all the villages. By the second decade of the twentieth century, African teachers administered the many churches in villages. In addition to the remarkable contribution of *vahembeki*, the growth of Christianity in twentieth-century Unyamwezi corresponded to the tireless efforts of lay women whose work among women was instrumental in fashioning a new Christian identity and creating spiritual connections. Lay women, too, taught children in Sunday schools, while others accompanied village teachers and launched home-visit campaigns to attract more Nyamwezi women to Christianity. Indeed, the task of the Nyamwezi women had parallels with the 'Bible women' of India because their home visits and administration of Sunday classes to children in village churches contributed to the spread of a Christian culture beyond missions.[1]

This chapter centres on the village outstations of the Moravians and Swedish Free Mission to explore the contribution of African teachers and laywomen to the growth of Christianity beyond mission stations. It seeks to show that with the knowledge of scripture, teachers and lay Nyamwezi women relied on the Protestant tradition of reading and personal interpretation of religious texts and used their ingenuity in 'translating the message'

---

[1] For details about the 'Bible women' of India and their home-visit campaign, see Jeffrey Cox, *Imperial Fault Lines: Christianity and Colonial Power in India, 1818–1940* (Stanford, CA: Stanford University Press, 2002), 105–7.

SLAVE EMANCIPATION, CHRISTIAN COMMUNITIES, AND DISSENT IN TANZANIA

to shape the development of Christianity.[2] In exercising their intellectual ingenuity, teachers established newspapers and festivals as integral podia to encourage congregants to read and share their experiences about scripture and evangelization across villages and as avenues to extend networks of friendship and support among Christians and teachers. The use of festivals to spread Christian culture and draw together a community of believers drew on the existing Nyamwezi culture of the neighbourhood. In the end, the chapter shows that the administration of village outstations and the tradition of reading and interpreting texts in twentieth-century Unyamwezi inspired African teachers and women not only to mount a rebellion against the influence of revivalism but also to develop ideas of self-governance (*kujitawala*) of the church that were to have an impact on the nationwide movement for independence – a topic to be dealt in the next chapter.

Teachers and Women in the Village Outstations

As we saw in Chapter 1, the Moravian missionaries established a chain of mission stations in southern Unyamwezi, in Kitunda, Kipembawe, Ipole, and Sikonge, creating a network that stretched from Lake Victoria to the Nyasa Province.[3] Subsequently, Moravian village outstations (*sinagogo*) developed on the periphery of southern Unyamwezi at some distance from Tabora town, from which it took days to reach them. For instance, it took about four days to walk on foot from Tabora town to the Sikonge mission and its surrounding village outstations. The distance from Tabora town to the Kitunda mission and its nearby village outstations took about six days. It was apparent that the distance from Tabora town to these two missions and village outstations required resident African teachers to manage the services in the villages, which the few European missionaries staying in missions could only rarely visit.[4] The exception was the village outstations of the Usoke mission,

---

[2] Lamin Sanneh, *Translating the Message: The Missionary Impact on Culture* (Maryknoll, NY: Orbis Books, 2009), 51.

[3] Aylward E.M. Shorter, 'Ukimbu and the Kimbu Chiefdoms of Southern Unyamwezi, the History and Present Pattern of Kimbu Social Organisation and Movement' (n.d.), WFA 11-03; Teofilo H. Kisanji, *Historia Fupi ya Kanisa la Kimoravian Tanganyika Magharibi* (Kipalapala: TMP, 1980), 37; J. Taylor Hamilton and Kenneth G. Hamilton, *History of the Moravian Church: The Renewed Unitas Fratrum, 1722–1957*, 2nd edn (Bethlehem, PA: Interprovincial Board of Christian Education, Moravian Church of America, 1983), 611; and Angetile Y. Musomba, *The Moravian Church in Tanzania Southern Province: A Short History* (Nairobi: IFRA, 2005), 85.

[4] Kisanji, *Historia Fupi*, 37.

where people lived along the central railway line that ran from the coast to Kigoma and along the main road from Tabora to Kigoma, making it easy for African teachers working in the villages to move between the Usoke mission and Tabora town.[5]

The dilemmas increased in the 1930s following the Great Depression, which caused uncertainties in life, unemployment, and low wages and made life in rural areas untenable. In Unyamwezi, many men who were used to working for a wage remained idle at home, and farmers sold their crops at reduced prices. As a result, there was a decline in the export of groundnuts, rice, sesame, cassava, maize, and other grains. Agricultural production further declined owing to the outbreak of the Second World War, which affected production and presented a more formidable challenge to the export of crops.[6] In addition to the economic difficulties of wartime, rinderpest broke out in the districts of Unyamwezi, the export of cattle was barred, and quarantine restrictions 'killed all prospect of cattle profit'.[7] Locusts were 'swarming over the country in numbers never known before', and prolonged drought continued to affect various parts of Unyamwezi.[8]

In addition to the economic difficulties, the prevalence of sleeping sickness (trypanosomiasis) in southern Unyamwezi forced people to abandon the affected villages. The displaced population moved into five concentrations to combat the disease (see Figure 10): 742 people moved into Ubagwe, 991 to Ushetu, 973 Ukumbi, 492 to Urambo, and 800 to Usagari. Other groups amounted to 450 in Usoke, 313 in Igalula, 271 in Morogoro (Sikonge), and 2,000 in Nyonga. Patients in the Tabora district received treatment at the sleeping sickness dispensaries of Urambo, Ushetu, Nzindalo, and Mambali, and the Moravian mission also administered treatment at the mission hospitals of Sikonge, Ipole, and Usoke.[9] The establishment of population concentrations

---

[5] Ibid., 52.

[6] Tabora District Book, Volume I, 'Movement of Produce by Rail in Tabora District in Tons, 1929–1943', TNA.

[7] F.J. Bagshawe, Esq., MBE, Provincial Commissioner, Western Province-Tanganyika Territory, Annual Reports for the Provincial Commissioners on Native Administration for the Year 1932, 63, UDSM EAF.

[8] H.C. Stiebel, Esq., OBE, Provincial Commissioner, Tabora Province-Tanganyika Territory, Annual Reports for the Provincial Commissioners on Native Administration for the Year 1931, 70, UDSM EAF. For general effects of the Great Depression in Tanganyika, see Report from the Governor's Deputy, Tanganyika Territory, 21 August 1934, UKNA CO 323/1257/9; 'Domestic Slavery in Tanganyika', Response to Maxwell's Memorandum, 10 August 1935, UKNA CO 323/1320/7 [Colonial No. 1901].

[9] 'Sleeping Sickness-Tabora (including Kitunda)', Tabora District Book, 1927 & 1929, TNA. For further details about the Moravian involvement in the treatment

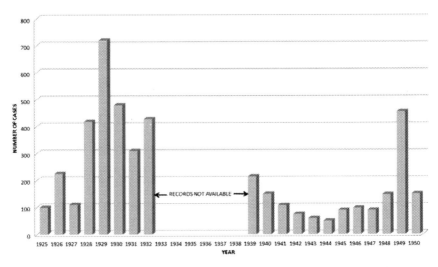

Figure 10 Incidence of Sleeping Sickness in Tabora District, c.1925–50.

proved successful in containing the spread of sleeping sickness in the region, and in only two years, between 1952 and 1954, reported cases from Kaliua, Ussoke, Usinge, Kitunda, Uyowa, Nguruka, Ibiri, and Mambali declined from 286 to 182.[10]

The persistence of trypanosomiasis and the consequent relocation of people halted the progress of Christianity and meant that those village churches that had gained momentum before the outbreak were doomed to collapse as people relocated to new areas and faced new challenges in building Christian communities.[11] We learn that the increasing cases of trypanosomiasis forced villagers to abandon the sleeping sickness-affected areas of the western parts of the Ugunda territory. Consequently, the people were moved to new settlements near Usoke called 'Tabora-Mpya' or 'Kakola II'. In response to the new settlements, the Moravian Church moved Paulo Kwiyamba Kolokoloni from Nsogolo village to these new villages. Later, Lotto Tandu joined Kolokoloni to work as a teacher. Eventually, the outstation they established to serve Tabora-Mpya, and Kakola II became one of the largest villages of the Moravian mission of Usoke. Before resettlement, the area occupied by the new mission had a substantial Muslim population. They appear to have

of sleeping sickness at Sikonge mission hospital, see H.C. Baxter, 'Medical Facilities', Tabora District Book, March 1938.

[10] Settlement Officer, Nguruka, to the Provincial Commissioner, Western Province, 29 September 1955, TNA 63/P4/66/Vol. IV/701.

[11] Francis P. Nolan, 'Christianity in Unyamwezi, 1878–1928' (PhD thesis, University of Cambridge, 1977), 306–8.

opposed the establishment of Christian missions because, as Teofilo Kisanji would later describe it, the area was 'hard soil' ('udongo mgumu'), implying that Christianity would not easily flourish there.[12] Of course, the conflict may not have been primarily about religion. After all, these Muslims were having their land taken away by the colonial state.

Sleeping sickness further forced the chiefly lineage to abandon the old headquarters of Mirambo at Iselamagazi. At the same time, people abandoned the villages, with young men seeking new opportunities in towns to make ends meet.[13] However, in the neighbouring territory of Usene, where there were no tsetse flies, people remained in their villages. In this territory, Nyamwezi farmers could keep cattle. The area also had the advantage of being on the road between Ujiji and the westernmost of Mirambo's towns. These villages thrived as they attracted many former residents of the abandoned villages that the Urambo mission had served.[14] In the 1940s, following reported cases of sleeping sickness, people in the outlying villages of the Moravian mission of Kitunda moved to 'safer areas' for resettlement in new villages.[15] As a consequence, villages grew because they attracted residents from abandoned villages that the Kitunda mission had formerly served. Indeed, the number of Christians in the Kitunda mission increased between 1931 and 1950, implying that sleeping sickness had no noticeable impact on that mission and its outlying villages and that people chose to remain.[16] The depopulation of villages and compulsory resettlement influenced Christians to relocate to other village outstations. Christians joined churches in the resettled villages and carried the ethos of the Christian community from their old missions and villages. The growing number of Christians increased the need for 'village teachers' (*bahembeki/vahembeki*).[17] As Christians established new village churches, they also sought ways of prospering and strengthening Christian communities to make them independent from chiefly control.[18]

The devastating impact of trypanosomiasis in Unyamwezi coincided with famine, affecting people in rural Unyamwezi – at Igalula, Uyowa, Ussoke, and Ussinge. People reported a shortage of rainfall between 1953 and 1958,

---

[12] Kisanji, *Historia Fupi*, 144.

[13] Ibid.

[14] E. Southon to Mr Whitehouse, Urambo, 29 November 1880, CWM/LMS/Box 3/ Folder 3.

[15] Kisanji, *Historia Fupi*, 222.

[16] *Bestand der Gemeinen in der Missionsprovinz* (Statistics of the Mission in Unyamwezi, 1931–1950), KFC.

[17] See, for instance, Kisanji, *Historia Fupi*, 30–44.

[18] 'Kuchukia ni kubaya, tutasimangwa kwa Mungu', *Lusangi*, No. 32, August 1938, KFC.

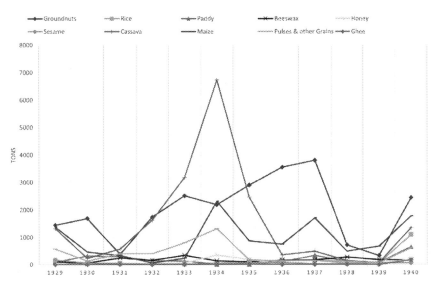

Figure 11 Movement of Produce by Rail in Tabora District in Tons, 1929–40.

culminating in poor harvests and famine.[19] The district authority prohibited people from removing food from the district and embarked on agricultural campaigns to remedy the effects of famine. However, villagers opposed it because of poor harvests and unpredictable rainfall. At Igalula in the chiefdom of Unyanyembe, the council (*baraza*) arrested seven villagers, accusing them of inducing others to refrain from the district authority's agricultural campaign (*kuwakataza kulima*).[20] Despite the state's response to dissidence in the villages, these actions demonstrated that people were not passive recipients of the policies imposed by the district authority. Many villagers who had attended mission schools could read and write and challenged state policies that did not consider the realities in the villages. In 1958, following increased dissent in the villages, the produce market declined considerably in Unyamwezi, forcing the district authority to close village markets to induce people to retain food supply (see Table 8 and Figure 11).[21]

[19] Barua ya Mtemi wa Uyui kwa District Commissioner, Tabora, 22 March 1958, TNA 47/A3/3/86; 'Barua ya District Commissioner kwa Mtemi N.S. Fundikira II', 8 January 1954, TNA 47/A3/9/245; 'Barua ya District Commissioner kwa Mkubwa wa Baraza la Ussoke', 19 November 1953, TNA 47/A3/9/248.

[20] 'Barua kutoka kwa Swetu Mshama, Mkubwa wa Baraza la Igalula, kwa Bwana District Commissioner wa Tabora', 12 January 1956, TNA 47/A3/3/74; 'Barua ya Swetu Mshama kwa Bwana District Commissioner wa Tabora', 4 January 1956, TNA 47/A3/3/71.

[21] 'Barua ya Agriculture Field Officer kwa Mabaraza yote ya Wilaya ya Tabora', 6 October 1958, TNA 47/A3/6/49.

Table 8 Movement of Produce by Rail in Tabora District in Tons, 1929–40.

PRODUCE	1929	1930	1931	1932	1933	1934	1935	1936	1937	1938	1939	1940
Groundnuts	1447	1690	383	1741	2514	2187	2901	3556	3805	723	332	2445
Rice	50	32	37	37	13	52	122	163	146	53	47	1097
Paddy	92	318	297	143	127	14	11	103	337	111	77	653
Beeswax	104	55	247	159	344	138	99	157	175	275	180	172
Honey	52	9	16	50	59	–	187[*]	27[*]	25[*]	18[*]	6[*]	208
Sesame	171	56	47	14	21	22	64	77	28	29	69	63
Cassava	1322	226	580	1629	3178	6735	2466	354	489	143	72	1351
Maize	1375	463	339	62	235	2314	875	751	1705	488	675	1778
Pulses and other Grains	573	132	396	404	804	1315	180	129	152	116	66	612
Ghee	–	–	–	–	7	10	20[*]	–	–	2[*]	2[*]	175
TOTAL	**5184**	**2981**	**2342**	**4239**	**7296**	**12787**	**7671**	**6044**	**7993**	**2213**	**1806**	**8554**

[*] Figures include Bukene and Isaka railway stations.

Source: Tabora District Book, Volume I, TNA. Note there was a sharp decline in the export of groundnuts, rice, sesame, cassava, maize, and other grains between 1929 and 1933 owing to the Great Depression and in the leadup to the outbreak of the Second World War in 1938–39.

Naming, Slave Antecedents, and the Creation of Christian Communities in Villages, 1930–50

The effects of slavery on formerly enslaved people and their descendants varied depending on the culture and society with which they were brought into contact in post-abolition Unyamwezi. By and large, formerly enslaved people remained ashamed of talking about their slave past. For former slaves who had earned positions in society, even mentioning their slave past could undermine their social standing.[22] Formerly enslaved people and their descendants risked losing freedom of expression, friends, kinship ties, and identity, and would be shunned even by members of their kin who wanted to distance themselves from the stigma of slavery.[23] Furthermore, the open contempt (*dharau*) and mockery created a feeling of inferiority among formerly enslaved people, who were perceived as 'weak'(*wanyonge*) and 'worthless' (*wasiokuwa na msaada*) and whose 'skulls of slavery' (*makovu ya utaumwa*) made it difficult for them to be reintegrated into Unyamwezi society.[24]

Some slaves in the Moravian missions and village outstations resorted to travelling to outlying villages where they were completely unknown in order 'to hide shame' (*kuficha aibu*). Moving to new villages, slaves believed, would automatically bring the dilemmas and anxieties of the slave past to a virtual halt.[25] However, others struggled for social recognition and incorporation into Unyamwezi societies in which they had been previously enslaved. The list of names of adult men and women who converted to Christianity in the missions and village outstations of Moravians between 1908 and 1934 provides insights into the various strategies employed by former slaves to rid themselves of the shame of their past in post-slavery Unyamwezi society (see Table 9). Birth names (commonly called *majina ya uji*) were context-based, providing clues into how shame translated into the names of formerly enslaved people. Names such as Mukombe (messenger or carrier of message) were prevalent among the formerly enslaved to challenge the negative connotations, contempt, and intimidation rooted in the society regarding slavery.[26] As we have seen in Chapter 4, in Unyamwezi society, *vakombe* or *bakombe* carried messages of the chief about war, drought, invasions, chiefly meetings,

---

[22] Interview with Paulo Mteba and Selemani Hamadi, Simbo village, 20 October 2021. See also Marc J. Schwartz, 'Shame, Culture, and Status among the Swahili of Mombasa', *Ethos*, Vol. 16, No. 1 (1988), 24.

[23] Interview with Ashura Fumbo Kambimbaya, Simbo village, 18 October 2021.

[24] Interview with Paulo Mteba and Selemani Hamadi, Simbo village, 20 October 2021.

[25] Interview with Elly Makenge, October 2019.

[26] Listi ya Vakristo Vahanya, Kanisa ya Sikonge Main Station III, entry 1433, 1944, KFC.

or any other important event that required the people's attention. Thus, adopting the name *mukombe* was a way of mitigating social uneasiness about slavery.[27] Some slaves, however, struggled for social recognition by adopting the name 'safisha' in response to the dominant discourses of slavery and post-slavery experiences.[28] The name Safisha was derived from the Kinyamwezi *kutema* to mean initiators of new settlements in Unyamwezi. Like new chiefs (*vatemi*), the formerly enslaved people cleared the brush, founded settlements, and bound communities together by maintaining robust networks of friendship, support, and social solidarity.

For some slaves, associating themselves with the chiefly line and other influential people was a way to disguise and overcome shame. Because chiefs commanded respect from the people, former slaves aspired to be part of their families. By adopting the birth name Munywasele on the register, for example, slaves could hide their shame by association with name of a chief in Unyamwezi. The name Munywasele, adopted by Yohana Masesa, shows that he took the name of the Unyamwezi chief, Mnwasele, to mask his slave past and connect himself to the chiefly line. In this way, Masesa became part of the chiefdom and could command society's respect. He had become part of the family of Mtemi Mnwasele.[29]

Some slaves adopted the names of prominent traders in Unyamwezi as they wrestled against the binaries imposed by the European 'civilizing mission'. In assuming names like Mulungwana or Kalungwana ('civilized'), as in the cases of Rode and Leonard Mumanywa, former slaves struggled for recognition by signalling cultural and economic status in society. The names suggest that the two former slaves adopted them to distinguish themselves from *vasenzi* ('uncivilized').[30] We have seen that in Unyamwezi, the term *valungwana* ('the civilized') was initially used to mean accumulating enough wealth to establish oneself as an independent trader, to gain the ability to marry, acquire livestock, or purchase slaves to work in one's household.[31] Hence, as porterage took hold in Unyamwezi, an occupational group, the *vandeva* (sing. *mundeva*), emerged as the 'civilized' or free gentlemen (*valungwana*), whose wealth provided them with a new source of social status and power.

---

[27] Interview with Oscar E. Kisanji, Tabora, 19 June 2017.

[28] Listi ya Vakristo Vahanya, Kanisa ya Sikonge Main Station III, entry 1433, 1944, KFC; List ya Vakristo Vahanya, Kanisa ya Mazinge, Sikonge, 1944, KFC.

[29] Listi ya Vakristo Vahanya, Kanisa ya Sikonge Main Station III, entry 1753, 1944, KFC.

[30] Listi ya Vakristo Vahanya, Kanisa ya Ulilwansimba, Sikonge, No. 3, 1944; Listi ya Vakristo Vahanya, Kanisa ya Ulilwansimva, No. I, 1944, KFC.

[31] Michelle R. Moyd, *Violent Intermediaries: African Soldiers, Conquest, and Everyday Colonialism in German East Africa* (Athens: Ohio University Press, 2014), 65.

Table 9 Names, Shame, and Slave Antecedents in Mission Registers, *c*.1937–44.

Entry	Names	Adopted Name	Meaning	Station	Baptismal Year
1433	Mose Mukombe	Mukombe	Messenger, carrier of chiefly message, an influential person in the society.	Sikonge Main Station III	1943
1753	Yohana Masesa Mnywasele	Mnywasele	Name of the chief of Unyamwezi, an influential leader in Unyanyembe.	Sikonge Main Station III	1943
240	Salome Tulikuvangi Matingabuli	Tulikuvangi	We live in a foreign land Suggests a slave who lived in Unyamwezi.	Sikonge Main Station IX	1943
413	Serebia Kalekwa	Kalekwa	Abandoned, orphan parents enslaved.	Kipanga I	1943
1496	Samweli Mukombe Safisha	Mukombe Safisha	Mukombe: Messenger, Safisha: One who clears bushes for settlements.	Mazinge, Sikonge	1938 (?)
2117	Rode Mpasa Kalungwana	Kalungwana	Civilized, exposed to coastal culture, wealth, and influence.	Ulilwansimba	1942
108	Samson Kamwelwe Msuluzya	Msuluzya	Trader, wealthy, influential in the society.	Ulilwansimba	1943
1977	Elisabeth Muzumya	Muzumya	One who accepts everything, including slave status.	Ulilwansimba	1943
527	Helena Nsimbo Muzumya	Muzumya	One who accepts everything, including slave status.	Vutyatya	1941
711	Lukasi Mufwalila Muzumya	Muzumya	One who accepts everything, including slave status.	Vutyatya, Sikonge	1944
508	Tomas Mayila s/o Eli Maganga Mayila	Mayila	Mayila: roads An influential trader who constantly moves between the interior and the coast. Wealthy trader in nineteenth- and twentieth-century Unyamwezi	Sikonge	1936

537	Zebedayo Kalungwana s/o Yakobo Kalembe Kalungwana	Kalungwana	Civilized, wealthy, powerful individual in the society.	Ilunga	1932
882	Dorothea Kalunde d/o Salomo Mwarabu	Mwarabu	She adopted the name Kalunde because she was a daughter of a formerly enslaved person. Her father adopted the name of his owner – Mwarabu, to earn respect.	Ilunga	1941
826	Neli Sizya s/o Marko Mwarabu	Mwarabu	The owner's name (Mwarabu) was adopted to earn respect and hide his slave antecedent.	Mukola	1940
841	Neli Sizya s/o Silas Barabara	Barabara	Like Mayila.	Mivono	1941
597	Yoas Muyema	Munyema	Munyema: suggests slave's origin (Manyema region in eastern Congo).		1937
nil	Hilda Kalekwa	Kalekwa	Orphan, abandoned.	Mivono	1937
1672	Petro Mulekwa	Mulekwa	Orphan, abandoned.	Igigwa	1939
1216	Sisilia Nzala	Nzala	Hunger. Enslaved owing to hunger and destitution.	Kipanga	1942
1137	Terese Kalekwa	Kalekwa	Orphan, abandoned.	Ulilwansimba	1938
2002	Maria Kalekwa	Kalekwa	Orphan, abandoned.	Kisanga	1942
1111	Herman Kafwimbe Kalungwana	Kalungwana	Civilized, wealthy, powerful individual in the society.	Sikonge	1944

Source: Compiled from '*Listi ya Vakristo Vahanya*' and '*Listi ya Vana Vakristo*' (Moravian Missions and Village Outstations, 1937–44) KFC.

160 SLAVE EMANCIPATION, CHRISTIAN COMMUNITIES, AND DISSENT IN TANZANIA

They had a well-connected network of elite and rich families, familiarity with Islam, the ability to speak Kiswahili, exposure to the coast and urban life, and the means to own slaves. By contrast, those who had not gone to the coast and who could communicate more in Kinyamwezi than in Kiswahili were often called 'savages' or 'barbarians' (*vasenzi*).[32] Because porterage was the source of power, wealth, and influence in Unyamwezi, it was common to find slaves in the village outstations taking names like Mayila ('roads'), Msuluzya ('trader'), Barabara ('road'), and Mulungwana, or Kalungwana ('civilized') to signal their aspiration to become 'big men' in Unyamwezi society.[33] Their new names also echoed those of nineteenth-century caravan porters and wealthy individuals who accumulated wealth, power, and influence through long-distance trade between the interior and the coast.[34]

In some villages, some of the formerly enslaved resorted to taking the names of their former owners to be assimilated into the post-slavery community. Because slave owners enjoyed socioeconomic positions in society, slaves believed that by embracing their names they would also ascend the social hierarchy. By contrast, children of former slaves dropped the names, trying to undo the strategy their parents had used to achieve social recognition. For their children and descendants, this naming strategy had become a liability. The name Mwarabu, appearing in the birth record entries of Dorothea Kalunde and Neli Sizya, suggests, first, that their parents, Salomo Mwarabu and Marko Mwarabu, were former slaves of an Arab slave owner and that Salomo and Marko adopted the name of their owners to earn social recognition.[35] Second, its absence in the names of Dorothea and Neli suggests

[32] Alfred Chukwudi Unomah, 'Economic Expansion and Political Change in Unyanyembe, c. 1840–1900' (PhD thesis, University of Ibadan, 1972), iv and 75; Stephen J. Rockel, 'Slavery and Freedom in Nineteenth Century East Africa: The Case of Waungwana Caravan Porters', *African Studies*, Vol. 68, No. 1 (April 2009), 88; John Iliffe, *A Modern History of Tanganyika* (Cambridge: Cambridge University Press, 1979), 64–74.

[33] Listi ya Vana Vakristo Kanisa ya Sikonge, entry 508, 1941, KFC; Listi ya Vana Vakristo, Kanisa ya Mivono, entry 841, 1941, KFC; Listi ya Vakristo Vahanya, Kanisa ya Ulilwansimba, listi no. 1, 1944, KFC; Listi ya Vakristo Vahanya, Kanisa ya Ulilwansimba, No. 1, entry 108, 1944, KFC; Listi ya Vana Vakristo, Kanisa ya Ilunga, entry 537, 1941, KFC; Moyd, *Violent Intermediaries*, 64–65.

[34] Listi ya Vana Vakristo, Kanisa ya Sikonge, 1941, KFC. See also Unomah, 'Economic Expansion', 75, Stephen J. Rockel, *Carriers of Culture: Labor on the Road in Nineteenth-Century East Africa* (Portsmouth, NH: Heinemann, 2006), 231.

[35] Listi ya Vana Vakristo, Kanisa ya Ilunga, entry 882, 1941, KFC; Listi ya Vana Vakristo, Kanisa ya Mukola, entry 826, 1940, KFC; Listi ya Vana Vakristo, Kanisa ya Mukola, entry 826, KFC.

that in Unyamwezi society, the name Mwarabu marked them as descendants of the formerly enslaved. To avoid shame, they omitted the name as soon as they joined the Moravian missions. The omission shows the effects of slavery across generations in western Tanzania in the post-slavery era, and how the naming strategies of formerly enslaved parents could attach the stigma of slavery to their descendants who then did all they could to disguise it.

For slaves who converted to Christianity, adopting new names meant embracing the new culture and civilization they encountered (*ustaarabu*). Vexed by the binaries and contempt, slaves in the village outstations stopped using their birth names, especially 'Mlekwa' or 'Kalekwa', in favour of Christian names such as 'Elisabeth', 'Elia', 'Sisilia', 'Eva', and 'Ema' to mention just a few examples.[36] The omission of the name of the male parent (*lina ise*), as was the norm in Nyamwezi naming tradition, suggests that slaves who had initially been called Kalekwa or Mlekwa were previously unfree dependents. Of course, society regarded slaves as orphans, thereby isolating them from parents and relatives and leaving them with virtually no ability to own or inherit property. Deprived of access to property, land, and ritual, slaves lived in Unyamwezi entirely as unfree dependents and pawns.[37] In dropping names with connotations of having been 'orphaned' or disavowed, former slaves and their descendants sought to counteract the traditional social animosity directed towards slaves. The mission register shows that names like Mugaywa ('one who is hated') and Kugaywa ('to be hated') fell into disuse as slaves converted to Christianity.[38]

While some slaves sought social recognition by adopting names of high-ranking leaders and individuals in Unyamwezi society, others adopted names that signified acceptance of the trauma, intimidation, and contempt embedded in slavery. The name Mzumya ('one who accepts') assigned to Elisabeth

---

[36] See, for instance, Listi ya Vakristo Vahanya, Kanisa ya Ulilwansimba (n.d.), KFC; Listi Listi ya Vakristo Vahanya, Kanisa ya Ulilwansimba, entry 421, 1942, KFC; Listi Listi ya Vakristo Vahanya, Kanisa ya Ulilwansimba, entries 1977 and 1137, 1943, KFC; Listi ya Vakristo Vahanya, Kanisa ya Vutyatya, entry 1419, 1942, KFC; Listi ya Vakristo Vahanya, Kanisa ya Kipanga I, No. I, 1944, KFC; Listi ya Vakristo Vahanya, Kanisa ya Mukolye, Sikonge, No. 2, 1944, KFC.

[37] For details about pawnship in African history, see Juhani Koponen, *People and Production in Late Precolonial Tanzania: History and Structures* (Helsinki: Finnish Society for Development Studies, 1988), and James L. Giblin 'Pawning, Politics and Matriliny in Northeastern Tanzania', in Toyin Falola and Paul Lovejoy (eds), *Pawnship in Africa: Debt Bondage in Historical Perspective* (Boulder, CO: Westview Press, 1994), 43–54.

[38] See, for instance, Listi ya Vakristo Vahanya, Kanisa ya Vutyatya, entry 7, 1943, KFC.

SLAVE EMANCIPATION, CHRISTIAN COMMUNITIES, AND DISSENT IN TANZANIA

Kalekwa, Helena Nsimbo, and Lukasi Mufwalila suggests that while a significant number of slaves in Unyamwezi struggled for social recognition, often using overt and covert strategies, others accepted their slave past and openly demonstrated this through naming.[39] The prevalence of female slaves with the name Mzumya in the baptismal register suggests that women in Unyamwezi were more willing to accept their slave past. Further, Salome's surname, Tulikuvangi ('we are in a foreign land'), implies that she maintained her former slave identity as an enslaved person from the interior who was formerly enslaved in Unyamwezi.[40]

Gender, Patronage, and Kinship Networks in Villages, 1930–50

By 1930, a sizeable number of Nyamwezi and formerly enslaved people had attended mission schools, achieving literacy and numeracy. Some now worked as teachers – and here I use 'teacher' as an umbrella term to mean an 'evangelist' in the Moravian and Swedish Free missions of Unyamwezi. After having worked for years in villages, teachers or evangelists could be ordained 'pastors'. Among the missions where teachers worked was the Swedish Free Mission at Nhazengwa, which opened in 1932.[41] With only two European missionaries, Erland Dahlquist and his wife, Esther, it was apparent that the 'great progress' of the village mission work rested on indigenous teachers.[42] The Nyamwezi teachers of the Swedish Free Mission toured the villages of Ndala, Nyawa, Nkinga, Isanzu, Itanana, Lowa, and Mpela, preaching in Kinyamwezi and singing *mimbo ga bupiji* (praise songs). Villagers were attracted to Christianity because they could hear the songs and the sermons in their native tongues.[43]

---

[39] Listi ya Vakristo Vahanya, Kanisa ya Ulilwansimba, Sikonge, Listi No. 2, entry 1977, 1944, KFC; Listi ya Vakristo Vahanya, Kanisa ya Vutyatya-Sikonge, Listi No 3, entry 527, 1944, KFC; Listi Listi ya Vakristo Vahanya, Kanisa ya Vutyatya-Sikonge, entry 711, 1944, KFC.

[40] Listi ya Vakristo Vahanya, Kanisa ya Sikonge Main Station IX, entry 240, 1944, KFC.

[41] Annual Report, Nzega District for 1933, TNA 967.823; interviews with Rev. Absalom Martin, FPCT Tabora, 21 November 2016, Rev. Paulo Mnangala, Nkinga FPCT, 19 November 2016, and Rev. Samweli Saimoni Mhoja, FPCT Tazengwa (Nhazengwa), 22 November 2016.

[42] Annual Report, Nzega District for 1933, TNA 967.823. The District Commissioner for Nzega District also expressed his concern to the pastor in charge that his limited knowledge of Kisukuma would limit the progress of his mission work. The dominant dialect in northern Unyamwezi is Kisukuma.

[43] Annual Report, Nzega District for 1950, TNA 967.823; Daft Annual Report for

Some Nyamwezi women of the Swedish Free Mission taught children in Sunday schools, while others worked as domestic workers for the missions. Raheli Musa Sengerema is an example of a female domestic servant who later became a Sunday school teacher. She initially worked in domestic service at the Nhazengwa mission, mostly caring for children at the missionary's home. But Raheli's experience as a domestic worker led her to advance to teaching catechumens and children in Sunday school. She recalled: 'I taught children prayer, singing, and reading the Bible passages by heart.'[44] Raheli's engagement in teaching was typical of the African women who helped consolidate and grow African Christianity.

In addition to domestic duties, Nyamwezi women in the Swedish Free Mission accompanied teachers to villages, often walking long distances from the Nhazengwa mission. On their way, they sang *mimbo ga bupiji* and preached in Kinyamwezi to the Isanzu, Tazengwa, Itanana, and Mpela residents. The teachers, including Harris Kapiga, organized home visits and offered sermons in villages.[45] But it was the women accompanying Kapiga who launched a campaign of home visits, offering clothes and other gifts to attract more women to Christianity.[46] The experiences of these village women indicate how being Christian enabled women not only to forge a new identity but also to enlarge the new Christian community by incorporating non-Christian women, including formerly enslaved people and other marginalized women.

Women also played a key role in extending Christianity by accompanying male Moravian African teachers when they visited villages to preach to the people. Each mission opened centres in villages where Christians and teachers would meet; these grew into village outstations, with the village Christians (*wananchi*) building outstation churches. The Moravian outstations remained under the guardianship of village teachers, commonly referred to as *vahembeki* or *bahembeki*.[47] These 'village teachers' had a basic knowledge of the scripture, which they learned before being sent to work in villages. At the

---

1955, TNA 967.823; interviews with Rev. Julius Kulwa Msubi, FPCT/SFM, Tazengwa, 23 November 2016, Rev. Azori Mapolu Fumbuka and Raheli Sengerema, FPCT, Ilolangulu, 21 November 2016, and Rev. Jonas Kulwa Msubi, FPCT, Tazengwa, 23 November 2016.

[44] Interview with Raheli Musa Sengerema, Ilolangulu, Tabora, 21 November 2016. In Kiswahili, 'niliwafundisha watoto kuomba, kuimba, kusoma Biblia, na kusoma aya kwa moyo'.

[45] Interview with Jonas Kulwa Msubi, Nhazengwa, FPCT/SFM, 23 November 2016.

[46] Interviews with Samweli Saimon Mhoja, Nhazengwa, 22 November 2016, and Jonas Kulwa Msubi, Nhazengwa, 23 November 2016.

[47] Kisanji, *Historia Fupi*, 73–74.

Moravian mission station of Urambo Kilimani, village teachers attended a course on scripture for a few weeks before they could work in villages. The training was intended to widen their scriptural knowledge and make them effective preachers.[48]

In addition to these women's creativity, the newspaper *Lusangi* became a platform for Moravian teachers to share their personal experiences of the progress of mission work in 1930s Unyamwezi. Contributors were mostly teachers in Moravian village outstations. Their language was simple, relying on everyday proverbs, sayings, and short stories. The newspaper was mostly read during religious sessions on Sundays or in the homes of catechumens and teachers.[49] The articles covered polygamy, adultery, concubinage, and problems caused by beer drinking and brewing – all central concerns African teachers addressed as they worked with villagers.[50]

Many Nyamwezi Christians found it hard to abide by monogamy because it deviated from the culture of 'big men' in Unyamwezi society, which carried power and prestige. As noted in previous chapters, becoming a 'big man' or respectable person in Unyamwezi meant among others the ability to accumulate wealth to marry, acquire livestock, and purchase slaves to work domestically or in the fields.[51] In Unyamwezi culture, as in many African cultures, large families with co-wives were sources of increased income and prestige.[52] It is no wonder that many Nyamwezi Christian men were accused of adultery and that some were excommunicated (*luduko*) from the mission churches and village outstations because it was difficult to ignore the culture in which they had been raised.[53] The increasing complaints reported in the *Lusangi* newsletter came from teachers worried about marriage conflicts arising from

[48] Ibid., 74.

[49] *Lusangi*, No. 33, September 1938, KFC. A Danish Moravian missionary, Frits Larsen, referred to African teachers as 'vandugu vane' ('my brethren') to differentiate them from others because they could read and write.

[50] See, for instance, Charles Pyagu, Igwamanoni, 'Kusikia kwa Kenge ni Mpaka Atokwe Damu Puani', *Lusangi*, No. 32, August 1938, KFC; Teofilo mwana Mapolu, 'Mtama Hauvunji Tumbo', *Lusangi*, No. 33, September 1938, KFC; and 'Uwasaidie Wazazi wawalee Watoto wao Vyema', *Lusangi*, No. 26, February 1938, KFC.

[51] Michelle R. Moyd, *Violent Intermediaries: African Soldiers, Conquest, and Everyday Colonialism in German East Africa* (Athens: Ohio University Press, 2014), 170.

[52] See Remi Clignet, *Many Wives, Many Powers: Authority and Power in Polygamous Families* (Evanston: Northwestern University Press, 1970).

[53] See for instance *Ivanza lya Chalo*, Usoke, 29 February 1964, MCWT/35/7; *Ivanza lya Chalo*, Usoke, 4 April 1964, MCWT/35/7; *Ivanza lya Chalo*, Usoke, 29 May 1965, MCWT/35/7.

adultery. Their concerns reached the attention of elders' councils (*mavanza ga chalo*) in villages and are suggestive of ways in which concubinage and promiscuity had dominated the social life of Nyamwezi Christian men and women. Teachers reported their experiences in villages and published short stories in the *Lusangi* newsletter, drawing examples from verses in the Bible in support of their moral teachings to readers about the social and religious implications of adultery for married men and women in Unyamwezi.[54]

Just as rejecting polygamy and adultery remained a challenging task for Nyamwezi Christians, so did abstaining from brewing and consuming alcohol. In the 1930s and 1940s, numerous cases reported in the *Lusangi* newsletter of Christians brewing and selling liquor caught the attention of teachers in villages in Unyamwezi. They too used short stories with moral teachings to show the gravity of the problem and the implications of brewing and called upon the elders' councils (*mavanza ga chalo*) to intervene. They cited 'fighting' (*magomvi*), 'insulting words' (*matusi*), 'excessive drinking' (*ulevi*), and that 'it disturbed social relations among Christians' (*iliharibu mahusiano ya Wakristo*) because of 'resultant implications of brewing in Christin life' (*madhara ya pombe katika maisha ya Kikristu*).[55] Nevertheless, addressing brewing and alcoholism was not an easy task, as the 'drinking culture' of men was part of the daily routine in villages and urban Tabora.[56] For women brewers (*wapika pombe*), beer making functioned as protest against oppression, as formerly enslaved women used it to seek refuge from chiefly abuses, the difficulties of enslavement, and ill-treatment in households.[57]

Further, African teachers were better equipped than European missionaries to engage with aspects of their own culture and could discuss them in Kinyamwezi. Presenting issues through everyday examples, riddles, and short stories made it easier to attract Nyamwezi candidates for instruction, baptism,

---

[54] See for instance, Hiyobo Nandu, Kitunda, 'Tunao Wakati wa Kutafakari' *Lusangi*, No. 33, KFC; September 1938; Charles Pyagu, Igwamanoni, 'Kusikia kwa Kenge ni Mpaka Atokwe Damu Puani', *Lusangi*, No. 32, August 1938, KFC; Tobias Kagusa, Kidugalo, 'Wanawake Wawili kwa Mwanamume Mmoja' *Lusangi*, No. 32, August 1938.

[55] See for instance, Teofilo mwana Mapolu, 'Mtama Hauvunji Tumbo', *Lusangi*, No. 33, September 1938, KFC.

[56] Justin Willis, *Potent Brews: A Social History of Alcohol in East Africa, 1850–1999* (Oxford: James Currey, 2002), 71.

[57] James L. Giblin, *A History of the Excluded: Making Family a Refuge from State in Twentieth-Century Tanzania* (Oxford: James Currey, 2005); and Helen Bradford, '"We Women Will Show Them": Beer Protests in the Natal Countryside, 1929', in Jonathan Crush and Charles Ambler (eds), *Brew and Labor in Southern Africa* (Athens: Ohio University Press, 1992), 208–34.

and confirmation. In one of his articles in *Lusangi*, Davidi Yongolo challenged Bishop Søren H. Ibsen of the Moravian church in Unyamwezi because he did not have a good grasp of the customs of the Nyamwezi who wanted to become Christians, saying, 'you [missionaries] are strangers who do not know our behaviours. It is good to ask the people before you provide certificates [of baptism] to Africans.'[58] Yongolo's challenge indicates that African teachers wanted authority to vet admission to the congregations of the communities in which they were working. It was, therefore, important to ask teachers and the people who knew the conduct of individuals aspiring to become Christians before granting baptismal certificates. Yongolo's insistence on good moral standing indicates that becoming Christian meant demonstrating good behaviour and good relations with others in their society. He cited Acts 5:1–11 about Anania and his wife to warn Christians to refrain from certifying admission to Christianity to those whose behaviour was not morally acceptable.[59]

The role of parents in nurturing children as a basis for the Christian family raised debates among African teachers, who used everyday examples to advance their viewpoints on parental care in Christian families. Damson Kazunga's article 'Uwasaidie Wazazi Wawalee Watoto Vema' ('You Should Help Parents to Bring up Children') was read by the Nyamwezi teachers in villages because it demonstrated the importance of parents and children in 'domesticating' or 'appropriating' Christianity by using familiar Nyamwezi examples, short stories, and cultural practices.[60] Of course, parents were expected to become role models to children in their everyday lives by avoiding family conflicts and attending the Sunday services.

[58] Davidi mwana Yongolo, 'Cheti cha Kikristo', *Lusangi*, No. 26, February 1938, KFC. Yongolo's challenge to Ibsen in Kiswahili: 'ninyi ni wageni hamuwezi kujua tabia zetu, ni vyema pale mnapoona tunakuja kuomba cheti, kabla hamjatoa muwaulize kwanza wenyeji'.

[59] Yongolo, 'Cheti', KFC; Acts 5:1–11 (RSV).

[60] Tobia Sizya, 'Uwasaidie Wazazi Wawalele Watoto Wao Vyema', *Lusangi*, No. 26, February 1938, KFC. For details about the 'domestication' or 'appropriation' of Christianity in African culture, see Elizabeth Elbourne, *Blood Ground: Colonialism, Missions and the contest for Christianity in the Cape Colony and Britain 1799–1853* (Montreal: McGill-Queen's University Press, 2002), 174; Elizabeth Prevost, *The Communion of Women: Missions and Gender in Colonial Africa and the British Metropole* (Oxford: Oxford University Press, 2010), 6; Gregory Maddox, 'The Church and Cigogo: Father Stephen Mulundi and Christianity in Central Tanzania', in Thomas Spear and Isaria Kimambo (eds), *East African Expressions of Christianity* (Oxford: James Currey, 1999), 151; and James L. Giblin, 'Family Life, Indigenous Culture and Christianity in Colonial Njombe', in Spear and Kimambo (eds), *East African Expressions*, 309.

Debates about paying tithes as a precondition for becoming Christian spread to many of the villages. The basis of the debate was whether teachers should exclude community members from churches for their failure to pay the tithe. Some villagers questioned whether it was morally correct to accommodate Christians who paid tithes but whose behaviour was not morally acceptable. Other villagers questioned whether Christians who could not afford to pay tithes should be accepted because their good behaviour was a model for others. Some teachers debated whether possession of money should exclude a person or whether wealth qualified people to become Christians regardless of their behaviour.[61] The root cause of these debates among villagers and teachers was the growing number of suspensions (*luduko*) for members who failed to pay tithes, which discouraged Christians from attending church services. In the Moravian missions of Kitunda, Ilalangulu, and Kamata, more than half of the Christians were suspended for failing to pay the tithe in 1946 and 1947.[62] Of course, the disruption of resettlement was a factor in the Nyamwezi Christians' failure to pay the tithe. Resettlement meant abandoning villages and farms and disrupting agricultural production.

Discussions about wealth, morality, and being Christian dominated the missions' sermons and Sunday services in the villages as teachers posed these questions. These debates stimulated discussion because European missionaries and religious texts drew the image of the poverty of Christ and the Christian renunciation of worldly wealth.[63] Yet wealth remained central to Nyamwezi chiefs and ordinary people as a mark of status, and their political and religious authority enabled chiefs to accumulate enough wealth to command their subjects' respect. For the lay Nyamwezi people, on the other hand, migrant labour in the sisal plantations in northeastern and east-central Tanzania opened a path for them to accumulate cash and goods and earn social respectability in Unyamwezi, particularly from the 1930s to the 1950s.[64] Indeed, the culture of migrant labour among Nyamwezi men was built on nineteenth-century caravan porterage, which 'laid the foundation for respectability back in Unyamwezi'.[65] In addition to social respectability, paying tithes was a significant motivation for labour migrants. Of course, a sizeable portion of Christians could not pay tithes, leading to excommunication (*luduko*).

---

[61] 'Barazani kuna Baba zako Wengi', *Lusangi*, No. 33, September 1938, KFC.

[62] Listi ya Vakristo Vahanya, Kanisaya Kamata, No. 14, 1946, KFC; Listi ya Vakristo Vahanya, Kanisa ya Ilalangulu, No. 8, 1946, Listi ya Vakristo Vahanya, Kanisa ya Kitunda, 1947, KFC.

[63] See, for instance, Brauer Sermons, January 1913, 14, KFC.

[64] Moyd, *Violent Intermediaries*, 67.

[65] Ibid., 73.

One of the villages concerned about tithing was Igwamanoni, where villagers questioned whether paying tithes and even possessing money really made them good Christians. Some churches went so far as to suspend members for their failure to pay tithes in the form of money. In response to these concerns, Charles Pyagu, a teacher in charge of the Moravian church in the village, decided to discuss the matter with other teachers in the pages of *Lusangi* before responding to the villagers.[66]

Many people could not meet the tithe obligations and did not attend church services. According to the teachers, some Nyamwezi Christians did not attend Sunday services and instead worked communally in their fields, a practice often rewarded with indigenous brewed spirits. Teachers argued that excessive drinking disturbed relations among Christians, causing them to fight amongst themselves and with non-Christians. The teachers said they also committed other 'shameful acts', such as adultery and stealing, thereby presenting a negative image of all Christians.[67] Teachers writing in *Lusangi*, such as Davidi Yongolo, were critical of those they did not consider good Christians. They called upon them to attend the services, emphasizing that serving both God and wealth was impossible.[68]

To address the moral and social implications of the 'drinking culture of men', adultery, and polygamous marriage, teachers called for the formation of village and parish councils of elders (*mabaraza ya wazee*; in Kinyamwezi, *mavanza ga chalo*).[69] As a tool of social and moral reform, the *baraza* was duty-bound to punish church members convicted of adultery and consequent pregnancy to achieve 'moral reform'.[70] The *baraza*'s formulation of Christian morality in Unyamwezi demonstrates the extent to which the Nyamwezi Christians expressed an older morality in new, Christian terms, which was, of

---

[66] Charles Pyagu, 'Barazani', *Lusangi*, No. 33, September 1938, KFC.

[67] Teofilo mwana Mapolu, Kakola, 'Mtama Hauvunji Tumbo', *Lusangi*, No. 33, September 1938, KFC; Charles Pyagu, Igwamanoni, 'Kusikia kwa Kenge ni Mpaka Atokwe na Damu', *Lusangi*, No. 32, August 1938, KFC.

[68] Davidi mwana Yongolo, Tabora, 'Wengine Furaha Wengine Huzuni', *Lusangi*, No. 32, August 1938, KFC; Matthew 6: 24.

[69] Hiobo Ng'andu, Kitunda, 'Tunao Wakati wa Kutafakari', Kitunda, *Lusangi*, No. 33, September 1938, KFC; Tobia Kagusa, Kidugalo, 'Wanawake Wakristo Wawili kwa Mwanamume Mmoja', *Lusangi*, No. 32, 1938, KFC. I have adopted the term 'drinking culture of men' from Justin Willis, 'Unpretentious Bars: Municipal Monopoly and Indigenous Drinking in Colonial Dar es Salaam', in James Brennan, Andrew Burton, and Yusufu Lawi (eds), *Dar es Salaam: Histories from an Emerging Metropolis* (Dar es Salaam: Mkuki na Nyota, 2007), 157–73; and see Willis, *Potent Brews*.

[70] Derek R. Peterson, *Ethnic Patriotism and East African Revival: A History of Dissent, c. 1935–1972* (Cambridge: Cambridge University Press, 2012), 173.

course, a way that teachers tried to gain control over the communities around the village outstations.

The expression of an older morality in new Christian teachings enabled councils to impose a six months' ban from the church and nonengagement in church affairs for those Christians found guilty of promiscuity. After the six-month ban, converts reported to the council of the elders and had to demonstrate that they had been morally reformed before they could be readmitted into the church.[71] The experience of one Maria of Usoke Moravian mission exemplifies the moral transformation of Christians excommunicated for promiscuous behaviour. A *baraza* excommunicated her from the church in 1940, but after a considerable period, elders readmitted her to the church because they were satisfied with her moral transformation.[72]

In addition to a six-month ban, *baraza* expelled Christians accused of adultery and pregnancy from their jobs at the mission schools and dispensaries. In the mission of Usoke and the village outstations of Imalaseko and Kalembela III, increased pressure from ordinary Christians, who accused teachers and some elders of the church of promiscuous behaviour with women, led to the dismissal of some of the accused from their duties in missions and outstations. Samweli Katala Pandisha, who worked at Usoke mission's *baraza* and served as an elder of the parish church (*mzee wa kanisa*), lost both positions because he had an affair with an unmarried Muslim woman for whom he had not paid bridewealth. Similarly, Mika Mbago, a teacher at Kauna mission school, lost his position because he had sexual relations with an unmarried young lady.[73] The loss of a job meant the loss of men's respectability before their in-laws, the church, and society. In Unyamwezi, a person's status in the family, before his in-laws, and in society was measured by his occupation and how well he could support his dependents, including his wife. This explains why men travelled to sisal plantations, a practice that opened a 'few paths to respectability' and allowed men 'to prove their masculine respectability' and 'dignity', and thus attain the 'civic virtue' necessary to 'assume adult responsibilities'.[74]

---

[71] See, for example, *Ivanza lya Chalo*, Usoke, 31 January, 28 February, and 4 April 1959, MCWT/35/7; *Ivanza lya Chalo*, Usoke, 26 March 1960 and 28 May 1960, MCWT/35/7.

[72] *Ivanza lya Chalo*, Usoke, 31 December 1960, MCWT/35/7.

[73] *Ivanza lya Chalo*, Usoke, 28 May 1960, MCWT/35/7; *Ivanza lya Chalo*, Usoke, 30 May 1960, MCWT/35/7. The names used in this context are pseudonyms.

[74] Moyd, *Violent Intermediaries*, 65; Giblin, *History of the Excluded*, 115–16; John Iliffe, *Honour in African History* (Cambridge: Cambridge University Press, 2005), 281; Peterson, *Ethnic Patriotism*, 33. I have adopted the concept 'civic virtue' from John Lonsdale to show how labour migration enabled men to assume power and responsibility in the society. For details about the concept,

The title of another article in *Lusangi*, 'In the Council of Elders, There Are Many Parents' ('Barazani kuna Baba zako Wengi'), suggests the kind of community the Nyamwezi Christians wished to build in the villages – one that transcended boundaries of kinship to encompass a larger family formed by members from different families. The new Christian community had obligations to nurture children and to support all Christians as members of the larger Christian community or family. In this way, the Christian community, not the familial kin, became the new Christian family in villages and missions. Yet one's obligations within these Christian families were like the expectations for members of traditional Nyamwezi families.[75] The article suggests that teachers and Christian villagers should present their concerns to councils of elders (*mavanza ga chalo*), and seek advice on doctrine and family relations in the larger, ideal Christian family.

The increasing circulation of the *Lusangi* newsletter among African teachers created a platform for sharing experiences from the villages where they worked. The newsletter was a guide for administering Sunday schools and increased the Christians' curiosity to read books to deepen their knowledge of social and religious affairs. In 1938, the editor of *Lusangi* informed readers that anonymous leaders of the Moravian Church had donated money to buy sixty-eight books that would be available to African teachers and other people who wished to read. They could borrow the books for one or two cents, cheap enough for everyone to afford. The editor said the price would allow the church 'to buy more new books each year to replace the worn-out books in the library' so that 'no one could be restricted in reading the books because of his or her poverty'.[76] The editor also reiterated that an account should be set up to accumulate money to buy more books. However, the report from the editor of the newsletter did not provide details about the kinds of books that were purchased or about their language or place of publication. It is reasonable to assume that the Tanganyika Mission Press, which had been active since 1925, might have published the books in western Tanzania and that they might have been written in Kiswahili or Kinyamwezi. Since interest in reading books increased, the first public library under the Moravian Church of Unyamwezi was established in Tabora town. The editor of *Lusangi* credited the library for Christian men and women in Unyamwezi as a means of widening their

---

see John Lonsdale, 'The Moral Economy of Mau Mau: Wealth, Poverty and Civic Virtue in Kikuyu Political Thought', in Bruce Berman and John Lonsdale (eds), *Unhappy Valley: Conflict in Kenya and Africa*, Bk 2, *Violence and Ethnicity* (London: James Currey, 1992), 326–29.

[75] 'Barazani kuna Baba zako Wengi', *Lusangi*, No. 33, September 1938, KFC.

[76] Mhariri, 'Vitabu vya Kuazima', *Lusangi*, No. 26, February 1938, KFC.

knowledge of the 'written word' to better understand their faith, its doctrines, and indeed God.[77]

With the mastery of the scripture, the Moravian Nyamwezi teachers in villages launched open-air meetings that, like the newsletter, were called *lusangi*. There, they emerged as eloquent preachers. The *lusangi*, originating from Nyamwezi culture, involved food sharing among neighbourhoods; families and strangers all got food. Thus, the African teachers in the Moravian missions and village outstations used these meetings to strengthen believers' commitment to Christianity.[78] Each parish organized *lusangi* that attracted people from far and wide. Teachers preached, baptized, and confirmed new members. At the end of each evening meeting, the people shared a communal meal that helped them create social networks and friendships. In the 1950s, these meetings became part of revivalist and crusade evangelism, combining open-air meetings and village house visits. The teachers preached about sin, salvation, and repentance. The change in *lusangi* devoted to crusade evangelism and preaching attracted more people and increased the attendance of villagers who had never attended Sunday services. These new teachings gained momentum because the East African revival movement spread across the East African region in the 1930s and 1940s.[79] The friendship networks that developed in these meetings stimulated the growth of Christian communities in villages, leading to marriages between young people who regularly attended the village *lusangi*.

On 28 August 1938, African teachers organized a *lusangi* festival at the Moravian mission of Kitunda. The people from Kitunda and the surrounding villages of Isuvangala, Matuli, Mafyeko, Ikonongo, and Mugombezi all attended the festival. The teachers preached the gospel, people sang together, and about eighty-three adults and thirty-eight children were baptized, while eleven children received the sacrament of confirmation at the following Sunday service.[80] The editor of the *Lusangi* newsletter reported that it was larger than most other festivals, for about eight hundred persons attended the festival, and about three hundred and forty received the Holy Sacrament (Holy

---

[77] Mhariri, 'Vitabu', *Lusangi*, No. 26, February 1938, KFC; Derek R. Peterson, 'Morality Plays: Marriage, Church Courts, and Colonial Agency in Central Tanganyika, ca. 1876–1928', *American Historical Review*, Vol. 111, No. 4 (2006), 1003–5.

[78] Interview with Esta Isaya Nkomabanhu, Erasto Kapera, Mateo Richard Mgalula, Charles Jeremiah Kinyonga, Mathiasi Aron Kiligito, and Edson Nhomba, Sikonge, 27 November 2016.

[79] Interviews with Oscar E. Kisanji, 30 November 2016, and Esta Isaya Nkomabanhu and Mathiasi Aron Kiligito, Sikonge, 27 November 2016.

[80] Mhariri, 'Sikukuu Kitunda', *Lusangi*, No. 34, October 1938, KFC.

Communion) during this *lusangi* festival. But the newsletter editor insisted that the Nyamwezi were disheartened because they were not served meat: *hawakupewa nyama*. The price of meat was high in Kiwere, making it hard to feed those who attended.[81] The complaints about the failure to be served meat during the *lusangi* festival suggest continuity with older ideas of hospitality, particularly the hospitality people would have expected from wealthy patrons and in gatherings of kin. It also reinforced the idea that the fulfilment of obligations to dependents was the basis of social status.

The activities of teachers in villages resulted in the growth of Christianity in the Moravian missions between 1930 and 1950, despite the relocation of some Christian communities due to the spread of tsetse fly. Table 10 shows changes in the number of baptized Christians in the Moravian missions. However, we do not know the size of the Moravian congregation between 1938 and 1946, probably because of the disruption caused by the Second World War. In some missions, the number of Christians dwindled. At Tabora, for example, the number of Christians sharply declined between 1934 and 1937. The reasons for the decline remain unclear. At Urambo, the number of Christians declined between 1934 and 1937 owing to sleeping sickness. The old mission of Urambo was closed in 1937, and teachers followed the people to new settlements that the government established some fifteen miles from Tabora. The Moravian mission of Urambo seems to have been active in the 1950s, so the table indicates that the number of Christians increased. By then, sleeping sickness had been contained, allowing people to return to their abandoned villages.

In the missions of Sikonge, Ipole, and Kitunda, which appear not to have been affected by sleeping sickness, the number of Christians increased steadily from 1931 to 1950. The number of Christians in all the Moravian missions in Unyamwezi increased from 2,268 in 1931 to 10,821 in 1950 (see Table 10 and Figure 12). The population increase throughout the region certainly contributed to the rise in the number of Christians. As a result some outstations grew to become mission stations. Among the new outstations were Mwamagembe, established in 1957, and Uyowa, established in 1958. The African teachers and ordained pastors were primarily responsible for the growth of Christianity in the villages. By 1950, only three European missionaries remained in Unyamwezi, and Africans led congregations in many villages and missions (see Figure 13 and Map 6).[82]

---

[81] 'Sikukuu', *Lusangi*, No. 34, October 1938, KFC.
[82] Sikonge Diary, 10 June 1956, KFC, Kisanji, *Historia Fupi*, 216.

Table 10 Baptized Christians in the Moravian Missions of Unyamwezi, 1931–50.

	1931	1932	1933	1934	1935	1936	1937	1946	1947	1948	1949	1950
Urambo	111	104	101	82	76	77	93	382	427	486	516	549
Usoke	213	258	277	281	304	384	405	777	808	821	844	545
Tabora	289	302	333	132	153	163	185	426	440	447	475	622
Sikonge	423	554	708	959	1235	1483	1636	2503	2556	2796	2999	3152
Ipole	616	710	837	962	1175	1256	1394	2098	2109	2233	2218	2412
Kitunda	616	634	691	730	963	1345	1597	2732	2876	2898	3022	3241
TOTAL	**2268**	**2562**	**2947**	**3146**	**3906**	**4708**	**5310**	**8918**	**9216**	**9681**	**10074**	**10821**

Source: Compiled from *Bestand der Gemeinen in der Missionsprovinz* (Statistics of the Mission in Unyamwezi, 1931–50), KFC.

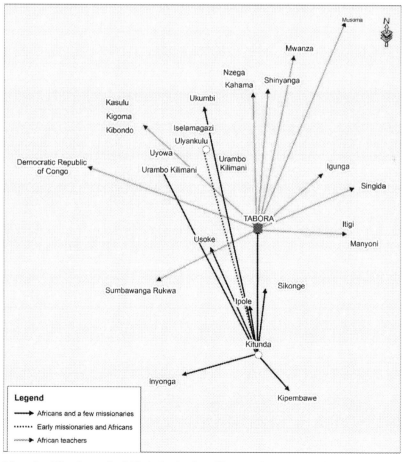

Map 6 The Spread of Christianity in Villages of Unyamwezi (Moravians).

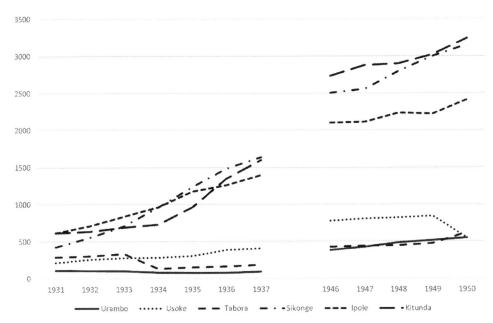

Figure 12 Baptized Christians in the Moravian Missions of Unyamwezi, 1931–50.

Figure 13 African-ordained Pastors in the Moravian Missions of Unyamwezi, 1940s–50s.

Conclusion

In 1962, Søren Haahr Ibsen, superintendent and bishop of the Moravian missions in Unyamwezi, published a memoir in Danish that looked back at the forty years of missionary work in Tanzania from 1922 to 1962. The biography, among other things, surveyed the remarkable development of the Moravian Church in Unyamwezi and praised the work of key pioneers, including Yohanesi Kipamila, a former mission porter and teacher in the Moravian church in southern Tanzania, whose contributions to the development of Christianity in southern Unyamwezi continue to shape the discourses of Christianization and missiology in the Moravian schools, colleges, missions, and village outstations.[83] The experience of Yohanesi Kipamila echoes the many porters and formerly enslaved people who laboured in Unyamwezi as teachers and pastors. Yet their contribution to the development of Christianity has always been relegated to the margins of the missionary enterprise.[84] Nevertheless, by the second decade of the twentieth century, it was evident that African teachers, formerly enslaved people, mission porters, and Nyamwezi men and women controlled the churches in the many villages. The *lusangi* festivals became essential platforms for congregants to network and share their experiences about scripture and evangelization, using a form that was deeply rooted in the Nyamwezi culture of the neighbourhood.[85] The *Lusangi* newsletter also attracted critical discussion on church policies, including tithes, excommunication, and the 'moral reform' of devotees.[86]

Despite the legal abolition of slavery in Tanganyika through the Involuntary Servitude (Abolition) Ordinance, the effects of slavery on formerly enslaved people and their descendants haunted their social life in post-abolition Unyamwezi.[87] For slaves who had earned positions in the society, talking about the slave past implied a loss of the social standing they had struggled to earn in Unyamwezi. Resettlement in distant villages where they were completely unknown became the coping strategy for the formerly enslaved 'to hide shame' ('kuficha aibu') and mitigate the dilemmas and anxieties of living with their slave past.[88] Yet for most slaves who remained in their villages, conversion to Christianity offered them 'refuge' from the shame and social

---

[83] Søren H. Ibsen, *Et Tilbageblik: Over 40 Års Virke I Tanzania, 1922–1922* (Forlaget Savanne, 1962).

[84] See, for instance, Hamilton and Hamilton, *History of the Moravian Church*.

[85] Mhariri, 'Vitabu vya Kuazima', *Lusangi*, No. 26, February 1938, KFC.

[86] See, for instance, Charles Pyagu, 'Barazani', *Lusangi*, No. 33, September 1938, KFC.

[87] *Tanganyika Territory Gazette*, Vol. III, 1922 [The Involuntary Servitude (Abolition) Ordinance, No. 13 of 1922], TNA.

[88] Interview with Elly Makenge, October 2019.

stigma associated with slavery and 'became a contingent social resource and survival strategy'.[89]

The result of festivals and the culture of reading and interpretation of Christian doctrines had a bearing on the growth of Christianity in villages beyond the missions. No sooner had Christianity become an important force than the East African revival, which had spread in rural Unyamwezi under born-again pastors and women, added a new dimension to African Christianity. In the Moravian missions, the influence of revivalism aroused tension and division between African teachers, evangelists, and lay Christians. The response from Christians to the spirit of revivalism differed from that in other parts of East Africa. In contrast, in Unyamwezi, members of older churches mounted opposition to the movement, preventing born-again pastors and evangelists from holding church services. Consequently, some Christians seceded from the mainstream Moravian churches to form their churches, selected their pastors, and drew dissatisfied Christians into the new congregations. Effective administration of village outstations, the tradition of reading and interpretation of texts, and rebelling against the East African revival in twentieth-century Unyamwezi inspired African teachers and women not only to mount a rebellion against the influence of revivalism but also encouraged ideas of self-governance (*kujitawala*), complete authority (*mamlaka kamili*), Africanization, and the quest for Tanganyikan independence.[90]

---

[89] Giblin, *History of the Excluded*; Priya Lal, 'Militants, Mothers, and the National Family: Ujamaa, Gender, and Rural Development in Postcolonial Tanzania', *Journal of African History*, Vol. 51, No. 1 (2010), 2.

[90] Oskar E. Kisanji, *Nimesema, Askofu Teofilo Hiyobo Kisanji: Baadhi ya Maandiko aliyoandika Hotuba alizotoa na Mahubiri aliyoyafanya kati ya mwaka 1955 na 1982* (Tabora: Frontex Associates, 2023), 25–27; Ronald Aminzade, *Race, Nation, and Citizenship in Post-Colonial Africa: The Case of Tanganyika* (New York: Cambridge University Press, 2013), 79–81.

CHAPTER 6

Christians, the Revival Movement, and Dissent in Moravian Missions and Villages, 1950–60

In much of western Tanzania, Africans initiated the new Christian faith, leading the people in prayers and Sunday services, preparing catechumens for baptism, and teaching children to read and write. The consequence of these activities was the growth of African Christianity in villages. This chapter explores Moravian Christians' experience with the revival movement in the 1950s and 1960s. Derek Peterson's authoritative work on the East African revival treats revivalists as theological, social, and political innovators who challenged a growing Christian establishment slow to respond to dramatic social change.[1] By contrast, revivalists became the target of critique in western Tanzania by innovators who saw the revivalists as a self-righteous establishment. Revivalists and their critics engaged in intricate theological disputes over the nature and process of salvation and the legitimacy of claiming to be 'born again'. While many born-again pastors in western Tanzania worked from within the established church, Christians critical of them seceded to form their own 'independent' churches, installing their pastors and recruiting adherents from the established churches. Both mission stations and village outstations became the sites of such dissent. The resulting social tensions were not so much resolved as lessened gradually over time, superseded by new political languages of independence, self-governance, and Africanization of churches which had dominated homilies and conversations in 1950s and early 1960s Unyamwezi.

Dissent in western Tanzania involved breaking away from the established mission churches and village outstations, causing tensions between born-again pastors who supported revivalism and Christians who opposed the movement. When reconstructing the history of dissent and resultant conflicts between the two groups of Christians in the Moravian church, this chapter relies

---

[1] Derek R. Peterson, *Ethnic Patriotism and East African Revival: A History of Dissent, c. 1935–1972* (Cambridge: Cambridge University Press, 2012).

primarily on diaries kept by pastors at the two missions of Tabora (also called Milumbani) and Sikonge. These diaries describe revivalism and dissent in the missions and village outstations between 1955 and 1958. The chapter also draws on the church newsletter *Habari za Kanisa*. Each issue had a column entitled 'From Our Records of the Moravian Church in Western Tanzania' (Kutoka Kumbukumbu Zetu za Kanisa la Moravian Tanganyika Magharibi), which reported on events in all the Moravian missions and villages, including revivalism and dissent.[2] In addition to primary sources, the chapter uses secondary sources and interviews with pastors who experienced revivalism firsthand. The primary and secondary sources offer glimpses that can help us understand revivalism in East Africa and the context in which it operated in Unyamwezi. Likewise, these sources allow us to see revivalism and dissent from the viewpoint of supporters of revivalism and that of Christians who seceded from the mainstream mission churches and village outstations in opposition to the movement.

The Rise and Development of the Revival Movement, 1930s–40s

The East African revival (*ulokole*) began in the 1930s at the evangelical wing of the CMS mission at Gahini in northern Rwanda. Its staff were evangelical missionaries recruited from Cambridge University's Christian Union. A missionary doctor, John Edward Church (alias Joe Church), became the most influential figure and preacher in the revival movement. His quest for a higher spiritual life under the influence of the Higher Life Movement, known as Keswick evangelicalism, and 'public confession' from the Oxford Group spread the spirit of revivalism beyond the mission hospitals. Joe Church stressed that Christians should experience a second transformation after being born again.[3] That Christians were called to experience the second

---

[2] Milumbani Diary, 1950–60, KFC; *Habari za Kanisa* (Gazeti la Kimoraviani, Unyamwezi), No. 3, July–September 1999, KFC.

[3] Adrian Hastings, *The Church in Africa, 1450–1950* (Oxford: Clarendon Press, 1996), 596; Jeffrey Cox, *The British Missionary Enterprise since 1700* (New York: Routledge, 2008), 250; Andrew Porter, 'Cambridge, Keswick, and Late-Nineteenth-Century Attitudes to Africa', *Journal of Imperial and Commonwealth History*, Vol. 5, No. 1 (1976), 14–16 and 25; Phillip A. Cantrell II, '"We are a Chosen People": The East African Revival and Its Return to Post-Genocide Rwanda', *Church History*, Vol. 83, No. 2 (2014), 429–30; Daewon Moon, 'The Conversion of Yosiya Kinuka and the Beginning of the East African Revival', *International Bulletin of Mission Research*, Vol. 41, No. 3 (2017), 204–5; Jason S. Bruner, 'The Politics of Public Confession in the East African Revival in Uganda, ca. 1930–1950' (PhD thesis, Princeton University, 2013), 2 and 53–67;

CHRISTIANS, THE REVIVAL MOVEMENT, AND DISSENT IN MORAVIAN MISSIONS

transformation was rooted in the Keswickian theology, which insists that after conversion, one must encounter the Spirit to progress into holiness. This second encounter with the Spirit, which is sometimes called 'the second blessing' or 'the second touch', echoes the Pentecostal doctrine of baptism in the Holy Spirit that embodies the 'enduement of power' and 'entire cleansing' and getting 'empty of sin' to believers.[4] Some Keswick teachers argued that 'sinless perfection could be possible after one received the second blessing'.[5] Proponents of holiness theology argued that the second experience inspired Christians to feel 'ensnared by wrongdoing, for they would have victory over sin' to inspire them to enjoy a 'higher spiritual life'.[6]

John Church worked with Simeoni Nsibambi, an affluent Ugandan landholder and health officer, Ezekieli Balaba, a schoolteacher, and Elisafati Matovu, a shopkeeper. This partnership culminated in an influx of young committed Baganda Christians and Christians from western Uganda to work at Gahini Hospital in Rwanda.[7] In due course, the three emerged as prominent preachers of the revival movement, moving across East Africa through Rwanda, southern Uganda, western Kenya, and northwestern Tanganyika, preaching about the public confession of sins and the new birth. These new teachings departed from the earlier traditions in established churches of silent and personal confession and sacramental requirements. They drew people from far and wide, with men, women, and students publicly confessing their sins at revival meetings and declaring themselves born-again Christians (*balokole*).[8]

Jason S. Bruner, 'Contesting Confession in the East African Revival', *Anglican and Episcopal History*, Vol. 84, No. 3 (2015), 253–55; Jason S. Bruner, *Living Salvation in the East African Revival in Uganda* (Rochester, NY: University of Rochester Press, 2017), 49–55.

[4] Donald W. Dayton, *Theological Roots of Pentecostalism* (Grand Rapids, MI: Baker Academic, 2011), 102–3.

[5] 'What is the Keswick movement, and is it biblical?' Got Questions, last updated 4 January 2022, https://www.gotquestions.org/Keswick-movement.html (accessed 3 October 2023).

[6] David W. Bebbington, *Evangelicalism in Modern Britain: A History from the 1730s to the 1980s* (London: Unwin Hyman, 1989), 151.

[7] Kevin Ward, '"Obedient Rebels" – The Relationship between the Early "Balokole" and the Church of Uganda: The Mukono Crisis of 1941', *Journal of Religion in Africa*, Vol. 19, Fasc. 3 (1989), 194.

[8] Peterson, *Ethnic Patriotism*, 115; Derek R. Peterson, 'Wordy Women: Gender Trouble and the Oral Politics of the East African Revival in Northern Gikuyu Land', *Journal of African History*, Vol. 42, No. 3 (2001), 470; Bruner, 'The Politics of Public Confession', 2–5; Bruner, *Living Salvation*, 4–9; Moon, 'The Conversion of Yosiya Kinuka', 204–10; Catherine E. Robins, 'Tukutendereza:

In 1950, revivalists held their first convention in Unyamwezi at Tabora Boys' Secondary School. Influential preachers from Uganda attended the meeting, including William Nagenda, Festo Kivengere, and Joe Church, who also led revival meetings with Ganda preachers in Bugufi in northwestern Tanzania. Preachers from Tanzania included Yohana Omari from Dodoma, who later became the Anglican bishop in the diocese of central Tanganyika.[9] These preachers used Kiswahili, Luganda, and English with the help of translators to deliver the new message of rebirth, salvation, and the public confession of sins. Revivalists believed that being born-again meant being saved from sins, and the new teachings became fundamental for being saved and becoming 'new Christians' (*wakristu wapya*). Preachers insisted that Christians abandon their old ways of living to become good people, emphasizing that Christians should confess their sins at revival meetings and declare that they would 'accept Jesus as [their] saviour'.[10]

While the records of the meeting at Tabora Boys' Secondary School do not reveal whether teachers and students were attracted to the revivalists' message, news about the meeting spread across Tabora town, and 'people and pastors were attracted to the teachings of revivalism'.[11] In due course, the revivalists became dominant in the Moravian missions and village churches in Unyamwezi. African pastors and evangelists at these institutions, including Teofilo Kisanji, Paulo Isai Misigalo, Erasto Kasoga, and Lukasi Masamalo, were drawn to the message of revivalism and declared themselves born again.[12] Of course, the success of these pastors in popularizing the revival movement stemmed from their earlier experience of preaching at *lusangi* festivals and open-air meetings.[13] Because pastors were well versed in the Nyamwezi culture of neighbourhood gatherings and food sharing which were

---

A Study of Social Change and Sectarian Withdrawal in the Balokole Revival of Uganda' (PhD thesis, Columbia University, 1975), 140–41; Hastings, *The Church*, 596–97; Cox, *The British Missionary*, 250; Elizabeth Isichei, *A History of Christianity in Africa: From Antiquity to Present* (Grand Rapids, MI: Eerdmans, 1995), 242.

[9] Teofilo H. Kisanji, *Historia Fupi ya Kanisa la Kimoravian Tanganyika Magharibi* (Kipalapala: TMP, 1982), 20.

[10] Interview with Oscar E. Kisanji, Kaze Hill, Tabora, 27 June 2017.

[11] Peterson, *Ethnic Patriotism*, 115; interview with Oscar E. Kisanji, Kaze Hill, Tabora, 27 June 2017.

[12] Kisanji, *Historia Fupi*, 207; interviews with Oscar E. Kisanji, Kaze Hill, Tabora, 27 June 2017, and Paulo Isai Misigaro, Tabora, 27 June 2017. Kisanji and Misigalo insisted in Kiswahili, 'watu na wachungaji walivutiwa na mafundisho ya uamsho'.

[13] See, for instance, Mhariri, 'Sikukuu Kitunda', *Lusangi*, No. 34, October 1938, KFC.

central to the Iusangi festivals, the use of the preexisting culture of Iusangi was requisite for them to extend the network of the revival among the Nyamwezi Christians in the Moravian village outstations and missions.[14]

As the revival meeting ended at Tabora Boys in 1950, teachers and evangelists returned to the missions and outstations determined to preach the message of the 'new birth', 'confession', and 'salvation'. African pastors of Tabora-Milumbani and Usoke missions invited William Nagenda, Joe Church, Festo Kivengere from Uganda, and Yohana Omari from Dodoma to preach their message of revivalism and attracted many Christians. Teofilo Kisanji of Tabora mission attended the revival convention in Maseno in western Kenya for two weeks and was inspired to establish a revival team to help spread revivalism in Unyamwezi. As he returned to Tabora, Kisanji held the first revival fellowship in Tabora mission and established a revival team of men and women consisting of himself as a pastor, Erick Kadelema, Timoteo Mgasa (a teacher at Tabora Railway School), Ester George, Kasanga Weja, Nelea Nikodemo Msogoti, Roda, and Martha.[15] This team, Sesilia Nikodemo Msogoti recalled, 'had been employed and earned cash; they were not poor. They drank tea whenever they met', which indicates that pastors and workers who had joined the revival movement had wealth enough to become patrons to provide food for themselves and the poor Christians who had joined the revival.[16]

This team preached the 'new revival gospel of salvation' (*injili mpya ya wokovu*) in the Moravian missions and outstations of Unyamwezi, including Kinhwa, Kakola II, Ugunda, Usoke, Kasenga, Mtendeni, and Uyui. In their daily meetings, they invariably sang the Luganda hymn 'Tukutendereza Yesu' ('We Praise Thee/Praise the Lord'). In due course, the song became a sign of greeting among revivalists and was used to distinguish born-again Christians from those not part of the movement. The consistent use of the hymn influenced dissenters in Unyamwezi to characterize the revival team as 'kikundi cha kutendereza' (literally, the group of praise).[17] The revival team meetings drew congregants from established churches. Rev. Misigalo

---

[14] Kisanji, *Historia Fupi*, 171 and 251.

[15] Milumbani Diary, 3 July and 23 December 1955, and 3 January 1956 KFC; interview with Sesilia Nikodemo Msogoti, Isevya-Tabora, 12 June 2018.

[16] Interview with Sesilia Nikodemo Msogoti, Isevya-Tabora, 12 June 2018. In Kiswahili, 'Walokole walikuwa na kazi na kipato chao, hawakuwa maskini. Walikuwa wanakunywa chai kila walipokutana'.

[17] Interview with Sesilia Nikodemo Msogoti, Isevya-Tabora, 12 June 2018; Robins, 'Tukutendereza', 6. For the words to the song, see 'Tukutendereza Yesu' (Luganda), in *Tenzi za Rohoni*, No. 138 (1968; repr. Musoma: Musoma Press, 2016).

182 SLAVE EMANCIPATION, CHRISTIAN COMMUNITIES, AND DISSENT IN TANZANIA

recalled how the discourses of revivalism in Usoke appealed to men and women, saying, 'women threw their decoration beads as a sign of being born-again'.[18] Further south, in the Sikonge and Ipole missions and the outstations of Ulilwansimba, Ugunda, and Iwensato I and II, the revival also took root, and Christians welcomed the message of revivalism.[19]

Ugome: Dissent in Missions and Village Outstations, 1955–59

No sooner had revivalism spread across Unyamwezi than some Christians from the mainstream Moravian churches responded negatively to the 'saved' and 'born-again' evangelists and pastors in families and the public. Sesilia Nikodemo Msogoti recalled how her sister, Nelea Msogoti, and other revivalists often met at their home, hoping to convince her to join the side of revivalism, but she refused. She said, 'They often came here at home to sing, but we had no interest in them … we always listened to them, but we left … we did not care, we concentrated on playing with other children … they were simply shouting at us.' Sesilia's recollection of her sister indicates that even some family members defied their revivalist relatives' attempts to convert them to born-again Christianity.[20]

The Mtendeni branch of the Tabora mission was the first outstation to oppose the teachings of 'born-again' teachers and evangelists. Mose Muhozya declared that the outstation would become the Tanganyika African Church (TAC). The TAC became the centre of dissent, influencing other missions and villages to mount similar rebellions (*ugome*) against the born-again pastors and evangelists (see Map 7).[21] Men and women at Mtendeni forbade Teofilo Kisanji, the pastor at Tabora, from either holding Sunday services or preaching, because he was among the saved pastors and was associated with revivalism in Unyamwezi. Kisanji described this incident in the church diary, saying that 'they [anti-revivalists] restricted me from doing all these things [preaching and offering Holy communion]'.[22] Christians also accused Kisanji of failing to visit them in their homes and called upon him to rectify his conduct. While

---

[18] Interview with Paulo Isai Misigalo, Tabora, 27 June 2017. In Kiswahili, 'wanawake walitupa shanga zao kama ishara ya kuokoka'.

[19] Milumbani Diary, 9 and 25 March and 6 and 22 April 1956; Sikonge Diary, 2, 6, and 10 July 1955, and 22 and 29 April and 13 July 1956, KFC.

[20] Interview with Sesilia Nikodemo Msogoti, Isevya-Tabora, 12 June 2018. In Kiswahili, 'walikuwa wanakuja kuimba hapa kwetu lakini sisi hatukuwa na interest nao', 'tulikuwa tunawasikia tunawaacha tu', 'walikuwa wanatupigia kelele tu', 'tulikuwa hatujali, tulikuwa tunakwenda kucheza'.

[21] Kisanji, *Historia Fupi*, 215.

[22] Milumbani Diary, 21 October 1956; *Habari za Kanisa*, No. 3, July–September

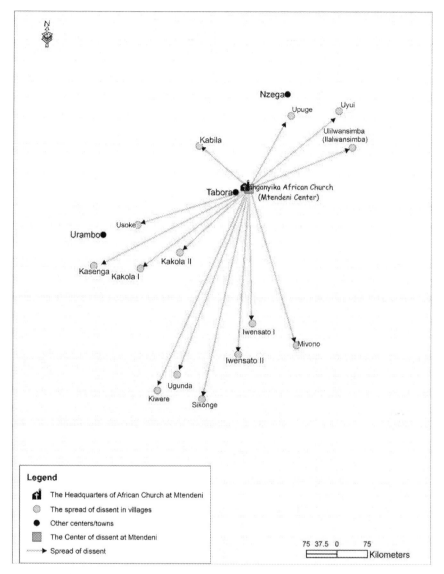

Map 7 The Spread of the Revival Movement and Dissent in Unyamwezi.

Kisanji admitted his failure to visit his Christians regularly, he maintained that he would not dissociate himself from revivalism. As a result, Christians of Mtendeni isolated him and ceased attending his services, leaving him with

1999, KFC. In Kiswahili, 'walinizuia nisifanye hayo yote [kuhubiri na kutoa ushirika]'.

only four members in the church. Commenting with discouragement about the dissent, he said, 'finally, only four members of the church attended the service while the rest seceded'.[23]

After the secession, the revivalist pastors immediately attempted to reconcile with the Christians of Mtendeni. At first, congregants appeared to moderate their stance on not attending the services,[24] but they continued to protest against the 'saved' pastors. In February 1957, they refused to attend a service led by Rev. Erasto Kasoga or cooperate with him because he was also 'saved'. They refused to take his bag into the church, remaining outside until he finished the service.[25] Dissent continued, and the elders' council (*ivanza lya chalo*) of Mtendeni refused to let born-again pastors and their bishop hold services in the church.[26] The elders issued a letter prohibiting Kisanji, Misigalo, and the bishop from holding services at Mtendeni because Christians at the outstation were against revivalism. Rev. Misigalo insisted upon leading a service, but only a few members attended. When he made a second attempt to conduct a service, dissenters prevented him from doing so and held their own service instead.[27]

The influence of dissent and the TAC at Mtendeni spread to many missions and villages of Unyamwezi. In some places, dissenters mobilized Christians against the 'saved' pastors. At Ikongolo, Absalomi Elia, an evangelist of the outstation, led his people in preventing the spread of revivalism in the area. In one instance, he decided against informing the people of Upuge about a service to be held by Rev. Erasto Kasoga. He also prevented Kasoga from holding a service at Ikongolo, and Kasoga returned to Tabora without holding the service, reporting that '[the Christians] protested against me and ... have made arrangements with the Christians of Mtendeni ... they said they don't want [me]'.[28] Frustrated by the dissent, Kasoga requested that the church council question Elia about his opposition to born-again pastors. Kasoga thought that Elia had no mandate to prevent him from holding a service in

---

[23] Milumbani Diary, 21 October 1956, KFC; *Habari za Kanisa*, No. 3, July–September, 1999, KFC. Kisanji reported with discouragement, 'mwisho tulishiriki na watu wanne, wengine walijitenga'.

[24] Milumbani Diary, 11 November 1956, KFC.

[25] Milumbani Diary, 3 February 1957, KFC.

[26] Milumbani Diary, 20 and 25 May, and 16 September 1958, KFC.

[27] Milumbani Diary, 25 and 30 Mach 1958, and 11 January 1959, KFC; *Habari za Kanisa*, No. 3, July–September, 1999 KFC; interview with Paulo Isai Misigalo, Tabora, 27 June 2017.

[28] Milumbani Diary, 19–20 May 1957, KFC. Erasto Kasoga reported, saying, 'walianzisha ugome wao kwamba wamepatana na chama cha Mtendeni ... walisema hawataki'.

the village and did not think that the anti-revivalist influence had come from Mtendeni, where he had been rejected in the previous months, but from Elia. In his diary, he asked himself: 'Mwinjilisti anayo madaraka gani ya kumzuia mchungaji asifanye kazi yake?' ('What authority does the evangelist have to prevent the pastor from exercising his duty?').[29]

Elsewhere, dissenters also prevented revivalist pastors from holding services. Congregants at Kasenga rejected Rev. Misigalo's effort to hold a service in the church and instead chose a young man, Paulo Katema, to preach, indicating their discomfort with revivalism. Recalling the people's discontent, Misigalo said, 'many people were angry at me'.[30] Christians at Uyui also took a strong stance against revivalism. Their decision went beyond preventing pastors from holding services. They announced plans to install their own pastor. They refused three times to allow Paulo Misigalo and Teofilo Kisanji to lead services in Uyui and told them that they were going to appoint another pastor. Teofilo Kisanji noted in the diary of the Tabora mission that 'those against revivalism would like to elect their pastor on 28/12/1958'. Although Kisanji did not indicate whether that plan succeeded, it was indeed a sign of opposition against the imposition of revivalism in their church.[31] It may well be that Kisanji's report about the attempt by dissenters to install their own pastor referred to Mose Muhozya, who at this time was administering his church at Mtendeni in Uyui.[32]

Dissent spread further south to the villages of the missions of Sikonge and Ipole, again causing tension between congregations and born-again pastors. At Iwensato I, the elders' council (*ivanza lya chalo*) opposed revivalism. There seemed to be an 'unwilling spirit' among the anti-revivalists concerning the tithe (*ifungu*) payment to the born-again pastor.[33] That same conflict between church members and born-again pastors was also reported at Iwensanto I and II. The church elders (*wazee wa kanisa*) gathered with the congregation. After a long conversation about tithes, the congregation said quite openly that they did not want to contribute any money as tithes or a harvest offering to

---

[29] Milumbani Diary, 19–20 May 1957, and see also 3 February 1957, KFC.

[30] Milumbani Diary, 21 and 28 September 1958, KFC; interview with Paulo Isai Misigalo, Tabora, 27 June 2017. He reported that 'watu wengi walikasirishwa sana'.

[31] Milumbani Diary, 26–27 September and 25 December 1958; *Habari za Kanisa*, 9, KFC. The diarist commented, 'nimesikia ikitangazwa kwamba hao wapinga revival wanataka kuwa na mchungaji wao tarehe 28/12/1958'.

[32] Interviews with Davidi Simoni Mwantandi and Selemani Mateo Chamlungu, Mtendeni-Tabora, 13 June 2018, and Sesilia Nikodemo Msogoti, Isevya-Tabora, 12 June 2018.

[33] Sikonge Diary, 28 October 1955, KFC.

186 SLAVE EMANCIPATION, CHRISTIAN COMMUNITIES, AND DISSENT IN TANZANIA

the revivalists because they opposed the revival movement.[34] While dissenters often opposed paying tithes as a precondition for attaining salvation, at Iwensato, they objected to paying tithes to a pastor they did not want.

Besides disputes over tithes, other tensions became apparent in the outstations as Christians opposed the born-again pastors. The Christians at Kavale village no longer wanted Elia Nsindi because he had become a *mwongofu* (born again). The elders' council in the Ugunda territory, which included Kavale village, demanded a new evangelist and forbade Nsindi to 'use the farms for cultivating', expressing their dislike of revivalism.[35] The villagers' refusal to let the pastor use church-owned fields for cultivation was an extension of the common tension between the rich farmers and poor villagers in the productive areas of Ipole and Sikonge missions in southern Unyamwezi. The concentration of people in these missions exacerbated conflict over the fertile land for cultivating maize, bananas, and rice.[36] Nsindi and a few other congregation members who had become born-again Christians were accused of 'causing a disturbance in the congregation' of the village. The church authority moved Nsindi to the Chabutwa outstation. The Christians in the village then waited for more than six months, from June to December 1957, before the new evangelist from Kitunda took charge of the outstation. The new evangelist calmed tensions and tried to dissociate himself from revivalism.[37]

The conflict between Christians and born-again pastors of Ipole and Sikonge led to the rejection of pastors who supported revivalism. At Iwensato II village, tensions mounted between the congregation and their pastor, Lukasi Masamalo, because he was involved in the revival movement. They demanded that the church board remove him, or they would not attend services. A meeting of the elders of Ugunda, which included Iwensanto I and II, was held at Iwensato II. The church board was at the top of the hierarchy of the Moravian church; under the board were pastors, elders of the church (*wazee wa kanisa*), and lay people who had to submit matters of the church in missions and villages to the board for decision.[38] At the meeting held at Iwensato II, a letter from the church board was read before the elders, after which they discussed it. The elders were quite disappointed that the letter did not reply to their request to transfer Rev. Lukasi Masamalo and install another pastor not associated with the revival movement. Most elders declared they would oppose any pastor connected to the revival movement. They also said they would

---

[34] Sikonge Diary, 13 July 1956, KFC.

[35] Sikonge Diary, 30 December 1957, KFC.

[36] Kisanji, *Historia Fupi*, 40.

[37] Sikonge Diary, 30 December 1957 and 13 April 1958, KFC.

[38] For details on the structure and functions of the Moravian church board, see Kisanji, *Historia Fupi*, 203–04.

CHRISTIANS, THE REVIVAL MOVEMENT, AND DISSENT IN MORAVIAN MISSIONS 187

refuse to be served by a born-again pastor at baptism and Holy Communion. In the end, the representative of the church board, Johannes Hansen, promised to work on their request to have Lukasi Masamalo transferred out of Ugunda territory.[39]

Soon, the council held another meeting with the board of the Moravian church at Iwensato I over the request of congregants to dismiss Lukasi Masamalo. This time, council members did not want him to be chair of the council. (Evangelists and pastors usually chaired the meetings held by the council in all missions and outstations.) The rejection of Rev. Masamalo and the call to prevent him from being the council chair was meant to deprive him of his influence on the church board. In the end, the council nominated Rev. Martin Isonda to replace Masamalo as head of the council.[40] At a third meeting at Iwensato II, the church board tried to lower the tension between the elders and Lukasi Masamalo, but Christians 'stood firm on their point, that they could not regard Lukasi as their pastor' and therefore asked for another pastor who was not involved in the movement.[41] In response to the demand from the church members, Rev. Lukasi Masamalo was transferred to Usoke. At the same time, Rev. Mateo Mchahumbi of Usoke took charge of the congregation of Iwensato I and II villages. Many people attended his service because Mchahumbi was uninvolved in the revival movement.[42]

The diarist reported tensions between dissenters and born-again pastors in various village outstations, suggesting opposition to the revival movement. In 1959, Rev. G.C. Sorensen and Rev. Paulo I. Misigalo visited the Christians of Uyui and Kasenga. They read the letter from Bishop Ibsen of 1 January as a new year's message to Christians. The letter, reported the diarist, 'was intended to appeal to Christians not to join the *ugome* of the people of Mtendeni', but Christians 'did not listen to the [Bishop's] words' ('hawaku-shika maneno').[43] On 11 January 1959, Rev. Misigalo went to the church of Mtendeni and beseeched the congregants to leave aside *ugome*, but dissenters 'refused to join him', and instead, 'they held their own service' ('waliendesha ibada yao').[44] Rev. Teofilo H. Kisanji attempted, on 1 March 1959, to influence the believers of Mtendeni to get rid of *ugome*, but when the dissenters (*wagome*) saw him, the diarist commented, 'they returned to their household and did not go back to the church'.[45] He returned to Mtendeni on 7 June

[39] Sikonge Diary, 17 August 1956, KFC.
[40] Sikonge Diary, 13 September 1956, KFC.
[41] Sikonge Diary, 10 October 1956, KFC.
[42] Sikonge Diary, 11, 23, and 28 November 1956, KFC.
[43] Milumbani Diary, 2 January 1959, KFC.
[44] Milumbani Diary, 11 January 1959, KFC.
[45] Milumbani Diary, 1 March 1959, KFC.

1959, and this time he held the meeting with women whose husbands had told them to dissociate themselves from revivalism and born-again pastors. However, his attempt yielded no substantial results because very few attended the meeting.[46] Those dissenters at Mtendeni refused to join the service on three occasions, challenging the revival movement and openly stating their dissatisfaction with born-again pastors.

Despite the acrimony between Christians and born-again pastors, annual *lusangi* celebrations continued to be held across the missions in Unyamwezi, bringing together born-again Christians and dissenters. At Iwensato I and II, many Christians attended the celebrations of 1955 and 1956, despite the trouble with their pastor, Lukasi Masamalo.[47] In 1956, many people attended the *lusangi* at Iwensato II. Rev. Erasto Kasoga held the Sunday service and baptized children on the second day of the *lusangi*.[48] Similarly, *lusangi* celebrations brought together Christians of Mivono and Sikonge. At Sikonge alone, the church was crowded, and about two hundred fifty worshipers received Holy Communion.[49] At Mtendeni in Tabora, said to be the centre of dissent, Christians could attend *lusangi* at Tabora mission. The large number of believers at the Tabora mission, which included Mtendeni outstation, indicated in 1956 the extent to which people still attended the gatherings despite the doctrinal tensions. Rev. Silasi M. Kisimi of Ichemba, evangelist Loto Tandu of Usoke, and evangelist Erasto Elia from Sikonge were invited as guest preachers.[50]

Doctrinal Controversies over Salvation, Sin, and Public Confession

Though the culture of *lusangi* attracted Christians and pastors to the revival movement, divergent interpretations of the teachings on salvation, sin, and public confession of sins divided revivalists and their born-again pastors on the one hand and the dissenters on the other. The main doctrinal teachings of the revivalists focused on ideas of salvation, sin, and confession.[51] They taught that salvation is required for accepting Jesus as the saviour. While salvation and the new birth were fundamental parts of the Christian belief, they constituted a mark of born-again Christians because preachers insisted that Christians could attain salvation while living in this world. Some born-again pastors quoted passages from the Bible, such as the Gospel of Luke

---

[46] Milumbani Diary, 7 June 1959, KFC.
[47] Sikonge Diary, 8 October 1955 and 11 November 1956, KFC.
[48] Sikonge Diary, 11, 23, and 28 November 1956, KFC.
[49] Sikonge Diary, 18 November 1955 and 10 October 1956, KFC.
[50] Milumbani Diary, 3 and 18 November 1956, KFC.
[51] Peterson, *Ethnic Patriotism*, 115.

19:9, which supported the assertion that a person can attain salvation in life.[52] These new ideas represented a doctrinal departure from how Christians and pastors believed and practised their faith. Before revivalism, pastors insisted that salvation was an ongoing process in the life of Christians and that it could only be attained after death. Probably Christians who opposed revivalism preferred the lines from the Gospel of Matthew about resisting temptations and abstaining from sin until the end of life as a necessity for attaining salvation.[53]

Divergent interpretations of individual salvation originated from the debate about tithing (*ifungu*), wealth, and salvation. From the 1930s, the Moravian church urged all Christians to pay the monthly tithe in the form of money. Formerly, tithing in crops had been common. Most Christians could not afford to pay the tithe in money, so church leaders excommunicated Christians from village churches.[54] At the village of Igwamanoni, for example, the church leadership suspended almost half of the village congregants for failing to pay tithes, which led church members to question whether being a true Christian should depend only on an individual's ability to tithe in the form of money, not on a person's behaviour.[55]

Congregants in the village of Igwamanoni became involved in the debate among teachers about whether Christians should use money to attain salvation. The debate gained momentum after Charles Pyagu, a teacher of Igwamanoni, reported the villagers' concern to the *Lusangi* newsletter. His question, 'Does money save people from sins?' stimulated debate among pastors and Christians over whether the money tithe was a prerequisite for individual salvation.[56] The *Lusangi* newsletter helped spread the debate about money and salvation

---

[52] In Luke 19:9 RSV we read that 'today salvation has come to this house, because this man too is a son of Abraham', which implies that Zacchaeus, in this case, could attain salvation following his repentance of sins.

[53] Interview with Oscar E. Kisanji, 6 August 2017; Matthew 24:13 RSV. The Book of Revelations 22:4–5 RSV also suggests this line of thinking about salvation: 'they shall see his face, and his name shall be on their foreheads. And night shall be no more; they need no light of lamp or sun, for the Lord God will be their light, and they shall reign forever and ever.'

[54] 'Barazani kuna Baba zako Wengi', *Lusangi*, No. 33, September 1938, KFC. For details on *luduko* (excommunication) cases in other villages, see Listi ya Vakristo Vahanya, Kanisaya Kamata, No. 14, 1946, KFC; Listi ya Vakristo Vahanya, Kanisa ya Ilalangulu, No. 8, 1946, KFC; and Listi ya Vakristo Vahanya, Kanisa ya Kitunda, 1947, KFC.

[55] Charles Pyagu, 'Barazani kuna Baba zako Wengi', 1938, KFC.

[56] Ibid. Charles Pyagu's question in Kiswahili, 'watu wanakombolewa na pesa?', provoked further discussion about the place of money in attaining individual salvation.

190 SLAVE EMANCIPATION, CHRISTIAN COMMUNITIES, AND DISSENT IN TANZANIA

to the many village outstations. These debates provided the grounds for the people to question revivalist teachings.

The debate over money, salvation, and becoming Christian increased during the Great Depression of the 1930s because many poor Christians could not afford to pay their tithe in money. Many people had become increasingly dependent on casual labour for rich farmers, while others resorted to labour migration to make ends meet, including paying the money tithe. It is no wonder that excommunication (*luduko*) of poor Christians from churches became common in village outstations because of the inability to pay the tithe,[57] which became a powerful motivation for opposing revivalism and arguing that wealth was not a necessary condition for individual salvation. Furthermore, dissenters opposed the money tithe because it suggested that rich people could use their wealth to guarantee salvation. Thus, dissenters protested the inequality between the rich and the poor in Unyamwezi society in matters of salvation because it violated the belief in the equality of all humans before God.[58] It is unclear from the existing documents and accounts of informants whether revivalists were for or against the payment of a money tithe. But since they worked inside the established churches, revivalists probably insisted that Christians pay tithes to make it possible to run the affairs of the churches, including the annual *lusangi*. The controversy over the money tithe and salvation increased dissent against revivalism, as dissenters questioned the role of wealth in salvation.[59]

Revivalists, recalled Sesilia Nikodemo Msogoti, 'did not establish separate churches, but we prayed together', which indicates that the Nyamwezi born-again Christians and pastors worked inside the established Moravian mission churches and village outstations.[60] In the established churches, the Nyamwezi *balokole* emphasized that Jesus literally 'washed' and 'carried

---

[57] See, for instance, Listi ya Vakristo Vahanya, Kanisaya Kamata, No. 14, 1946; Listi ya Vakristo Vahanya, Kanisa ya Ilalangulu, No. 8, 1946, KFC; and Listi ya Vakristo Vahanya, Kanisa ya Kitunda, 1947, KFC.

[58] There are several Bible passages that support equality of all humans before God. In Matthew 22:16 RSV, we read that the Pharisees asked Jesus about paying taxes to Caesar, saying 'Teacher we know that you are true … [and] you do not regard the position of men', which implies that Jesus did not care about the social status of individuals; in Acts 10:34 RSV, we also read that Peter said to the crowd, 'I perceive that God shows no partiality'; and in Romans 10:12 RSV, we read that 'For there is no distinction between Jew and Greek; the same Lord is of all and bestows his riches upon all who call upon him'.

[59] See, for instance, 'Barazani kuna Baba zako Wengi', 1938, KFC.

[60] Interview with Sesilia Nikodemo Msogoti, Isevya-Tabora, 12 June 2018. In Kiswahili, 'hawakuwa na Kanisa ila tulikuwa tunasali pamoja'.

their sins', permitting those who confessed their sins publicly to move from 'darkness' to 'walking in the light'.[61] This assertion might have come from the first letter of John 1:7, which reads, 'but if we walk in the light … Jesus his son cleanses us from all sin'.[62] The *balokole* also used statements that appear to come from the Gospel of John, including 'The light shines in the darkness, and the darkness has not overcome it', and professed that Jesus is 'the light of the world', distinguishing themselves from Christians who were not saved.[63] They considered themselves to be the light that could shine on Christians who had not been saved, seeing them instead as 'people of darkness' because 'they did not walk in the light' and as 'people not belonging to Jesus'.[64] Indeed, the analogy of light and darkness to distinguish themselves from their fellow Christians who were not part of the movement was an innovation in Christian belief and practice.

As for public confession, revivalists invited Christians to confess their sins before those who attended the revival meetings and to give testimonies of their conversion.[65] Revivalists' insistence on public confession seems to have been influenced by some verses in the Bible, especially the first letter of John 1:9, which reads: 'If we confess our sins, he … will forgive our sins and cleanse us from all the unrighteousness'. For revivalists, the phrase 'If we confess our sins' implied a call for individuals to confess their sins before the crowd.[66] Before revivalism took root in Unyamwezi, Christians confessed their sins secretly during collective prayer. Still, for revivalists, a collective prayer was not a 'real' form of confession because it did not allow church members to acknowledge their specific wrongdoings. In addition to confession during revival meetings, the Nyamwezi *balokole* launched home-visit campaigns, preaching and urging members of households to confess their sins and accept Jesus as their saviour.[67]

Unlike revivalists, who preached that salvation saved people from sin, dissenters did not believe that being born again prevented people from committing

---

[61] Interview with Oscar E. Kisanji, Kaze Hill, Tabora, 27 June 2017. See also Bruner, *Living Salvation*, 50 and 58.

[62] John 1:7–9 RSV.

[63] John 1:9 and 9:5 RSV.

[64] Interview with Sesilia Nikodemo Msogoti, Isevya-Tabora, 12 June 2018. In Kiswahili, 'watu wa gizani', 'siyo watu wa Yesu', na 'wasiotembea nuruni'.

[65] Robins, 'Tukutendereza', 6–7. Jason Bruner supports this verse from the first letter of John to imply public confession. See for details, Bruner, *Living Salvation*, 53.

[66] John 1:9 RSV.

[67] Interview with Sesilia Nikodemo Msogoti, Isevya-Tabora, 12 June 2018. In Kiswahili, 'alikuwa anatualika kuwasikiliza'.

sins. They believed that Christians could attain salvation only after death. They interpreted the teaching of revivalists about being free from sin as blasphemy (*kufuru*) and did not accept the revivalists' teaching that a person could be born again and accordingly be saved from sins (*mtu hawezi kuokoka*; in Kinyamwezi to be saved is *kulokoka*). Instead, they ridiculed the born-again teachers and pastors who attempted to convince Christians to join the revival.[68] That dissenters opposed the revivalist view of salvation corresponded to the theology of soteriology as a 'finished work of Christ which includes not only deliverance from the penalty of sin but also from the power of sin'. The theology of 'the finished work of Christ' hinged in part on Jesus' last words on the cross to show that Jesus had finished the work of salvation and that there was 'nothing left to be done to provide salvation [to people]'.[69] They also seem to have challenged the theology of higher life or the Keswick theology that 'sinless perfection is possible after one receives the second coming'.[70] For public confession, dissenters argued that, as Majaliwa Andrea put it, 'no one should stand in the way of people confessing sins'.[71] Pastors and teachers insisted on using a joint prayer to maintain secrecy during confession. Even as revivalism gained momentum in Unyamwezi, dissenters relied on the practice of confessing sins in private. They believed that sins were personal and should not be declared publicly.[72] Among the dissenters who defied the revivalists' teachings on individual salvation was Mose Muhozya. He did not believe in individual salvation or that being born again freed a person from sin. Muhozya and other dissenting Christians ridiculed born-again pastors, arguing that the teachings of revivalists about salvation and public confession of sins were blasphemous.[73]

The experience of Paulo Isai Misigalo at Mtendeni and Usoke reveals that differences in the concepts of salvation culminated in disputes between born-again pastors and dissenters. In his sermons at Mtendeni, Rev. Misigalo

---

[68] Interview with Oscar E. Kisanji, Kaze Hill, Tabora, 27 June 2017; Kisanji, *Historia Fupi*, 214.

[69] 'Soteriology – The Doctrine of Salvation', Bible.org, 2023, https://bible.org/article/soteriology-doctrine-salvation (accessed 4 October 2023). See also John 19:30.

[70] 'What is the Keswick movement, and is it biblical? Got Questions, last updated 4 January 2022, https://www.gotquestions.org/Keswick-movement.html (accessed 4 October 2023).

[71] Interview with Majaliwa Andrea, TAC, Kabila, 4 August 2018. In Kiswahili, 'hakuna kusimama mbele ya watu kukiri dhambi'.

[72] Ibid.

[73] Interview with Oscar E. Kisanji, Kaze Hill, Tabora, 27 June 2017; Kisanji, *Historia Fupi*, 214–15.

CHRISTIANS, THE REVIVAL MOVEMENT, AND DISSENT IN MORAVIAN MISSIONS   193

testified that 'Jesus had saved him', but church members became angry and mocked him, saying he could not be saved. Similarly, at Usoke, his salvation testimony brought him into dispute with his mother, who thought the preachers, including her son, were insulting the people. He recalled his mother's reaction: 'My mother was angry because she thought we were uttering insults.'[74] Her reaction demonstrates the extent to which lay Christians understood the teachings of revivalists about salvation and public confession of sins as insults to Christians who did not join revivalism and shows how some people found it hard to believe the concepts of salvation and public confession, considering them a 'mockery'. Recalling the public, Misigalo said that 'people became angry', indicating that they did not accept the teachings of revivalism.[75]

Mose Muhozya, the Tanganyika African Church (TAC), and Dissent

The rebellion of Christians against the revival movement owed much to the influence of Mose Muhozya. Available sources do not reveal his date of birth or region of origin. Still, we know he worked at the Ipole Moravian mission in the 1920s, teaching at the mission school with Mateo Mwinyi, Yonathan Njawa, and Yohanesi Ivata.[76] Muhozya subsequently transferred to the Tabora mission (Milumbani), where he worked for thirteen years as a teacher between 1927 and 1940. At Tabora, Muhozya was a hard-working teacher and knew the Bible 'more than other teachers', which accounted for his considerable influence.[77]

Muhozya's work in the Tabora mission convinced Søren H. Ibsen, the superintendent of the Moravian missions in Unyamwezi, to ordain him as pastor on 8 December 1940; he became the first Nyamwezi pastor in the Moravian Church of Western Tanzania. Given his hard work and because Ibsen feared that the Second World War would leave no European missionaries in western Tanzania, the ordination of Muhozya was meant to prepare him to become the superintendent of all the Moravian missions if the British troops interned all German missionaries.[78] Nevertheless, although the war affected the missions' activities, a few European missionaries continued to work in Unyamwezi with African teachers. Consequently, Muhozya never

---

[74] Interview with Paulo Isai Misigalo, Tabora, 27 June 2017. In Kiswahili, 'mama yangu alikasirika sana, alihisi tulikuwa tunazungumza matusi'.
[75] Ibid. In Kiswahili, 'watu walikasirishwa sana'.
[76] Kisanji, *Historia Fupi*, 151.
[77] Ibid., 185. In Kiswahili that '[Mose Muhozya] aliwazidi wenzake'.
[78] Ibid., 163.

became a superintendent but continued to work as a pastor at Tabora mission and its surrounding outstations.[79]

While serving as a teacher and later as pastor in Tabora, Muhozya, together with Isai Mgunda and Isai Maganga, revised the translation of the Kinyamwezi Bible using the common vocabulary and sayings of daily conversation. The translation of the new Kinyamwezi Bible took Muhozya and his colleagues about ten years before its completion in the late 1940s. In 1951, the newly translated Kinyamwezi Bible was published by the British and Foreign Bible Society in Dodoma and titled *Ilagano Ipya: Mhola ya Chelu yamwa Guku na Mupizya Wiswe Yesu Kristo* – literally 'The New Testament: Good News of the Grandfather (the Lord) and our Savior Jesus Christ'.[80]

In due course, Muhozya became critical of the church's authority and consequently could not get along with Bishop Ibsen. Indeed, he had a personal hatred of church leaders and invariably accused them of embezzling the church's funds, including tithes.[81] In response to Muhozya's criticisms, Ibsen and other church leaders excommunicated him 'because [he was] against the church's regulations'.[82] Muhozya formed the TAC at Mtendeni in Uyui in 1958 and became its first bishop. In the eastern part of Tabora town, Mtendeni was an outstation of the Tabora Moravian mission where teachers and pastors, including Muhozya, led the Sunday services. The church drew many Christians from the Moravian mission of Tabora and Mtendeni. Muhozya thought born-again preachers 'did not spread the message of salvation but hatred among Christians'. In his homilies, said elders who remember him, he invariably asked the question, 'If a person is saved, then why should he or she show hatred toward others?'[83] Muhozya accused born-again preachers of fomenting hatred and division among Christians (*balokole* and dissenters) and declared that their teachings did not constitute the ideals of salvation.[84] In

---

[79] For details about the effects of the Second World War on the activities of the Moravian missions in Unyamwezi, see J. Taylor Hamilton and Kenneth G. Hamilton, *History of the Moravian Church, the Renewed Unitas Fratrum 1722–1957*, 2nd edn (Bethlehem, PA: Interprovincial Board of Christian Education, Moravian Church of America, 1983), 621.

[80] *Ilagano Ipya: Mhola ya Chelu yamwa Guku na Mupizya Wiswe Yesu Kristo* (Dodoma: The Bible Society of Tanzania, 1951).

[81] Interview with Oscar E. Kisanji, Kaze Hill, Tabora, 27 June 2017. Kisanji repeatedly said during the interview that 'Mose Mhozya alikuwa na chuki binafsi kwa viongozi wa kanisa'.

[82] Kisanji, *Historia Fupi*, 215.

[83] Interviews with Davidi Simoni Mwantandi and Selemani Mateo Chamlungu, Mtendeni-Tabora, 13 June 2018, and Sesilia Nikodemo Msogoti, Isevya-Tabora, 12 June 2018.

[84] Interview with Davidi Simoni Mwantandi, Mtendeni-Tabora, 12 June 2018.

1959, Mose Muhozya opened the Tanganyika African Church at Kilimatinde in central Tanganyika for 'Christians who had dissented from the CMS'.[85]

The division became apparent between revivalists and dissenters as born-again preachers warned their followers against shaking hands with Christians who had not yet been saved because they regarded them as sinners. Emphasizing the division, Davidi Mwantandi, the current bishop of the TAC, rhetorically asked, 'Sasa wewe umeokoka unashindwaje kumpa mkono?' ('If you are born again, why shouldn't you shake hands with those who are not saved?'), indicating the extent to which born-again Christians engendered a sense of division among Christians.[86] Instead, Muhozya preached what Mwantandi calls 'the gospel of unity'. His emphasis on unity and 'sticking to the Word' ('kufuata neno lilivyo') attracted Christians from different socio-cultural backgrounds to his services in the TAC at Mtendeni.[87] His gospel of unity reinforced the persistent ethos of community, inclusiveness, and relative equality among the communities of formerly enslaved people in missions. Indeed, as we have seen, mission communities had integrated the runaway slaves, orphans, and older people by creating kinship relations based not on bonds made through blood or marriage but developed through 'fictive' or 'networked' kinship founded on the shared experiences of enslavement and conversion to Christianity.[88]

Muhozya made Mtendeni, located in a suburb of Tabora town, the centre of the TAC because it had many Moravian believers dissatisfied with revivalism. These congregants were formerly members of the Mtendeni Moravian outstation. The outstation was close to where Muhozya lived in Uyui, making it easy for him to establish himself as an independent preacher in the area.[89] As a bishop of the TAC, Muhozya installed elders of the church (*wazee wa kanisa*) and teachers (*wainjilisti*) to lead prayers and Sunday services at Mtendeni and the village branches of the TAC. Simoni Mwantandi was among the first ordained pastors of the TAC who administered the church at Mtendeni together with Muhozya. His son, Davidi Simoni Mwantandi, was also attracted to the church and aspired to become a pastor. After ordination, Davidi went to Igombewani and Kabila villages to open outstations of the TAC.[90] Although

---

[85] Milumbani Diary, 25 October 1959, KFC.

[86] Interview with Davidi Mwantandi, Mtendeni-Tabora, 13 June 2018.

[87] Ibid. In Kiswahili, Muhozya 'alihubiri mfungamano wa injili' na 'kufuata neno lilivyo'.

[88] Elisabeth McMahon, *Slavery and Emancipation in Islamic East Africa: From Honor to Respectability* (Cambridge: Cambridge University Press, 2013), 196.

[89] Interviews with Davidi Simoni Mwantandi, Mtendeni-Uyui, 13 June 2018, and Sesilia Nikodemo Msogoti, Isevya-Tabora, 12 June 2018.

[90] Interviews with Davidi Simoni Mwantandi, Mtendeni-Uyui, 13 June 2018, and

Muhozya and many dissenters seceded from the Moravian mainstream church, the liturgy in the TAC retained Moravian songs and prayers. The use of well-known songs and liturgy allowed outstations of the TAC to attract Moravians. The Kabila outstation of the TAC is an example of a church where Moravians joined the TAC for Sunday services from the late 1950s to the 1970s. Later they returned to the Moravian church in the village.[91]

Some teachers and evangelists who had resigned from the mission churches for lack of funding worked in the outstations of Muhozya's church and found other jobs to make ends meet. To support the running of the church, Muhozya established a hotel at Mtendeni. Most customers were members of the TAC who had seceded from the Moravian church. But Muhozya's 'gospel of unity' opened the hotel to everyone, including born-again Christians from the Moravian outstation of Mtendeni and Uyui. The establishment of the hotel reflected the spirit of egalitarianism among the dissidents. Profits from the hotel were used to fund church activities, including meetings, the payment of teacher salaries, and travel to the different outstations of the TAC in villages. Muhozya's opposition movement against born-again pastors and teachers spread to other missions and villages. In some villages, including Usoke, Kabila, Kipalapala, and Ikongolo, Muhozya established outstations of the TAC, serving members who wished to leave the mainstream Moravian churches.[92]

The Decline of Revivalism and Dissent, 1960

In 1960, the influence of revivalism and dissent experienced a relative decline in Unyamwezi. One development contributing to the decline was the opening of a dialogue between Christians and elders in missions and outstations where dissent had taken root. The second factor was the growing interest in national independence, meaning that 'people began thinking about independence even in churches' (to be discussed in the next section).[93] The movement for national independence spread in the villages, with pastors and lay Christians including discussions about independence during homilies and normal conversations.

Sofia Bernardo Nzige, Kabila, 4 August 2018.

[91] Interviews with Kenedi Mateo Kambele and Janeti Mgawe, Kabila village, 13 June 2018, and John Bella, Sofia Bernardo Nzige, and Jane Mgawe, 4 August 2018.

[92] Interviews with Davidi Mwantandi, Mtendeni-Tabora, 13 June 2018, Kenedi Mateo Kambele, Janeti Mgawe, and Majaliwa Andrea, Kabila village, 13 June 2018.

[93] Interview with Oscar E. Kisanji, Kaze Hill, Tabora, 27 June 2017. Kisanji remarked, 'hata kanisani watu walikuwa wanafikiria uhuru'.

CHRISTIANS, THE REVIVAL MOVEMENT, AND DISSENT IN MORAVIAN MISSIONS   197

Third, annual *lusangi* celebrations continued in each mission, despite the waves of revivalism and dissent. Christians from villages assembled for two days to read, sing, and attend the services. The growing influence of yearly *lusangi* celebrations diminished the influence of revivalism and maintained the ideals of friendship, togetherness, and neighbourhood, which were integral qualities of Unyamwezi culture. Thus, from 1960 onwards, the mission journals of Tabora and Sikonge rarely mentioned revivalism and dissent in missions and outstations, indicating a decline in the conflict over revivalism.[94]

In the outstations of Kasenga and Uyui, the dissent that had taken root following the Christians' rejection of Paulo Misigalo and Teofilo Kisanji had almost fizzled out by 1960. In 1960, the two pastors administered Holy Communion to Christians without encountering dissent. For instance, when Teofilo Kisanji held a service at Kasenga, he noted that 'yote yalikuwa shwari kabisa' (everything was okay).[95] Similarly, Paulo Misigalo, who had been rejected several times at Mtendeni, held the service at Mtendeni for the first time in 1960 with no opposition from congregants and administered baptism and confirmation.[96] However, Mose Muhozya continued serving followers who opposed revivalism in the TAC at Mtendeni. Misigalo reported that 'Mose Muhozya also administered Holy Communion to his followers in their church', indicating that Muhozya's TAC at Mtendeni was still active in 1960, with dissenters attending his Sunday services. The TAC at Mtendeni continued to attract many Christians and remained the headquarters of its village outstations for years.[97] Rev. Misigalo and Yeremia Kavombwe made frequent tours in some villages where the influence of *ugome* had become strong, and held talks with Christians. Still, they did not encounter strong opposition from dissenters. They also embarked on house-to-house visits, and again their mission progressed unopposed.[98]

Sunday services at Sikonge, Ntumbiri, Mulenda, Mkolye, Kidugalo, and Kisanga, which attracted dissenters, were well attended. After Bishop Søren Ibsen departed from the Sikonge mission on 27 May 1959, no diary record was regularly kept, and so we know no more about revivalism and dissent in

---

[94] Milumbani Diary, 15 April 1960, KFC.
[95] Milumbani Diary, 17 April and 7 June 1960, KFC.
[96] Milumbani Diary, 17 April 1960, KFC.
[97] Milumbani Diary, 15 and 17 April 1960, KFC. Misigalo reported in Kinyamwezi, 'nawe wizaga kuwapa vagome viye kiwembo mu ifuluka holyene valisomela' ['naye alikuja kuwapa wapingaji chakula cha Bwana katika kibanda chao wanachosalia'], interview with Davidi Simoni Mwantandi, Mtendeni-Tabora, 13 June 2018.
[98] Milumbani Diary, 22–23 June 1960, KFC.

Unyamwezi.[99] Reports about the Sikonge mission did not resume until 1968. Between the final entry in the diary in 1960 and 1968, an independent Moravian church was established in western Tanzania, with much of the work in the mission placed in the hands of African pastors. Despite the absence of records, dissent continued at Mtendeni, Kabila, and in some villages of Sikonge mission where the TAC had already established outstations. At Kabila village, Christians who had seceded from the Moravian mainstream church continued to attend Sunday services, attracting even the Moravian Christians.[100]

Nationalism, Africanization, and Divisions among the Moravians, 1955–60

The aftermath of *ugome* in Unyamwezi coincided with the wave of Africanization and nationalism in Tanganyika, whose influence also filtered into village and mission churches. The Second World War had already weakened the Moravian church in Rungwe, bordering the Moravian Church in Western Tanzania to the north, placing all the mission work 'almost entirely under African control'.[101] In the villages and mission stations of southern Unyamwezi, teachers and pastors formed the Unity of Kiwere Tribal Association (UKTA) because European missionaries had showed no concern for the problems they faced in the villages. Between 1947 and 1950, the association attracted membership from far and wide and served as a platform for congregants to voice their grievances. The UKTA demanded that residents of Kiwere have access to better healthcare and education and that Africans be promoted to leadership positions in mission schools and hospitals.

Nevertheless, the management of dispensaries and schools created tension between missionaries and members of the UKTA. While, for instance, advisors to the UKTA desired that the proposed construction of the dispensary at Kiwere be under the patronage of members and the 'native' authority as a solution to growing social inequalities, missionaries opposed the plan, arguing that they would appoint the doctor in charge and that people would be asked to pay money for treatment so long as the mission treasury paid the doctor. In the end, the disputes between the UKTA and Moravian missionaries greatly

---

[99] Sikonge Diary, 27 May 1959, and 7 October 1960, KFC.

[100] Milumbani Diary, 29 March 1959, and 15 April 1960; Sikonge Diary, January 1968, KFC; interviews with Davidi Mwantandi, 13 June 2018, and Kenedi Mateo Kambele, 13 June 2018.

[101] John Iliffe, *A Modern History of Tanganyika* (Cambridge: Cambridge University Press, 1979), 546.

affected the membership of the association because the Nyamwezi Christians were divided over the reasonings of missionaries and advisors.[102]

In 1955, Bishop John Foy from England, who had visited the Moravian church of Rungwe, reported in the newspaper of the Moravian Board (*gazeti la Bodi*) about the 'effective African control' of mission and village churches but made a rather negative comment on the Moravian church in Unyamwezi, complaining that 'the church found its people hard to control' ('walikuwa wazito kutwaa madaraka') and that 'they did not have the motive to grow' ('wasiokuwa na hamu ya kukua'), implying that they were pleased with missionaries' control of the church in western Tanganyika. Nevertheless, Bishop Foy drew his conclusions based on rumours that did not consider the realities on the ground. Pastors and teachers openly challenged the report and called it 'scandalous' ('kashfa') because 'it degraded the status of our diocese' ('iliondoa hadhi ya Jimbo letu').[103]

Foy's unsubstantiated report enraged members of the UMCC because it dismissed their work as ineffective and so exasperated teachers and pastors in missions and villages. In 1957, partly in response to the report, members of the Church Board (Halmashauri ya Kanisa) at Usoke held a 'private meeting without missionaries' ('walipata faragha bila wamisionari'). They talked at length about how they were tired of being 'harassed' ('kunyanyaswa') and of the increasing animosity between European missionaries and African teachers. They decided that 'a party or council of *wananchi*' be established to help them 'rise from their present conditions' to the level that would enable them to 'assume the authority of managing their affairs to become self-reliant' ('kutwaa madaraka na kujitegemea wenyewe').[104] The same year, African pastors and teachers formally established the Unyamwezi Moravian Church Council (UMCC), or Baraza la Kanisa la Moravian Unyamwezi. In his letter to Bishop Foy, Teofilo Kisanji, the organizing secretary of the UMCC, made it clear that although Foy's words hurt the Nyamwezi pastors and teachers, they had challenged him to think about their position in the church, and Kisanji declared that, 'in future, we will keep your words in all our achievements towards the self-supporting status of the Moravian church in Unyamwezi'.[105] Kisanji's response indicated the determination of Nyamwezi teachers and

---

[102] Assistant Secretary to Secretary UKTA Rungwe, Kiloli, 3 July 1947; Teofilo H. Kisanji, secretary to UKTA, to the advisor, 26 July 1947.

[103] Oscar E. Kisanji, *Nimesema, Askofu Teofilo Hiyobo Kisanji: Baadhi ya Maandiko aliyoandika Hotuba alizotoa na Mahubiri aliyoyafanya kati am waka 1955 na 1982* (Tabora: Frontex Associates, 2023), 13.

[104] Kisanji, *Historia Fupi*, 169–70.

[105] Teofilo Kisanji, Organizing Secretary of UMCC to Rev. J.H. Foy, 13 January 1958, KFC.

pastors to take the church into their own hands. While the Moravian Board approved the UMCC's formation, all missionaries, including the superintendent of the Moravian missions in Unyamwezi, Bishop Søren Ibsen, were displeased with it, arguing that the council 'consisted of Africans only' ('lilikuwa la wanakanisa wananchi tu') and that this would split the church and deprive the church board of its authority in the region.[106]

Despite the fear and unwelcoming response from the church authority, which teachers and pastors expected, the UMCC pushed its agenda of self-governance and attracted a membership of educated Christians and lay congregants in villages, Tabora town, and beyond Unyamwezi. In 1958, the council presided over by Pastor Abraham Iteo appointed Silas Kisimi as vice president and Mwalimu Adam Erasto Kaombwe as secretary general of the general assembly of Chabutwa.[107] From 27 to 29 October 1958, the council held a meeting at Chabutwa that was attended by thirty-one pastors from Kivele, Mpanda and Inyonga, Ugunda, Ngulu (Sikonge), Tabora, Usoke, Urambo, Ichemba, and Usukuma, including the superintendent of the Moravian missions of Unyamwezi, Bishop Ibsen, whom they listed as an 'invited guest' ('mgeni mwalikwa').[108] In his speech to the council, Ibsen expressed his qualms about the functions of UMCC, which in his view were similar to those of the Church Conference.[109] But in response to his reservations, the president of UMCC ardently stated that 'we have only one objective' ('lengo letu ni moja tu'), which is 'to stand on our own' ('kusimama wenyewe').[110] As part of its programme of self-governance, the UMCC solicited contributions from Christians across Unyamwezi missions and villages to run the daily affairs of the council and the general assembly. By October 1958, Christians had contributed the sum of TZS 2,848.90 to the council, which had set up a bank account in Tabora.[111]

The general assembly deliberated on four agendas linked to nationwide nationalism and Africanization. First, the meeting deliberated on Christians' proposal that the membership cards and regulations governing the council be printed for Christians to buy. But the council objected to the proposal that

---

[106] Ripoti ya Unyamwezi Moravian Church Council ya Mwaka 1957, KFC.

[107] 'Minuti zya mkutano gwa Unyamwezi Moravian Church Council' [Miniti za Mkutano wa U.M.C.C. Na. 2, Chabutwa 27, 28, 29, 1958], KFC.

[108] 'Minuti zya mkutano', October 1958, KFC.

[109] 'Hotuba yamwa Superintendent Bishop S.H. Ibsen hambele na ivanza lya U.M.C.C. Chabutwa, lusiku lwa Jumatano', 29 October 1958, KFC. See also Letter from Ibsen to Teofilo Kisanji, Organizing Secretary of UMCC, 28 November 1958, KFC.

[110] 'Minuti zya mkutano', October 1958, p. 1, KFC.

[111] Ibid., p. 1.

CHRISTIANS, THE REVIVAL MOVEMENT, AND DISSENT IN MORAVIAN MISSIONS 201

membership cards be bought. While the reasons for this objection remain unclear, it seems that the gathering objected to the idea in favour of free distribution, to reach as many Christians as possible. The assembly also consented that the missions of Kivele, Mpanda and Inyonga, Ugunda, Ngulu (Sikonge), Tabora, Usoke, Urambo, Ichemba, and Usukuma were to use the logo of the UMCC and that all people living beyond Unyamwezi 'be informed about the existence of the UMCC'.[112] Second, because the UMCC desired to take control of the church, there was an urgent need for an educated elite (*vasomi*) that could take up leadership and administrative positions. In the end, members subscribed to the proposal that middle-school teachers advise students that 'the church needs educated people too.'[113] Third, members audaciously stated in front of Bishop Ibsen that the council planned to propose to the Mission Board in Europe that the 'Superintendent [in Unyamwezi mission field] be African' because the church had grown with a substantial number of African Christians.[114]

In an undated document entitled 'Some thoughts about the future of two Moravian fields in Tanganyika', Amos James Nsekela, who later served as a diplomat and chairperson and managing director of the National Bank of Commerce, saw the need for the Moravian church to 'work ahead of politics' because the church ought to 'remodel [its] thinking in terms of a Moravian Church in Tanganyika'.[115] He called on the Moravian church to think about itself as a church capable of enriching people's existence and life in a self-governing Tanganyika. To be able to do this, insisted Nsekela, '[the] two Moravian fields in Unyamwezi and the Southern highlands must come closer together and be able to work hand in glove'.[116] Nsekela's appeal for mutual aid between the Moravian churches in Unyamwezi and the Southern Highlands effectively pushed the agenda for autonomous churches. Further, the regular correspondence between African pastors in the two mission fields, as well as in the CMS Diocese of Central Tanganyika, whose independence and self-governance of the churches became dominant in the late 1950s, called for the establishment of a newspaper that would provide them with a platform to deliberate and share experiences across the vast areas of the territory.[117]

---

[112] Ibid., p. 2.

[113] Ibid., p. 3.

[114] Ibid., p. 3.

[115] Amon J.A.S. Nsekela, 'Some thoughts on the future of our two Moravian fields in Tanganyika', n.d., KFC.

[116] Ibid.

[117] See, for instance, Mr A.J. Nsekela, CMS Mvumi kwa Makanisa ya Moravian, Unyamwezi na Southern Highlands, 8 November 1957, KFC.

The push for Africanization of the church dominated the churches of Unyamwezi for almost a decade, and the response from the UMCC was not immediate. Silas Kisimi Masalu, who was working as resident pastor of Chabutwa, recalled to his fellow pastors Bishop Ibsen's rhetorical question of 1940, 'When will you Nyamwezi stand on your own?' ('Wanyamwezi lini mtasimama wenyewe kwa miguu yenu?'), as a wake-up call to get them to think about assuming control of the church.[118] This question, which had lingered in the minds of pastors for almost a decade, inspired the UMCC's invitation of Bishop Ibsen to the general assembly to demonstrate that they were ready to administer the church with an African superintendent. By the 1950s, complaints that Africans were 'denied complete authority' ('hawaku-pewa madaraka kamili') had become common in churches, education, and healthcare institutions because European missionaries 'accomplished tasks which Africans could easily do'.[119]

Under mounting pressure, the UMCC made four resolutions at its general meeting in Chabutwa. First, members acceded to the demand that Africans with the required qualifications for higher administrative positions be installed with 'immediate effect' ('sasa hivi') so that they could learn from European missionaries.[120] That teachers had to take higher administrative positions immediately corresponded to the nationwide drive for Africanization that, in *sensus stricto*, meant to replace foreign expatriate workers (non-Africans) with Africans.[121] Second, the council called upon European missionaries holding higher positions to allow Africans to assume these posts without hesitation. European missionaries' indecisions about letting Africans assume higher administrative positions caused the advancement of African pastors to come to a standstill in some churches, schools, and hospitals. Ibsen's response to Teofilo Kisanji, the organizing secretary of the UMCC, that 'it is totally impossible' ('kigakaa kabisa') to assume 'complete authority of Superintendship in one year' ('madaraka ya kuwa Superintendent kamili katika mwaka mmoja') and that 'I do not want to be a teacher for a task that cannot be accomplished in one year' ('sikubaliani mimi kuwa mwalimu wa kazi ambayo haiwezekani kufundishwa kwa mwaka mmoja') reflected the opinions of missionaries on granting complete authority to Africans in Unyamwezi.[122] Third, missionar-

---

[118] Silas Kisimi Masalu kumwa mudugu wane Rev. Teofilo Kisanji, Ichemba, 15 December 1958, KFC.

[119] 'Minuti zya mkutano', October 1958, p. 4, KFC.

[120] Ibid., p. 4.

[121] Iliffe, *A Modern History*, 542; Paul Bjerk, *Building a Peaceful Nation: Julius Nyerere and the Establishment of Sovereignty in Tanzania, 1960–1964* (Rochester, NY: University of Rochester Press, 2015), 73.

[122] Bishop S.H. Ibsen to Teofilo Kisanji, the Organizing Secretary, UMCC, 28

ies' reservations about ceding complete authority over the church, schools, and health services prompted the council to propose that Europeans remain as advisors, preparing and mentoring Africans for administrative and leadership positions, with the expectation that, after a short transition, they would leave the church and its institutions in the hands of Africans. Finally, members agreed to sponsor a scholarship for Africans to learn about administrative work (*kazi za madaraka*) and get acquainted with the proper management of the church.[123]

Teachers working in all Moravian-run schools across the region founded the Moravian Unyamwezi Teachers' Union (MUTU) as an effective podium, in addition to the UMCC, for voicing their concerns about church authority over educational affairs. As a union of *vasomi* (the literate), teachers across the Unyamwezi mission field used MUTU to uphold the ideals of teaching, fulfil the standards imposed by the department of education, and act as a collective bargaining platform 'to channel their grievances in one voice' ('kupeleka malalamiko yao kwa sauti moja') against the inequalities entrenched in the church and the education system.[124] Initially, the union met with resistance from the church leadership because of its dissident character. Still, teachers persevered through fear and intimidation and sustained the union as the only effective means of collectively facing down the power of the church leadership and the department of education. The union became an important organ 'for the development of the Unyamwezi Moravian mission field' ('kwa manufaa kwa maendeleo ya Idara hiyo katika jimbo').[125]

In May 1959, the African Inland Mission marked the fiftieth anniversary of missionary work in the Lake Region. Its leadership invited Pastor Teofilo Hiyobo Kisanji from the Moravian Church of Western Tanganyika to attend the celebrations at Nasa in Mwanza. Again, the independence and Africanization of churches in Tanganyika dominated the anniversary discussions. In his speech for the golden jubilee, Kisanji told the congregants that nationalism had become the household name for both TANU leaders and Africans in churches. Therefore, it was inevitable to talk about it as 'it had entered the hearts of Africans' in Tanganyika.[126] Because nationalism had dominated the religious and political spheres of the 1950s, Kisanji observed, it had aroused 'the attitude of self-governance' ('moyo wa kutaka kujitawala') among Christians in missions and villages. His insistence that 'it is better to have poverty and suffering in independence than richness and prosperity

---

November 1958, KFC.

[123] 'Minuti zya mkutano', October 1958, p. 4, KFC.

[124] Kisanji, *Historia Fupi*, 220.

[125] Ibid.

[126] Kisanji, *Nimesema*, 2.

in enslavement and colonialism' shows how Christians and Tanganyikans in general imagined colonialism as a form of enslavement that had shaped socioeconomic, political, and religious circumstances in nineteenth- and twentieth-century Unyamwezi.[127] In breaking with the past of enslavement and colonialism, Kisanji encouraged pastors, teachers, and Christians to overcome the fear and doubt that might arise while discussing the independence and self-governance of churches in Tanganyika. He emphatically stated that the Bible 'does not legalize colonization and *enslavement*', and therefore that '[it is not] sinful for people to govern themselves'.[128]

Kisanji's citation of the Bible as a primary source was meant to encourage pastors, teachers, and Christians to join in TANU's quest for majority rule in Tanganyika. It stemmed from his experience in Unyamwezi, where the pursuit of independence and Africanization divided Christians and the Moravian church. While pastors in Unyamwezi pushed for these agendas, some leaders in churches and Christians in villages and missions held back their support. Instead, they 'helped the colonial authority to prevent Africanization' ('walisaidia serikali kuzuia kujitawala kwa wananchi'), and slowed down the 'devolution of power' in churches and governments at provincial, district, and local levels.[129] He told the audience that on 3 May 1959, one African preacher (whose name he did not disclose) preached against the need for independence in Tanganyika, citing Matthew 6:33 ('But seek first his kingdom and his righteousness, and all these things shall be yours as well'). Another preacher cited the book Genesis 9:20–27 about curses and enslavement if people demanded independence and self-governance.[130] But Kisanji rebutted preachers of this sort and referred to them as 'quislings' because 'they openly [sold] the right for independence by flattering the whites!' ('[waliuza] haki ya uhuru kimachomacho kwa kujipendekeza kwa Wazungu!').[131] Kisanji called upon Christians and African pastors who had attended the anniversary of the African Inland Mission to rid themselves of divisive and cowardly preachings, urging them to put the demands for 'independence first and then religion later' ('uhuru

---

[127] Ibid., 5. In Kiswahili, 'heri umasikini na shida katika uhuru kuliko mali na raha katika utumwa wa kutawaliwa'.

[128] Ibid., 2. In Kiswahili, 'hata Wakristo wanapopeleleza katika imani yao inayofafanuliwa katika Biblia, hawaoni sheria au kanuni ya haki inayoweza kuleta sababu ya kuwafanya wakae chini ya utawala wa wageni'.

[129] Ibid., 6–7.

[130] The preacher in question frequently cited Genesis 9:25, 'Cursed be Canaan; a slave of slaves shall he be to his brothers', and verses 26 and 27, 'Blessed by the Lord my God be Shem; and let Canaan be his slave' and 'God enlarge Japheth, and let him dwell in the tents of Shem; and let Canaan be his slave'.

[131] Kisanji, *Nimesema*, 7.

CHRISTIANS, THE REVIVAL MOVEMENT, AND DISSENT IN MORAVIAN MISSIONS   205

kwanza dini baadaye') and that these teachings would enable 'European missionaries to turn [Africans] secretly into their slaves' ('wazungu kuwageuza [Waafrika] kuwa watumwa wao kisirisiri').[132] Kisanji concluded his speech with words 'Haya, Kanisa, Amka! Shika Usukani Utuegeshe Bandarini' ('Now, church, take charge! Steer the boat and dock us safely!'), as a wake-up call for Christians to be at the forefront of Tanganyika's campaign for majority rule.[133]

Kisanji's relentless call for Africanization persisted and dominated his speeches of the late 1950s, and he used opportunities available in the church to push for this agenda. On 15 May 1961, Kisanji read a speech before delegates of the British Mission Board and the Danish Brethren Mission in Christianfield, Denmark. Africanization constituted the main theme of his talk for the Moravian Church in Western Tanganyika. He told delegates that the need for Africanization of the Moravian church in Unyamwezi paralleled Tanganyika's demand for independence, and just as the people in the territory aspired to achieve what they called 'our own ways' ('njia zetu wenyewe') so too were the church's aspirations for Africanization to determine 'its ways' ('njia zake lenyewe').[134] He fervently told the delegates that the 'political turns' ('mageuko'), characteristic of the increasing wave of independence, had spread in urban and rural Tanganyika and showed that Tanganyika would soon gain its majority rule. The signs that Tanganyikan independence was at hand, Kisanji argued, would have been deemed meaningless had the church not made strides to define its 'own ways' ('njia zake lenyewe'), 'identity' ('utambulisho'), and 'regulations to sustain its independence' ('kanuni zake na kuendeleza uhuru wake').[135] Thus, on 28 December 1961 – nineteen days after Tanganyika's independence – the British Mission Board sent a telegram to the Moravian authority in western Tanganyika, stating that, effective from 1 January 1962, the church would have complete authority over its own synodal proceedings, constitution, and provincial board.[136]

In the same year, in 1962, the Synod elected Kisanji Superintendent of the Moravian Church in Western Tanganyika, becoming the first African to hold this position. He was elected bishop of the Moravian Church in Tanzania in 1965. His consecration took place on 27 November 1966 at Tabora under Bishop Ibsen, his predecessor, as the main celebrant, assisted by Bishop

[132] Ibid., 8.
[133] Ibid., 13.
[134] Teofilo Kisanji, Speech delivered at the BDM/BMB in Christiansfeld, Denmark, 15 May 1961, KFC. See also Kisanji, *Nimesema*, 18–19.
[135] Teofilo Kisanji, Speech delivered at the BDM/BMB in Christiansfeld, Denmark, 15 May 1961, KFC; Kisanji, *Nimesema*, 19 and 21.
[136] Kisanji, *Nimesema*, 26.

John Madinda of the Anglican Church, Diocese of Central Tanganyika, Bishop Josiah Kibira of the Evangelical Lutheran Church in Northwestern Tanganyika, and Bishop John Foy. As the first African bishop, Kisanji was entrusted to serve the Moravian Church in Western Tanganyika. He was also duty-bound to serve the Moravian Church in Southern and Southwest Tanzania until Anosisye Jongo became bishop of Southern Tanzania in 1979 and Yohana Wavenza became bishop of Southwest Tanzania in 1982.[137]

Conclusion

In his pastoral letter to all clerics of the Moravian Church in Western Tanzania of 25 July 1970, Bishop Teofilo Hiyobo Kisanji reported that Mose Muhozya, who had decamped from the Moravian Church of Western Tanzania, had passed away on 21 July 1970 at the Tabora regional hospital. The bishop communicated this message to all pastors in missions and villages, admitting that although Muhozya established his church, his legacy was worth acknowledging in the Moravian Church of Unyamwezi because 'he was the first African to be ordained in the church on 8 December 1940'.[138] His ordination signalled an important epoch in the Moravian enterprise in western Tanzania since 1898, when the first missionaries took over the mission work of the LMS missionaries at Urambo.[139] Therefore, his ordination was part of the church's attempt to 'read the signs of the times', that is, the wave of nationalism and Africanization that penetrated rural Tanganyika under the banner of the TANU. Chief Abdallah Fundikira of the Chiefdom of Unyanyembe stood as TANU's candidate for the elections of 1958–59, and his position as a Nyamwezi chief helped the party gain influence in the region.[140]

In 1958, TANU held an annual conference in Tabora and resolved to spread the party's message 'until the smallest child in the village should know the meaning of TANU and freedom', and after the resolution, a series of meetings and conversations followed in villages 'until TANU had announced itself at every house in every village'.[141] These strategies filtered into churches and called for more African pastors to take up positions in the church hierarchy. In addition to nationalism, the ordination of Mose Muhozya was also a response

[137] Rev. Angolwisye Isakwisa Malambugi, 'Kisanji, Teofilo Hiobo, 1915–1982', *Dictionary of African Christian Biography*, 2007, https://dacb.org/stories/tanzania/kisanji/ (accessed 5 October 2023).

[138] Barua ya Teofilo H. Kisanji kwa Wachungaji Wote, MCWT, 25 July 1970, KFC.

[139] W. Draper to Rev. G. Bousins, Urambo, 24 January 1898, CWM/LMS/Box 10/Folder 1/No. 9.

[140] Iliffe, *A Modern History*, 560.

[141] Ibid., 558.

CHRISTIANS, THE REVIVAL MOVEMENT, AND DISSENT IN MORAVIAN MISSIONS 207

to Bishop Ibsen's rhetorical question of 1940, asking Nyamwezi pastors when they would be ready to stand on their own in running the church.[142] Indeed, the increasing number of African pastors that followed Muhozya's ordination suggested that the need for Africanization of the church would in no time be 'breaking the chain' of the authority of Moravian missionaries at 'its weakest link' because the quest for nationalism and self-governance in Tanganyika had reached the point of no return in the 1950s, and African pastors and teachers expressed 'the desire to speak with unity in an independent state'.[143]

Therefore, Muhozya's dissent from the Moravian mainstream church was both an attempt to find an 'African expression of Christianity' and the drive for the independence of African pastors from the control of missionaries in churches, education, and health institutions.[144] His daring challenge to the missionaries' administration of the church and the systemic inequality between African pastors and missionaries in churches, schools, and hospitals was motivated by his desire for an independent platform on which to practice his Christian faith. It is no wonder that as doctrinal conflicts increased in the Moravian churches, Muhozya seceded and established the TAC, attracting many Christians from the Moravian missions of Tabora and Mtendeni. Eventually, Mtendeni in Tabora became the centre of dissent, influencing other Christians in missions and villages to mount similar oppositional actions against pastors and evangelists.

The complete authority of the church in Unyamwezi over its own synodal proceedings, constitution, and provincial board signalled a new era in the administration of the missions and village outstations. That African pastors would have complete authority over the church in western Tanzania implied that their efforts in pushing for the Africanization of the church had paid off with great *éclat*. In 1971, the Moravian Church in Western Tanzania marked the tenth anniversary of its administration. As Africans assumed total control of the church, which was then recognized as a synodal province, they had the right to representation at the Unity Conference held in Cape Town in South Africa in August 1962. The church also sent two African delegates to the Moravian Unity Synod in Potstejn, Czechoslovakia, from 6 July to 4 August

---

[142] Silas Kisimi Masalu kumwa mudugu wane Rev. Teofilo Kisanji, Ichemba, 15 December 1958, KFC.

[143] John Iliffe, 'Breaking the Chain at its Weakest Link: TANU and the Colonial Office', in Gregory H. Maddox and James L. Giblin (eds), *In Search of a Nation: Histories of Authority and Dissidence in Tanzania* (Oxford: James Currey, 2005), 168–93; Iliffe, *A Modern History*, 546.

[144] For more details about 'African expressions of Christianity', see Thomas Spear and Isaria N. Kimambo (eds), *East African Expressions of Christianity* (Oxford: James Currey, 1999).

1967. Africans also had the authority to hold synodal conferences that provided pastors across the Unyamwezi missions with avenues to discuss various aspects of governing the church, including the new constitution, which would correspond to the needs and challenges of the people in Unyamwezi. By 1971, the new constitution of the Moravian Church of Western Tanzania was already being used in the Moravian missions and villages.[145]

[145] Kisanji, *Nimesema*, 26.

Conclusion

The experiences of formerly enslaved people in nineteenth- and twentieth-century western Tabora leave no doubt that the abolition of slavery and the creation of communities involved various forces, ranging from individual initiatives to the influence of missionaries and government intervention. Although missionaries and the colonial state played an undeniable role in emancipation, their strategies were insufficient to eliminate the institution of slavery, as it was so entrenched in the social system. Instead, the end of slavery, as Deutsch reiterated, was due to a 'prolonged struggle between owners and slaves, in which slaves tried to make the best of the limited choices and opportunities available to them'.[1] In particular, the use of public declarations and witnesses, which developed in mission communities as a prerequisite for certification of freedom, was one strategy that demonstrated slaves' intellectual creativity in shaping the legal procedure for emancipation. Public pronouncements and oath-taking became the legal prerequisites for freedom and signalled the slaves' desire to begin a new life in missions and villages. The use of such statements and the calling of witnesses shows that slaves were not passive subjects of the laws imposed by the colonial state; instead, their actions helped shape the legal system in Tanganyika, ultimately leading the British colonial state, which took over the administration of German East Africa after the war, to enact the Evidence Act and the Oaths and Affirmations Act in 1920.[2]

In Unyamwezi, early converts were primarily formerly enslaved people who did not come from well-established families. Thus, in Unyamwezi, the assimilation of Christianity reflected the concerns of people who were seeking to escape marginalization under existing social hierarchies. One of the ways they expressed their vision of Christianity was through the translation of religious texts. Additionally, the Nyamwezi practice of *lusangi* provided

---

[1] Jan-Georg Deutsch, *Emancipation without Abolition in German East Africa, c.1884–1914* (Oxford: James Currey, 2006), 242.

[2] Alison Russell, *The Laws of Tanganyika Territory*, Vol. 1 (London: Waterlow & Sons, 1929), 10.

opportunities to build social networks and communities. Weekly dances in Catholic missions and the annual *lusangi* meetings among the Moravians provided avenues for extending networks of friendship and support among the Nyamwezi Christians in villages. The formation of the Unity of Kiwere Tribal Association (UKTA), Unyamwezi Moravian Church Council (UMCC), and Moravian Unyamwezi Teachers' Union (MUTU) offered a means by which teachers and Christians in villages could protest social inequality and endorse the rising demand for Africanization. These organizations embodied collective action for the welfare of congregants as bona fide citizens.[3]

The demand for complete authority over the churches and associated institutions dominated the religious public sphere of 1950s western Tanzania. Africans proved beyond a reasonable doubt – by their ability to administer mission and village churches as pastors, catechists, and teachers – that they could accomplish the administrative and leadership 'tasks' independently of the control of European missionaries.[4] Thus, the formation of the UMCC was part of Africans' quest for Africanization of the church in the region and a direct challenge to the preconceptions of men like Bishop Foy, who condescendingly assumed that Africans in Unyamwezi would find it 'hard to assume the authority of the church' ('walikuwa wazito kutwaa madaraka') because 'they did not want to grow' ('hawakutaka kukua').[5] In due course, the UMCC became an important means of confronting the entrenched inequalities between Africans and missionaries in mission churches, schools, and health institutions. Its existence in missions and villages demonstrated that the aspirations for the development of African Christianity under the leadership of Africans had won great favour among teachers and congregants who faced the daily challenges of living under the authority of European missionaries. The UMCC proved an effective vehicle by which to 'assume the authority of managing their affairs to become self-reliant'.[6]

Of course, the road to Africanization and self-governance of the church in western Tanzania was not easy because of the divisions between pastors and congregants over how this self-governance should be pursued. These divisions transcended the limits of churches as a few Africans emphasized the

---

[3] Secretary to District Commissioner of Tabora, 7 April 1947, KFC UKTA; Minuti zya mkutano gwa Unyamwezi Moravian Church Council, No. 2, Chabutwa 27, 28, 29, 1958, KFC; Teofilo H. Kisanji, *Historia Fupi ya Kanisa la Kimoravian Tanganyika Magharibi* (Kipalapala: TMP, 1980), 220.

[4] 'Minuti zya mkutano', October 1958, 4, KFC.

[5] Oscar E. Kisanji, *Nimesema, Askofu Teofilo Hiyobo Kisanji: Baadhi ya Maandiko aliyoandika Hotuba alizotoa na Mahubiri aliyoyafanya kati ya mwaka 1955 na 1982* (Tabora: Frontex Associates, 2023), 13.

[6] Kisanji, *Historia Fupi*, 169–70.

difficulties the change presented and 'helped the colonial authority' to slow down the 'devolution of power'.[7] Notwithstanding the reservations of the few Africans who were not for change, the move gained momentum in the mid-1950s because decolonization in Tanganyika had reached a point of no return, providing a solution to the problems of increased colonial exploitation. TANU nationalists capitalized on the spirit of dissent and the devolution of power, which had spread in the missions and villages of Unyamwezi, channelling the ambitions for Tanganyikan independence into the churches.[8] No sooner had ideas of independence filtered down into rural Unyamwezi than catechists and teachers demanded greater recognition and a greater role in the administration of churches in villages and mission stations. The Moravian teachers, riding the wave of Tanganyikan nationalism, increased the pace of the movement for self-governance, demanding complete authority over synodal proceedings and the provincial board within the Moravian Church of Western Tanganyika.[9]

Gender, Authority, Adaptation, and the Making of Christianity

Undoubtedly, women and girls in nineteenth- and twentieth-century Unyamwezi constituted most of the slaves who joined mission communities.[10] With the increasing conflicts in the nineteenth and early twentieth century in Unyamwezi, many slave women from various parts of the East African interior laboured in the region as domestic and field slaves and adapted themselves to the Nyamwezi culture and language. While some enslaved men had limited opportunities available to them to form marronage villages, most slave women resorted to joining mission communities because the location of mission and orphanage centres – which were built close to the central caravan route – made them more easily reachable both by slaves seeking refuge and

---

[7] Kisanji, *Nimesema*, 6–7.

[8] Interview with Oscar E. Kisanji, Tabora, 4 March 2020. See also Salvatory S. Nyanto, 'Priests without Ordination: Catechists and their Wives in Villages Beyond Missions, 1948–1978', *Catholic Historical Review*, Vol. 108, No. 3 (2022), 571.

[9] Kisanji, *Nimesema*, 25–27.

[10] See for instance Jan-Georg Deutsch, 'Notes on the Rise of Slavery and Social Change in Unyamwezi, c. 1860–1900', in Henri Médard and Shane Doyle (eds), *Slavery in the Great Lakes Region of East Africa* (Athens: Ohio University Press, 2007), 92; Edward A. Alpers, 'The Story of Swema: Female Vulnerability in Nineteenth-Century East Africa', in Claire C. Robertson and Martin Klein (eds), *Women and Slavery in Africa* (Madison: University of Wisconsin Press, 1983), 185.

orphans whose parents had been taken into slavery. Because of the strategic locations of their missions, missionaries were less responsive to the chiefs and, therefore, less useful as a source of chiefly legitimacy. Indeed, the list of slave names and orphan girls recorded from missionary sources and their young and productive ages suggest that 'being female made one especially vulnerable to enslavement' in nineteenth- and twentieth-century East Africa.[11]

Because slaves and orphans lived entirely dependent on what the missions could provide to maintain their precarious existence, missionaries became 'patrons and protectors'.[12] The range of manual labour that characterized the lives of formerly enslaved people in the missions did not reflect the kind of freedom they had longed for in joining mission communities. They encountered *new* communities of various sizes, compositions, and degrees of discipline. Despite the diversity, mission communities functioned as places where European culture rather than the culture of formerly enslaved people controlled the daily routine.[13] Very often, teenagers and children with what the missionaries called 'intolerable behaviour' lived under close supervision until they reached the age of marriage, after which they were allowed to leave the community and live in nearby villages.[14] Furthermore, close supervision and a strict timetable for the range of activities in the mission separated residents from the wider village life, culture, and friends.[15]

In the end, formerly enslaved people adapted themselves to the culture of mission communities and Nyamwezi society. Weekly dances and *lusangi* festivals bound formerly enslaved people to Christian and Nyamwezi culture because they offered them opportunities to be integrated into mission communities and villages.[16] While some slaves assimilated to the new culture by retaining their names with slave antecedents, others did not accept the practice and chose Christian names as a periphrasis of their former identity.[17]

---

[11] F. van Vlijmen, 'The Origins of the Archdiocese of Tabora' (Unpublished manuscript, Ndala, 1990), 39; Adrian Hastings, *The Church in Africa 1450–1950* (Oxford: Clarendon Press, 1996), 213; Alpers, 'The Story of Swema', 186.

[12] Andreana C. Prichard, *Sisters in Spirit: Christianity, Affect, and Community Building in East Africa, 1860–1970* (East Lansing: Michigan State University, 2017), 59.

[13] Hastings, *The Church*, 214.

[14] Interview with Tekla Herman, Ushirombo, 5 December 2016.

[15] Kathleen R. Smythe, *Fipa Families: Reproduction and Catholic Evangelization in Nkasi, Ufipa, 1880–1960* (Portsmouth; NH: Heinemann, 2006), 80.

[16] Interview with Mhoja, Nhazengwa, 22 November 2016.

[17] Listi ya Vakristo Vahanya, Kanisa ya Ulilwansimba, Sikonge, Listi No. 2, entry 1944, KFC; Listi ya Vakristo Vahanya, Kanisa ya Vutyatya-Sikonge, Listi No 3, entry 527, 1944, KFC; and Listi Listi ya Vakristo Vahanya, Kanisa ya Vutyatya-Sikonge, entry 711, 1944, KFC.

The hiding of slave status through name changes increased from the second decade of the twentieth century due to generational change, as formerly enslaved people and their descendants joined missions as adult members. The population increase in mission communities shaped social relations and binaries in post-abolition Unyamwezi society, such as the opposition between 'indigenous' (*wazawa*) and 'foreigners' (*wakuja*) and between 'Nyamwezi Christians' and 'former slaves' and their descendants, who were marked as 'simply slaves' (*watumwa tu*).[18] While recourse to new names became prevalent among slaves as a means of camouflaging their slave past, the names also reveal the hardships slaves endured and reflect the social binaries that dominated social life in Unyamwezi, impeding the incorporation of formerly enslaved people into Unyamwezi society.[19]

Catechists and Teachers as Carriers of Christian Culture

While the effects of slavery lingered in post-slavery Tabora, the contribution of the formerly enslaved in shaping the course of Christianity remained significant. The ongoing interactions between missionaries and residents around missions formed the basis for a Nyamwezi intelligentsia, producing first-generation African teachers and catechists and causing missions to become melting pots for developing African Christianity. Nevertheless, the small number of missionaries meant that many villages remained isolated from the new Christian culture. Catechists and teachers took on the task of spreading Christian culture in their villages and used their own intellectual and cultural creativity in shaping its development and reception. The tasks of teaching and administering village outstations influenced teachers to become independent agents rather than simple followers of the missionaries' instructions. Teachers and catechists helped congregants reconcile Christianity within the existing Nyamwezi culture. Ultimately, they became 'carriers of Christian culture' in villages with almost no missionary influence.[20]

As carriers of Christian culture, catechists administered catechesis, led the congregation in Sunday services, and translated religious texts into the indigenous languages using the knowledge they had acquired in missions and schools. Their families became exemplary Christian families, laying the foundation for African Christianity's development in the villages. While European missionaries intended to prepare catechists, teachers, and their wives to

---

[18] Interviews with Eli William Makenge, Tabora, 4 October 2021, and Issa Ndima Kipakila, Kipalapala village, 11 March 2020.

[19] Issa Ndima Kipakila, Kipalapala village, 11 March 2020.

[20] Stephen J. Rockel, *Carriers of Culture: Labor on the Road in Nineteenth-Century East Africa* (Portsmouth, NH: Heinemann, 2006).

embody the values of the model Christian family, the range of activities performed in the village outstations helped them to extend their networks beyond blood relations and build lasting communities based on their shared experiences.[21] In due course, communities grew, and people sought to articulate interpretations of Christianity that reinforced the ethics of Nyamwezi communities. In the Moravian Church, where there was a tradition of believers reading and interpreting scripture for themselves, there was more opportunity for formerly enslaved people and dependents to form their own interpretations than in the Catholic churches, where clerical control was stronger.

The work of shaping interpretations of scripture that corresponded to the communities' aspirations for solidarity and prosperity continued into the twentieth century as African teachers and clerics increasingly took over the responsibility for running village churches and outstations. Utilizing the knowledge they had acquired from mission schools, Nyamwezi teachers and catechists established schools in the villages, becoming 'village teachers' (*vahembeki*), literate 'elites' (*vasomi*), and 'masters of the new ways'.[22] Nyamwezi women joined these intellectuals as 'teachers and catechists' and were decisive in shaping the growth of African Christianity; their lives provided a model of Christian womanhood that attracted women in villages to Christianity, and they also found that the practices of 'home visits' and 'neighbourhood' (*lusangi*) gatherings were ways of making Christianity more attractive by drawing on established traditions in Unyamwezi society. The culture of *lusangi* – with its core tenets of solidarity and mutual assistance – was particularly effective in encouraging solidarity in communities of diverse origins. For former slaves-turned-teachers and preachers who spoke Kinyamwezi but had relatively shallow roots in Nyamwezi networks of kinship, it provided an accessible model of Christian belief in everyday life. Consequently, pastors and rich individuals emerged as new patrons, filling the role formerly played by chiefs as providers of food and support to poor Christians.

Dissent from Below: Translation, Authority, and the East African Revival

Formerly enslaved people and porters who lived in the mission communities played an undeniable role in translating texts into Kinyamwezi – the language they had adopted as a *lingua franca* because they had originated from

---

[21] See, for instance, Ndala, 31 July 1960, AAT 325.299.

[22] Brauer's Sermons, 1913, 21, KFC; 'The Origins and Role of Catechists in the Archdiocese of Tabora, 1879–1967' [31 August 1967], 12–13, AAT 325.297; *Fibula ja Kinyamwezi, Fibel der Nyamwezisprache* (Herrnhut: Missionsanstalt der Envagelischen Brüder-Unität, 1911), 38; Kisanji, *Historia Fupi*, 73–74.

different language communities inhabiting the East African interior. Their mastery of culture and language enabled catechists and evangelists in the villages of western Tanzania to form 'the basis for the modern intelligentsia' by becoming 'scripture readers' and translators.[23] By employing linguistic skills and some rudimentary training from the mission schools, Africans 'crossed linguistic and cultural boundaries to spread the faith' into the villages.[24] In this way, translation became a form of dissent, and the Kinyamwezi language and culture were influenced by the experiences of formerly enslaved people, porters, residents, and missionaries. Translation of texts into the Kinyamwezi language embodied African adaptation and agency in making Christianity in nineteenth- and twentieth-century western Tanzania because Africans integrated the Nyamwezi culture, social relations, and chiefly authority into the translated versions of the religious texts. As the translated texts filtered into villages, missionaries were encouraged to translate their Sunday homilies into Kinyamwezi. The sermons were written a few days before Sunday service in consultation with the Nyamwezi Christians, mission residents, porters, and friends.[25]

Between the 1950s and 1960s, Tabora dissent dominated the religious sphere. It manifested in various ways, involving disputes between Christians and church authorities on one hand and between church authorities and teachers and catechists on the other. In particular, the experiences in Catholic and Moravian missions in western Tanzania indicate that an understanding of revivalism and dissent should consider historically and culturally constructed forces within their specific settings. Dissent against the influence of revivalism and recognition in the Moravian Church of Western Tanganyika was attributable to the strong solidarity among Christians, the translation and independent interpretation of texts, and community building based on shared experiences of slavery and post-emancipation mission life. Thus, the doctrinal controversies between revivalists and dissenters further demonstrated that a culture of independent interpretation of religious texts had taken hold in Unyamwezi. It also reveals that Christians were not passive recipients of the teachings and practices imposed by revivalists. Instead, their intellectual and cultural experience of shaping the interpretation of texts encouraged them to scrutinize the doctrines imposed by revivalists. Further, the commitment to community building remained potent throughout the twentieth century, making Christians reluctant to break away from mainstream churches. Even those who seceded

---

[23] J.D.Y. Peel, *Religious Encounter and the Making of the Yoruba* (Bloomington: Indiana University Press, 2000), 156–61.

[24] Paul Kollman and Cynthia Toms Smedley, *Understanding World Christianity: Eastern Africa* (Minneapolis, MN: Fortress Press, 2018).

[25] Kisanji, *Historia Fupi*, 43.

for good maintained the ideals of community, neighbourly solidarity, and liturgy entrenched in their culture and mission experience.

Dissent among catechists in Catholic missions and village outstations shows that strong affinity, kinship networks, and community building in missions and villages became important forces in shaping the course of Christianity in twentieth-century western Tanzania. The catechists' experiences also reveal the persistent struggle for equality and recognition of their work in the villages. The agency of catechists in translating texts, catechetical instruction, and leading congregants in missions and village outstations helped them create an idealized community based on these experiences. The shared challenges of village life, inequality, and dilemmas of the catechesis were to impact how they challenged church authority. Thus, dissent among catechists suggests that they were neither passive nor simply 'examples of the missionary enterprise' in western Tanzania; rather, they were active and self-reliant leaders who questioned and sometimes directly challenged church authority in their pursuit of equality and respect for their mission work.[26] The audacity of catechists in mounting a rebellion against church authority further suggests that, to borrow Jonathon Glassman's words, they produced a 'consciousness fashioned out of fragments of the hegemonic ideologies which they had found at hand'.[27] The networks of friendship and creation of networked kinship relations that bound catechists to village life filtered into rural areas and shaped how they interacted with congregants in building and maintaining 'affective communities' based on village and spiritual experience.[28] The transcendence of dissent beyond the realm of catechists suggests that the 'fictive' and 'networked' kinship relations created by catechists in village outstations had a bearing on congregants who joined with them in pressing for their demands.

[26] Letter of catechists, 21 February 1961, AAT 325.298; Mgomo wa Makatekista, 20 February 1961, AAT 325.298.

[27] Jonathan Glassman, 'The Bondsman's New Clothes: The Contradictory Consciousness of Slave Resistance on the Swahili Coast', *Journal of African History*, Vol 32, No. 2 (1991), 277.

[28] On 'affective community', see Andreana C. Pritchard, *Sisters in Spirit: Christianity, Affect, and Community Building in East Africa, 1860–1970* (East Lansing: Michigan State University Press, 2017).

Appendix

Table 11 Names of Women, Girls, and Children at the White Sisters' Convent, 1909–10.

1.	Bertha	31.	Appolonia	61.	Pungo
2.	Christina	32.	Seonora	62.	Catharina
3.	Victoria	33.	Daria	63.	Madakare
4.	Elisa	34.	Margarita	64.	Madalena
5.	Paulina	35.	Sophia	65.	Ernestina
6.	Sabina	36.	Henrika	66.	Brigitta
7.	Maria	37.	Monika	67.	Ndoto
8.	Rosa mkubwa	38.	Anastasia	68.	Kalekwa
9.	Clerisia	39.	Getruda	69.	Nyawile
10.	Victoria	40.	Salome	70.	Kuz
11.	Regina	41.	Paulina mkubwa	71.	Sinzo
12.	Agatta	42.	Franciska	72.	Nywile
13.	Odylia	43.	Gengetta	73.	Karunde ndogo
14.	Rosa ndogo	44.	Marina	74.	Sinzo
15.	Martina	45.	Lucia	75.	Kalekwa ndogo
16.	Cecilia	46.	Mariamu	76.	Sinzo Nyamizi ndogo
17.	Cecilia Petero	47.	Valery	77.	Kigema
18.	Sidurina	48.	Herman Joseph	78.	Karunde Ndogo
19.	Agnesi	49.	Helena	79.	Namamsumna mkubwa
20.	Tecla	50.	Lucia Mkubwa	80.	Nyamizi
21.	Martina	51.	Mariana	81.	Kumbo
22.	Elisabella	52.	Odriana	82.	Vumilia
23.	Ngambetta	53.	Sumuni	83.	Massasa
24.	Mkangirwa	54.	Nyanza	84.	Kakundi
25.	Mamaaskari	55.	Thime	85.	Nyamilwa
26.	Simi	56.	Kapemba	86.	Kadala
27.	Zeno	57.	Hagila	87.	Kamulwa
28.	Marihema	58.	Kianza	88.	Sizia
29.	Mwamulwa	59.	Sikujua	89.	Mwilwa
30.	Kasinde	60.	Kamili	90.	Dora

Sources: Noms des femmes, filles et enfants à Notre Dame 1909–10 [Names of women, girls, and children redeemed by the White Sisters], AAT 350.002; Noms des autres réfugiées à Notre Dame, 1909–10 [Names of Refugee women], AAT 350.002.

Table 12   Former Slaves in Christian Communities, Vicariate of Unyanyembe, 1907–10.

	Mission Station	Resident Catechists	Baptism		Marriage	Schools		Orphanages
			Adults	Children	Total	Boys	Girls	Total
1.	Ushirombo	35	47	72	28	23	-	2
2.	Msalala	17	19	30	2	26	-	1
3.	Ndala	6	27	13	2	18	-	1
4.	Tabora	2	9	7	1	36	-	2
5.	Ulungwa	5	26	4	3	20	-	2
6.	Usambiro	1	0	7	1	28	-	1
7.	Muyanga	4	15	8	3	47	-	1
8.	Mugera	-	46	15	5	50	-	2
9.	Buhonga	-	33	5	3	28	40	2
	Total	70	222	161	48	276	40	14

Source: Annual Reports, 1906–08, AAT 322.399.

Table 13   Redeemed Slaves, Village Communities, and Christians in the Vicariate of Unyanyembe, 1906–07.

	Mission station	Redeemed enslaved people	Village communities	Total Christians
1.	Ushirombo	16	3	211
2.	Msalala	0	1	68
3.	Ndala	0	1	9
4.	Tabora	0	2	25
5.	Ulungwa	11	2	27
6.	Usambiro	2	1	26
7.	Muyanga	0	2	16
8.	Mugera	0	2	18
9.	Buhonga	5	1	23
	Total	34	15	423

Source: Annual Reports, 1906–08, AAT 322.399.

Bibliography

Primary Sources

Interviews

I conducted interviews with descendants of former slaves and men and women in the villages of western Tanzania between 2016 and 2017 as part of my doctoral project, and between 2020 and 2021 as part of my postdoctoral fellowship.

Manuscript and Archival Collections

Archives of the Catholic Archdiocese of Tabora

AAT 526.503, Freibriefe, Nos 3–1297, 1897–1914.
AAT 350.002, Mission statistique (Ndala), année 1907–08.
AAT 322.399, Rachats d'esclaves, 1908–1909.
AAT 355.108, 'Ndala: rapport sur l'esclavage', 15 June 1913.
AAT 350.002, Notre Dame de Tabora, 1 July 1909–1 July 1910.
AAT 350.002, Noms des femmes, filles et enfants à Notre Dame 1909–10, 1 July 1910.
AAT 526.502, 1922–23.
AAT 325.299, 1928–61.
AAT 350.002, Statistiques annuelles,1937–56.
AAT 322.399, Statistics, Tabora Archdiocese, 1930–50.
AAT 350.002, 1950–51.
AAT 325.299, 1952–64.
AAT 325.297, 1956, 1967.
AAT 325.298, 1957–70.
AAT 526.502, 'Slave Trade in East Africa', 1974.
AAT 23.01, F. van Vlijmen, 'The Origins of the Archdiocese of Tabora' (unpublished manuscript, 1990).
AAT 361.000, Henny W. Blockland, 'Two Nyamwezi Texts: An Exercise in Translation and Understanding', 1987.

Cadbury Research Library Special Collections, University of Birmingham
CMS/B/OMS/C A6/O/3–109/1878–1883.
G3 A6/O/1883 [Missing] Nyanza Mission Précis, 1883–84.

BIBLIOGRAPHY

CMS/B/OMS/G3 A6/O/1884–1885.
CMS/ACC 212/F 8. E.G. Hampel, 'A Short Narrative of the Work and Growth in the First 25 Years of Kilimatinde Hospital 1928–1953', 1954.

Kisanji Family Collection, Kazeh-Hill, Tabora

KFC, Rev. Max Brauer's Sermons, Ipole mission, 1912–13.
KFC, *Lusangi*, Nos 26–34, 1938.
KFC, *Nimbo zya Kikristo*, 1912.
KFC, *Nimbo zya Kikristo*, 1938.
KFC, *Nimbo zya Kikristo, 1958.*
KFC, *Nyimbo za Kikristo*, 1988.
KFC, *Bestand der Gemeinen in der Missionsprovinz* (Statistics of the Mission in Unyamwezi), 1931–50.
KFC, Diary, Moravian Mission Sikonge, 1939–68.
KFC, Diary, Moravian Mission Milumbani, 1940–60.
KFC, 'Listi ya Vakristo Vahanya', 1946–47.
KFC UKTA, 1947–49.
KFC, 'Minuti zya mkutano', October 1958
KFC, *Habari za Kanisa*, No. 3, July–September 1999.
UKTA, Unity of Kiwere Tribal Association, 1930–54.

Moravian Church in Western Tanganyika

MCWT/35/7, *Ivanza lya Chalo*, Usoke, 1959–65.

National Archives of the United Kingdom at Kew, London

UKNA CO 1071/366/1920–1927.
UKNA CO 691/117/1930.
UKNA CO 323/1257/1934–1935.

School of Oriental and African Studies (SOAS), University of London

CWM/LMS Central Africa/Box 1/1878.
CWM/LMS Central Africa/Box 2/1879.
CWM/LMS Central Africa/Box 3/1880.
CWM/LMS Central Africa/Box 5/1883.
CWM/LMS Central Africa/Box 6/1885.
CWM/LMS/ Central Africa/Box 7/1888.
CWM/LMS Central Africa/Box 8/1891.
CWM/LMS Central Africa/Box 9/1895.
CWM/LMS Central Africa/Box 10/1898.

BIBLIOGRAPHY 221

Tanzania National Archives, Dar es Salaam

TNA, *Tanganyika Territory Gazette*, Vol. III, 1922 (The Involuntary Servitude [Abolition] Ordinance, No. 13 of 1922).

TNA, Tabora District Book, 1928.

TNA, Tabora Provincial Book, 1955.

TNA, Tabora Regional Book (Western Province), 1929.

TNA 47/A3/3/71, 'Barua ya Swetu Mshama kwa Bwana District Commissioner wa Tabora', 4 January 1956.

TNA 47/A3/3/74, 'Barua kutoka kwa Swetu Mshama, Mkubwa wa Baraza la Igalula, kwa Bwana District Commissioner wa Tabora', 12 January 1956.

TNA 47/A3/3/86, 'Barua ya Mtemi wa Uyui kwa District Commissioner', Tabora, 22 March 1958.

TNA 47/A3/6/49, 'Barua ya Agriculture Field Officer kwa Mabaraza yote ya Wilaya ya Tabora', 6 October 1958.

TNA 47/A3/9/245, 'Barua ya District Commissioner kwa Mtemi N.S. Fundikira II', 8 January 1954.

TNA 47/A3/9/248, Barua ya District Commissioner kwa Mkubwa wa Baraza la Ussoke, 19 November 1953.

TNA, Nzega District Book, volume I, 1946.

TNA 967.821.01, Annual Report, Nzega Division, Kahama District, 1941.

TNA 967.823, Annual Report, Nzega District, 1930–31.

TNA 967.823, Annual Report, Nzega District, 1933.

TNA AB 47/Vol. III/10873/1936–1953.

TNA 967.823, Annual Report on Native Affairs, Nzega District, 1949.

TNA 967.823, Annual Report, Nzega District for 1950.

TNA 47/T5/Minutes, Provincial Office, 1952.

TNA 63/P4/66/Vol. III/1953.

TNA 47/T5/Miscellaneous, 1954.

TNA 967.823, Draft Annual Report for 1955.

TNA 63/P4/66/Vol. IV/1955.

TNA 63/P4/66/Vol. III/1954–1955.

University of Dar es Salaam History Resources

UDSM/History Resources Room, Translated German Documents (Annual Report about the Development of German East Africa, 1905–06).

University of Dar es Salaam Main Library, East Africana

UDSM/EAF Tanganyika Provincial Commissioners Annual Reports 1932–49.

White Fathers Archives, Atiman House, Dar es Salaam

WFA 01.43, Ndala Diary, 1896–1979.

WFA 01.43, Ushirombo Diary, 1891–1946.

WFA Rel 74, Jubilee Usongo na Igumo: Matukio ya Kila Siku, 1980.

WFA 11-03, Aylward E.M. Shorter, 'Ukimbu and the Kimbu Chiefdoms of Southern Unyamwezi: The History and Present Pattern of Kimbu Social Organisation and Movement', n.d.

Printed Primary Sources

American Bible Society. *The Bible: Revised Standard Version* (RSV). New York: American Bible Society, 1971.

Bennett, Norman R. (ed.). *Stanley's Despatches to the New York Herald, 1871–1873, 1874–1877*. Boston, MA: Boston University Press, 1970.

Bible Society of Tanzania. *150 Years of Kiswahili Bible Translations*. Dodoma: Bible Society of Tanzania, 1994.

Broyon, Phillipe. 'Description of Unyamwesi, the Territory of King Mirambo, and the Best Route Thither from the East Coast'. *Proceedings of the Royal Geographical Society*, Vol. 22, No. 1 (1877–78), 28–38.

Burton, Richard F. 'The Lake Regions of Central Equatorial Africa, with Notices of the Luna Mountains and the Sources of the Nile; Being the Results of an Expedition Undertaken under the Patronage of Her Majesty's Government and the Royal Geographical Society of London, in the Years 1857–1859'. *Journal of the Royal Geographical Society of London*, Vol. 29 (1859), pp. 1–454.

——. *The Lake Regions of Central Africa: A Picture of Exploration*, 2 vols. Longman, Green, Longman, and Roberts, 1860.

——. *Zanzibar: City, Island, and Coast*, 2 vols. London: Tinsley Brothers, 1872.

Coulbois, François. *Dix années au Tanganyika*. Limoges, 1901.

Diesing, E. 'Eine Reise in Ukonongo'. *Globus*, Vol. 95 (1909), 309–12, 325–28.

Fibula ja Kinyamwezi/Fibel der Nyamwezisprache. Herrnhut: Missionsanstalt der Envagelischen Brüder-Unität, 1911.

Hore, Edward. *Missionary to Tanganyika 1877–1888: The Writings of Edward Coode Hore, Master Mariner*. Edited by James B. Wolf. London: Frank Cass, 1971.

Ibuku lya nimbo zya mukanisa/Kleines Gesangbuch für Unyamwezi. Herrnhut: Missionsanstalt der Envagelischen Brüder-Unität, 1912.

Ilagano Ipya: Mhola ya Chelu yamwa Guku na Mupizya Wiswe Yesu Kristo. Dodoma: The Bible Society of Tanzania, 1951.

Matthäus-Evangelium auf Kinyamwezi (Deutsch-Ost-Afrika). Herrnhut: Missionsanstalt der Envagelischen Brüder-Unität, 1907.

Migani ja vutemi vwa Mulungu: Geschichten aus dem Reiche Gotte. Herrnhut: Evangelische Brüder-Unität, 1910.

Muhola ja Tjelu ja Ilagano Lipya Jakundulwa Mugati na Mupizya Wiswe Jesu Klisto Jatonilwe Mukijombele Tja Kinyamwezi. Translated by L.R. Stern. London and Herrnhut, 1909.

Nimbo zya Kikristo. Moravian Church in Western Tanganyika, 1958.

Rebman, Yohanes. *Engili ya Lukasi Iliofasirika Kua Maneno ya Kisuaheli*. St Chrishona, 1876.

Speke, John H. *Journal of the Discovery of the Source of the Nile*. Edinburgh and London: William Blackwood and Sons, 1863.

Stanley, Henry M. *How I found Livingstone: Travels, Adventures, and Discoveries in Central Africa, Including an Account of Four Month's Residence with Dr. Livingstone*. New York: Scribner, Armstrong & Co., 1872.

Steere, Edward. 'On East African Tribes and Languages'. *Journal of the Anthropological Institute of Great Britain and Ireland*, Vol. 1 (1871), cxliii–cliv.

——. *Anjili kwa Yohana: Kiswahili*. London: British and Foreign Bible Society, 1875.

——. *Anjili ya Bwana na Mwokozi Wetu Isa Masiya kwa Mattayo: Maneno ya Kiswahili*. London: British and Foreign Bible Society, 1876.

——. *Anjili kwa Marko: Kiswahili*. London: British and Foreign Bible Society, 1879.

——. *The Kinyamwezi Language as Spoken in the Chiefdom of Unyanyembe*. London: Society for the Promotion of Christian Knowledge, 1882.

——. *Kitabu cha Agano Jipya la Bwana na Mwokozi wetu Isa Masiya Kimefasirika katika Maneno ya Kwanza ya Kiyonani*. London: Kimepigwa Chapa kwa British and Foreign Bible Society, 1883.

Tenzi za Rohoni. 1968; repr. Musoma: Musoma Press, 2016.

Weule, Karl. *Native Life in East Africa: The Results of an Ethnological Research Expedition*. Translated by Alice Werner. 1909; repr. Westport, CT: Negro University Press, 1970.

Secondary Sources

Books and Articles

Abrahams, Raphael G. *The Peoples of Greater Unyamwezi, Tanzania (Nyamwezi, Sukuma, Sumbwa, Kimbu, Konongo)*. London: International African Institute, 1967.

——. *The Political Organization of Unyamwezi*. Cambridge: Cambridge University Press, 1967.

——. *The Nyamwezi Today: A Tanzanian People in the 1970s*. Cambridge: Cambridge University Press, 1981.

Alpers, Edward. 'The Story of Swema: Female Vulnerability in Nineteenth-Century East Africa', in Claire C. Robertson and Martin Klein (eds), *Women and Slavery in Africa*, pp. 85–219. Madison: University of Wisconsin Press, 1983.

Aminzade, Ronald. *Race, Nation, and Citizenship in Post-colonial Africa: The Case of Tanganyika.* New York: Cambridge University Press, 2013.

Barnstone, Willis. *The Poetics of Translation: History, Theory, Practice.* New Haven, CT: Yale University Press, 1993.

Bassnett, Susan. 'The Translator as Cross-Cultural Mediator', in Kirsten Malmkjær and Kevin Windle (eds), *The Oxford Handbook of Translation Studies*, pp. 94–107. Oxford: Oxford University Press, 2011.

Bebbington, David W. *Evangelicalism in Modern Britain: A History from the 1730s to the 1980s.* London: Unwin Hyman, 1989.

Behrend, Heike. *Alice Lakwena and the Holy Spirits: War in Northern Uganda, 1986–1997.* Oxford: James Currey, 1999.

Bennett, Norman R. 'The London Missionary Society at Urambo, 1878–1898'. *Tanzania Notes and Records*, Vol. 65 (1966), 43–52.

Berger, Anna Maria Busse. *The Search for Medieval Music in Africa and Germany, 1891–1961: Scholars, Singers, Missionaries.* Chicago, IL: University of Chicago Press, 2021.

Bjerk, Paul. *Building a Peaceful Nation: Julius Nyerere and the Establishment of Sovereignty in Tanzania, 1960–1964.* Rochester, NY: University of Rochester Press, 2015.

Bolton, Caitlyn. 'Making Africa Legible: Kiswahili Arabic and Orthographic Romanization in Colonial Zanzibar'. *American Journal of Islamic Social Sciences*, Vol. 33, No. 3 (2016), 61–78.

Borg, Marcus J. *Conflict, Holiness and Politics in the Teachings of Jesus.* New York: Edwin Mellen, 1984.

Bradford, Helen. '"We Women Will Show Them": Beer Protests in the Natal Countryside, 1929', in Jonathan Crush and Charles Ambler (eds), *Brew and Labor in Southern Africa*, pp. 208–34. Athens: Ohio University Press, 1992.

Bruner, Jason S. 'Contesting Confession in the East African Revival'. *Anglican and Episcopal History*, Vol. 84, No. 3 (2015), 253–78.

——. *Living Salvation in the East African Revival in Uganda.* Rochester, NY: University of Rochester Press, 2017.

Callaci, Emily. *Street Archives and City Life: Popular Intellectuals in Postcolonial Tanzania.* Durham, NC: Duke University Press, 2017.

Cantrell II, Phillip A. '"We are a Chosen People": The East African Revival and Its Return to Post-Genocide Rwanda'. *Church History*, Vol. 83, No. 2 (2014), 422–45.

Ceillier, Jean-Claude and François Richard, *Cardinal Charles Lavigerie and the Anti-Slavery Campaign*. Rome: Society of the Missionaries of Africa, 2012.

Clignet, Remi. *Many Wives, Many Powers: Authority and Power in Polygamous Families*. Evanston: Northwestern University Press, 1970.

Comaroff, Jean and John. *Of Revelation and Revolution: Christianity, Colonialism and Consciousness in South Africa*, Vol. 1. Chicago, IL: University of Chicago Press, 1991.

Cory, Hans. 'The Buswezi'. *American Anthropologist*, Vol. 57, No. 5 (1955), 923–52.

Cox, Jeffrey L. *Imperial Fault Lines: Christianity and Colonial Power in India, 1818–1940*. Stanford, CA: Stanford University Press, 2002.

——. *The British Missionary Enterprise since 1700*. New York: Routledge, 2008.

Creary, Nicholas M. *Domesticating a Religious Import: The Jesuits and the Inculturation of the Catholic Church in Zimbabwe, 1879–1980*. New York: Fordham University Press, 2011.

Dayton, Donald W. *Theological Roots of Pentecostalism*. Grand Rapids, MI: Baker Academic, 2011.

Deutsch, Jan-Georg. *Emancipation without Abolition in German East Africa c.1884–1914*. Oxford: James Currey, 2006.

——. 'Notes on the Rise of Slavery and Social Change in Unyamwezi, c.1860–1900', in Henri Médard and Shane Doyle (eds), *Slavery in the Great Lakes Region of East Africa*, pp. 76–110. Athens: Ohio University Press, 2007.

——.'Prices for Female Slaves and Changes in their Life Cycle: Evidence from German East Africa', in Gwyn Campbell, Suzanne Miers, and Joseph C. Miller (eds), *Women and Slavery*, Vol. 1, *Africa and the Western Indian Ocean Islands*, pp. 129–46. Athens: Ohio University Press, 2007.

Dube, Saurabh. 'Conversion to Translation: Colonial Registers of a Vernacular Christianity'. *South Atlantic Quarterly*, Vol. 101, No. 4 (2000), 807–32.

——. *After Conversion: Cultural Histories of Modern India*. New Delhi: Yoda Press, 2010.

Ebner, Elzear. *The History of the Wangoni and their Origin in South African Bantu Tribes*. Ndanda and Peramiho: Benedictine Publications, 1987.

Elbourne, Elizabeth. *Blood Ground: Colonialism, Missions, and the Contest for Christianity in the Cape Colony and Britain, 1799–1853*. Montreal: McGill-Queen's University Press, 2002.

Etherington, Norman. 'Mission Station Melting Pots as a Factor in the Rise of South African Black Nationalism'. *International Journal of African Historical Studies*, Vol. 9, No. 4 (1976), 592–605.

Fabian, Johannes. *Language and Colonial Power: The Appropriation of Swahili in the Former Belgian Congo 1880–1938*. Cambridge: Cambridge University Press, 1986.

Feierman, Steven. *Peasant Intellectuals: Anthropology and History in Tanzania*. Madison: University of Wisconsin Press, 1990.

——. 'Explanation of Uncertainty in the Medical World of Ghaambo'. *Bulletin of the History of Medicine*, Vol. 74, No. 2 (2000), 317–44.

Frankl, P.J.L. and Yahya Ali Omar. 'The Idea of "The Holy" in Swahili', *Journal of Religion in Africa*, Vol. 29, Fasc. 1 (February 1999), 109–14.

Gaarde, Nis H. 'A Brief Report of Unyamwezi for the Year 1921'. *Periodical Accounts Relating to Moravian Missions*, Vol. 11, No. 3 (June 1922), 129–41.

Giblin, James L. *The Politics of Environmental Control in Northeastern Tanzania, 1840–1940*. Philadelphia: University of Pennsylvania Press, 1992.

——. 'Pawning, Politics and Matriliny in Northeastern Tanzania', in Toyin Falola and Paul Lovejoy (eds), *Pawnship in Africa: Debt Bondage in Historical Perspective*, pp. 43–54. Boulder, CO: Westview Press, 1994.

——. 'Pre-Colonial Politics of Disease Control in the Lowlands of Northeastern Tanzania', in Gregory H. Maddox, James L. Giblin, and Isaria N. Kimambo (eds), *Custodians of the Land: Ecology and Culture in the History of Tanzania*, pp. 127–51. London: James Currey; 1996.

——. 'Family Life, Indigenous Culture and Christianity in Colonial Njombe', in Thomas Spear and Isaria Kimambo (eds), *East African Expressions of Christianity*, pp. 309–22.

——. 'Divided Patriarchs in a Labour Migration Economy: Contextualizing Debate about Family and Gender in Colonial Njombe', in Colin Creighton and C.K. Omari (eds), *Gender, Family and Work in Tanzania*, pp. 177–99. Aldershot: Ashgate, 2000.

——. *A History of the Excluded: Making Family a Refuge from State in Twentieth-Century Tanzania*. Oxford: James Currey, 2006.

Glassman, Jonathon. 'The Bondsman's New Clothes: The Contradictory Consciousness of Slave Resistance on the Swahili Coast'. *Journal of African History*, 32, no. 2 (1991), 277–312.

Guha, Ranajit and Gayatri C. Spivak (eds). *Selected Subaltern Studies*. New York: Oxford University Press, 1988.

Gunderson, Frank. *Sukuma Labor Songs from Western Tanzania: 'We Never Sleep, We Dream of Farming'*. Leiden and Boston: Brill, 2010.

Hamilton, J. Taylor and Kenneth G. Hamilton. *History of the Moravian Church: The Renewed Unitas Fratrum 1722–1957*. 2nd edn. Bethlehem, PA: Interprovincial Board of Christian Education, Moravian Church of America, 1983.

Hastings, Adrian. *The Church in Africa, 1450–1950*. Oxford: Clarendon Press, 1996.

Haustein, Jörg. *Islam in German East Africa, 1885–1918: A Genealogy of Colonial Religion*. London: Palgrave Macmillan, 2023.

Heintze, Beatrix. 'Translations as Sources for African History'. *History in Africa*, Vol. 11 (1984), 131–61.

Hobsbawm, Eric. 'Introduction: Inventing Traditions', in Eric Hobsbawm and Terence Ranger (eds), *The Invention of Tradition*, pp. 1–14. Cambridge: Cambridge University Press, 2012.

Hoehler-Fatton, Cynthia. *Women of Fire and Spirit: History, Faith and Gender in Roho Religion in Western Kenya*. Oxford: Oxford University Press, 1996.

Hodgson, Dorothy. *The Church of Women: Gendered Encounters between Maasai and Missionaries*. Bloomington: Indiana University Press, 2005.

Hölzl, Richard. 'Educating Missions: Teachers and Catechists in Southern Tanganyika, 1890s–1940s'. *Itenerario*, Vol. 40, No. 3 (2016), 405–28.

Hunter, Emma. 'Language, Empire and the World: Karl Roehl and the History of the Swahili Bible in East Africa'. *Journal of Imperial and Commonwealth History*, Vol. 41, No. 4 (2013), 600–616.

——. *Political Thought and the Public Sphere in Tanzania: Freedom, Democracy and Citizenship in the Era of Decolonization*. Cambridge: Cambridge University Press, 2015.

Ibsen, Søren H. *Et Tilbageblik: Over 40 Års Virke I Tanzania, 1922–1922*. Forlaget Savanne, 1962.

Iliffe, John. *A Modern History of Tanganyika*. Cambridge: Cambridge University Press, 1979.

——. *Honour in African History*. Cambridge: Cambridge University Press, 2005.

——. 'Breaking the Chain at its Weakest Link: TANU and the Colonial Office', in Gregory H. Maddox and James L. Giblin (eds), *In Search of a Nation: Histories of Authority and Dissidence in Tanzania*, pp. 168–93.

Isichei, Elizabeth. *A History of Christianity in Africa: From Antiquity to Present*. Grand Rapids, MI: Eerdmans, 1995.

Janzen, John M. *The Quest for Therapy in Lower Zaïre*. Berkley: University of California Press, 1978.

Kabeya, John B. *Mtemi Mirambo: Mtawala shujaa wa Kinyamwezi*. Nairobi: East African Literature Bureau, 1971.

King, Fergus J. 'Nyimbo za Vijana: Biblical Interpretation in Contemporary Hymns from Tanzania', in Gerald O. West and Musa W. Dube (eds), *The Bible in Africa: Transactions, Trajectories, and Trends*, pp. 360–73. Leiden: Brill, 2000.

Kiriama, Herman O. 'The Landscapes of Slavery in Kenya'. *Journal of African Diaspora Archaeology and Heritage*, Vol 7, No. 2 (2018), 192–206.

Kisanji, Teofilo H. *Historia Fupi ya Kanisa la Kimoravian Tanganyika Magharibi*. Kipalapala: TMP, 1980.

Kisanji, Oscar E. *Nimesema, Askofu Teofilo Hiyobo Kisanji: Baadhi ya Maandiko aliyoandika Hotuba alizotoa na Mahubiri aliyoyafanya kati ya mwaka 1955 na 1982*. Tabora: Frontex Associates, 2023.

Kjekshus, Helge. *Ecology Control and Economic Development in East African History: The Case of Tanganyika, 1850–1950*. Berkley: University of California Press, 1977.

Kodesh, Neil. *Beyond the Royal Gaze: Clanship and Public Healing in Buganda*. Charlottesville: University of Virginia Press, 2010.

Kollman, Paul V. *The Evangelization of Slaves and Catholic Origins in East Africa*. Maryknoll, NY: Orbis Books, 2005.

Kollman, Paul and Cynthia Toms Smedley. *Understanding World Christianity: Eastern Africa*. Minneapolis, MN: Fortress Press, 2018.

Koponen, Juhani. *People and Production in Late Precolonial Tanzania: History and Structures*. Helsinki: Finnish Society for Development Studies, 1988.

——. 'War, Famine, and Pestilence in Late Precolonial Tanzania: A Case for Heightened Mortality'. *International Journal of African Historical Studies*, Vol. 21, No. 4 (1988), 637–76.

——. *Development for Exploitation: German Colonial Policies in Mainland Tanzania, 1884–1914*. Helsinki: Finnish Historical Society, 1994.

Kopytoff, Igor and Suzanne Miers. 'African "Slavery" as an Institution of Marginality', in Suzanne Miers and Igor Kopytoff (eds), *Slavery in Africa: Historical and Anthropological Perspectives*, pp. 3–81. Madison: University of Wisconsin Press, 1979.

Kunene, Daniel P. Introduction to Thomas Mofolo, *Chaka*, trans. Daniel P. Kunene. London: Heinemann, 1981.

Lal, Priya. 'Militants, Mothers, and the National Family: Ujamaa, Gender, and Rural Development in Postcolonial Tanzania'. *Journal of African History*, Vol. 51, No. 1 (2010), 1–20.

Lamden, S.C. 'Some Aspects of Porterage in East Africa'. *Tanganyika Notes and Records*, Vol. 61 (1963), 155–64.

Liebst, Michelle. 'African Workers and the Universities' Mission to Central Africa in Zanzibar, 1864–1900'. *Journal of Eastern African Studies*, Vol. 8, No. 3 (2014), 366–81.

——. *Labour and Christianity in the Mission: African Workers in Tanganyika and Zanzibar, 1864–1926*. Woodbridge: James Currey, 2021.

Lonsdale, John. 'The Moral Economy of Mau Mau: Wealth, Poverty and Civic Virtue in Kikuyu Political Thought', in Bruce Berman and John Lonsdale (eds), *Unhappy Valley: Conflict in Kenya and Africa*, Bk 2, *Violence and Ethnicity*, pp. 315–504. London: James Currey, 1992.

Low, Donald A. and John Lonsdale, 'Introduction: Towards the New Order 1945–1963', in D.A. Low and Alison Smith (eds), *Oxford History of East Africa*, Vol. 3, pp. 1–64. Oxford: Oxford University Press, 1976.

Luna, Anita de. 'Evangelizadoras del Barrio: The Rise of the Missionary Catechists of Divine Providence'. *U.S. Catholic Historian*, Vol. 21, No. 1 (Winter 2003), 53–71.

Maddox, Gregory H. 'The Church and Cigogo: Father Stephen Mulundi and Christianity in Central Tanzania', in Thomas Spear and Isaria Kimambo (eds), *East African Expressions of Christianity*, pp. 150–63.

Maddox, Gregory H. and James L. Giblin (eds). *In Search of a Nation: Histories of Authority and Dissidence in Tanzania*. Oxford: James Currey, 2005.

Malambugi, Rev. Angolwisye Isakwisa. 'Kisanji, Teofilo Hiobo, 1915–1982', in *Dictionary of African Christian Biography*, 2007. https://dacb.org/stories/tanzania/kisanji/ (accessed 5 October 2023).

Masele, Esther J. and Venkatachalam Lakshmanan. 'Manifestations of Power and Marginality in Marriage Practices: A Qualitative Analysis of Sukuma Songs in Tanzania'. *Journal of International Women's Studies*, Vol. 22, No. 1 (2021), 386–98.

Maxwell, David. *Christians and Chiefs in Zimbabwe: A Social History of the Hwesa People*. Westport, CT: Praeger, 1999.

McMahon, Elizabeth. *Slavery and Emancipation in Islamic East Africa: From Honor to Respectability*. Cambridge: Cambridge University Press, 2013.

Mofolo, Thomas. *Chaka*. Translated by Daniel P. Kunene. London: Heinemann, 1981.

Moon, Daewon. 'The Conversion of Yosiya Kinuka and the Beginning of the East African Revival'. *International Bulletin of Mission Research*, Vol. 41, No. 3 (2017), 204–14.

Morton, Fred. *Children of Ham: Freed Slaves and Fugitive Slaves on the Kenya Coast, 1873 to 1907*. Boulder, CO: Westview Press, 1990.

Moyd, Michelle R. *Violent Intermediaries: African Soldiers, Conquest, and Everyday Colonialism in German East Africa*. Athens: Ohio University Press, 2014.

Mugane, John M. *The Story of Swahili*. Athens: Ohio University Press, 2015.

Musomba, Angetile Y. *The Moravian Church in Tanzania Southern Province: A Short History*. Nairobi: IFRA, 2005.

Nyanto, Salvatory S. 'Waliletwa na Kengele ya Kanisa: Discourses of Slave Emancipation and Conversion at Ndala Catholic Mission in Western Tanzania, 1896–1913', *Tanzania Journal of Sociology*, Vol. 2/3 (2017), 69–84.

———. 'Society, Conversion, and Frustrations in the CMS and LMS Missions of Unyamwezi, Western Tanzania, 1878–1898'. *Tanzania Journal of Sociology*, Vol. 4 (June 2018), 66–80.

———. 'Empire, Religious Conflicts, and State Intervention in Buha and Unyamwezi, Colonial Tanganyika, 1920s–1960'. *Tanzania Journal of Sociology*, Vol. 5 (June 2019), 72–86.

———. 'Priests without Ordination: Catechists and their Wives in Villages beyond Missions, 1948–1978'. *Catholic Historical Review*, Vol. 108, No. 3 (2022), 560–600.

Nyanto, Salvatory S. and Felicitas M. Becker. 'In Pursuit of Freedom: Oaths, Slave Agency, and the Abolition of Slavery in Western Tanzania, 1905–1930'. *Law and History Review,* Vol. 42, Special issue 1: 'African Legal Abolitions' (February 2024), 119–41.

Nyerere, Julius K. 'Ujamaa Tanzania na Dini: Hotuba aliyotoa Rais Julius K. Nyerere siku ya Kufungua Semina ya Viongozi wa Madhehebu mbalimbali ya Dini huko Tabora', unpublished, 27 July 1970.

———. 'Socialism and Rural Development', in *Freedom and Development: Selection from Writings and Speeches* (Dar es Salaam: Oxford University Press, 1973).

———. 'Nyufa: Mazungumzo ya Mwalimu Julius K. Nyerere Kwenye Klabu ya Waandishi wa Habari wa Tanzania, Hoteli ya Kilimanjaro', Dar es Salaam, 13 March 1995, in Mwalimu Julius Kambarage Nyerere, *Chemchemi ya Fikra za Kimapinduzi* (Dar es Salaam: Mkuki na Nyota, 2022).

Pallaver, Karin. 'Nyamwezi Participation in the Nineteenth-Century East African Long-Distance Trade: Some Evidence from Missionary Sources'. *Africa*, Vol. 61, Nos 3/4 (2006), 513–31.

———. 'A Triangle: Spatial Processes of Urbanization and Political Power in 19th-Century Tabora, Tanzania'. *Afriques: Débats, méthodes et terrains d'histoire*, Vol. 11 (2020), https://doi.org/10.4000/afriques.2871.

Peel, J.D.Y. *Religious Encounter and the Making of the Yoruba*. Bloomington: Indiana University Press, 2000.

Peterson, Derek R. 'Translating the Word: Dialogism and Debate in Two Gikuyu Dictionaries'. *Journal of Religious History*, Vol. 23, No. 1 (1999), 31–50.

———. 'Wordy Women: Gender Trouble and the Oral Politics of the East African Revival in Northern Gikuyu Land'. *Journal of African History*, Vol. 42, No. 3 (2001), 469–89.

———. *Creative Writing: Translation, Bookkeeping, and the Work of Imagination in Colonial Kenya*. Portsmouth, NH: Heinemann, 2004.

———. 'Morality Plays: Marriage, Church Courts, and Colonial Agency in Central Tanganyika, ca. 1876–1928'. *The American Historical Review* 111, no. 4 (2006): 983–1010.

——. *Ethnic Patriotism and East African Revival: A History of Dissent, c. 1935–1972*. Cambridge: Cambridge University Press, 2012.

Porter, Andrew. 'Cambridge, Keswick, and Late-Nineteenth-Century Attitudes to Africa'. *Journal of Imperial and Commonwealth History*, Vol. 5, No. 1 (1976), 5–34.

Prevost, Elizabeth. *The Communion of Women: Missions and Gender in Colonial Africa and the British Metropole*. Oxford: Oxford University Press, 2010.

Prichard, Andreana C. *Sisters in Spirit: Christianity, Affect, and Community Building in East Africa, 1860–1970*. East Lancing: Michigan State University Press, 2017.

Rafael, Vicente. *Contracting Colonialism: Translation and Christian Conversion in Tagalog Society under Early Spanish Rule*. Ithaca, NY: Cornell University Press, 1988.

Ranger, Terence O. 'Godly Medicine: The Ambiguities of Medical Mission in Southeastern Tanzania, 1900–1945', in Steven Feierman and John M. Janzen (eds), *The Social Basis of Health and Healing in Africa*, pp. 256–82. Berkely: University of California Press, 1992.

Ranger, Terence O. and Isaria N. Kimambo (eds). *The Historical Study of African Religion*. Berkley: University of California Press, 1972.

Raum, O.F. 'German East Africa: Changes in African Life under German Administration, 1892–1914', in Vincent Harlow and E.M. Chilver (eds), *History of East Africa*, Vol. 2, pp. 163–207. Oxford: Clarendon Press, 1965.

Reid, Richard. 'Mutesa and Mirambo: Thoughts on East African Warfare and Diplomacy in Nineteenth Century'. *International Journal of African Historical Studies*, Vol. 31, No. 1 (1998), 73–89.

——. *War in Pre-Colonial Eastern Africa: The Patterns and Meanings of State-Level Conflict in the Nineteenth Century*. Oxford: James Currey, 2007.

Renault, François. *Lavigerie: L'Esclavage Africain et L'Europe, 1868–1892*, Vol. 2, *Campagne Antiesclavagiste*. Paris: Éditions E. De Boccard, 1971.

Rigby, Peter. *Cattle and Kinship among the Gogo: A Semi-Pastoral Society of Central Tanzania*. Ithaca, NY: Cornell University Press, 1969.

Roberts, Andrew. 'The Nyamwezi', in Andrew Roberts (ed.), *Tanzania before 1900*, pp. 117–50. Nairobi: East African Publishing House, 1968.

——. 'Political Change in the Nineteenth Century', in Isaria N. Kimambo and Arnold J. Temu (eds), *A History of Tanzania*, pp. 57–84. Nairobi: East African Publishing House, 1969.

——. 'Nyamwezi Trade', in Richard Gray and David Birmingham (eds), *Pre-Colonial African Trade: Essays on Trade in Central and Eastern Africa before 1900*, pp. 39–74. London: Oxford University Press, 1970.

Robertson, Claire. 'Slavery and Women in Africa: Changing Definitions, Continuing Problems', in William H. Worger, Charles Ambler, and Nwando Achebe (eds), *A Companion to African History*, pp. 143–60. Hoboken, NJ: Wiley, 2019.

Rockel, Stephen J. '"A Nation of Porters": The Nyamwezi and the Labour Market in Nineteenth-Century Tanzania'. *Journal of African History*, Vol. 41, No. 2 (2000), 173–95.

——. *Carriers of Culture: Labor on the Road in Nineteenth-Century East Africa*. Portsmouth, NH: Heinemann, 2006.

——. 'Slavery and Freedom in Nineteenth-Century East Africa: The Case of Waungwana Caravan Porters'. *African Studies*, Vol. 68, No. 1 (2009), 87–109.

——. 'Between Pori, Pwani and Kisiwani: Overlapping Labour Cultures in the Caravans, Ports and Dhows of the Western Indian Ocean', in Abdul Sheriff and Engseng Ho (eds), *The Indian Ocean: Oceanic Connections and the Creation of New Societies*, pp. 95–122.

——. 'The Home and the World: Slavery and Domestic Labor in a Nineteenth-Century East African Caravan Town', in James Williams and Felicitas Hentschke (eds), *To be at Home: House, Work, and Self in the Modern World*, pp. 125–31. Berlin and Boston: De Gruyter, 2018.

Russell, Alison. *The Laws of Tanganyika Territory*, Vol. 1. London: Waterlow & Sons, 1929.

Rwelamira, Juvenalis B. *Tanzanian Socialism-Ujamaa and Gaudium et Spes: Two Convergent Designs of Integral Human Development*. Rome: Academia Alfonsiana, 1988.

Sakai, Naoki *Translations and Subjectivity: On Japan and Cultural Nationalism*. Minneapolis: University of Minnesota Press, 2008.

Sanneh, Lamin. *Translating the Message: The Missionary Impact on Culture*. Maryknoll, NY: Orbis Books, 2009.

Schwartz, Marc J. 'Shame, Culture, and Status among the Swahili of Mombasa'. *Ethos*, Vol. 16, No. 1 (1988), 21–51.

Scott, James C. *Weapons of the Weak: Everyday Forms of Peasant Resistance*. New Haven, CT: Yale University Press, 1985.

Sheriff, Abdul. *Slaves, Spices, and Ivory in Zanzibar: Integration of an East African Commercial Empire into the World Economy, 1770–1873*. 1987; repr. Oxford: James Currey, 2000.

Sheriff, Abdul and Engseng Ho (eds). *The Indian Ocean: Oceanic Connections and the Creation of New Societies*. London: Hurst, 2014.

Shivji, Issa G. *Development as Rebellion: A Biography of Julius Nyerere*, Vol. 3: *Rebellion without Rebels*. Dar es Salaam: Mkuki na Nyota Publishers, 2020.

Shorter, Aylward. 'Nyungu-Ya-Mawe and the "Empire of the Ruga-Rugas"'. *Journal of African History*, Vol. 9, No. 2 (1968), 235–59.

———. 'The Migawo: Peripheral Spirit Possession and Christian Healing'. *Anthropos*, Vol. 1/2 (1970), 110–26.

———. *Chiefship in Western Tanzania: A Political History of the Kimbu*. Oxford: Clarendon Press, 1972.

———. 'Symbolism, Ritual, and History: An Examination of the work of Victor Turner', in Terence O. Ranger and Isaria N. Kimambo (eds), *Historical Study of African Religion*, pp. 139–48.

———. *East African Societies*. London: Routledge & Kegan Paul, 1974.

———. *Cross and Flag: The 'White Fathers' during the Colonial Scramble (1892–1914)*. Maryknoll, NY: Orbis Books, 2006.

Smythe, Kathleen R. *Fipa Families: Reproduction and Catholic Evangelization in Nkasi, Ufipa, 1880–1960*. Portsmouth, NH: Heinemann, 2006.

Spear, Thomas 'Introduction: Toward the History of African Christianity', in Tomas Spear and Isaria N. Kimambo (eds), *East African Expressions of Christianity*. Oxford: James Currey, 1999.

Spear, Thomas and Isaria N. Kimambo (eds). *East African Expressions of Christianity*. Oxford: James Currey, 1999.

Sperling, David C. and Jose H. Kagabo. 'The Coast Hinterland and the Interior of East Africa', in Nehemia Levtzion and Randall L. Pouwels (eds), *The History of Islam in Africa*, pp. 273–97. Athens: Ohio University Press, 2000.

Stilwell, Sean. *Slavery and Slaving in African History: New Approaches to African History*. Cambridge: Cambridge University Press, 2014.

Sutton, John E.G. and Andrew Roberts. 'Uvinza and its Salt Industry'. *Azania*, Vol. 3 (1968), 45–86.

Thornton, John K. *Africa and Africans in the Making of the Atlantic World, 1400–1800*. Cambridge: Cambridge University Press, 1998.

Topan, Farouk M. 'Swahili as a Religious Language'. *Journal of Religion in Africa*, Vol. 22, Fasc. 4 (Nov. 1992), 331–49.

Turner, Victor W. *The Ritual Process: Structure and Anti-Structure*. 1969; repr. New Brunswick, NJ: Aldine Transaction, 2008.

———. 'Liminality and Communitas', in Ronald L. Grimes (ed.), *Readings in Ritual Studies*, pp. 511–19. Upper Saddle River, NJ: Prentice Hall, 1996.

URT. *Population and Housing Census*. Dar es Salaam: Ministry of East African Cooperation, 2012.

Unomah, Alfred C. and J.B. Webster, 'East Africa: The Expansion of Commerce', in John E. Flint (ed.), *The Cambridge History of Africa*, Vol. 5, *From c.1790 to c.1870*, pp. 270–318. Cambridge: Cambridge University Press, 1977.

Ward, Kevin. '"Obedient Rebels" – The Relationship between the Early "Balokole" and the Church of Uganda: The Mukono Crisis of 1941'. *Journal of Religion in Africa*, Vol. 19, Fasc. 3 (1989), 194–227.

Ward, Kevin and Emma Wild-Wood (eds). *The East African Revival: History and Legacies*. Farnham: Ashgate, 2012.

Willis, Justin. 'Unpretentious Bars: Municipal Monopoly and Indigenous Drinking in Colonial Dar es Salaam', in James Brennan, Andrew Burton, and Yusufu Lawi (eds), *Dar es Salaam: Histories from an Emerging Metropolis*, pp. 157–73. Dar es Salaam: Mkuki na Nyota, 2001.

——. *Potent Brews: A Social History of Alcohol in East Africa, 1850–1999*. Oxford: James Currey, 2002.

Wright, Marcia. *Strategies of Slaves and Women: Life-Stories from East/Central Africa*. London: James Currey, 1993.

Unpublished Theses

Bruner, Jason S. 'The Politics of Public Confession in the East African Revival in Uganda, ca. 1930–1950'. PhD thesis, Princeton University, 2013.

Giblin, James L. 'Famine, Authority, and the Impact of Foreign Capital in Handeni District, Tanzania, 1840–1940'. PhD thesis, University of Wisconsin-Madison, 1986.

Hartfield, Colby R. 'The Nfumu in Tradition and Change: A Study of the Position of Religious Practitioners among the Sukuma of Tanzania, East Africa'. PhD thesis, Catholic University of America, 1968.

Maddox, Gregory H. 'Leave Wagogo, You Have no Food: Famine and Survival in Ugogo, Tanzania, 1916–1961'. PhD thesis, Northwestern University, 1988.

Magaya, Aldrin T. 'Christianity, Culture, and the African Experience in Bocha, Zimbabwe, c. 1905–1960s'. PhD thesis, University of Iowa, 2018.

Nolan, Francis P. 'Christianity in Unyamwezi, 1878–1928'. PhD thesis, University of Cambridge, 1977.

Robins, Catherine E. 'Tukutendereza: A Study of Social Change and Sectarian Withdrawal in the Balokole Revival of Uganda'. PhD thesis, Columbia University, 1975.

Rockel, Stephen J. 'Caravan Porters of the Nyika: Labor, Culture, and Society in Nineteenth-Century Tanzania'. PhD thesis, University of Toronto, 1997.

Salaita, John. 'Colonialism and Underdevelopment in Unyanyembe, 1900–1960'. MA thesis, University of Dar es Salaam, 1975.

Taylor, Rachel J. 'Crafting Cosmopolitanism: Nyamwezi Male Labor, Acquisition of Honor, c. 1750–1914'. PhD thesis, Northwestern University, 2018.

Unomah, Alfred C. 'Economic Expansion and Political Change in Unyanyembe, c.1840–1900'. PhD thesis, University of Ibadan, 1972.

Yusuf, Imtyaz. 'Islam and African Socialism: A Study of the Interactions between Islam and Ujamaa Socialism in Tanzania'. PhD thesis, Temple University, 1990.

Web-Based Sources

Gtiau, Wanjiru. 'The Life Work of Andrew Walls for African Theology: Re-centering Africa's Place in Christian History', November 2022. Lausanne Movement. https://lausanne.org/global-analysis/the-lifework-of-andrew-walls-for-african-theology-2 (accessed 11 April 2024).

'Soteriology – The Doctrine of Salvation', Bible.org, 2023, https://bible.org/article/soteriology-doctrine-salvation (accessed 4 October 2023).

'Msemo wa "mzigo mzito mpe mnyamwezi" una maana gani?' JamiiForums, 25 April 2018, … (accessed 1 May 2019).

'Swali la "Mzigo mzito mpe Mnyamwezi" limejibiwa na Naibu Waziri Kilimo Dr Mwanjelwa', blog, 22 June 2018, http://millardayo.com/2wwddd/ (accessed 1 May 2019).

'What is the Keswick movement, and is it biblical?' Got Questions, last updated 4 January 2022, https://www.gotquestions.org/Keswick-movement.html (accessed 3 October 2023).

Index

Abolition of slavery   14, 26, 69, 70, 175, 209

African Inland Mission (AIM)   203, 204

Africanization   13, 35, 176, 198, 200, 202, 203, 204, 205, 206, 207, 210

'Ajamī (Ajamiyya)   9, 33, 97, 99, 103

Ambrose Mhaliga (Fr.)   135

Anti-Slavery Campaigns   70

Banangwa (mwanangwa)   105, 106, 107, 108, 111

Bandeba (Vandeva)   47, 49, 113, 157

Balokole   12, 17, 179, 190, 191, 194

Barbarism   110, 113

Barugaruga   51, 55

Born-again Christians   179, 181, 186, 188, 190, 195

Brauer, Max (Rev.)   108, 109, 110, 111, 112, 113, 118, 121

Bulungwa   27, 28, 130, 134, 135, 139

Burundi (also Urundi)   2, 72, 78, 84, 85, 90

Caravan porters   22, 36, 39, 49, 52, 63, 160

Caravans   27, 43, 45, 46, 47, 49, 50, 51, 54, 55, 56, 84, 86, 99

Catechesis   147, 213

Catechism   4, 104, 121, 122, 123, 126, 128, 130, 132

Catechist School (Ndala)   139, 142, 144

Catechists   3, 4, 5, 6, 7, 9, 11, 13, 14, 119, 21, 22, 34, 98, 122, 123, 124, 125, 126, 127, 128, 129, 130, 131, 132, 133, 134, 135, 139, 141, 142, 143, 144, 146, 147, 148, 210, 211, 213, 214, 215, 216

Catechumens   13, 126, 129, 133, 141, 144, 163, 164, 177

Certificate of freedom   72, 85, 70, 75, 76, 77, 85, 93, 94

Changilo   109, 111

Chief Fundikira   46, 139, 206

Christian Community (also Christian Communities)   1, 3, 7, 8, 15, 22, 31, 61, 62, 84, 97, 115, 120, 122, 128, 147, 152, 153, 156, 163, 170, 171, 172

Church elders   185

Church, Joe   178, 180, 181

Church Missionary Society (CMS)   20, 26, 27, 60, 61, 68, 101, 103, 178, 195, 201

Civilization (ustaarabu)   79, 110, 113, 147, 161

Civilized   11, 52, 113, 157, 160

Confession of sins   5, 18, 19, 178, 179, 180, 181, 188, 191, 192, 193

Congo   1, 2, 41, 47, 72, 79, 84, 85, 90, 91, 126

Council (Baraza)   101, 154, 168, 169, 170, 199

Diocese of Central Tanganyika (DCT)   180, 201, 206

Dissent   1, 6, 8, 11, 12, 13, 14, 17, 18, 19, 22, 32, 35, 36, 37, 59, 60, 97, 98, 99, 122, 134, 141, 143, 154, 176, 177, 178, 182, 183, 184, 185, 188, 190, 193, 196, 197, 198, 207, 211, 215, 216

Domestic slaves   52, 53, 76

Elders council   165, 184, 185, 186

Elephantiasis   62, 63, 64

Emancipation   1, 4, 15, 61, 62, 69, 76, 77, 86, 93, 96, 209, 215

INDEX 237

Enslavement 3, 11, 25, 36, 52, 54, 55, 59, 76, 78, 84, 86, 88, 165, 195, 204, 212
Evangelism 3, 171
Evangelists 3, 6, 7, 16, 19, 22, 25, 146, 162, 176, 180, 181, 182, 187, 196, 207, 215
Evangelization 64, 97, 146, 147, 150, 175

Female slaves 57, 72, 77, 78, 79, 84, 85, 162
Field slaves (also shamba slaves) 33, 36, 48, 53, 57, 211
Foy, John (Bishop) 199, 206, 210
Freibrief 72, 79
Freibriefe 4, 72, 75, 76, 85, 93, 95, 96
Fugitive slaves 4, 14, 57, 58, 71, 92

German boma 4
German colonial officials 71
German colonial state 4, 71, 72, 75
German East Africa 70, 71, 72, 99, 209
Germans 71, 79

Higher life 178, 192
Hwami 31, 42, 43

Ikulu 26, 31, 32, 66
Iliffe, John 37, 40, 59
Independence (of Tanganyika) 6, 7, 14, 34, 42, 57, 94, 150, 176, 177, 196, 201, 203, 204, 205, 207, 211
Individual flight 4, 15, 69, 71
Inega, Benedicto 130, 135
Ipole mission 8, 101, 103, 109, 110, 111, 112, 117, 151, 172, 182, 180, 185, 193
Iraku (Mbulu) 140
Iselamagazi 26, 31, 153
Itaga 124, 130, 139, 144
Ivory 23, 26, 33, 36, 37, 40, 43, 45, 46, 47, 48, 49, 56, 61, 78, 84, 112

Kabeya, John (Fr.) 135
Kaniha mission 130, 134, 135
Keswickian theology *see* higher life

Kinship 2, 10, 22, 33, 37, 55, 61, 78, 84, 88, 106, 107, 108, 110, 111, 116, 117, 119, 121, 129, 156, 170, 195, 216
Kinyamwezi 2, 3, 4, 5, 9, 11, 18, 19, 20, 21, 23, 33, 34, 51, 83, 84, 85, 86, 96, 97, 98, 99, 100, 101, 102, 103, 104, 105, 106, 108, 109, 111, 114, 115, 116, 117, 118, 119, 120, 121, 123, 128, 130, 134, 135, 147, 157, 160, 162, 163, 165, 168, 192, 194, 214, 215
Kipalapala 4, 8, 27, 28, 89, 92, 124, 139, 196
Kipamila, Yohanesi 101, 193, 175
Kisanji, Teofilo 153, 180, 181, 182, 185, 197, 199, 202
Kiswahili 99, 102, 103, 110, 115, 116, 120, 121, 127, 128, 130, 160, 170, 180
Kitunda mission 8, 101, 103, 109, 150, 152, 153, 167, 171, 172, 186

Lavigerie, Charles Allemand (Cardinal) 70
LMS missionaries 61, 64, 65, 66, 109, 206
Luduko 117, 146, 164, 167, 190
Lusangi 5, 10, 89, 164, 165, 166, 168, 170, 171, 172, 175, 180, 181, 188, 189, 190, 197, 210, 212, 214

Marronage 11, 36, 52, 57, 60, 211
Masamalo, Lukasi (Rev.) 117, 180, 186, 187, 188
Mbulu (Kahama) 139, 144
Mihayo, Marko (Archbishop) 146
Mirambo 25, 26, 29, 30, 31, 41, 42, 46, 47, 49, 51, 54, 55, 64, 65, 66, 67, 100, 135, 140, 141, 153
Misigalo, Paulo (Rev.) 180, 181, 184, 185, 187, 192, 193, 197
Mission stations 2, 3, 5, 6, 8, 29, 33, 34, 35, 61, 92, 122, 123, 135, 139, 140, 141, 142, 144, 147, 148, 149, 150, 172, 177, 198, 211
Missionaries of Africa *see* White Fathers
Missions 1, 3, 4, 5, 6, 7, 9, 10, 11, 12, 13, 15, 16, 19, 20, 21, 22, 26, 29, 31, 33,

34, 60, 61, 62, 65, 68, 69, 75, 76, 78, 79, 84, 85, 86, 87, 88, 89, 90, 91, 92, 93, 94, 95, 96, 97, 98, 99, 101, 102, 103, 104, 109, 111, 114, 117, 120, 121, 122, 123, 124, 125, 126, 127, 132, 133, 134, 135, 139, 140, 141, 142, 143, 145, 149, 150, 153, 156, 161, 162, 163, 167, 169, 171, 172, 175, 176, 177, 178, 180, 181, 182, 184, 186, 187, 188, 193, 194, 195, 196, 197, 199, 200, 201, 203, 204, 206, 207, 208, 209, 210, 211, 212, 213, 215, 216

Moravian Church of Western Tanganyika   7, 203, 211, 215

Moravians   5, 6, 7, 8, 10, 12, 13, 19, 20, 27, 34, 35, 61, 89, 98, 101, 102, 103, 104, 108, 109, 111, 114, 117, 121, 132, 146, 149, 150, 151, 152, 153, 156, 161, 162, 163, 164, 166, 167, 168, 169, 170, 171, 172, 175, 176, 177, 178, 180, 181, 182, 186, 187, 189, 190, 193, 194, 195, 196, 198, 199, 200, 201, 203, 204, 205, 206, 207, 208, 210, 211, 214, 215

Mpandashalo   41, 42

Msalala (Ngaya)   4, 27, 28, 31, 41, 42, 43, 88, 134, 140

Mtemi   29, 31, 42, 43, 47, 55, 100, 116, 119, 139, 157

Mtemi Ntabo (Matolu)   31

Mtendeni   181, 182, 183, 184, 185, 187, 188, 192, 194, 195, 196, 197, 198, 207

Mugunda Mkali   63

Muhozya, Mose   182, 185, 192, 193, 195, 197, 206

Ndala mission   1, 2, 4, 9, 31, 71, 79, 85, 86, 87, 88, 90, 91, 124, 130, 134, 142, 143

Ndonno (also Ndono)   124, 125, 130, 140, 142

New birth   179, 181, 188

Nyamwezi   5, 8, 9, 10, 13, 14, 18, 19, 21, 22, 23, 33, 34, 36, 38, 39, 43, 44, 45, 26, 47, 48, 49, 50, 51, 52, 53, 55, 58, 61, 62, 65, 66, 71, 78, 85, 86, 89, 92, 97, 98, 99, 100, 101, 102, 104, 105, 106,

108, 109, 110, 111, 112, 113, 114, 115, 116, 117, 118, 119, 120, 121, 124, 125, 126, 130, 133, 134, 135, 144, 145, 146, 149, 150, 153, 162, 163, 164, 165, 166, 167, 168, 170, 171, 172, 175, 180, 181, 190, 191, 193, 199, 202, 206, 207, 209, 210, 211, 212, 213, 214, 215

Nyamwezi porters   22, 43, 44, 45, 46, 48, 49, 22, 100, 101

Nyamwezi women   5, 34, 149, 163, 214

Nyamwezisprache   21, 214

Nyerere, Julius   145

Nyungu ya Mawe   46, 49, 51, 54, 55

Orphanage Centers   2, 4, 27, 69, 79, 87, 88, 89, 90, 91, 93, 211

Orphans   2, 9, 27, 69, 78, 86, 87, 88, 90, 91, 139, 161, 195, 212

Patronage   22, 60, 112, 115, 116, 162, 198

Patrons   45, 58, 79, 116, 172, 181, 212

Porterage   36, 37, 43, 44, 46, 47, 48, 49, 113, 157, 160, 167

Porters   5, 6, 18, 22, 33, 39, 42, 43, 44, 45, 46, 48, 49, 52, 56, 63, 96, 98, 100, 101, 102, 104, 108, 109, 120, 122, 149, 160, 175, 215

Post-Abolition   1, 16, 19, 156, 175, 213

Postulants   141

Public declarations   4, 15, 69, 72, 75, 95, 96, 209

Redemption   72, 92, 93

Resident catechists   19, 124, 126, 127

Revival   176, 177, 178, 179, 180

Revival movement   6, 12, 19, 34, 89, 171, 177, 178, 180, 181, 183, 185, 186, 187, 188, 193

Revivalism   5, 6, 12, 17, 18, 150, 176, 177, 178, 180, 181, 182, 183, 184, 185, 186, 188, 189, 190, 191, 192, 193, 195, 196, 197, 215

Rituals   40, 113

Runaway slaves   1, 2, 9, 11, 14, 27, 51, 60, 69, 71, 72, 77, 195

Rwanda   2, 11, 72, 84, 90, 178, 179

Salvation   5, 12, 19, 116, 171, 177, 180, 181, 186, 188, 189, 190, 191, 192, 193, 194
Self-governance   6, 7, 13, 14, 57, 200, 201, 210
Sikonge mission   8, 22, 47, 101, 109, 117, 143, 150, 151, 172, 178, 182, 185, 186, 188, 197, 198, 200, 201
Sins   5, 34, 179, 180, 189, 191, 192, 193
Slave women   52, 69, 78, 84, 211
Slavery   2, 5, 9, 11, 15, 18, 19, 25, 26, 27, 32, 33, 35, 52, 53, 54, 57, 58, 59, 60, 69, 70, 71, 75, 78, 84, 85, 93, 95, 96, 117, 118, 121, 127, 156, 157, 161, 175, 176, 209, 212, 213
Slaves   1, 2, 3, 4, 5, 8, 9, 10, 11, 14, 15, 16, 18, 19, 26, 27, 32, 33, 34, 36, 37, 40, 41, 46, 47, 48, 50, 51, 52, 53, 54, 55, 56, 57, 58, 59, 60, 61, 62, 63, 67, 69, 70, 71, 72, 76, 77, 78, 79, 84, 86, 87, 88, 91, 92, 93, 94, 96, 100, 104, 120, 122, 123, 143, 144, 148, 156, 157, 160, 161, 162, 164, 175, 195, 205, 209, 211, 212, 213
Smallpox   62, 63, 68
Southon, Ebenezer John (MD)   23, 24, 25, 29, 64, 66
Spirits   39, 40, 106, 117, 168
Spirituality   16
Steere, Edward (Bishop)   20, 46, 99, 102
Stern, Rudolf   8, 102, 104
Swedish Free Mission   10, 34, 149, 162, 163

Tabora   4, 6, 8, 9, 10, 18, 22, 25, 26, 27, 41, 46, 47, 48, 52, 53, 54, 63, 69, 71, 72, 75, 76, 77, 78, 79, 84, 85, 86, 87, 88, 92, 93, 94, 100, 109, 124, 125, 126, 132, 133, 134, 139, 140, 142, 144, 145, 146, 150, 151, 152, 154, 165, 170, 172, 178, 180, 181, 182, 184, 185, 188, 193, 194, 195, 197, 200, 201, 205, 206, 207, 209, 213, 215
Tabora Boys' Secondary School   180, 181

Tanganyika African Church (TAC)   182, 193, 195, 196, 198
Tanganyika African National Union (TANU)   6, 7, 145, 203, 204, 206, 207, 211
Tazengwa   163
Teachers (*Vahembeki*)   1, 3, 4, 5, 6, 7, 10, 11, 13, 19, 21, 34, 98, 101, 104, 105, 106, 108, 109, 117, 121, 122, 123, 134, 135, 148, 149, 150, 151, 153, 162, 163, 164, 165, 166, 167, 168, 169, 170, 171, 172, 175, 176, 179, 180, 181, 182, 189, 192, 193, 194, 195, 196, 198, 199, 200, 201, 202, 203, 204, 207, 210, 211, 213, 214, 216
Tithes (*Zaka*)   12, 167, 168, 175, 185, 189, 190, 194
Translation   3, 4, 5, 9, 11, 16, 17, 18, 19, 20, 21, 22, 33, 96, 97, 98, 99, 100, 101, 102, 103, 104, 108, 109, 110, 111, 113, 115, 116, 117, 118, 119, 120, 121, 122, 194, 215

Uganda   17, 22, 27, 56, 72, 84, 179, 180
Ugogo   48, 50, 75, 76
Ugome   182, 187, 197, 198
Ujamaa   7, 13, 145, 146
Ujiji   15, 22, 26, 41, 92, 153
Ukimbu   51, 25, 39, 40, 49, 51, 76, 78
Unity of Kiwere Tribal Association (UKTA)   198, 210
Universities Mission to Central Africa (UMCA)   13, 199, 200, 201, 202, 203, 210
Uncivilized   157
Unyamwezi   2, 4, 6, 7, 8, 11, 12, 13, 20, 21, 23, 24, 25, 26, 27, 28, 29, 31, 32, 33, 34, 35, 36, 37, 38, 39, 40, 41, 42, 43, 45, 46, 47, 48, 49, 50, 51, 52, 53, 55, 56, 57, 58, 59, 60, 61, 62, 63, 64, 67, 68, 75, 76, 77, 78, 79, 84, 85, 92, 98, 99, 100, 101, 102, 103, 105, 106, 107, 108, 109, 110, 111, 113, 114, 115, 116, 117, 118, 119, 120, 121, 123, 124, 125, 126, 134, 135, 139, 141, 143, 144, 145, 147, 149, 150, 151, 153, 154, 156, 157,

159, 160, 161, 162, 164, 165, 166, 167,
168, 169, 170, 172, 173, 174, 175, 176,
177, 178, 180, 181, 182, 183, 184, 186,
188, 190, 191, 192, 193, 196, 197, 198,
199, 200, 201, 202, 203, 204, 205,
206, 207, 208, 209, 210, 211, 213, 214
Unyamwezi Moravian Council
(UMCC) 13, 199, 200, 201, 202, 203,
210
Unyanyembe 9, 23, 27, 41, 45, 46, 47,
48, 50, 53, 54, 56, 63, 79, 99, 100, 154,
160, 206
Ushirombo 4, 8, 9, 15, 27, 31, 69, 76,
78, 79, 84, 86, 87, 88, 89, 90, 91, 92,
93, 94, 126, 133, 134

Usukuma 78, 79, 200, 201
Uyui 22, 24, 26, 27, 31, 32, 41, 47, 56,
63, 68, 79, 84, 101, 102, 103, 123, 134,
181, 185, 187, 194, 194, 195, 196, 197

Vasomi (literate people) 201, 203, 214
Volunteer catechists 123, 132, 133, 134

White Fathers 8, 13, 15, 27, 31, 61, 66,
70, 92, 127, 140, 144, 146
White Sisters 69, 78, 79, 84, 87, 92,
93, 94, 95
Witchcraft 39
Witches 106, 110
Witnesses 4, 26, 72, 95, 96, 209

Previously Published Titles in the Series

Violent Conversion: Brazilian Pentecostalism and Urban Women in Mozambique, Linda van de Kamp (2016)

Beyond Religious Tolerance: Muslim, Christian & Traditionalist Encounters in an African Town, edited by Insa Nolte, Olukoya Ogen and Rebecca Jones (2017)

Faith, Power and Family: Christianity and Social Change in French Cameroon, Charlotte Walker-Said (2018)

Contesting Catholics: Benedicto Kiwanuka and the Birth of Postcolonial Uganda, Jonathon L. Earle and J.J. Carney (2021)

Islamic Scholarship in Africa: New Directions and Global Contexts, edited by Ousmane Oumar Kane (2021)

From Rebels to Rulers: Writing Legitimacy in the Early Sokoto State, Paul Naylor (2021)

Sacred Queer Stories: Ugandan LGBTQ+ Refugee Lives and the Bible, Adriaan van Klinken and Johanna Stiebert, with Sebyala Brian and Fredrick Hudson (2021)

Labour & Christianity in the Mission: African Workers in Tanganyika and Zanzibar, 1864–1926, Michelle Liebst (2021)

The Genocide against the Tutsi, and the Rwandan Churches: Between Grief and Denial, Philippe Denis (2022)

Competing Catholicisms: The Jesuits, the Vatican & the Making of Postcolonial French Africa, Jean Luc Enyegue, SJ (2022)

Islam in Uganda: The Muslim Minority, Nationalism & Political Power, Joseph Kasule (2022)

Spiritual Contestations – The Violence of Peace in South Sudan, Naomi Ruth Pendle (2023)

Mystical Power and Politics on the Swahili Coast, Nathalie Arnold Koenings (2024)

Religious Plurality in Africa: Coexistence, Conviviality, Conflict, edited by Marloes Janson, Kai Kresse, Benedikt Pontzen, and Hassan Mwakimako (2024)

Printed in the United States
by Baker & Taylor Publisher Services